DECISION AT SEA

ALSO BY CRAIG L. SYMONDS

Navalists and Antinavalists
A Battlefield Atlas of the Civil War
A Battlefield Atlas of the American Revolution
Joseph E. Johnston: A Civil War Biography
Gettysburg: A Battlefield Atlas
The Naval Institute Historical Atlas of the U.S. Navy
Stonewall of the West: Patrick Cleburne and the Civil War
Confederate Admiral: The Life and Wars of Franklin Buchanan
The American Heritage History of the Battle of Gettysburg

EDITED BY CRAIG L. SYMONDS

Charleston Blockade
New Aspects of Naval History
Recollections of a Naval Officer
A Year on a Monitor and the Destruction of Fort Sumter
Jubal Early's Memoirs
Jefferson Davis: A Memoir by His Wife
The Civil War Recollections of Ellis Spear
The Civil War Reader, 1862
The Lost History of Gettysburg

DECISION AT SEA

Five Naval Battles
that Shaped American History

—

CRAIG L. SYMONDS

To Roy,
With Very Best Wishes,
Craig L. Symonds
Nov 15, 2009

OXFORD
UNIVERSITY PRESS

OXFORD
UNIVERSITY PRESS

Oxford University Press, Inc., publishes works that further
Oxford University's objective of excellence
in research, scholarship, and education.

Oxford New York
Auckland Cape Town Dar es Salaam Hong Kong Karachi
Kuala Lumpur Madrid Melbourne Mexico City Nairobi
New Delhi Shanghai Taipei Toronto

With offices in
Argentina Austria Brazil Chile Czech Republic France
Greece Guatemala Hungary Italy Japan Poland Portugal Singapore
South Korea Switzerland Thailand Turkey Ukraine Vietnam

First published by Oxford University Press, Inc., 2005
198 Madison Avenue, New York, NY 10016

www.oup.com

First issued as an Oxford University Press paperback, 2006

Library of Congress Cataloging-in-Publication Data
Symonds, Craig L.
Decision at sea : five naval battles that shaped American history /
Craig L. Symonds.
p. cm. Includes bibliographical references.
ISBN 978-0-19-531211-9 (PBK.)
1. United States—History, Naval—Anecdotes.
2. Naval battles—United States—History. I. Title.
E182.S995 2005 359.4'773—dc22 2004029394

Book design and composition by Mark McGarry, Texas Type & Book Works
Set in Minion

9 8 7 6 5 4 3 2
Printed in the United States of America
on acid-free paper

For those in peril on the sea

[CONTENTS]

[ACKNOWLEDGMENTS]

My initial acknowledgment must go to the late Tom Buell, who originally conceived of this project—or at least a project similar to this one—and who invited me to take up the challenge of making it a reality. If the final product is very different from what Tom had in mind, his vision informed the way I attacked and presented the material. Nevertheless, all the conclusions and interpretations offered in this volume, as well as any errors that may have crept in, are mine alone.

I also want to thank Bob Pratt, the excellent cartographer at *National Geographic*, who produced the maps in the book; Tim Wooldridge and Janis Jorgensen of the U.S. Naval Institute Photo Archives, Claudia Jew at the Mariners' Museum, and Scott Harmon, director of the Naval Academy Museum, all of whom helped me with the illustrations; and, at Oxford, Peter Ginna, my superb editor, who had faith in the project from the start, as well as the efficient and accomplished Furaha Norton. Finally, I offer thanks to Barbara Breeden, Barbara Manvel, and the wonderful staff at the Nimitz Library at the United States Naval Academy.

Prologue. I am indebted to my friend John Hattendorf, the Ernest J. King Chair of Maritime History at the Naval War College, who read the Prologue and made several helpful suggestions about my treatment of the Battle of the Capes.

Part One: Lake Erie. Gerard Altoff, the park historian at the Perry Memorial and International Peace Monument at Put-in-Bay, Ohio, very generously shared with me the results of his many years of research about the Battle of Lake Erie and offered valuable criticism on, and corrections

to, an early draft of the text. His generosity of spirit defines academic colle-
giality.

Thanks are due as well to John C. Dann, director of the William L.
Clements Library on Early Americana at the University of Michigan, who
allowed me to quote from the Oliver Hazard Perry Papers, and to Elisabeth
Proffen, the special collections assistant at the Maryland Historical Society,
for allowing me to quote from the Samuel Hambleton Diary.

Part Two: Hampton Roads. Dr. Francis J. DuCoin of Stuart, Florida,
who has made the technical aspects of the *Monitor* a special study, helped
me to appreciate the fine details of Ericsson's revolutionary vessel, particularly the characteristics of the pilothouse. John W. Hinds of Shoreline,
Washington, helped me with information about Hawthorne's visit to the
Monitor just after the battle. Versions of this chapter were presented orally
at various meetings of the Civil War Weekend at the Mariners' Museum,
and I wish to thank all those whose comments and observations helped
me sharpen my argument, including William C. "Jack" Davis, David Min-
dell, and John Quarstein. I benefited as well from a collaboration on the
construction of the CSS *Virginia* with Harold Holzer, Lincoln scholar and
vice president for communications at the Metropolitan Museum of Art.

The Hagley Museum and Library in Wilmington, Delaware, generously
granted permission to use the Samuel F. Du Pont Papers; the P. K. Yonge
Library at the University of Florida gave permission to use the Stephen
Mallory Papers; and the Research Collection at the Mariners' Museum, the
final resting place for the remains of the USS *Monitor*, generously allowed
me access to its extended holdings about the Battle of Hampton Roads.

Part Three: Manila Bay. Rich Baker at the U.S. Army War College Military History Institute aided me in finding and identifying the Wayne Longnecker Papers. My friend and Naval Academy colleague Fred Harrod
brought my attention to several important sources about the Spanish-
American War and offered valuable comments on the manuscript that
helped me rethink critical aspects of the battle.

Part Four: The Battle of Midway. Vice Admiral William D. Houser, USN
(ret), and Captain Jack Crawford, USN (ret), Midway veterans and stewards of the history of the Battle of Midway, not only provided oral remi-

niscences but directed me to other Midway veterans who helped me get a better feel for this pivotal battle. Otis Kight, who (like Jack Crawford) served aboard *Yorktown* during the battle, helped me with several details of that vessel's operations, as did Ronald W. Russell. Not only was Paul Still-well, head of the oral history collection at the U.S. Naval Institute, the mid-wife of this project, but in addition his oral histories of Midway veterans provided much of the raw material for this section. Thanks, too, to Bar-bara Manvel, who guided me to the Action Reports microfilm collection in Nimitz Library.

Part Five: Praying Mantis. I am grateful to Lieutenant Commander Don Donegon, USN, a former student of mine at the Naval Academy and now a friend, who conducted two interviews with Persian Gulf veterans aboard the USS *Carl Vinson*. Thanks as well to Lieutenant Commander Tom Cut-ler, USN (ret), a friend and former colleague at the Academy and author of the *Bluejacket's Manual,* who tipped me to several useful sources. Members of the Naval Academy History Department's Works-in-Progress seminar read a draft of the chapter and made their usual insightful observations. In particular, Commander Steve Bates, USN, Commander Dan Redmond, USN, and Lieutenant Commander Scott Herbener, USN, all helped explain the intricacies of the weapons technology. Robert W. Love Jr. and Joseph Stanik each read the entire text carefully and made a number of valuable suggestions.

Part Five could not have been written at all without the generous coop-eration of the many participants of the Persian Gulf conflict who agreed to be interviewed or who supplied firsthand information to the author. They are listed here along with the job each held in April 1988: the Hon. Colin Powell, general, USA (ret), President Reagan's national security advisor; the Hon. William J. Crowe Jr., admiral, USN (ret), chairman of the Joint Chiefs of Staff; Captain James Chandler, USN (ret), commanding officer of USS *Wainwright*; Captain Jerry O'Donnell, USN (ret), commanding offi-cer of USS *Thach*; Captain Henry "Hank" Sanford, USN (ret), executive officer on USS *Merrill*; Captain James "Red" Smith, USN, lieutenant on USS *Thach*; Commander Alfred Eakins, USN (ret), lieutenant on USS *Cal-ifornia*; Commander Leo Carling, USNR (ret), lieutenant on USS

Wainwright; Senior Chief Petty Officer Ruben Vargas, USN, operations specialist first class on USS *Wainwright*; Mr. Richard Molck, weapons technician second class on USS *Wainwright*; and Chief Petty Officer Walter Brown, USN, yeoman second class on USS *LaSalle*.

Though I have never met him, I want to acknowledge the journalistic work of William Matthews of the *Navy Times,* whose careful reporting from the Gulf helped provide the chronological structure for this chapter.

Epilogue. Lieutenant Commander Randy Balano, USNR, and Lieutenant Commander Scott Herbener helped verify some of the factual information in this section, but I need to emphasize that although my views about the U.S. Navy's role in the twenty-first century are a product of thirty years of teaching, speaking, and writing about American naval history, and therefore dependent on the insight provided by colleagues, students, and others, both in and out of uniform, I am solely responsible for the interpretive conclusions offered here and indeed throughout the book.

As always, my most insightful editor was my wife, Marylou, a partner in all my writing efforts as well as in everything else in my life, to whom I owe more than I can ever repay.

CRAIG L. SYMONDS
ANNAPOLIS, MARYLAND

[AUTHOR'S NOTE]

The original idea for this book belonged to Thomas B. Buell, a retired naval officer and respected historian. Early in 2002 he envisioned a book that examined the changing nature of warfare at sea by describing three critical sea battles of American history: Lake Erie, Hampton Roads, and the Naval Battle of Guadalcanal. Tom composed a proposal based on this idea and won a contract from Oxford University Press for a book to be called *The Sea Warrior Trilogy*. Soon thereafter, Tom's doctor informed him that he had leukemia.

Though it was hardly his first thought upon hearing this devastating news, Tom was disappointed that his vision for this book would go unfulfilled. It was a mutual friend, Paul Stillwell, who in conversation with Tom suggested that perhaps I might take over the project. Tom and I had known each other since the 1970s when we had both served in uniform at the Naval War College, and he was immediately enthusiastic about the idea. After several phone conversations during which we discussed the project, Tom sent me a small package containing some preliminary notes he had made and a few of the books he was consulting. Two days after I received that package, Tom died.

This is, of course, a very different book from the one that Tom would have written. For one thing, I decided not to include the Naval Battle of Guadalcanal, and I have added three other battles: Manila Bay, Midway, and the Persian Gulf. I made these decisions for reasons that I think are compelling and which are explained in the Prologue. But if the coverage is different, I tried to be faithful throughout to Tom's notion that a key element in the analysis of any naval battle should be a consideration of the impact of warfare on the individual officer and sailor. Some idea of how Tom felt about those ideas is evident in the Foreword, drawn from Tom's original proposal, which follows this note.

[FOREWORD]

by Thomas B. Buell

A large stained-glass window in the Naval Academy chapel depicts a newly commissioned ensign in dress white uniform reading his commission, held reverently in his outstretched hands. A seascape occupies the background, and a figure of Christ rises on the horizon. This vision inspired me when I worshiped there as a midshipman. I perceived the naval profession as a special calling that demanded selfless devotion to the United States Navy and the nation. The spirit of naval heroes was everywhere, in portraits, banners, murals, busts, monuments, and memorials. The essence of the Naval Academy was clear and unmistakable: a naval officer was part of an elite society of which much was expected, and he led a life governed by ethics, morals, and certitudes. While he was *in* the world, he was not *of* it.

As I matured in the profession, reality replaced imagery through observation and study. Though I recognized that naval leaders were fallible, they continued to fascinate me. There were two principal reasons. One was that as a career naval officer, my professional goal was command at sea, and I recognized that such an aspiration required the ability to lead under stress. I studied in order to learn from the masters. The other reason was intellectual inquiry: to learn how the great naval leaders developed their talents, how they thought and reasoned, and what compelled their actions. How did they manage the responsibilities and tension of high command? How did they prepare themselves for war, reflect about war, and behave when they made war? To discover the answers, I read—and eventually I wrote— naval history, for although history is a constantly changing tableau, it is also a seamless cloth, and by understanding how sea warriors in the past attempted to answer these questions, I could discern the essential nature of war at sea.

The antagonists in the battles described in this book first had to contend with the sea. The sea's most fundamental characteristic is its vastness, for the oceans cover 75 percent of the earth's surface. While army officers think in terms of kilometers over terrain ranging from deserts to mountains, naval officers think in terms of transit time over great distances, hundreds and even thousands of nautical miles over a uniform water surface disturbed only by the wind. Naval officers prefer the freedom of the open seas, though they must nonetheless sometimes fight at close quarters in restricted waters, forcing them to think three-dimensionally by considering the depth of water under the keel as well as the precise distances between ship and shoals. By the middle of the twentieth century their warfare environment included carrier-launched airplanes, and by the end of that century it embraced orbiting satellites as naval warfare became genuinely global.

Alfred Thayer Mahan notwithstanding, no one navy can truly control the sea, for a fleet is but a pinprick upon 135 million square miles of water. It may be a fleet of great power, able to defeat any enemy within range of its weapons and thus temporarily control an area within its combat radius, but when the fleet moves on, the sea in its wake is again open to other ships to pass undisturbed. Hence there is no equivalent to the trenches, fortifications, and front lines of land warfare, which allow armies to remain in place and in control indefinitely. Barclay "controlled" Lake Erie until defeated by Perry; the *Virginia* seized "control" of Hampton Roads for a day, only to lose it the next; in the western Pacific, Japanese "control" of the waters around the Philippines proved almost equally fleeting. In the Persian Gulf, and in the modern world generally, the "control" of any sea is an elusive and ephemeral quality.

The accountability of command, however, is absolute. This sometimes leads naval officers to be careful, even meticulous—their degree of caution (or boldness) contingent upon their willingness to take calculated risks. But sea duty also instills a sense of enormous confidence and independence first experienced when a junior qualifies as an officer of the deck under way and assumes the burden of responsibility for the ship while the captain is below. Decisions must often be made instantaneously, and as a junior officer makes those decisions and exercises his authority, he may over time come to feel more liberated than inhibited by the mantle of authority. Once in command, a captain's authority becomes nearly as absolute as his accountability.

In the midst of battle, that authority must be exercised in an environment that is both chaotic and constantly changing. War is messy. The orderly battle line disintegrates into a melee. The eternal question for captains engaged in combat is one of assigning priorities. Which of the many crises a captain confronts must be dealt with first? Does he maneuver to conform to instructions that seem to have been overtaken by events, or does he exercise his authority and independently close with the enemy? At the Battle of Trafalgar in 1805, the great British hero of the Age of Sail, Horatio Lord Nelson, informed his commanders that "no captain can do very wrong if he places his ship alongside that of an enemy." Nelson encouraged independent thought among his subordinates, and that day, at least, it paid off for him—and for England. Despite dramatic improvements in communication since Nelson's day, the central dilemma remains, and both responsibility and accountability continue to reside with the ship's commanding officer.

Each of the battles discussed in this book provides insight into the essential features of naval combat and command at sea. From the Age of Sail to the modern era, the one constant element is fighting spirit. While there have been many personalities among the Navy's great commanders, from the flamboyance of "Bull" Halsey to the reticence of Raymond Spruance, fighting spirit has always been the one essential characteristic of them all. Without the warrior ethic, without courage under fire, a naval officer cannot command.

DECISION AT SEA

PROLOGUE

—

Naval Battles and History

History is about change, and more than any other human activity, war both causes and accelerates change. War propels history into fast forward, precipitating social and cultural transformation so swiftly and profoundly that often it is that transformation, rather than the object that provoked hostilities in the first place, that emerges as the principal consequence of war. Occasionally the change is self-conscious, the product of deliberate revolution, such as the one that took place in France in 1789. More often, however, change is a by-product of war, unforeseen and even unimagined, as in the dramatic social and cultural revolution that resulted from the mass mobilization and ghastly bloodletting in Europe from 1914 to 1918. Despite the best efforts of policy makers who struggle to fulfill the Clausewitzian dictum that wars ought to be a means by which nations secure clear and discrete national policy objectives, wars create a momentum of their own that constantly threatens to seize control of events from the hands of the decision makers and send history careening forward like a runaway train.

War also *reflects* change. Indeed, because war places society under pressure, it casts a bright light onto the values and character of the societies engaged in it. War invites—even demands—that citizens sacrifice their time, their treasure, their very lives, to the object of the war, however ill defined or imperfectly understood that object might be. In consequence, it is in the midst of war that citizens are most frequently called upon to embody the dominant values of their culture. The archaic chivalry of medieval warfare, where one army commander might politely offer another the opportunity to strike the first blow, reflected one set of values; the cold-blooded matter-of-factness with which the German *Einsatzgruppen* conducted the mass execution of Soviet Jews in 1942 reflected another. Once begun, war often becomes the dominant governmental and cultural concern, and because of that, war most accurately reflects both the prevailing technology and the dominant culture of the societies engaged in it.

As is the case with all nations, the history and culture of the United States have been both defined by and reflected in its several wars. From the earliest days of the Republic, war delineated the stages of American transformation as the country evolved from a frontier society along the Atlantic seaboard to become first a continental power, then a world power, and eventually the greatest power in history. At each stage of this metamorphosis, America's wars reflected the dominant national focus of its generation. In the early nineteenth century, America's wars focused on defending the frontier and protecting its overseas trade; at midcentury, the Civil War resolved a fundamental disagreement about the nature of American democracy and began a social and political revolution as profound as any in the country's history; at the end of the century, the United States defeated Spain in a war that marked America's emergence as a world power. In the twentieth century—the American century—the United States confirmed its status as world power as it participated in two world wars, and by the end of that century many Americans accepted as a matter of course that the United States had both the right and the responsibility to act as the world's policeman and to extend its military power into every corner of the globe. All these profound changes were the product of wars; all of them are likewise reflected in the way the nation conducted those wars.

These changes were not instantaneous, nor were they the product of a single event. Still, it is possible to identify one battle from each epoch to serve as a useful historical milestone that illuminates the nature of these changes. No less an authority than Winston Churchill, who knew a thing or two about both history and war, insisted that "battles are the landmarks of secular history." Churchill was referring to land battles when he made the remark, but as a "former naval person," he surely would not have dissented from the assertion that naval battles, too, are milestones of historic change. For Britain, the defeat of the Spanish Armada in 1588, the victory at Trafalgar in 1805, and the victory over the U-boat menace in 1943 were all crucial and historic moments, marking as they did the dawn, apex, and sunset of British naval supremacy. For the United States, too, the stages of national transformation can be identified with specific naval battles that both reflected and provoked cultural and societal change. This book is based on the premise that five landmark naval battles were milestones not only of American *naval* history but also of the country's *national* history.

- Oliver Hazard Perry's victory on Lake Erie in 1813 was a rare fleet engagement for the U.S. Navy in the Age of Sail and a bracing bit of good news in an otherwise disappointing war. But more importantly, Perry's frontier navy, itself constructed of the trees of the western forests, secured the American claim to the Northwest Territory and was therefore an essential prerequisite for the subsequent westward expansion that would eventually make the United States a continental power.

- The Battle of Hampton Roads in 1862 was the world's first engagement between armored warships, and in that respect it foreshadowed the age of machine warfare, but in the process it also demonstrated the industrial strength and economic resilience of the Union states, factors that helped ensure the survival of the Union itself and launched the reunified United States into the age of industry.

- The Battle of Manila Bay in 1898 was the nation's first that involved the oceangoing steam and steel warships of what historians have labeled "the New Navy." It also marked America's debut as a nascent world power and secured a series of overseas possessions that dramatically altered America's place in world politics. After that, the national insularity that many Americans had taken for granted would prove impossible to sustain, and the United States became, if not quite an empire, then at least a major power on the world stage.

- Midway was not the world's first carrier battle, but it was the carrier battle that changed the course of the Second World War, not only in the Pacific but globally, and put the United States on the path to superpower status.

- Operation Praying Mantis in 1988—the most obscure of the battles profiled here—not only revealed the capabilities of a new generation of electronically integrated missile systems but fixed the United States at the center of the Middle East political struggle and marked the emergence of the United States in its new role as the world's policeman, a role it would continue and expand upon in the twenty-first century.

Technologically as well as culturally and politically, each of the battles described in this book marked a departure from an existing paradigm— all but the first. The Battle of Lake Erie occurred near the end of an era in which the dominant model of naval warfare had remained relatively static for two and a half centuries. Ever since the end of the sixteenth century, warships had been essentially floating platforms for artillery. War at sea entailed maneuvering wooden-hulled, sail-driven vessels in such a way as to bring their broadsides of cast iron guns to bear against the enemy. The most effective way to do that was for warships to sail single file in a long column, what was called a line ahead. Because a line is no stronger than its weakest element, it soon became evident that only those ships carrying more than fifty guns should occupy a position in this line. They were called ships of the line. They carried their heavy guns in two (or sometimes three) long rows along each side, and when those guns were fired all at once this was known as a broadside. There were smaller warships, too: frigates carried fewer guns (usually between twenty and forty) in one row on the weather deck and were used to scout for the enemy battle fleet or to escort merchant ships from port to port. Even smaller vessels, sloops and brigs with twelve to twenty guns, carried dispatches from place to place and harried the trade of others. But in the European wars of the seventeenth and eighteenth centuries, it was the ships of the line that won or lost wars.

The product of three centuries of evolution, ships of the line were magnificent engines of war. Each of them carried between sixty and one hundred guns (though seventy-four eventually became standard), and each required a crew numbering up to a thousand men. With their three towering masts, complex webs of ropes, lines, and cables, and hand-carved and gilded filigree (especially around the stern), they were works of art as well as engines of war, and it is no wonder that they have been the focus of painters and model builders ever since. The French in particular built beautiful ships. If pressed, many British naval officers would admit that French ships were often better than their own. But during the century and a quarter of almost continuous warfare between the two countries after 1689, many of those beautiful French ships ended up flying the British ensign. This was because what mattered most in a fleet engagement during the Age of Sail was not the beauty of the design or the sophistication of the technology but the skill and discipline of the crew. Because France, as a continental power, necessarily focused on land war, her naval crews were often less experienced than those of Britain, and in battle after battle, British fleets with fewer ships and fewer guns outperformed their French counterparts.

Throughout all those wars, a pattern or template of naval warfare emerged that served to guide the naval officers who were charged with the command of war fleets. The keys to success, they learned, were:

1. A fleet commander had to maintain strict control over his ships, deploying them in a well-ordered line-ahead formation so that an enemy fleet would face an unbroken wall of cannon. Such a battle line might number anywhere from a half dozen to three dozen ships of the line, and when so many vessels were arrayed end to end a cable's length apart (two hundred yards), the battle line might extend for several miles. A watchful fleet commander would maintain the discipline of this extended battle line by signal flags, enjoining each captain to keep his ship in its proper place.

2. British commanders, at least, also sought to gain and hold the "weather gage"—that is, they tried to ensure that the wind blew away from their fleet and toward that of the enemy. The side with

the weather gage could control the action. No fleet could attack upwind, so whoever held the weather gage could choose the moment of attack.* In addition, the wind blew the white smoke from hundreds of cannons on the ships with the weather gage into the faces of their adversaries. These well-understood advantages often led to elaborate maneuvering before the battle as each fleet commander sought to gain the weather gage.

3.   Finally, once the two fleets were side by side sailing in parallel lines a half cable's length apart (one hundred yards), victory or defeat depended on how quickly the gunners could fire their guns. Other factors being equal, a ship whose crew could fire a round every three minutes was likely to defeat a ship whose crew could fire only every five minutes. Aiming the guns was a very imprecise science. But given the close range at which the ships fought, pointing the gun in the general direction of the enemy was often all the aiming that was required.

To be successful in all three of these predictors, the secret was constant drill: drill in fleet maneuvers, in station keeping, and in gunnery. Service in war fleets of the Age of Sail, therefore, meant endless days of nearly constant drill: officers called for the men to make sail, shorten sail, clear for action, secure from quarters, and fire as the target bears. But sometimes, too, success depended on the willingness of a bold commander to violate these time-tested rules of engagement and do the unexpected.

The archetypal naval battle of the Age of Sail was the victory of Lord Nelson over the combined fleets of France and Spain off Cape Trafalgar on October 21, 1805, a victory that certified England's undisputed command of the seas during the Napoleonic Wars and which is still celebrated annually in England. For the United States, however, the most important naval battle of this era was the one that took place twenty-five years earlier, on

---

* For their part, the French were often happy to accept the lee gage because frequently their objective was not the destruction of the enemy fleet but rather the protection of a convoy, and holding the lee gage allowed them to break off the action when their immediate goal had been achieved.

A modern drawing of a British ship of the line in combat depicts many of the elements of naval warfare in the Age of Sail. At left a gun crew manhandles a gun into firing position while the gun captain sights along the barrel; in the center a powder monkey (perhaps a midshipman given his uniform) runs toward the crew with a new round of ammunition; and at right officers carry on a shouted conversation amidst the din. (U.S. Navy)

September 5, 1781, off the entrance to Chesapeake Bay. No Americans participated in this battle, and by the standards of the age it was neither a very big battle nor tactically decisive. Nevertheless, the Battle of the Capes was the battle that secured American independence, for it prevented the rescue of Lord Cornwallis and his trapped army at Yorktown and was the proximate cause of his surrender. Though it may be technically incorrect to cite this as one of America's great naval battles, a short description of it is appropriate here, for not only did it contribute significantly to American victory in the Revolutionary War, but it provides a useful benchmark for the consideration of the subsequent battles that are discussed in this book, and in that respect it is a useful prototype of naval warfare at the apex of the Age of Sail.

A Prototype of Naval War: The Battle of the Capes

On the morning of September 5, 1781, the British frigate *Solebay* was sailing southward, running before the wind, as it approached the entrance to Chesapeake Bay. At nine o'clock a lookout stationed in the foretop called down to the deck to report that he could see a fleet of warships anchored just inside the southern headland, Virginia's Cape Henry. The *Solebay*'s captain, Charles H. Everitt, was skeptical. He suspected that the lookout was fooled by the bare trunks of trees on the edge of the American wilderness. Taking a long glass with him, Everitt climbed the rigging to have a look himself. As he steadied himself in the foretop and the image swung into view through his glass, he could no longer doubt. There were indeed a number of large warships anchored there—and they were ships of the line. Since all British ships of the line were accounted for, these vessels could only be French. He counted them as his own vessel drew closer. When he got to eight, he thought it must be the squadron of Admiral de Barras from Newport, though how the Frenchman came to be there, he could not imagine. Then he kept counting, and when he reached the mid-teens, he knew that it could only be the French main battle fleet of the comte de Grasse from the West Indies. After returning to the deck, Everitt sent signal flags whipping up the halyards of the *Solebay* to be read by the flag lieutenant on the British flagship *London*, several miles astern, where the news then became the problem of the British fleet commander, Rear Admiral Thomas Graves.[1]

The sequence of events that brought the fleets of Graves and de Grasse to Chesapeake Bay in the first week of September 1781 had begun more than a year earlier when Major General Charles Cornwallis initiated a lengthy land campaign in the Carolinas that was designed to pacify the southern colonies. Harassed by irregular forces commanded by Thomas Sumter (the Gamecock) and Francis Marion (the Swamp Fox), Cornwallis's small army nevertheless worked its way north from Charleston, fighting a series of small and indecisive battles with American forces at places such as Camden in South Carolina and Guilford Courthouse in North Carolina before entering Virginia in the spring of 1781. In late July Cornwallis marched his army to Yorktown on Chesapeake Bay to await support from the Royal Navy. Instead, on August 26 it was the French fleet of Admiral de Grasse that arrived.[2]

The arrival of de Grasse's fleet at that time and place was one of the most unlikely and at the same time consequential events of the whole war.

The Franco-American alliance signed three years before, in 1778, had prompted George Washington to nurture a hope that with French naval support he might at last be able to win a decisive victory over the British. Washington knew that as long as the Royal Navy commanded the sea, the British army could never be pinned down and defeated unless it foolishly ventured inland (as John Burgoyne had done at Saratoga). Because the Royal Navy did command the sea, whenever British land forces got into trouble, they headed for the coast, where their navy could resupply, reinforce, or if necessary evacuate them. But with the French alliance, the Americans, too, had a fleet—or at least a fleet that was on their side. To make maximum use of it, however, the Franco-American allies would have to achieve a kind of coordination that was virtually unprecedented in the Age of Sail, and in the end it took more than two years to achieve it.

The first piece of the puzzle—the key piece—was the fleet of Admiral François-Joseph-Paul, marquis de Grasse-Tilly (or simply the comte de Grasse) in the West Indies. De Grasse's orders specified that the protection of French possessions in the West Indies was his first priority. After all, most Europeans held the sugar islands of the Lesser Antilles to be of far greater value than all of the mainland American colonies combined. But in midsummer of 1781, de Grasse received a letter from the French general Jean-Baptiste de Rochambeau, who wrote him from Newport that the American Revolution was foundering, and that swift action by de Grasse and his fleet might be essential to sustain it. Boldly de Grasse took it upon himself to ignore his orders and focus instead on the needs of his American allies. "I believe myself authorized to take some responsibility on my own shoulders for a common cause," he wrote. Despite the pleas of French merchants in the Caribbean, and the risk to his own career, de Grasse decided to take his entire fleet to the American coast.[3]

On August 14, 1781, Washington received a letter from de Grasse indicating that he planned to arrive at the mouth of Chesapeake Bay at the end of the month. Washington then made a decision that was as bold as de Grasse's. Leaving a small covering force to keep an eye on the British in New York, he started south with an army of seven thousand men, over half of them French soldiers under Rochambeau. This combined force of

French and Americans marched overland across New Jersey and into Pennsylvania, then through Philadelphia, and southward to the head of the Elk River at the top of Chesapeake Bay. There, some embarked on barges and small boats to finish the trip by water, while others continued the march through Baltimore and across the Potomac into Virginia, then along the banks of the York River to join the marquis de Lafayette's covering force at Williamsburg outside Yorktown. At the same time, de Barras left Newport with six ships of the line, plus four frigates and eighteen transport ships carrying Rochambeau's artillery. For Washington's plan to work, all these elements—the troops marching overland, those going by sea, de Barras's squadron with the siege artillery, and, most important of all, de Grasse's battle fleet—had to arrive at the same place at more or less the same time without encountering any British forces en route.

The key element in all this was de Grasse's battle fleet, which consisted of twenty-eight ships of the line, including his flagship, the *Ville de Paris*, the largest warship in the world at the time. The British suspected that de Grasse might send some portion of his fleet to aid the Americans, but they also assumed that he would have to leave at least half of it in the West Indies, and as a result they sent only fourteen ships of their own after him, under the command of Sir Samuel Hood. The British might have sent more ships from the home fleet to reinforce their American holdings, but threatening French naval movements in European waters convinced the decision makers at Whitehall to keep the home fleet close to Britain.

Hood guessed at once that de Grasse was heading for Chesapeake Bay, and he set a direct course for Virginia. He arrived at the entrance to Chesapeake Bay on August 25 and looked in past the capes to discover that the French were not there. Hood then made another assumption: if de Grasse wasn't in the Chesapeake, he must have headed instead for New York. He therefore immediately sped away to the north to join his commander, Thomas Graves, in New York harbor. A few days after Hood disappeared over the northern horizon, the first of de Grasse's vessels loomed over the southern horizon. Unlike Hood, who had taken the direct route to the Virginia coast, de Grasse had gone first to Spanish Cuba (Spain was a French ally in the war against Britain) and then hugged the American coastline as he worked his way north. As a result, he did not arrive off the Cape Henry headland until August 29, dropping anchor in Lynnhaven Bay just inside Cape Henry. Over the next few days he landed fifteen hundred troops and an equal number of sailors to join the American army under the marquis de Lafayette, thereby ensuring that Cornwallis would remain trapped in Yorktown until Washington's army arrived. With de Grasse holding the entrance to the bay and a Franco-American army holding the lines around Yorktown, Cornwallis was in a box. His survival depended entirely on whether or not the Royal Navy could drive off the French fleet, regain control of Chesapeake Bay, and resupply or reinforce him.

When Hood arrived at New York on September 1, he found that the French fleet was not there, either. He instantly concluded that he had been right the first time and that de Grasse had sailed for the Chesapeake after all, though he could not imagine how he had missed him. He pressed Admiral Graves, who was senior to him, to join forces and return to the Chesapeake to challenge de Grasse. Graves concurred, but he was able to contribute only five of his eight ships, and as a result the British fleet headed south with a total of nineteen ships of the line plus a handful of frigates. Since Graves assumed that de Grasse had no more than fourteen ships—at most twenty if he had somehow managed to join forces with de Barras—he counted on superior British gunnery to overwhelm the French. Not until he read the signal flags from the *Solebay* on the morning of September 5 did Graves realize that de Grasse had not fourteen or even twenty ships of the line, but twenty-eight.

To his credit, the news from the *Solebay* did not deter Graves from his objective. At ten o'clock in the morning he ordered his ships to clear for action. This involved not only casting loose the guns and bringing up powder and shot from the magazine but also knocking down temporary bulkheads to provide an uninterrupted gun deck, lashing up the hammocks to get them out of the way and to provide a cushion for the woodwork (splinters were a major cause of injury in a naval engagement), and throwing sand on the decks so that the gunners did not slip on the blood that would soon be flowing. This complicated evolution usually took between four and six minutes, and then with everyone in place, Graves watched while the French, too, prepared for battle.

De Grasse learned of the approach of the British fleet at about the same time that Graves learned of the presence of the French. The Frenchman could have stayed where he was and tried to defend the entrance to the bay—control of the Chesapeake, after all, was the object of the whole campaign—but he knew that de Barras was coming south from Newport with the siege artillery, and he feared that if he did not go out to fight the British, they might intercept and capture de Barras's whole squadron. Since his ships were at anchor, the first thing to do was get under way. Hauling up the heavy anchors took too much time, so de Grasse ordered his captains to slip their anchors—that is, to tie the anchor line to a buoy so that the anchor could be found later, then cut the line with an ax. While that was taking place, other hands climbed the towering masts to loosen the sails. Though routine, this was always dangerous work, for after climbing to the yards some sixty or eighty feet above the deck, the men then had to edge out on the footropes suspended below the yards, holding on to the yard itself, until they could reach the knots that kept the sails furled. They then untied the knots and shook the heavy canvas sails loose so that other men on the deck below could haul in on the lines and pull them taut.

De Grasse ordered his ships to form a battle line as best they could ("promiscuously" was the word he used) without worrying about the previously established order of sailing. This led to a kind of race in which the most eager captains with the fastest ships sought to take the lead, while others whose ships were less nimble or who had to round the shoal water off Cape Henry fell to the rear. In an age when personal honor was reflected by a captain's willingness to put himself (and his men) in the position of maximum danger, this was a race for distinction and preferment as well as pride. With evident satisfaction, de Grasse later reported, "All the captains applied themselves [and] the fleet was under sail in less than three quarters of an hour."[4]

As the French ships straggled out of the bay in no particular order, Graves's fleet continued to close the range, their ships in precise alignment under topsails and jib. The French admired the precision of the British line. One French officer later wrote, "They came down upon us with a following wind and with an assurance which made us think they did not know our strength."[5] But even as the English fleet bravely sailed toward the enemy, Graves worried about the tactical problem of bringing all the enemy ships to battle in accordance with the prescribed formula. The two fleets were approaching each other on opposite tacks; if they continued as they were, the battle would be a passing engagement. In order to put all of his own ships alongside those of the enemy on the same tack, Graves would have to turn his column around to head east. At a few minutes past two, therefore, Graves's flagship hoisted the signal for all ships to wear together. This was when the months and even years of constant drill paid off: All nineteen ships in the British line of battle executed the same maneuver at the same time, only two hundred yards apart, as each ship put down its helm, the yards swinging round, and the ships settled back into

The van of de Grasse's fleet (at left), sailing in the requisite line-ahead formation under top-sails, engages the British van (at right) in the opening phase of the Battle of the Capes. With the lee gage, the French fired to cripple the British rigging, while the British (with the weather gage) fired into the hull of the French ships. Despite the disorganization of the French line of battle, the British failed to achieve their usual victory, in part because of Graves's inability to signal his intentions to his subordinates. (U.S. Navy)

line on the port tack, but now in reverse order. By three o'clock the two fleets were side by side, two miles apart, sailing eastward.

The French had a clear numerical advantage. De Grasse had left four of his ships behind to watch the York and James Rivers, but that still gave him twenty-four ships of the line to Graves's nineteen. More importantly, the French also had five hundred more guns (two thousand to fifteen hundred), and at least two of the English ships (*Terrible* and *Ajax*) were leaking so badly that they had their pumps going even before the battle began. Indeed, their leaks made them so unseaworthy that they kept falling out of position until Graves fired three shots to leeward to punctuate the signal: "Keep better station." But to balance these weaknesses, there was the long tradition of superior British gunnery and the fact that de Grasse had sent fifteen hundred of his sailors ashore, which meant that several of his ships were severely shorthanded. And of course there was the evident disorganization of the French battle line. The first four or five French ships that rounded the Cape Charles headland sorted themselves out into a passable line of battle, but much of the rest of the fleet was bunched up well to the rear. The French van was isolated and, in Hood's view, ripe for the picking.

Hood's division, which had initially occupied the British van, was now in the rear. Graves's order to wear together had reversed the order of the British fleet, and Hood waited impatiently for Graves to signal general chase, which would release him (and all other commanders) from the discipline of the line-ahead formation in order to fall upon the disorganized French. Instead Graves kept the signal for line ahead flying, though he decreased the interval to a half cable's length (one hundred yards) to tighten up the formation. Later Hood wrote with obvious disapproval that the French disorder "afforded the British fleet a most glorious opening for making a close attack . . . but it was not embraced."[6]

In fact, far from dashing at the enemy, Graves deliberately waited until the French ships had successfully rounded Cape Henry and organized themselves into a more or less coherent battle line before issuing the order to attack. His notion of a fleet engagement was so tied to the concept of parallel battle lines that he felt compelled to wait until all ships, on both sides, were in their proper station before the battle could begin. Finally at four o'clock Graves raised the signal for close action, but he also kept the signal for line ahead flying.

Graves's difficulty was that the flag hoist system allowed him to send only very specific orders. Lord Howe had issued a new set of signal codes when he arrived in New York in July 1776, only a week after the American Declaration of Independence was signed. These had been modified by Vice Admiral Marriot Arbuthnot and adopted by Graves, who issued them to Hood. But even these revised codes gave commanders very limited options. Each set of signals was coded to a particular order in the Royal Navy's signal book. The signal for close engagement, for example, was a white pendant over a blue and white checkered square. What Graves wanted was for his whole fleet to ease down gradually against the enemy battle line so that each vessel took on its opposite number. But there was no signal for such a maneuver. Improvising, Graves ordered the signals for engage the enemy *and* line ahead at the same time, hoping that his captains would figure it out.*

They didn't. As the British van (commanded by an admiral with the historic name of Francis Drake) edged down toward the French van to engage, the rest of the British battle line remained locked in its tight line-ahead formation, so the opposing battle lines formed an acute angle to one another. Even after the lead vessels began firing broadsides, the ships in the rear of both lines remained out of range. Eager as he was for a fight, Hood felt obligated to remain a well-disciplined half cable's length behind the ship in front of him. He was not happy about it. He was angry that Graves had not pounced on the isolated French van when he had the chance; he was angry that Graves kept the signal for line ahead flying even after the action opened; above all, he was angry that Graves did not set "an example of close action" (in his words) by adopting a less conventional and more aggressive plan for the battle.[7]

---

* The use of signal flags to issue orders to a fleet under way was still evolving in the late eighteenth century. Not until 1790 did the Royal Navy adopt Lord Howe's system as standard. Even then it was sometimes necessary to spell out nonstandard orders. At Trafalgar, in 1805, Nelson kept his signal officers busy during the long approach to battle by ordering them to spell out the now-famous order "England expects that every man will do his duty."

The ships at the front of the two columns hammered away furiously at each other, though this time the British did not dominate the gunnery duel, as they so often did. In part this may have been because the most eager French captains had charged to the front when de Grasse ordered them under way, so the French ships that constituted the van of their fleet were those led by the most aggressive French commanders. Moreover, the British van contained several of the ships that entered the battle already in a weak condition, including the leaky *Terrible* and *Ajax*. At four-fifteen Graves hauled down the signal for line ahead, but the rest of his fleet never did get fully involved. At five o'clock, with the sun already low in the sky, de Grasse ordered his fleet to bear away, and at six the firing died out. Though no one knew it yet, the battle was over.

For whatever reason, the British had got the worst of it. The lead British ship, the *Shrewsbury*, suffered twenty-six killed and forty-six wounded, including the ship's captain, who lost a leg. The second ship in the line, the *Intrepid*, counted sixty-five shot holes in her starboard side, in addition to which her sails and rigging were badly cut up, and both her mainmast and foremast were so weakened that they threatened to go over the side.* Altogether, the six ships in the British van suffered 54 killed and 153 wounded, whereas in the six ships of Hood's rear division there were no casualties at all. French casualties were comparable, a total of 209 killed and wounded, but their ships were relatively undamaged.[8]

For the next three days the two fleets maneuvered as each sought to gain (or keep) the weather gage. At the same time, the British worked furiously to repair their battered and crippled vessels while Graves tried to figure out his duty under these unusual circumstances. When he ordered his ships to prepare for battle on the sixth, several captains replied that they were in no condition to renew the fight. When Graves sent to Hood for his advice, that officer was icily correct and altogether unhelpful: "I dare say,"

---

* Eventually the *Intrepid* lost its weakened mainmast and the captain of the *Terrible* reported that his pumps could not keep up with the water, which was rising at the rate of eight feet per hour. On September 11, six days after the battle, Graves decided to abandon the *Terrible*, and after the crew was removed, it was burned.

Hood replied, "Mr. Graves will do what is right." On September 10, five days after the battle, Graves called for a conference of flag officers on board the *London*. At that conference, when Graves asked Hood why he had not engaged during the fight, Hood replied, "You had the signal up for the line." When Graves asked Drake why he *had* engaged, Drake replied, "On account of the signal for action." Graves turned back to Hood: "What say you to this?" Hood replied, "The signal for the line was enough for me."⁹

As the English admirals engaged in this kind of unprofitable bickering, de Grasse managed to maneuver his ships into the windward position. Then he disappeared. Graves literally lost sight of him. The next day Hood wrote Graves a formal note suggesting that de Grasse must have returned to Chesapeake Bay (as indeed he had) and implying that since this was the object of the whole campaign, the British should head there as well. Hood got no answer to that, but on the thirteenth he received an equally formal note that, along with Hood's response, speaks volumes about the character of formal communications in the eighteenth century, as well as the thinly disguised tension that existed between the beleaguered Graves and his frustrated subordinate:

On Board HMS London, Thursday Morning, 6 o'clock: *Admiral Graves presents his compliments to Sir Samuel Hood, and begs leave to acquaint [him] that . . . the French fleet are at anchor above the Horse Shoe [Shoal] in the Chesapeake, and desires his opinion what to do with the fleet.*

#

Barfleur, Thursday Morning, 7 A.M.: *Rear Admiral Sir Samuel Hood presents his compliments to Rear-Admiral Graves. Is extremely concerned to find by his note just received that the French fleet is at anchor in the Chesapeake . . . , though it is no more than what he expected. . . . Sir Samuel would be very glad to send an opinion, but he really knows not what to say in the truly lamentable state we have brought ourselves.*¹⁰

That afternoon, in a council of war on board the *London*, the British commanders agreed to return to New York, refit, and make another try of it later.

Lord Cornwallis, whose cornered army was the focus of the whole campaign, still hoped that the Royal Navy might give it another try, but the odds had become much longer. Washington had arrived at Yorktown with the rest of the American army. Worse, while Graves and de Grasse had maneuvered further and further away from the Virginia capes, de Barras had arrived with eight more French ships of the line and had slipped into the bay, giving de Grasse a total of thirty-six such vessels. Moreover, de Barras brought the heavy siege artillery the Franco-American allies needed to isolate Yorktown completely. Just as there was a studied formality to engagements at sea, so, too, was there a regular procedure for sieges ashore. With heavy siege guns, Washington and Rochambeau could begin working their way, yard by yard, toward the British lines. And finally, Cornwallis was running out of food and supplies. On October 3 he ordered two hundred horses drowned in the York River because he did not have enough forage to keep them alive.[11]

In New York the British made great efforts to patch together a relief expedition. Eventually they gathered some twenty-five ships of the line plus an equal number of transports crammed with an embarked army of over seven thousand men. The sailing date was set for October 19, but though the British in New York could not have known it, on that very day outside Yorktown, the British army marched out of its lines to lay down its arms in formal surrender. When Graves reached Chesapeake Bay two days later, he learned that not only had Cornwallis surrendered his army, but a total of thirty-six French ships of the line now occupied the bay. True to his character, Hood wanted to remain on station and blockade them. But with the odds so long, and with seven thousand embarked soldiers to feed, blockade was an unlikely stratagem. Graves had to face the fact that he was too late. The next day he led his armada back to New York.

Graves lost his job. His command of the American station had always been a temporary one, though he might have kept it had he won a victory. Instead the arrival of Rear Admiral the Hon. Robert Digby ended his short tenure, and Graves was ordered to Jamaica to serve under Vice Admiral Sir Peter Parker. Whether or not this was meant as a chastisement, Graves took it as one. "I must beg to state to the their lordships in my own behalf," he wrote, "that being superceded [*sic*] by a junior officer, and sent to another station where I can only be second and possibly third in command ... imply's [*sic*] such a disapprobation of my conduct as will certainly discredit me." It was characteristic of his generation and his station in society to express as much concern about how his transfer would affect his reputation as he did about the loss of Cornwallis's army. After all, he seemed to ask, what was his crime? He had followed the rules precisely. In responding to Hood's subsequent criticism of his conduct of the battle, he replied, "My aim was to get close, to form parallel, and attack together." Wasn't that precisely what a fleet commander was supposed to do?[12]

If Graves had played by the rules, de Grasse had bent them: first in virtually abandoning the West Indies to bring his entire fleet to Chesapeake Bay, second by going out to meet the British challenge rather than trying to defend the bay, and finally by discarding the hoary rules of combat to improvise when necessary. Then, too, while Graves and Hood had bickered over whose fault it was that de Grasse had got away, de Grasse and his subordinates engaged in a genuine exchange of ideas about how best to react to the British challenge. A quarter century later Lord Nelson would emphasize the importance of command cooperation, and he christened his subordinate captains "a band of brothers." In the Battle of the Capes, it was the French high command, and not the British, that behaved in accordance with this new concept of cooperative command.

For the French and the British, the Battle of the Capes was simply one more fleet engagement in a long list of such encounters. But for the Americans it was epochal. Though it was part of a complex global strategy involving naval and land forces separated by thousands of miles, in the end Graves's failure to drive de Grasse from the Virginia Capes was the proximate cause of Cornwallis's capitulation, the event that led directly to American independence. In London, George III wanted to continue the fight for his North American colonies, but his prime minister, Lord North, knew better. He knew that after this disaster, the country would not sustain a continued war. When he heard that Cornwallis had surrendered, he cried out, "Oh God! It is all over."

For the United States, however, it was only the beginning.

[PART ONE]

WOODEN WARSHIPS
AND THE WESTERN FRONTIER

—

The Battle of Lake Erie
September 10, 1813

LAKE ERIE IS THE SOUTHERNMOST OF THE FIVE GREAT LAKES. At its western end it is fed by the Detroit River, which carries the discharge from the three largest of those lakes (Superior, Michigan, and Huron), and at its eastern end it is drained by the Niagara River, which spills spectacularly into Lake Ontario. Along its southern shore, connected today by the asphalt ribbon of Interstate 90, is a string of cities historically associated with the coal-and-steel-based industry of the late nineteenth century: Buffalo, Erie, Cleveland, Toledo, and Detroit. Modern Americans are likely to conceive of this region as the "rust belt," an area where the "old economy" flourished in the nineteenth and early twentieth centuries, where brick chimneys spilled black smoke into the sky, and where endless trains of boxcars and flatcars carried the products from a hundred factories to the world's consumers. Given that, it is difficult to envision Lake Erie the way Americans did in the early nineteenth century: as a distant frontier of dense forests and untracked wilderness, a body of water whose shores were largely unpopulated if not in some areas virtually unexplored. The town of Erie was a tiny frontier settlement on Presque Isle Bay, Cleveland had fewer than a hundred residents, and Detroit was Fort Detroit, a garrisoned western outpost for trappers and traders. In 1813 Lake Erie represented not the East but the West, and it was the key to the great western empire granted to the United States by the British in the Treaty of Paris in 1783.

That treaty had been a diplomatic coup for the United States. Not only did it acknowledge the United States to be "free, sovereign, and independent," it also established the national boundaries of the new country as extending "to the river Mississippi," thus granting to the new nation a western empire beyond the hopes of all but the most optimistic. Of particular interest was the area west of the Alleghenies and north of the Ohio River, a region called simply "the Northwest," an area that would eventually encompass the states of Ohio, Indiana, Illinois, Michigan, Wisconsin, and part of Minnesota. The treaty called for British troops to be evacuated "with all convenient speed" from this territory, but the British seemed to find any speed inconvenient. This infuriated Americans, who had always suspected that the British government intended to keep them hemmed in along the coastline. One of the charges that Americans had leveled against George III in the Declaration of Independence was that he had encouraged "the merciless Indian savages" to attack American settlements on the western frontier. If that was not literally true, it was certainly true that the British hoped to limit American expansion in the West even after independence, and they sought to achieve this goal by encouraging the aspirations of the native tribes. In some small part this may have been due to British concern for their erstwhile Indian allies, but primarily it was because the British recognized that a thriving and commercially vibrant United States would pose a threat to British mastery in the Atlantic.

Because there were so few roads in the Northwest, the lakes and waterways were crucial. Travelers from the East Coast to the western frontier generally ascended the Hudson River to Albany, then worked their way westward along the Mohawk River Valley to Lake Ontario and along its southern shore to Lake Erie, which provided communication with Ohio and Michigan Territory. The ability to move men and supplies across the western lakes determined control of not only the Northwest but also "Upper Canada": the southernmost part of modern Ontario. In 1813 whoever controlled Lake Erie controlled the West, and with it the future course of American history. On the tenth of September in 1813, that future was decided in a battle between two small squadrons of sailing vessels on Lake Erie. It was America's most important engagement during the Age of Sail, and if the numbers involved were relatively modest, the strategic consequences were enormous.

—

A T F I R S T L I G H T on September 10, 1813, the two brigs and seven small gunboats that constituted the American naval squadron on Lake Erie lay quietly at anchor in the sheltered waters of Put-in-Bay in the lee of South Bass Island. As dawn spread slowly across the surface of the lake, a sailor stationed at the crosstrees of the mainmast on the flagship

Lawrence peered into the gray mist to the northwest, the direction from which the enemy was most likely to approach. As the sky brightened, he noted a small irregularity that emerged from the gray curtain, and with the sun at his back he discerned the glint of sunlight off canvas. He did not wait for the image to solidify. Cupping his hand around his mouth, he shouted down to the deck below: "Sail ho!"

"Where away?" the deck officer called back.

"Off Snake Island," came the reply. Then the sailor cried out again: "Sail ho!" Then again: "Sail ho! Six sail in sight."[1]

In his cabin at the stern of the *Lawrence*, twenty-eight-year-old Master Commandant Oliver Hazard Perry was on his feet even before the deck officer could formally relay the news. He knew at once that the appearance of six sail could only mean that the British fleet was out and approaching. He rushed topside from his cabin and began issuing the commands that would get the *Lawrence* and the eight other vessels of his command out of the bay and into the open waters of Lake Erie, where they could meet the enemy. A single gun boomed out from the *Lawrence*—the prearranged signal to get under way—bo'suns' pipes twittered, and the ship came to life. Sailors spat into their hands before grasping the capstan bars and leaning into them to heave up the ship's anchor; other sailors climbed outboard of the rails to ascend the rope ladders, called ratlines, to the horizontal spars or yards, then edged out onto the footropes slung below the yards in order to loose the sails. A few of them moved gingerly, looking down as they placed their bare feet on the single strand of rope. Watching from the deck below were other "sailors" who only weeks before had been members of the militia army of General William Henry Harrison and who found themselves aboard a ship now only because of Perry's desperate need for manpower. As the sails were sheeted home the ship began to move, almost imperceptibly at first, and the helmsman gently tested the feel of the tiller as the ship's keel bit into the water. These activities were duplicated throughout the squadron as, one by one, the vessels of Perry's command got under way.[2]

Perry had been anticipating this moment for over five months, ever since he had arrived at Presque Isle on the lake's southern shoreline in late

March with orders to oversee the completion of a squadron of warships. Now his nervous energy was evident in his body language as he paced back and forth on the small quarterdeck, glancing upward to see how the sails were drawing, peering around him at the activity within the squadron, and turning occasionally to steady his glass on the approaching enemy. The fact that the British were out and apparently determined on a fight was the good news; Perry had been seeking just such a fight ever since his squadron had been completed in late July. The bad news was that the wind was blowing from the southwest, which would give the British the weather gage. As long as the wind blew from the British toward the Americans, the British commander could decide when—or even if—to engage, and, more importantly, at what range. Both of Perry's big ships were armed primarily with short-range carronades: stubby, short-barreled guns that were deadly at close range but useless at a distance. If the British held the weather gage, they could remain at whatever range they preferred and pick him to pieces with their long guns. Perry wanted a fight at close range, preferably at the traditional half cable's length—about one hundred yards—from which distance he was confident that he could blast the English ships to kindling. But the contrary wind made that unlikely. Almost certainly the British commander had chosen this moment to seek battle precisely because the wind direction would allow him to dictate the character of the fight.

Perry was reluctant to surrender such an advantage without a struggle. As the vessels of his squadron straggled out of the bay in a rough line-ahead formation, he set a course to gain a westerly heading in an effort to seize the weather gage. For three hours, from seven to ten, he tried to force his square-rigged two-masted brigs into the teeth of a seven-knot breeze, tacking back and forth with a great expenditure of time and effort. The novice sailors on the *Lawrence* struggled mightily to brace the yards as close to the wind as the geometry of wind and sail would allow, then at Perry's command they swung the yards around by brute force as the tiller went over and the ship heeled grudgingly onto the other tack. Forward progress was measured in feet. At times it seemed that the contrary wind was pushing the American ships sideways, and meanwhile the British ships were coming ever closer. They were easily visible from the deck now, and the surgeon's mate on board the *Lawrence* was impressed by the display: "The vessels were freshly painted," he recalled, "and with the morning sun shining upon their broadsides, and their red ensigns gently unfolding to the breeze, they made a very gallant appearance."[3]

At midmorning, with the British squadron hull up and closing, Perry reluctantly conceded the weather gage to the enemy. He abandoned the idea of a fight from close range and gave the order to wear ship to put the *Lawrence* and the rest of the squadron on an easterly heading. It would give the British a serious, perhaps even decisive tactical advantage, and the *Lawrence*'s sailing master, William Taylor, was bold enough to say so. "I don't care!" Perry shot back. "To windward or to leeward, they shall fight today!"[4]

Then Perry's luck changed. The southwest wind weakened and died, and then, almost imperceptibly, it began to blow from the southeast. At once Perry countermanded the order to wear ship, and as the new breeze strengthened and the sails on the *Lawrence* stiffened, the American vessels settled comfortably on a northwesterly course with the wind to their backs. In that moment, the tactical advantage shifted dramatically and unpredictably from the British to the Americans. His spirits soaring, Perry ordered the battle flag that he had prepared raised to main truck of the *Lawrence*. It was a large black square on which a sailor's widow had stitched white block letters to form the words DONT GIVE UP THE SHIP. Every man on board knew that this was more than command guidance. They were the dying words of James Lawrence, captain of the ill-fated American frigate *Chesapeake,* who had been mortally wounded in a duel with the British frigate *Shannon* on the first of June, and in whose honor Perry's flagship had been named. Perry no doubt meant the flag to be an inspiration as well as an injunction, and when it broke at the top of the mast and could be read, it elicited a rousing cheer from the crew. If nothing else, the flag was a symbol of Perry's determination to bring things to a decisive conclusion. Perry knew that in the next few hours the men on board the two squadrons now swiftly closing on each other would decide the control of Lake Erie and with it the outcome of the campaign for mastery of the American Northwest.[5]

The war that brought Perry to Lake Erie had its roots in the continuing—indeed, seemingly endless—series of wars between Britain and France that dated back to 1689. The latest chapter in this epic struggle had begun in 1793, a decade after the end of the American Revolution, and by the dawn of the new century, the armies of France were being led by an inspired and unpredictable genius named Napoleon Bonaparte. By then, the British had developed a well-worn strategy for conducting their wars against France. Counting on their continental allies to keep the French army occupied on land, the British themselves relied heavily—if not quite exclusively—on their navy: to blockade the coast of France, to harry its trade, and to seize its colonies. Only in Spain, where the future duke of Wellington fought a war of attrition and maneuver with the French occupiers, did Britain commit its soldiers to the land war.

On one hand, such a strategy took maximum advantage of Britain's superiority at sea and minimized British casualties, but on the other hand, it was enormously expensive. To maintain a worldwide fleet of nearly a thousand warships required not only money but also manpower, and as a result, the Royal Navy had an unquenchable need for sailors, or at least for men who could be turned into sailors. To get them, Royal Navy captains fitting out ships for service were authorized to press men into service—that is, simply to take them—in whatever public place they could be found: lounging on the docks, having a pint or a smoke at the pub, even sleeping in the rented room of a boardinghouse. The press gang could not, however, enter a man's home; that, at least, was sacrosanct. Ignorance of the maritime profession provided no security from the press gangs. Even those who had never been to sea were fair game. Rated as "landsmen" and assigned the most rudimentary tasks, they were expected simply to learn on the job. The justification for this draconian policy was the presumption that every British citizen owed service to his king whenever the security of the nation was at risk. The press was the British counterpart of the French levée en masse that secured the cannon fodder for Napoleon's armies.

After the end of the brief Peace of Amiens in 1803, with the war already in its second decade, the pickings had become pretty scarce along the waterfront, and Royal Navy captains had to be increasingly creative to secure a crew. Royal Navy warships stopped inbound British merchant ships at the harbor's mouth, and the men on board who had been eagerly looking forward to setting foot on shore after a long voyage instead found themselves pressed into the Royal Navy. This practice extended into the open sea as well and became so common that British merchant captains, like their French counterparts, often fled at the sight of a Royal Navy warship on the horizon. Of course, flight aroused the suspicions of warship captains, who set out in pursuit and soon caught and stopped the slower merchant vessels. Sometimes the warship only "spoke" the vessel, with officers literally shouting across the intervening distance to discover the identity and nationality of the suspicious merchantman. But often the captain of the warship decided to send a boat for a closer inspection. When the boat bumped alongside, a Royal Navy lieutenant, generally a young man in his early twenties, would climb onto the deck and ask the skipper for his papers. Once satisfied that the vessel was not French or bound for a French port, the lieutenant might ask the captain to muster his crew. Any likely-looking sailor, particularly one with a seaman's pigtail or tattoo, would then and there be pressed into service: taken off the merchantman and carried back to the warship to serve for the duration of the war. If the warship was seriously shorthanded, men might be pressed into service whether they had previous naval experience or not, or even if they claimed not to be British citizens.

What rankled Americans was that this practice of impressment often included American vessels. Stopping American ships at sea to check their papers was annoying enough, but when the British began conscripting able-bodied Americans off those ships, it was intolerable. The British insisted that they took only men who could be identified as British citizens, men who by their English birth owed service to their king by British law. But men who had been born in the British Isles and subsequently emigrated to America did not think of themselves as British subjects. Besides, Royal Navy captains who were desperate for manpower inevitably stretched the definition of "British subject." Any bloke with an accent, or for that matter anyone who could not prove that he *wasn't* British, was likely to be pressed into service. Eventually some ten thousand men who claimed to be Americans were pressed into service to feed the insatiable manpower demands of the Royal Navy.[6]

American protests over this practice nearly boiled over into war fever in 1807 when the British frigate *Leopard* stopped the American warship *Chesapeake* just outside its namesake bay. James Barron was the *Chesapeake*'s commanding officer, and because he did not expect to encounter a hostile environment until he arrived in the Mediterranean, he was apparently unconcerned that the *Chesapeake*'s deck was littered with crates of supplies, its guns secured, and its powder and shot stowed below.* When the *Leopard* signaled that it had dispatches to deliver, Barron obligingly hove to and waited for the small boat containing a blue-coated lieutenant to be rowed across. The "dispatches" turned out to be a letter from the British captain demanding that three men, all of them deserters from the Royal Navy whom he believed to be on board the *Chesapeake*, be turned over to him. Barron was convinced that there were no British deserters on his ship and refused the request. The lieutenant made it clear that he was under specific orders and that serious consequences might result if Barron did not accede. When Barron remained adamant and sent the lieutenant back to his ship, the *Leopard* opened fire. Unable to reply due to the disorganized state of the gundeck, the officers and men on the hapless *Chesapeake* simply absorbed the punishment until finally a single gun could be fired in a gesture of defiance before Barron ordered the flag lowered. As the white smoke from the guns drifted away, the lieutenant returned and claimed his three deserters, and the *Leopard* departed.[7]

News of this outrage raced through the States. Impressing sailors from merchant vessels was bad enough, but opening fire on an American ship of war elevated the dispute to a crisis. President Thomas Jefferson came under tremendous pressure to do something. Jefferson, however, saw little

---

* Technically, Barron was the commodore of the Mediterranean squadron and Charles Gordon was the captain of the *Chesapeake*. But Barron was the senior officer present afloat (SOPA) and therefore responsible for the decisions made during the encounter with the *Leopard*. Afterward it was Barron and not Gordon who was court-martialed and suspended from the service for five years for taking the vessel to sea in such an unready state.

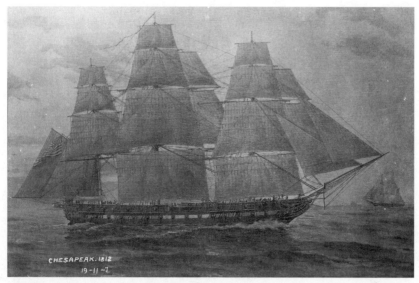

The unlucky American frigate USS *Chesapeake* under way. The *Chesapeake* not only was the victim of HMS *Leopard* in 1807 but was subsequently defeated and captured by HMS *Shannon* in the War of 1812 in the battle that claimed the life of James Lawrence. Lawrence's dying words—"Don't give up the ship"—inspired the flag that Perry flew during the Battle of Lake Erie. (U.S. Navy)

national benefit, other than the mitigation of hurt pride, to be gained from a war with England, and his reaction was muted. Still, his complaints were sufficient to secure an apology from the British, who were no more eager for war than he was. The British commodore who had ordered the recovery of the deserters was recalled, and two of the seized men were returned (one had already been hanged for desertion). Nevertheless, American anger and bitterness lingered as British "insults" to American nationality and pride continued.

Less dramatic but equally divisive were the disputes between America and Britain over economic policy. By 1806 Britain had gained unquestioned command of the sea, due largely to Lord Nelson's spectacular victory at Trafalgar in October 1805 over the combined fleets of France and Spain. For their part, the French had gained dominance on land due to Napoleon's equally spectacular victories over the Austrians and Russians at Austerlitz (1805) and the Prussians at Jena-Auerstadt (1806). The British were masters of the sea; the French were masters of the land. Because neither side could effectively threaten the other, each side sought to apply indirect pressure through economic sanctions. Napoleon began the economic warfare by declaring from French-occupied Berlin that no European nation would henceforth be allowed to trade with England (the so-called Berlin Decrees). England reciprocated with an Order in Council proclaiming that all nations trading with France or its allies would be treated as hostile. Caught in the middle of these opposing declarations was the neutral United States. Jefferson tried to avoid entanglement by declaring an embargo on all American trade, a policy that failed to influence the great powers abroad and which led to widespread smuggling at home before it was finally repealed in 1809.[8]

A third source of conflict between the United States and Britain was British sympathy for and support of several of the western Indian tribes in the Old Northwest. Despite the terms of the Treaty of Paris, which ceded the territory north of the Ohio and east of the Mississippi to the United States, the British maintained close relations with the native tribes of the Northwest, and particularly the Iroquois. On one hand, such a policy was intended to keep the peace and protect the handful of Canadian trappers and traders who ventured into the region of the Great Lakes, but in addition, British support for the Indians was a deliberate strategy to counterbalance American influence in the area. Americans resented the continued British influence in the Northwest and suspected that British agents were deliberately encouraging Indian raids against American outposts.[9]

American suspicions increased in 1808 when the Shawnee war chief Tecumseh, brother of the visionary leader known as the Prophet, met with British officials at Fort Malden, on the Canadian side of the Detroit River, to urge that they form a military alliance to drive the Americans from the region. The British did not say yes, but neither did they say no. Tecumseh met with the Americans, too. In 1810 he told the American militia general William Henry Harrison that the western Indians would not sign any more treaties that gave away Indian lands, and that further encroachments by the Americans on those lands would be met with force. When Indian raids against American outposts continued, Harrison organized a campaign to capture and punish those who were conducting the raids. As his militia army approached the Prophet's village on the Tippecanoe River in what is now central Indiana, the Indians struck. The Prophet had assured the warriors that American bullets could not harm them, and they attacked fearlessly, if improvidently. In the Battle of Tippecanoe (November 7, 1811) they suffered horrible losses, but they also killed or wounded nearly two hundred Americans before they were driven off, and the next day Harrison's men burned the Prophet's village.[10]

Frustrated and embittered by his brother's defeat, Tecumseh again appealed to the British. This time he arrived at Fort Malden bearing a beaded belt, or wampum, that the British had given the Iroquois years earlier, after the French and Indian War, as a token of permanent friendship and support. Brandishing this token, Tecumseh called upon the British to honor their pledge. This time the British were more receptive. Having decided that war with America was now likely if not imminent, the British agent, Matthew Elliott, sent off a request for five hundred British troops to act in concert with the Indians in an attack on Fort Detroit once war commenced. Americans in the area were now convinced that this Anglo-Indian alliance was a direct threat to their security. In March 1812 the *Niles Weekly Register* declared flatly that the Indian raids on the frontier "are instigated and supported by the British in Canada."[11]

The convergence of these events in Europe, on the high seas, and in the forests of the American Northwest brought the crisis in Anglo-American relations to a climax. One group of mostly western and southern congressmen, soon dubbed the "War Hawks," argued that because British dominance at sea was insurmountable, the best means of bringing England to account was to threaten her Canadian possessions. It was obvious that the United States lacked the resources to create a navy that could confront the British on the high seas. But the British commitment to the ongoing European war meant that British Canada was weakly garrisoned. The War Hawks argued that the invasion and occupation of Canada would not only suppress the Indian raids but also enable the Americans to hold Canada as a bargaining chip in the subsequent negotiations concerning both impressment and the hated Orders in Council. One of the prominent War

Hawks, House Speaker Henry Clay, wrote a friend in 1813: "When the war commenced, Canada was not the end but the means; the object of the war being the redress of injuries, and Canada being the instrument by which that redress was to be obtained."[12]

This new bellicosity led Congress to enact a number of measures during the winter of 1811–12 designed to put the country on a war footing. One act authorized an increase in the size of the regular army from ten thousand to thirty-five thousand; another authorized the president to call out a hundred thousand militia volunteers. When it came to naval preparations, however, Congress balked. A bill introduced by South Carolinian Langdon Cheves to build ten new frigates failed to pass in either house, not because members believed that war could (or should) be avoided but because they perceived that the coming war was likely to be fought along the Canadian border and not on the high seas. Many congressmen were instinctively suspicious of standing naval forces and argued that a permanent naval establishment was likely to become a tool of oppression. After all, wasn't British tyranny on the high seas the source of the current problem? "Navies," Congressman William Bibb of Georgia insisted, "are calculated to produce mischief."[13]

The British were not intimidated by the American preparations, but neither were they eager to add one more nation to their long list of foes in a war that had been going on intermittently for nearly two decades. In June 1812, therefore, the British repealed the Orders in Council, but it was too late. That same month the U.S. Congress declared war.

—

The American decision to declare war was astonishingly reckless. To be sure, Britain was engaged in a world war with Napoleonic France, which would prevent her from focusing all of her national strength against the United States, but the disparity in power between Britain and America, particularly at sea, was an unbridgeable gulf. The U.S. Navy in 1812 consisted of a total of 17 ships of war and 165 harbor defense gunboats, most of which carried only a single cannon and which could not operate on the high seas. By contrast, the Royal Navy had over 1,000 warships on its navy list, 719 of them in commission, 261 laid up in ordinary, and 62 more under construction. And many of those ships were double- or triple-deck ships of the line carrying up to a hundred or more guns each. A fair measure of the disparity in naval power between the opponents is the fact that the Royal Navy had three times as many *ships* as the United States Navy had *guns*.[14]

The War Hawks insisted that this didn't matter. They hoped to seize Canada with a militia army and hold it as a hostage for future negotiations, and they insisted that the conquest would be an easy one: "a mere matter of marching," as more than one described it. The War Hawks noted that Britain had wrested Canada from the French less than fifty years before, and they insisted that the allegiance of the population to British rule was questionable. In fact, Americans convinced themselves that the Canadians would not fight, or at least that they would not fight effectively. One congressman described them as "a debased race of poltroons" who would bolt and run at "the mere sight of an army of the United States."[15] But in order to overawe the "poltroons" of Canada, the United States would first need an army, and in spite of congressional authorization to raise new troops, its army was no more ready for war than its navy.

In 1812 the U.S. Army comprised two very different elements: a "frontier constabulary" consisting of small garrisons strung out across the western frontier to keep an eye on the Indians, and a quite separate body of men who were assigned to the coastal artillery along the Atlantic seaboard.[16] But there was no field force; no "army" that could march to Canada or anyplace else. Where would this "army of the United States" come from? The answer was the militia.

The American citizen soldier was then (and to a certain extent remains today) part of American popular culture. The prototype was the Minuteman who stood on Lexington Green to defy the redcoats in 1775. Despite Washington's subsequent skepticism about the value of militia troops during the Revolutionary War, an American myth emerged about the fighting prowess of the militia. According to this myth, America's security depended on its farmer-soldiers, men who in time of danger would seize their muskets from over the mantelpiece, muster on the village common, and march off to war to defend the Republic from either the heathens on the frontier or the hired legions of a European enemy.* By 1812 the idea that the nation's military strength rested in its militia had become a matter of faith. In fact, the militia had never performed all that well in battle, and in any case by 1812 the leaders of the various militia units were either superannuated leftovers from the Revolution or, more often, ambitious politicians who had obtained militia commissions for their social cachet or political value. A militia army meant indifferent discipline, insecure logistic support, and questionable leadership.

Despite that, American optimism was not entirely misplaced, for Canada was indeed vulnerable. In 1812 Canada was not the continental giant it is today; it consisted primarily of a series of towns and villages along the valley of the St. Lawrence River. Some likened British Canada to a tree lying on its side: the "roots" of this tree spread out from the Gulf of St. Lawrence, past Newfoundland, and into the Atlantic Ocean; the "trunk" was the St. Lawrence River, reaching inland past Quebec and Montreal to the "branches" of the tree, which were the five Great Lakes. "Lower Canada" referred to Quebec and the lower reaches of the St. Lawrence near the roots of the tree (even though they appear above the rest of Canada on a map), and "Upper Canada" meant the area south and west of Montreal bounded by Lakes Ontario and Erie to the south and Huron to the north. To kill this tree, it was fairly obvious that Americans should aim to sever the trunk, and the obvious place to apply the ax was Montreal. An American thrust up the traditional invasion route of the Hudson River Valley and along the axis of Lake Champlain to the St. Lawrence would cut the upriver settlements off from the life-giving river, and Canada would fall.[17]

But it didn't happen that way. A number of factors conspired to wreck this strategic plan before it even got started. First of all, the absence of a standing U.S. Army meant that a militia field army had to be assembled,

* This symbolism survives today in the Army Reserve, which employs the silhouette of a Minuteman as its official emblem. The mythology of the citizen soldier survives in popular culture as well. A film of the 1980s entitled *Red Dawn* reflected the patriotic anti-Communism of the Cold War era by depicting a handful of high school students with shotguns and pickup trucks defending Colorado from a Soviet invasion.

and that took time. While time passed, Americans were distracted by other wartime demands. Most importantly, the British deliberately diverted attention from the vulnerable trunk of the Canadian tree to its branches by unleashing the Indian threat in the Northwest. The campaign that should have begun at Montreal, therefore, began instead at Detroit. And it began badly.

—

In June of 1812, while Congress debated a declaration of war against England and Napoleon launched his ill-fated invasion of Russia, an American brigadier general named William Hull was marching what he grandly called the "American Army of the Northwest" through the forests of Ohio and Michigan toward Detroit, cutting a military road as he went. A Revolutionary War veteran and governor of Michigan Territory, Hull had enough military experience and knowledge of the local geography to realize the dangers of launching an invasion of Upper Canada before gaining naval control of Lake Erie, and his first instinct was to postpone an offensive until the lake was secured. But under pressure to act quickly, Hull decided that an American conquest of the lake's north shore would deny British warships their bases and thereby secure naval control without a navy. His first instinct was the correct one.

If Hull's advance to Fort Detroit was less disastrous than Napoleon's march to Moscow, his campaign was nevertheless a strategic calamity of the first order for the United States. To begin with, Hull chose to build his road through the Black Swamp, which slowed his progress considerably. Even more ill-considered was his decision to send his sick, and all of his baggage, ahead on the small schooner *Cuyahoga* across Lake Erie. On the very day that the *Cuyahoga* set sail, news arrived at British-held Fort Malden at the mouth of the Detroit River that Congress had declared war. When the *Cuyahoga* sailed blithely past Fort Malden en route to Detroit, six British soldiers in a rowboat stopped it, clambered on deck, and declared it to be a prize of war. The British thereby obtained not only a number of American prisoners, as well as most of the American army's entrenching equipment and all of its baggage, but also a copy of Hull's orders, his personal correspondence, and the army's muster rolls. Only after Hull arrived at Detroit in early July did he learn that war had been declared and that he had already suffered a serious setback. The news bred caution in a man who was already supremely cautious.[18]

It was Napoleon Bonaparte (now en route to Moscow) who asserted that "in war, it is not men who make the difference, but the man." What won battles, in other words, was not numbers but leadership. Whether that was true of Napoleon's victories (and his defeats), it was certainly true of the campaign along the banks of the Detroit River in the summer of 1812. Though Hull commanded an army of twenty-six hundred men, including one regular U.S. Army regiment, he lacked the will to use his army effectively. By contrast, his British opponent, Major General Isaac Brock, had only about seven hundred men, half of them Canadian militia, but he possessed both a burning determination and a willingness to take risks.

Hull began his campaign by issuing a proclamation to the Canadians announcing that he bore them no hostility and offering "Peace, Liberty, and Security" as long as they did not interfere with his invasion. If they did, however, he promised "instant destruction." Alas, Hull's actions did not match his words. Once he finally crossed the Detroit River into Canadian territory to begin his march toward the British outpost at Fort Malden, he moved slowly and cautiously, stopping en route to build a blockhouse. Because the British controlled the waters of both Lake Erie and the Detroit River, all of Hull's supplies had to come overland, which made them vulnerable to raids, and when Brock's Indian allies raided his supply lines, Hull concluded that he was overextended. While a bolder man might have pressed on, Hull decided, as he said later, "that an attempt on Malden should never be made until there was an absolute certainty of success," though he should have known as well as anyone that in war there is no such thing as "an absolute certainty." Even so, Hull decided to give up his advance and fall back across the river to Fort Detroit.[19]

Brock had planned to evacuate Fort Malden if the Americans arrived in force. But upon learning of Hull's retreat, he decided instead that an aggressive show of force now not only would allow him to keep the initiative but also might attract more Indian allies to his side. Despite the long odds, therefore, he decided to follow up Hull's retreat and invade the United States. His decision was as bold as Hull's was cautious, for Fort Detroit was a substantial citadel in that distant frontier. Its log-and-earth walls were twenty-two feet thick and protected by twenty-six artillery pieces. Undaunted by that reality, Brock crossed the river and invested Detroit from the landward side, sending the schooner *Queen Charlotte* (with eighteen guns) and the brig *General Hunter* (with ten) to block the Detroit River. Though Brock had only about four hundred regulars, an equal number of militia, and some six hundred Indian allies—barely half of Hull's strength—he declared that Detroit was under siege. His claim was more than bluff. With British ships controlling the river and Brock's Indian allies making the overland supply routes uncertain, Detroit was cut off from either supplies or support. Hull was terrified that if the siege proved successful, Brock would not be able to control his Indian allies and the families inside Fort Detroit would be butchered. When Brock promised safe passage for the Americans if they surrendered, Hull accepted.[20]

The impact of this disaster spread ripples all across the frontier and changed American strategy in Washington as well. Throughout the Northwest, the British success at Detroit emboldened the native tribes, and violence exploded all along the frontier from Ohio to Indiana. Hull himself was court-martialed, found guilty of neglect of duty and cowardice, and sentenced to die, though President Madison commuted his sentence in recognition of his Revolutionary War contributions. The fall of Detroit also provoked a dramatic change in U.S. grand strategy. The initial American thrust toward Montreal fizzled when an American militia army under Major General Henry Dearborn reached the Canadian border in November and the New York militia, which made up the bulk of his command, refused to leave their state. Even before that absurd denouement, President James Madison and Secretary of the Navy Paul Hamilton decided it was essential to refocus national attention on the northwest frontier, regain Detroit, and pacify the western Indians.

Hull's fate underscored the reality that for an American army to operate effectively on the northwest frontier, it would first be necessary to gain naval superiority on Lake Erie. Alas, when Brock captured Detroit, he also captured the only armed vessel the United States had on that lake: the fourteen-gun brig *Adams*, which the British renamed *Detroit* and added to their fleet of four other small warships to make up a squadron totaling fifty-seven guns. As long as the British controlled the lake, they also controlled all the lands that were washed by it from Ohio to Michigan. To defeat the Indians, therefore, it would first be necessary to build a fleet that could wrest control of Lake Erie from the British. "Without the ascendancy over those waters," Madison wrote, "we can never have it over the savages." Ironically, then, the land war against Canada would depend on the Navy after all.[21]

In fact, in the war so far, the tiny American Navy on the high seas had provided the only news that Americans could cheer about. Only three days after William Hull had ignominiously surrendered Detroit to the British, his nephew and adopted son Isaac Hull, in command of the frigate *Constitution* (forty-four guns), revived American morale as well as the family honor by winning a decisive victory over the British frigate *Guerriere* (thirty-eight guns) south of Newfoundland. It was in this fight that some of the British cannonballs allegedly bounced off the side of the stoutly built *Constitution*, giving her the immortal nickname "Old Ironsides." Soon afterward, even as the vaunted American invasion of Canada was collapsing, other single-ship victories by American frigates helped boost American morale at home. In October, Stephen Decatur in the *United States* (forty-four guns) defeated the British *Macedonian* (thirty-eight guns), and in December, it was the *Constitution* again, this time commanded by William Bainbridge, defeating the *Java* (forty-four guns) in a brutal slugfest off the coast of Brazil. After that, the British Admiralty ordered Royal Navy frigate commanders to avoid one-on-one engagements with the large American frigates. These American successes did not significantly affect the overall strategic situation, however, and within months a tightening British blockade of the American coast kept most of the U.S. warships imprisoned within their harbors. While those vessels sat idle, the United States had no ships at all on Lake Erie, where they were now so desperately needed.

To bring energy and a sense of purpose to the American naval presence on both Lake Ontario and Lake Erie, Madison appointed forty-year-old Navy veteran Isaac Chauncey to command American naval forces on both western lakes. Though Chauncey had little experience with naval combat, he had served a tour as commander of the New York Navy Yard and was knowledgeable about the construction and repair of ships, which was precisely the skill most needed in the fall of 1812. Chauncey's orders granted him wide latitude. He was to do whatever was necessary "to obtain command of the Lakes Ontario & Erie, with the least possible delay," and to achieve that, his orders gave him "unlimited authority" to "*purchase, hire, or build*" any vessels that he thought necessary. He could appropriate any supplies he needed and commandeer all the manpower he wanted, including "ship carpenters, caulkers, riggers, Sailmakers &c as may be required." Though Chauncey would have command on both lakes, he could not be in both places at the same time, so Hamilton ordered him to choose one of the lakes for his own headquarters and send some "officer in whom you can confide" to take command of the other. Chauncey set up his own headquarters at Sackett's Harbor at the eastern end of Lake Ontario, and to take command on Lake Erie he chose Lieutenant Jesse Duncan Elliott.[22]

Elliott was thirty years old in the fall of 1812 when he arrived on the shores of Lake Erie. A broad-faced man of middle stature, he had gotten something of a late start in his profession. Whereas most professionally ambitious young men received a midshipman's warrant in their teens, Elliott did not become a midshipman until he was twenty-one, an age when many young officers were already prepping for their lieutenant's exam. Perhaps because of that, he was a man in a hurry, eager for the public and professional glory that adhered to those who achieved military success. Like many officers during the Age of Sail, he was prone to measure his own worth by the yardstick of professional comment and public opinion. After all, not only were public acclaim and promotion gratifying, they were tangible evidence and validation of one's honor. In the nineteenth century, having "honor" not only required the demonstration of certain personal characteristics, such as bravery and truthfulness, but those values had to be confirmed and validated by the publicly expressed opinions of others; an unwitnessed act of honor was of little importance. Having been promoted from midshipman to lieutenant only two years before, Elliott looked to his assignment on Lake Erie as an opportunity to make his name in the service, gain promotion, and, not incidentally, validate his honor.[23]

Elliott arrived in Buffalo in the first week of September 1812. Before he could challenge the British for command of the lake, he first had to build a fleet. Moreover, that fleet would have to be built from scratch: vessels could not be brought from Lake Ontario because of Niagara Falls, and there were no existing facilities on Lake Erie for building warships. The entire American naval effort on Lake Erie would depend on conjuring a fleet out of the standing timber of the American forest. Worse, talks with the local militia commanders convinced Elliott that there was no suitable place on the shores of Lake Erie where a squadron of American gunboats might be built. All of the potential harbors along the southern (American) coastline either were too shallow to accommodate a shipyard or, if they were deep enough, could not be defended from British raids.[24] Still, he would have to set up shop someplace, and the place he selected was the small frontier town of Black Rock on the American side of the Niagara River, a few miles north of Buffalo. Elliott was aware that the site had severe limitations. First of all, there was no hope of building an American fleet in secret there: the Niagara River was so narrow that not only could the British on the north bank watch his activities, but soldiers on the two sides could actually shoot at each other. Worse, the western exit from the Niagara River into Lake Erie was commanded by a British fort (Fort Erie) on the northern shore. Even if Elliott managed to build his ships literally under the hostile eyes of his enemy, those vessels would be trapped in the Niagara River as long as the British commanded the exit. But the American militia general, Stephen Van Rensselaer, assured him that was not a problem, for he could "remove that difficulty" simply by taking possession of the British fort. Of course, this was before it had become evident that American militia might be unwilling to leave their state of origin.[25]

So Elliott got to work. Chauncey had ordered him to construct two 300-ton ships, which would make them the biggest warships on the lake (the *Queen Charlotte*, the largest of the British warships, displaced 255 tons), as well as six small gunboats. Getting started was relatively easy. He hired men to fell trees, strip them of their branches and bark, and begin sawing them into thick planks. But progress was slowed by a shortage of skilled carpenters, fitters, and joiners, and he lacked most of the matériel necessary to outfit a ship of war, including sails, rigging, blocks, anchors, cables, and of course guns, all of which had to be brought overland from the East Coast. Elliott chafed at the delays, and in October he planned an operation that would enable him to obtain the nucleus of an American squadron in one swift blow.

That month, two British warships of the Canadian Provincial Marine dropped anchor off Fort Erie. They were the three-gun brig *Caledonia* and the fourteen-gun *Detroit* (formerly the U.S. brig *Adams*, captured at Detroit). At about the same time, Elliott learned that a number of American sailors, forwarded from Lake Ontario by Chauncey to serve as crew for Elliott's vessels, were only a day's march away. Elliott decided to use the new arrivals to surprise the two British ships and capture them. On the

This nineteenth-century painting depicts the capture of HMS *Detroit* (in the foreground) and HMS *Caledonia* (at left) by Elliott's bold cutting-out expedition off Fort Erie in October of 1812. The feat made Elliott a hero, though his public reputation would suffer greatly after his behavior during the Battle of Lake Erie. (U.S. Naval Academy Museum)

night of October 8 he gathered about a hundred men in Buffalo Creek and embarked them onto two barges. Rowing across the mouth of the Niagara River in the darkest hours of the night, the Americans approached the two British vessels silently, then swiftly clambered up the sides of the two ships in a rush and captured them both. Locking the prisoners in the hold, Elliott ordered the anchor cables cut and raised the topsails, and within minutes the two vessels were moving downriver toward the American base at Black Rock.

But they were not moving very fast. The wind died to a flat calm, and British gunners on the northern bank of the river opened "a constant and destructive fire" with grape and canister. Elliott managed to get the smaller *Caledonia* to a safe anchorage under the American battery at Black Rock, but the larger *Detroit* proved unmanageable in a dead calm on a narrow river. After carrying on a running fight with British gunners for several hours and practically annihilating a boarding party of British soldiers that tried to retake the vessel, Elliott decided to abandon the *Detroit*, which by then had become a perfect wreck.[26]

This daring exploit was not a complete success, but it made Jesse Elliott a hero, the first American hero of the war in the Northwest (though Hull and Van Rensselaer provided little competition for such an accolade). Congress voted him a ceremonial sword, and a grateful Navy Department promoted him to master commandant over the heads of twenty-two other lieutenants who were senior to him. Elliott had gambled and won. He had weakened the British squadron on Lake Erie by capturing two of its five vessels, and simultaneously strengthened the American squadron. Not incidentally, he had won honors and promotion for himself. Surely it would not be long before he would be hailed again as the conqueror of Lake Erie.[27]

But Elliott was not the only naval officer dispatched to Lake Erie to build an American squadron. In early September, only days after Hamilton ordered Chauncey to take command on both of the western lakes, Daniel Dobbins showed up in Washington. Dobbins was a merchant ship captain who made a living bringing supplies to American outposts in the

Northwest. He and his vessel, the *Salina*, had been captured by the British when they seized the American outpost on Mackinac Island between Lake Michigan and Lake Huron. In the nineteenth century it was a fairly common practice to grant prisoners what was called "parole": a system in which the captive pledged himself not to bear arms against the enemy that had captured him unless by some arrangement both sides agreed to negotiate an exchange. Even if some prisoners occasionally defaulted on their parole, such a system avoided the expense and inconvenience of transporting, housing, and feeding large numbers of prisoners. So along with the rest of the American garrison at Mackinac, Dobbins was granted parole, and the British used Dobbins' vessel as a cartel to send the paroled American prisoners to Detroit. When Detroit fell in July, he was accused of having violated his parole, and he had to flee, hiding out in a schooner that was taking paroled prisoners to Cleveland. From there, Dobbins made his way along the lake shore to Erie, then overland to Washington, where he arrived in early September bearing the news of Hull's capitulation.[28]

Secretary of the Navy Paul Hamilton grilled Dobbins about British strength on the lake. Dobbins reported that the British had four armed vessels (they actually had five) plus another eight small schooners and sloops that could be converted to military use. Galvanized by Dobbins' report, Hamilton fired off another letter to Chauncey (who had already left for Sackett's Harbor), telling him that while he was to build ships on both lakes, the effort on Lake Erie should now be considered paramount. At the same time, Hamilton appointed Dobbins a sailing master in the Navy and sent him back to the northwest frontier with orders to build four gunboats in Presque Isle Bay near Erie, Pennsylvania, about ninety miles west of Elliott's base at Black Rock.[29]

Elliott was not happy to hear of Dobbins's arrival. He made sure that Dobbins understood who was in charge and told him bluntly that Presque Isle was utterly unsuitable as a building site, for there was a shallow bar across the mouth of the bay that would make it all but impossible to get warships from the building site out into the lake.[30] In part, Elliott's objections were genuine; he had considered Presque Isle as a base and rejected it. But in addition, he resented Hamilton's interference with his authority as the senior naval officer on Lake Erie. Elliott's pique never had a chance to blossom into open hostility, however, for in November Chauncey's shipwrights at Sackett's Harbor on Lake Ontario completed and launched a twenty-four-gun frigate that Chauncey named *Madison* after the president, and Chauncey picked Elliott to be her commander. Elliott thereupon quit his outpost at Black Rock and moved over to Lake Ontario. Technically, that left Dobbins in "command" of the American naval effort on Lake Erie. In the long run this clearly would not do. Someone with higher rank than that of sailing master had to be found for such a crucial theater of war. Coincidentally, that same month twenty-seven-year-old master commandant Oliver Hazard Perry applied to the Navy Department for active service.

—

Pudgy and baby-faced, with dark curly hair and sideburns, Oliver Hazard Perry looked much too young to be a master commandant with fourteen years of service in the United States Navy. Partly this was because he simply looked younger than he was, but partly, too, it was because Perry had started his naval career at a young age. His father, Christopher Raymond Perry, had been a successful privateer during the Revolutionary War, and by the time of the so-called Quasi War with France in 1798 the elder Perry was a post captain, the highest rank then available in the U.S. Navy. Perry senior managed to get a midshipman's warrant for his thirteen-year-old son, and young Oliver served in that capacity on board his father's ship. After the war, the teenage Oliver stayed in the Navy and served in the Mediterranean, where he was one of a handful of junior officers who fought with distinction under Edward Preble during the Barbary Wars and came to be known as "Preble's Boys." He made lieutenant at age twenty-one and commanded his own ship two years later. Since then, however, most of Perry's professional service had involved the more mundane service of constructing and maintaining coastal defense gunboats.[31]

Like most officers of his generation, Perry disliked gunboat service. Indeed, he disliked the whole idea of relying on gunboats for the nation's naval defense. Gunboats were small (usually sixty to eighty feet long) and lightly armed (most carried only a single gun forward); rigged with a single mast, they often had to be rowed from place to place, functioning more like floating artillery than actual warships. This was not the kind of service Perry had envisioned when he chose the Navy as a career. He petitioned the secretary of the navy for command of the brig *Argus*, but when that was not forthcoming, he accepted the nomination for service on Lake Erie with "great satisfaction."[32]

A baby-faced Oliver Hazard Perry painted at about the time of his victory on Lake Erie. Despite his youthful appearance, at the time of the battle Perry had spent half of his twenty-seven years as an officer in the U.S. Navy. (Painting by John Wesley Jarvis, U.S. Naval Academy Museum)

Though Perry got his orders to go to Lake Erie in the dead of winter, he started out at once, traveling overland from Newport to Albany accompanied by his thirteen-year-old brother, Alexander (who had his own warrant as a midshipman), and a black family servant named Cyrus Tiffany. At Albany, Perry caught up with his commanding officer, Isaac Chauncey, and they traveled together up the Mohawk River Valley to Sackett's Harbor on Lake Ontario before Perry pressed on to Black Rock on the Niagara River. Perry's first look at Black Rock convinced him that its close proximity to British soil made it unsuitable for an American shipyard, and he directed that all useful materials there should be forwarded to Presque Isle. Then he was off again, traveling the additional seventy-five miles further west to Presque Isle Bay near the town of Erie, Pennsylvania, where Dobbins was constructing four gunboats, and where the naval contractor Noah Brown had started work on two twenty-gun brigs.[33]

Perry's trip from Black Rock to Erie illuminated the difficulties that he would encounter in trying to build a war fleet on the banks of a frontier lake. The few roads that existed were all but impassable, rutted and soggy with melting snow. He started out in a horse-drawn sleigh that was dragged over the thin sheet of ice along the southern shore of the lake. But the ice was untrustworthy in late March, and the horses occasionally broke through the crust. Eventually he had to abandon the ice and trust to the sloppy roads ashore. Finally, on March 27, his party arrived at Erie, and he got his first glimpse of the shipyard where he was to supervise the construction of an American fleet.[34]

Erie itself was a pleasant little town consisting of about ninety buildings clustered near Presque Isle Bay, which was formed by an arm of the land that reached out into the lake. That peninsula shielded an arrowhead-shaped body of water some two miles wide, extending nearly five miles into the forest to a picturesque waterfall whose cascade provided a constant musical backdrop. On its shores, the keels of two twenty-gun brigs had been laid, the ribs of each vessel sticking up like the bones of a skeleton. Workers were in the process of nailing thick planks onto those ribs. But Noah Brown, the New York shipbuilder who had the government contract to build the brigs, was very nearly at the end of what he could do in this wilderness shipyard without iron fittings, cordage, sails, guns, or anchors. Nor did he have the carpenters, blacksmiths, joiners, and other experts necessary to complete the detail work on the two vessels. And finally, even if somehow all these obstacles could be overcome, there were no officers or sailors to man the ships if and when they were finished. All these elements necessary to success—the materials, the skilled workers, guns, officers, and a crew—would have to be found and brought to Erie along various routes at least as tortuous as the one Perry had just traveled.

Daunting as all that was, what astonished Perry most was that the site was completely unprotected. There were no fortifications to defend the bay from a British raid, and the only cannon at the site was an old iron boat howitzer that had been found on the beach and which locals used to celebrate the Fourth of July. The only security force was provided by a half dozen civilians who had been hired to watch the ships at night. An observer who arrived a few days after Perry noted in his diary that "a Sergeant's command . . . might destroy the whole [place] in an hour."[35]

Perry tackled the security problem first. He sought out the local militia commander, David Mead, and begged him to call out his command. Mead did so, but only seven men responded. Eventually, Pennsylvania governor Simon Snyder, in response to a plea from the secretary of war, formed a provisional regiment of infantry, and soon nearly eight hundred armed men swarmed about the shipyard. They repaired the tumbledown block-house at the foot of the bay, and when some cannon finally arrived, they mounted them there. At times the Pennsylvania militiamen must have seemed like dubious security. Like most militiamen, the soldiers consid-ered themselves free agents, and they chafed at the imposition of any kind of discipline. Their elected officers felt the need to be friendly with the vol-unteers under their "command," which made it all but impossible for them to give unwelcome orders. The officers and men played cards together, drank together, and engaged in footraces and wrestling matches. But at least there were now enough armed men around the shipyard to prevent it from being destroyed by a "sergeant's command."[36]

Perry's next problem was finding the guns to arm his vessels once they were completed. Cannon could not be manufactured in the wilderness; they had to be brought from the East. Assuming that guns could be found at all, they would have to be dragged by brute force over abysmal forest roads or smuggled by boat across a lake that was regularly patrolled by the British. Dobbins managed to acquire two long twelve-pounders in Black Rock, which he successfully transported to Erie in an old salt boat, sailing only at night and keeping close to the U.S. side of the lake. Perry himself traveled overland to Pittsburgh, where he secured four more guns, which had to be dragged by sledge overland. It was ruinous on the animals. One contemporary estimated that a total of thirty-two hundred horses died over the winter hauling materials from Albany to Sackett's Harbor, to Buf-falo, and finally to Erie. When Lieutenant Thomas Holdup arrived at Erie with two midshipmen and forty sailors, Perry welcomed them effusively, then ordered Holdup back to Buffalo for guns, powder, and shot. In a few days he returned with two more thirty-two-pounders and, just as vital, some sails. Carronades, the heavy, short-barreled guns that made up the bulk of Perry's firepower, were forged in Georgetown, near Washington,

DC. Other pieces of ordnance were located, acquired, and either dragged along frontier roads or smuggled by boat into Presque Isle Bay.[37]

Meanwhile, construction work continued on the two brigs and four small gunboats at the shipyard. Each morning teams of men went out into the forest to cut timber. Horses dragged the felled trees to the edge of the bay, where other teams cut them into planks. After that, it got more complicated, for besides Brown and Dobbins, there were few at Erie with the expertise necessary to turn a wooden shell into a living warship. On the very day he had arrived at Erie, Perry had sent an urgent dispatch to Philadelphia begging for carpenters and blacksmiths, but it would take weeks for them to arrive. And he knew that as soon as the ice melted, the British squadron would try to blockade his shipyard and make it difficult, if not impossible, to get any more guns or supplies. He knew, too, that the British were hard at work constructing a big warship of their own at their base on the Detroit River. Whoever completed their new ships first, armed them, manned them, and got them into the lake would gain an enormous advantage. There was no time to worry about making the brigs into works of art with figureheads or scrollwork. Perry insisted that good was good enough: "plain work" was what was needed. The contractor, Noah Brown, put his finger on the key issue when he noted that the ships "will be needed for one battle; if we win that is all that is wanted of them."[38]

In May, Perry learned of a pending attack on Fort George, downriver from Niagara Falls on the Canadian side of the river; eager for action, he left the construction work in the hands of the contractor and departed from Erie in a four-oared boat. Landing near Buffalo, he completed the journey by pony, his long legs nearly dragging on the ground as he rode. He took part in the successful attack on May 27, then busied himself recruiting sailors for his Lake Erie squadron. Returning to Erie via Black Rock, he determined to bring the five gunboats still languishing there to join his squadron at Presque Isle. It took several days to work the small craft upriver through the rapids, but finally in mid-June the last vessel cleared the rapids and Perry set sail for Erie. It was a risky journey, for at any moment the British squadron might appear over the horizon and blast his little squadron of five boats into pieces. Only later did he find out how close it was. On one occasion, a man from shore watched the British squadron disappear over the horizon in one direction just as Perry's little flotilla hove into sight from the other direction to anchor in the same spot. Only a thick haze prevented the British from spotting the vulnerable Americans.[39]

Combined with the four gunboats built in Presque Isle Bay, the five boats Perry brought from Black Rock gave the Americans a total of nine vessels for their Lake Erie "fleet."* None of them, however, carried more than four guns, and most carried only one. The two brigs were the key to everything. Without them, the Americans could not contest the British for command of the lake. Thankfully, the carpenters and blacksmiths had finally arrived from Philadelphia, and they began to put the finishing touches on the two large hulls. Upon his return to Presque Isle, Perry was delighted to discover that both brigs were now afloat and that the riggers were busy aloft. At about the same time, he learned from a British deserter that the enemy's big ship would not be ready for at least a month. It began to appear that he might win the shipbuilding race for the control of the lake.[40]

Even without their new ship, the British were becoming bolder. Beginning in mid-July, the British squadron began appearing almost daily off Presque Isle Bay. The enemy ships came close in toward the shore, as if about to execute a landing, or they exchanged fire with the small American gunboats that dropped down the harbor to meet them. Then they sailed off again over the horizon. Unable to take the sea, Perry could only watch and wonder when they might next appear.

Perry had assumed a commodore's privilege by giving names to the small schooners whose construction he had supervised. But the new secretary of the navy, William Jones, sent him names for the two brigs. One was to be named *Niagara*, and the other was to be the *Lawrence* in honor of James Lawrence, who had been killed in a frigate duel off Boston on June 1. In honor of the martyred Lawrence, Perry ordered all the flags of the

---

* Two of the nine gunboats, the small schooners *Ohio* and *Amelia*, were used as supply vessels and did not participate in the subsequent naval action.

squadron to half mast, and directed that each man was to wear a strip of black crepe around his left arm (the arm nearest the heart). Soon thereafter he ordered the preparation of a large black wool flag bearing the last words of the dying Lawrence: DONT GIVE UP THE SHIP.[41]

Of course, the problem of manpower still persisted. Perry sent letter after letter pleading for sailors, his frustration evident as he repeatedly expressed his "mortification." He had fewer than 150 men with him at Erie, and he wrote Secretary Jones that he would need a minimum of 403 officers and men to fit out the vessels in his squadron. Jones replied that 500 men were on their way and should arrive shortly. But instead of 500, only 65 arrived, along with one lieutenant and three midshipmen. A week later 53 more arrived, but the total was still less than a quarter of the promised 500. The source of the discrepancy was obvious. All of the men had been sent first to Sackett's Harbor, and Chauncey had kept most of them for his own squadron, forwarding only those he felt he could spare. As might have

This hand-made flag of white letters sewn on black wool bore James Lawrence's dying words. Perry flew this flag from the mainmast of the *Lawrence* during the Battle of Lake Erie and carried it with him when he transferred to the *Niagara*. (U.S. Naval Academy)

been expected, the few who arrived at Erie were not the pick of the litter. Perry complained to Chauncey that they were "a motley set [of] blacks, Soldiers and boys."[42]

Chauncey was unapologetic. He said he would send more men "as soon as the public service will allow me to send them from this Lake." In other words, he would send them only after his own campaign on Lake Ontario had been decided. Indeed, far from apologizing, Chauncey charged Perry with bigotry, picking up on his reference to "blacks, Soldiers and boys" and responding: "I have yet to learn that the Colour of the skin, or cut and trimmings of the coat, can affect a man's qualifications. . . . I have nearly 50 Blacks on board of this Ship and many of them are amongst my best men."[43] Chauncey was deliberately changing the subject. Perry's complaint was not fundamentally racial—about 10 to 15 percent of the men he had brought with him from Rhode Island were black, roughly the same percentage of blacks in the U.S. Navy. Perry's complaint was not that Chauncey had sent him black sailors but that he had forwarded the least experienced hands.*

In fact, Chauncey's letter struck Perry as so judgmental and censorious that Perry read it as a calculated insult. In that age of tender sensibilities, even the most carefully worded criticism threatened an officer's public honor. After reading the letter several times, Perry decided that he could not serve under a man who could write such a letter, "in every line of which there is an insult." He sent Secretary Jones his resignation, declaring, "I cannot serve longer under an officer who has been so totally regardless of my feelings." Jones was new in the job, but he was used to this kind of touchiness, and he replied with a letter designed to both assuage Perry and remind him of his duty: "The indulgence of such feelings must terminate in the most serious injury to the service," Jones wrote. "It is the duty of an

---

* Navies in the early nineteenth century, including both the U.S. Navy and the Royal Navy, made very little distinction about either race or nationality when it came to recruiting crews. In consequence, both navies had black sailors who worked alongside white sailors. Moreover, because quarters were crowded aboard ship, and because the nature of the work precluded segregated work teams, black and white sailors slept, ate, and worked together. There were, however, no black officers in the U.S. Navy until the Civil War.

Officer . . . to sacrifice all personal motives & feeling when in collision with the public good."[44]

Jones knew his man. Perry swallowed his anger and got about the business of doing the "public good." If Chauncey would not send him the men he needed, he would simply have to find them elsewhere. Perry had handbills printed asking for volunteers and circulated them among the militia forces. Aware of how much his own success depended on Perry's, William Henry Harrison also gave Perry permission to recruit among the soldiers of his army and even to draft soldiers who had sea experience whether they volunteered or not, though Perry balked at this latter suggestion, since it sounded too much like impressment. In the end, some sixty militiamen volunteered to transfer to the Navy, and Perry convinced another sixty to sign up for a single cruise, expecting that the issue would very likely be resolved in a single cruise anyway. These volunteers gave Perry a total of just over three hundred men. He was still shorthanded, but he calculated that he had just enough to man the vessels. The men might be inexperienced, but then much of the work aboard warships in the Age of Sail involved the application of human muscle: hauling on a rope, loosing (or furling) a sail, or levering a cannon around a deck. For those things, soldiers would do almost as well as sailors, as long as there was someone to tell them which rope to haul on.

The soldiers hardly knew what they were getting into. As Richard Henry Dana wrote in his classic account *Two Years Before the Mast*, "There is not so helpless and pitiable an object in the world as a landsman beginning a sailor's life." Captain George Stockton of the Pennsylvania militia would have agreed. After a few days on board, he sent Perry a note stating that he had volunteered in good faith, but that his "totle ignorance of this servis" meant that he had come on board without "the preparation nessessery." Some of the soldiers, he wrote, were "naked for clothes . . . no money to buy sope or any article of grocery." He wondered if it were "concistant with my duty heare" if he could "return to camp for a few days to make provisions for the soldiers."[45]

Perry's success in finding the necessary manpower created yet another problem: he now had over three hundred mouths to feed. A survey of the rations that had been forwarded from Pittsburgh showed that much of the bread supply was "mouldly & unfit for men to eat." The beef was "putrid and covered with vermine." Of course, shipboard rations in the Age of Sail were notoriously bad, but Perry's squadron wasn't even at sea yet. Nevertheless, in late August Perry had to reduce the bread ration to twelve ounces per day per man, and a week later he decreed that every other day the men would receive raw flour instead of bread. All this must have made Captain Stockton wonder what he had gotten himself into.[46]

By the end of July, Perry had a virtually complete naval squadron of two twenty-gun brigs, seven small gunboats, and two supply schooners, all of which were at last afloat, armed, and manned, even if the manpower was largely inexperienced. The two brigs were the most powerful vessels on Lake Erie, or at least they would be if he could get them into the lake, for as yet they were still inside Presque Isle Bay. Back in the spring when Dobbins had first set up shop there, Jesse Elliott had criticized the site because a shallow sand bar stretched across the mouth of the bay. While that barrier helped protect the shipyard from British raids, it also kept Perry's ships trapped inside. Perry had been aware of this from the beginning, of course, and he had a plan to deal with it. He would float his ships across the bar by using what were called "camels." These were specially built scows or barges deeply laden with ballast or filled with water. The filled barges were secured alongside the ship to be moved, then emptied out so that they acted like giant water wings, virtually lifting the vessel up and over the bar. In order to lighten the vessels as much as possible, however, it would be necessary to take the heavy guns off the ships first. If the British fleet showed up while the unarmed vessels were being floated over the bar, it could be disastrous.

All through July the British had appeared off Presque Isle Bay almost daily. They were there again on July 31, though they sailed away that night, and the next morning Perry directed his squadron down to the head of the bay to get ready for the tedious and labor-intensive process of crossing the bar. He positioned the small gunboats to guard the entrance, then set his men to work. One crew sounded and marked the deepest water, while others attached block and tackle to the big guns on the *Lawrence*, hoisted them over the side, and lowered them gingerly into small boats, which took them to the beach. The next day the previously prepared "camels" were secured alongside the ship. Some fifty feet long, ten feet wide, and eight feet deep, the barges were about half the size of the brigs themselves. They each had square holes cut in the bottom and were virtually submerged, with only their gunwales showing. Sailors maneuvered them along each side of the *Lawrence* and then ran long, heavy beams through the sweep ports of the *Lawrence* to rest atop the thwarts of the scows. Once everything was in place, the sailors plugged the holes in the bottom of the camels and began pumping out the water. Slowly, inch by inch, the *Lawrence* rose out of the water.[47]

But not enough. The crew on the *Lawrence* gently coaxed it forward over the bar until, halfway across, it suddenly lurched to a stop, aground in just over six feet of water. Somehow more weight had to be removed. Working all night, the men hoisted out the rest of the ship's guns, took off the cables and anchors, and even lowered the spars and topgallant yards and sent them all to the beach. Then the entire process was repeated, this time with the support beams resting on large blocks of wood that were set atop the camels to give the brig more clearance over the shoal. Again the *Lawrence* rose from the water; foot by foot it eased forward. Finally, just after dawn on August 4, it came safely to anchor in deep water. The barges were submerged again, and the whole process was repeated with the *Niagara*. It went more quickly the second time. By 11:00 A.M. the *Niagara*, too, was across the bar.[48]

Just as Perry was beginning to breathe a bit easier, lookouts on the *Lawrence* called down that the British fleet was approaching. Five vessels, led by the *Queen Charlotte*, were standing toward them "with every sail set." The timing could hardly have been worse. The two American brigs were at last in deep water, but they were completely unprepared for battle. The *Lawrence* had most of its guns remounted on their carriages, but the *Niagara*'s guns still lay useless on the beach. It was an extraordinary moment. All that Perry and others had worked so long and so hard to accomplish might be undone in a moment simply due to bad luck. Still, it would be several hours before the enemy ships were within range, and

Perry was determined to play the game out. He called upon the men to perform what one called "the most uncommon and extraordinary exertions" to return the guns to the *Niagara* and prepare it for action. The boats plied back and forth from the beach as men who had been up all night for two consecutive nights worked on pure adrenaline to restore the last of the guns, raise the topgallant mast and spars, and reset the rigging. Even if they succeeded, Perry knew that he did not have enough men on board to handle the guns in a fight. He appealed to the militiamen for help, and those who volunteered were rowed out to the brigs. One of Perry's officers, watching them take up positions on the deck of the *Lawrence*, suspected that until that moment, two-thirds of them "had probably never seen water except in their own wells." Still, there was nothing to do but bluff it out.[49]

The bluff worked. Seeing the American fleet apparently over the bar and ready for a fight, the British did not press the issue. After exchanging a few long-range shots with the gunboats, they turned and sailed back up the lake. Having narrowly avoided disaster, Perry changed at once from prey to predator. Once the *Niagara* was fully restored to readiness, he resolved to pursue the English squadron and defeat it before it could be augmented. That night he wrote to Jones to explain his decision. "I have great pleasure in informing you," he wrote in his bold, flowing script, "that I have succeeded after almost incredible labor and fatigue to the men, in getting all the vessels I have been able to man over the bar. . . . They are neither well officered or manned, but as the emergency of Genl Harrison, and the whole western country is such, I have determined to proceed on Service. My government, should I be unsuccessful, I trust will justly appreciate the motives which have governed me in this determination."[50]

The next morning he directed his ships toward Long Point, directly across the lake, where he suspected the British had gone. But after looking into the harbor there and seeing no enemy vessels, he concluded that they had returned to the safety of Fort Malden, near Amherstburg. Unwilling to try his untested crews with such a challenge, he returned to the anchorage off Erie. At dinner that evening, which he ate on board the *Lawrence* with his purser, Samuel Hambleton, Perry confessed that he was not sure what to do next. He knew the country was watching and waiting for news and that much was expected of him. He knew, too, that Harrison was waiting for support. But he feared that his undermanned and inexperienced crews would not be able to stand up to a pitched battle with the British. In Hambleton's words, he felt "the danger of delay [but] he is not insensible to the hazard of encountering an enemy without due preparation." Then, even as Perry talked, a midshipman entered the cabin to deliver a letter from Lieutenant Jesse Elliott, the hero of the Black Rock affair and the former commander on Lake Erie. The letter announced Elliott's imminent arrival at the head of almost a hundred sailors from Lake Ontario. Chauncey had finally caved in to Perry's repeated pleas for manpower. Hambleton reported to his diary that Perry was "electrified by the news . . . , declared that he had not been so happy since his first arrival; that now he had a commander, just such a one as he wanted, for the *Niagara*, he was at ease and would sail as soon as they arrived."[51]

The fleet sailed on August 12. It was a harrowing experience for the militiamen, most of whom became deathly seasick at once and remained in that condition for the whole of the cruise. The first stop was the entrance to Sandusky Bay near the campsite of General William Henry Harrison's American army. On August 19 Harrison himself came on board the *Lawrence*, bringing with him a dozen officers and a handful of friendly Indians. The Indians were fascinated by Perry's "big canoes," and especially by the heavy iron cannon, which fired a salute to Harrison. They were also impressed by the ship's spyglass, which brought the shore so much closer just by looking through it. Perry and Harrison had a valuable interview, the best part of which, from Perry's viewpoint, was Harrison's offer to send him another hundred volunteer soldiers to use as marines on board the ships of the squadron.[52]

With his ships now fully manned, Perry gave orders for the squadron to make sail for the British base at Amherstburg at the mouth of the Detroit River, where it would seek battle with the British for the command of Lake Erie.

One hundred thirty miles due west of Erie, at the northwest corner of the lake, Fort Malden guarded the entrance to the Detroit River. That fort, and the nearby town of Amherstburg, had been the object of William Hull's disastrous campaign exactly one year before. Now it was the base of Robert Barclay's small British squadron on Lake Erie. At twenty-seven (a year younger than Perry), Barclay bore the temporary rank of commander. But despite his age, Barclay had plenty of battle experience behind him. He had fought at Trafalgar as a teenage midshipman, and like his idol, Lord Nelson, he had lost his left arm in combat. In preparing his squadron for the confrontation with the Americans, Barclay had experienced virtually all of the same logistical and manpower problems that had plagued Perry. If anything, Barclay's difficulties had been greater. To begin with, Amherstburg was even more geographically isolated than Erie, and the roads, trails really, along the north shore of the lake were virtually impassable, meaning that all communication with the rest of Canada depended on use of the lake. In addition, Barclay's superiors provided him with even less support than Perry got from Jones or Chauncey. A pair of modern scholars comment astutely that Barclay began his operations on Lake Erie "not only without a left arm . . . but also with his right one figuratively tied behind his back." Still, Barclay was determined and energetic, and he vowed to do what he could.[53]

His command consisted of the seventeen-gun ship-rigged *Queen Charlotte*, the brig *General Hunter* (ten guns), and the schooner *Lady Prevost* (thirteen guns), plus a handful of smaller (and mostly unarmed) schooners and sloops. While this squadron was sufficient to command the lake in June, when Barclay arrived, he knew it would not be able to stand up to the two big American brigs once they were completed. His great hope was the *Detroit*. Named for the vessel captured by Elliott off Black Rock and destroyed in the ensuing fight, this was a one-hundred-foot-long, twenty-gun vessel currently under construction at the Amherstburg shipyard. Designed as a ship (with three masts), as opposed to Perry's brigs (which had two), it was otherwise a virtual match for either the *Lawrence* or the *Niagara*. Technically, at 490 tons, it would be the largest warship on the lake, since Perry's brigs displaced 480 tons each. Barclay felt that with the *Detroit* and the *Queen Charlotte*, he would have a good chance to match up with Perry's twin brigs.[54]

But although the British had begun work on the *Detroit* in December 1812, before the Americans got serious about their two brigs, progress was slow. In part this was because unlike Noah Brown, who encouraged "plain work" on the *Lawrence* and *Niagara*, the British contractor, William Bell, took perhaps too much pride in his careful craftsmanship. But in addition to that, the work lagged because the British in Amherstburg were even more destitute of supplies and matériel than the Americans at Erie. Manpower, too, was a bottleneck problem. If Perry was frustrated with Chauncey for sending him only about 260 sailors, Barclay got none at all from his theater commander, Sir James Yeo. Like Perry, Barclay recruited what men he could from the army, obtaining infantrymen from the British 41st Regiment and militiamen from the Royal Newfoundland Regiment. But he was less than enthusiastic about them. Unconsciously echoing Perry's complaint to Chauncey about "blacks, Soldiers and boys," Barclay wrote Yeo: "I am sure, Sir James, if you saw my Canadians, you would condemn every one (with perhaps two or three exceptions) as a poor devil not worth his Salt."[55] Except for the nineteen sailors he brought with him, Barclay had no experienced navy men at all. And finally, he lacked both powder and shot, as well as cordage, sails, anchors, or even matches to fire the guns. Once at sea, the crews on some of his ships had to fire their cannon by shooting at the touchholes with pistols because the slowmatch was unusable.

Barclay appealed for help, writing the governor general, Sir George Prevost, that "if prompt assistance is not sent up . . . the great superiority of the enemy may prove fatal." There was still hope, he insisted. "The *Detroit* will [soon] be ready to launch . . . , but there is neither a sufficient quantity of ordnance, Ammunition or any other stores—and not a man to put in her." Prevost replied that he would encourage Yeo to send whatever men he could, but he did not hold out much hope. "You must be sensible of the impossibility in the present state of the Country . . . of supplying you with all the articles of which you stand in need." And he ended with an astonishing instruction: "you must endeavor to obtain your Ordnance and

Naval Stores from the Enemy." In other words, Prevost expected Barclay to capture whatever supplies he needed from the Americans. In the end, Barclay managed to cobble together a mixed battery of nineteen guns for the *Detroit,* including eight nine-pounders, six twelve-pounders, two eighteen-pounders, and three twenty-four-pounders. It had no thirty-two-pounders at all, guns that constituted the main battery on both the *Lawrence* and the *Niagara.*[56]

Barclay's best hope was to keep the American squadron pinned up inside Presque Isle Bay until the *Detroit* was finished. During his reconnaissance in late July in the *Queen Charlotte,* he saw that the two American brigs were nearly complete, and he returned in the first week of August with his whole squadron to establish a blockade. But when he arrived on August 4, the Americans were already over the bar and into the open lake—or so it appeared to him. Unaware that Perry's ships were woefully unready for a fight, Barclay decided that there was no reason to provoke a fight with the *Detroit* so near completion, so he turned his squadron around and headed back to Fort Malden.

Barclay was now in a quandary, with few good options available to him. The presence of a superior American squadron on the lake meant that the British could no longer use the lake to bring supplies or reinforcements to Amherstburg. By September supplies in the fort and navy yard were already dwindling. Barclay had his own crews on half rations, and the circumstances were exacerbated by the presence of large numbers of Indian "allies" who encamped about the town and expected to be fed. If those expectations were not met, the Indians might easily change sides. Barclay's only chance was to regain naval superiority on the lake, which would allow the British once again to move supplies across its surface. As he expressed it later, he felt "obliged . . . to fight the Enemy . . . to enable us to get supplies and Provisions." As soon as the *Detroit* was completed, assuming that he could find enough men to put in her, he would have to offer battle.[57]

When Perry set out for Fort Malden in late August, his goal was to establish a blockade of Amherstburg. Only a few days out, however, sickness broke out on board most of the ships in the American squadron. The surgeon's mate on the *Lawrence,* Usher Parsons, called it "Bilious Remit-

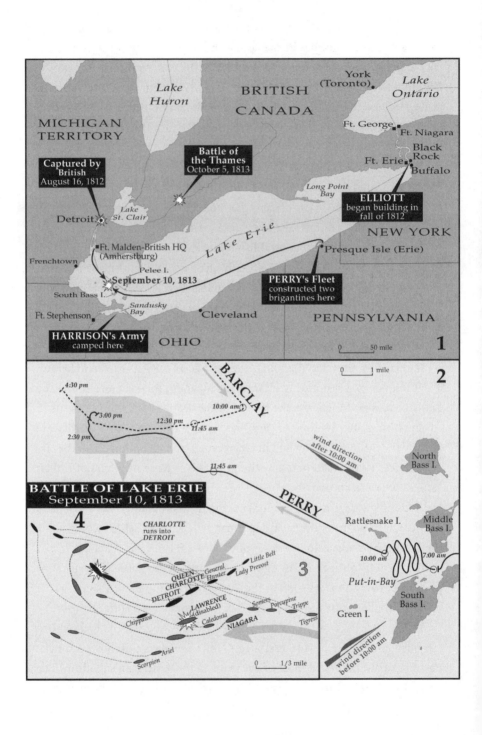

Lake Huron

BRITISH CANADA

York (Toronto)

Lake Ontario

MICHIGAN TERRITORY

Ft. George

Ft. Niagara

Black Rock

Ft. Erie

Buffalo

Battle of the Thames
October 5, 1813

Captured by British
August 16, 1812

Long Point Bay

ELLIOTT
began building in fall of 1812

Lake St. Clair

Detroit

NEW YORK

Presque Isle (Erie)

Ft. Malden-British HQ (Amherstburg)

Frenchtown

Lake Erie

Pelee I.

September 10, 1813

PERRY's Fleet
constructed two brigantines here

South Bass I.

Sandusky Bay

Ft. Stephenson

Cleveland

PENNSYLVANIA

HARRISON's Army camped here

OHIO

0   50 mile

1

0   1 mile

2

4:30 pm

BARCLAY

3:00 pm

10:00 am

12:30 pm

11:45 am

2:30 pm

wind direction after 10:00 am

North Bass I.

11:45 am

BATTLE OF LAKE ERIE
September 10, 1813

PERRY

Rattlesnake I.

Middle Bass I.

4

10:00 am

7:00 am

Put-in-Bay

CHARLOTTE runs into *DETROIT*

Little Belt

QUEEN CHARLOTTE   General Hunter   Lady Prevost

DETROIT

3

LAWRENCE (disabled)

Somers

Porcupine   Trippe

Chippawa

Caledonia

NIAGARA

Tigress

South Bass I.

Ariel

Green I.

Scorpion

wind direction before 10:00 am

0   1/3 mile

tent Fever" and attributed it to drinking the unhealthy water of Lake Erie, but whatever it was, it ran quickly through the squadron and struck Perry himself, who, for all his eagerness, had to confine himself to his cot. He gave orders for the squadron to find a safe anchorage at Put-in-Bay, a well-known harbor near Bass Island, not quite halfway between Fort Malden and Long Point. He knew that as long as his squadron occupied Put-in-Bay, the British could not use the lake route for their supplies. Eventually, Barclay would have to come out to drive the Americans away.

On September 10 he did.

The early phases of a fleet engagement in the Age of Sail proceeded in a well-established pattern and with a certain pageantry. Upon sighting and identifying the foe, the opposing commanders first ordered their ships cleared for action. The order was signaled by a drummer who beat the long roll: a bass-voiced trilling that sent a shiver up the spine of every sailor who ever heard it. This produced a profound reaction throughout the ship as the hands scrambled to take their preassigned stations. The gunners gathered around their giant iron weapons, casting them loose from their bindings. The marines went aloft, their rifles slung over their shoulders as they carefully ascended the ratlines; once positioned in the "fighting top," they would use their shoulder arms to pick off officers or other targets of opportunity on the enemy's deck. Other marines, including all the volunteer soldiers, took up positions on the more stable main deck. The most inexperienced men (and both squadrons had plenty of these) were assigned to carry the powder and shot to the guns from the magazine below or to assist in heaving the great guns into position, for although there were pulleys and ropes (known as block and tackle) to assist, any movement of the guns was done mainly by brute force.

The officers took their stations, too. The midshipmen and the lieutenants each commanded a section of guns, and it was their duty to ensure that all the men were in their places, that they had all the equipment necessary, including lit matches, and that once the fighting started, they stayed focused on their tasks. The ship's captain took a position on the quarter-

deck near the helmsman, who was usually the quartermaster when at battle stations. Perry's thirteen-year-old brother, Midshipman Alex Perry, also
stayed on the quarterdeck, since Perry planned to use him as a kind of aide
to relay messages and orders. While the drums rolled and men rushed to
their positions, there was a hurricane of action aboard the ship. Then
when everyone was in place, the officer of the deck, often the captain himself, would shout, "Silence about the deck!" and the whole ship would suddenly become still. Only the creaking of the masts interrupted the artificial
silence.

Everything was now ready, and there was nothing more to do but wait
for the enemy to come within range. In the relatively light airs on Lake
Erie, Perry's squadron approached the British at an almost glacial pace,
about three knots. During sea battles in the Age of Sail, there were
moments of frantic activity often followed by long periods when there was
nothing to do but wait, watch the slow approach of the enemy, and contemplate one's own mortality. Aboard the *Lawrence*, a sailor named David
Bunnell recalled that "we neared the enemy very slowly, which gave us a
little time for reflection." The men "stood in awful impatience—not a
word was spoken—not a sound heard, except now and then an order to
trim a sail, and the boatswain's shrill whistle." To Bunnell, "it seemed like
the awful silence that precedes an earthquake." Another thought it was like
"the stillness of the atmosphere that precedes the hurricane."[58]

To break that silence (and the tension), Perry stepped onto the top of a
gun slide so that he could be seen. Holding up the flag he had prepared, he
called out: "My brave Lads, this Flag contains the last words of the brave
Capt. Lawrence. Shall I hoist it?" It drew the desired response, and amidst
the cheering, Perry had it run up to the masthead. Then to make sure that
the men didn't have to fight on an empty stomach, he ordered that the
noontime bread and grog ration be distributed early. While the men ate
and drank, he went round the ship to check on each gun and gun crew to
see that everything was in order and to spread confidence. At each gun he
exchanged a few words with the gun captain, generally a senior enlisted
man. "Well, boys," he would remark, "are you ready?" And they would

reply cheerfully: "All ready, your honor!" Finding one gun manned by veterans who had come with him all the way from gunboat service in Narragansett Bay, he exclaimed, "Ah! Here are the Newport boys! They will do their duty, I warrant."[59]

More privately, Perry consulted with his purser, Samuel Hambleton, asking him to take charge of his personal papers in the event of his death. The ship's official papers Perry placed in a canvas sack, adding a lead bar as a weight so that the package could be tossed overboard in the event of disaster. Perry also found a job for his African American servant, Cyrus Tiffany. Handing him a musket and a bayonet, he told "Old Tiffany" to go down to the berth deck and guard the passageway so that once the shooting started, skulkers could not find safe haven below the waterline.[60]

Both squadrons were sailing in the traditional line-ahead formation. In the American squadron, the small schooners *Scorpion* and *Ariel* led, followed by the *Lawrence* and *Caledonia*, with the *Niagara* and four more small vessels bringing up the rear. Perry passed orders by trumpet and followed them with a signal flag that read: "Engage as you come up, every one against his Opponent in the line."[61] As Perry envisioned it, he would take on the British flagship, the brand-new *Detroit*, with his own vessel, leaving the *Queen Charlotte* to Elliott in the *Niagara*. Whatever happened in the fight between the smaller vessels, Perry knew that it was the duel between the two big ships on each side that would decide the outcome.

At fifteen minutes before noon, with the opposing squadrons about a mile apart, Barclay opened the action by firing a shot from one of the long twenty-four-pounders on the *Detroit*. The shot fell short, and Perry did not bother to reply. Most of his guns were stubby thirty-two-pounder carronades that fired a huge iron ball but had a relatively short range. He believed it was crucial to get as close as possible as quickly as he could. Carrying mainsail, topsail, and topgallant sails, Perry sailed boldly toward the enemy line, signaling to the other vessels to do the same. For a quarter of an hour, as the American fleet closed on the British line, the men on the *Lawrence* simply had to take the fire of the British long guns without any real opportunity to reply except with their single twelve-pound long gun.[62]

The three lead ships in the American line of battle (*Scorpion, Ariel,* and *Lawrence*) all closed with the British. The fourth ship, the *Caledonia*, was slow and soon fell behind. Elliott in the *Niagara* kept his own vessel in line behind it, and as a result, the five trailing ships in the American squadron did not come up as quickly. Just as Hood's division in the Battle of the Capes failed to come up to support Graves, so now did Elliott remain in the line of battle well beyond effective range. In fact, because of the range, Elliott ordered his carronades to cease firing and employed only his single long gun. That created an opportunity for Captain Robert Finnis in the *Queen Charlotte*. Seeing that the *Niagara* was staying out of range, Finnis brought his ship up just behind the *Detroit* to join her in pounding Perry's *Lawrence*.

Now the battle became a slugfest between the *Lawrence* and the two British big ships. Men on both sides loaded and fired as fast as possible. The recoil of each shot sent the guns leaping backward to jerk against the restraint of the gun tackle. Then the gun crews swarmed over their weapons, sponging out the burning embers of the last round, jamming a sack of premeasured black powder into the muzzle, and rolling a thirty-two-pound iron ball in after it. If wadding was available, they added that to hold the ball in place. All of this was then rammed home down the muzzle of the gun. Then the gun had to be "run out," which simply meant that the men of the gun crew had to lay hold of the ropes and haul away until the muzzle pointed out the gun port. A long pin or wire called a vent pick was inserted down through the vent on top of the breech to prick the bag of powder in the gun barrel, and a quill primer—a kind of narrow straw filled with fine-grain powder—was inserted into the vent. The gun captain trained the gun on the target, peering down the length of the barrel, essentially aiming by sight line. Then he stood aside as a slow match was touched down on the powder. A flash from the priming powder was followed almost instantly by the explosion of the powder in the barrel, and the gun leaped backward again to restart the process. It was exhausting work.

It was also dangerous. Though Perry's *Lawrence* was supported by the

This rendering of Perry's victory on Lake Erie decorates the stairwell of the U.S. Senate chamber in the Capitol in Washington. In order to show the whole battle, the artist has dramatically condensed the action into a small area; both American brigs are shown heavily engaged with shot holes through their topsails, though in fact the *Niagara* stayed out of the heavy fighting until Perry transferred his flag to it. (U.S. Navy)

Ariel (four guns) and *Caledonia* (two guns), it was taking a terrible beating from the two British big ships. At such close range, the slaughter was fearful. The dead were moved aside to be out of the way; the wounded were assisted below decks to the wardroom, which Surgeon's Mate Parsons was using as a hospital. Almost at once there was confusion at the main hatch, as those assisting the wounded below were stopped by a defiant Cyrus Tiffany brandishing his bayoneted musket. Only Perry's personal intercession convinced Tiffany to let the wounded go below and receive treatment. Even then, there was little safety in the surgeon's cockpit. Not only did the wounded have to suffer the ministrations of nineteenth-century medicine, but the *Lawrence*'s shallow draft meant that Parsons had to do his work above the waterline, so even as he worked to splint fractures or tie off arteries, cannonballs occasionally came crashing through his work area.

Parsons had just applied a splint to Midshipman Henry Laub when a ball punched through the bulwark, struck the midshipman full in the chest, "and dashed him against the other side of the room, which instantly terminated his sufferings."[63]

Above on the gun deck, the battle continued in full fury. David Bunnell, who moments before had stood in "awful impatience," now watched as a cannonball smashed through the bulwarks and cut both legs off the man who was standing next to him. Only minutes later, another cannonball struck another member of his gun crew in the head, covering Bunnell with brains and causing him to wonder momentarily if they were his own. One shot struck fair on the muzzle of a gun, sending bits of iron flying in all directions. Bunnell recalled that "one man was filled full of little pieces of cast iron from his knees to his chin." Even more fearful than the cannonballs themselves were the giant splinters—some of them several feet in length—ripped from the ship's hull and sent flying across the deck. Then there was "grape," clusters of nine iron balls, roughly the size of golf balls, that were fired at close range like giant buckshot. As a counterpoint to these terrors, one shot struck the hammocks on the *Lawrence* and exploded a mattress, which caused feathers to drift down on the perspiring men like snow. Another shot smashed the cooking pot and sent green peas rolling about on the deck. The terrible and the mundane combined to present the ghastly image of one of the ship's pigs, with both of its rear legs shot off, dragging itself across the deck to gobble down the spilled peas.[64]

Though land warfare has its own terrors, the confined space of a ship of war focuses the violence of combat. With no possible avenue of escape, with the guns firing every few minutes, and with missiles of all kinds flying across the deck, time itself lost meaning. Within an hour, five of the eight men assigned to Bunnell's gun were down, killed or wounded. To keep the guns in action, the officers stepped forward and joined the gun crews, straining against the ropes and lifting in the cannonballs like ordinary seamen.[65]

After two hours, the fire from the *Lawrence* began to slacken. Some twenty men were dead, and more than three dozen were wounded. Out of a crew of 150, many of whom still suffered the effects of bilious fever, more than half the ship's complement was out of action. Most of the guns had been put out of action, too, their carriages shattered or the guns themselves dismounted. There weren't enough able-bodied men left to work the few guns that still functioned; there were no men to bring powder and shot up from the magazines. Desperate for ammunition, the survivors of Bunnell's gun crew fired a crowbar and a brass swivel gun from their cannon.[66]

It was the sailing master on the *Lawrence*, William Taylor, who first asked the question that many may have been thinking: where was the *Niagara*? That vessel had not only dropped further astern but was moving inexorably to windward, passing by on the unengaged side and thus putting the *Lawrence* between itself and the enemy. Lieutenant Dulany Forrest pointed this out to Perry: "That Brig . . . will not help us, see how that fellow keeps off—he will not come to close action."[67]

Looking about his own ship and glancing over at the *Niagara*, Perry contemplated his circumstances. Though he did not know the precise numbers, he could see that over half his crew was killed or wounded. Indeed, he and his brother Alex were the only officers still unscathed. Taylor described the scene in a letter to his wife: "Every gun [was] dismounted, [gun] carriages knocked to pieces—every strand of rigging cut off—masts & spars shot & tottering over head & in just an unmanageable wreck." It was obvious that the *Lawrence* was no longer capable of offering resistance, much less defeating the enemy. Whatever firepower remained in the American squadron existed in the still-undamaged *Niagara*.[68]

Perry came to a decision. From his station on the gun deck, Bunnell heard him call out, "Man the boat!" and a small party of the able-bodied did so, bringing a small boat alongside. Perry ordered a sailor to haul down the black flag with Lawrence's dying words stitched on it, though the American flag continued to fly from both the foremast and the spanker gaff. Perry then met quietly with Lieutenant John Yarnall, whose face was covered with blood from a head wound, and told him to take command of the ship, but telling him also not to sacrifice lives unnecessarily. Then Perry took his flag down into the boat and ordered the men to shove off.

It took fifteen minutes to row the half mile from the *Lawrence* to the

Perry's bold move from the shattered *Lawrence* (at left) to the undamaged *Niagara* (at right) is dramatically depicted in this nineteenth-century oil painting by Thomas Birch. The original is in the Pennsylvania Academy of Fine Arts. (U.S. Navy)

Niagara. The small boat immediately became the target of every gun in the British fleet that could bear on it, and shot splashes erupted nearby, though none hit. Tradition has it that Perry stood during the trip, just as George Washington is supposed to have stood during the crossing of the Delaware, and contemporary evidence suggests that in that age of the grand gesture, he did indeed begin the trip standing. But the four rowers soon begged him to sit, for both his own safety and theirs, and after that Perry sat prudently in the sternsheets. Finally the boat bumped alongside the *Niagara* and Perry scrambled up the side. There he was met by Captain Elliott.

Elliott's first words were to ask how the day was going, as if he were some kind of neutral observer. Perry might have responded sharply to such a question, but instead he replied simply that it was going badly. Almost as if to punctuate that remark, the sound of cheering drew the attention of both men, who saw that the *Lawrence* had struck its flag, and the British were cheering their victory. Perry then asked Elliott why the gunboats were so far astern. Elliott said he did not know, but he volunteered to find out and bring them into the fight. No doubt happy to see him go, Perry gave his permission, and Elliott, like Perry, left his own ship in a small boat to go round up the strays.[69]

According to Alexander Slidell Mackenzie, Perry's first order on the *Niagara* was to "back the main topsail . . . , brail up the main trysail, put the helm up, and bear down before the wind, with squared yards, for the enemy."[70] In layman's terms, he turned the ship to starboard and sailed directly at the British squadron.

On board the *Detroit*, Barclay was still savoring his hard-fought victory over the *Lawrence*, which had come at a terrible cost, when he spied this new threat bearing down on him. Because his own ship was nearly as damaged as the *Lawrence*, his port battery virtually wrecked, he tried to wear ship so that he could present his starboard broadside to the charging *Niagara*. But his maneuver was too complicated for a badly damaged ship and an exhausted crew. Moreover, it completely confused the *Queen Charlotte*, which was close astern. The *Charlotte* had lost both its captain (Robert Finnis) and its first lieutenant (Thomas Stokoe), leaving it in command of a provisional (Canadian) lieutenant named Robert Irvine. As Barclay later expressed it, Irvine's "experience was much too limited to supply the place of such an officer as Finnis," and the combination of Barclay's maneuver and Irvine's inexperience soon resulted in the two British ships becoming tangled up with each other. Into the midst of this self-inflicted confusion came Perry in the *Niagara*. After two and a half hours of being pounded, he was about to turn the tables.[71]

Passing through the British line of battle, the *Niagara* fired its first full broadsides of the battle in both directions. They were devastating. The starboard broadside swept the length of the two British vessels that had become tangled together. Barclay, who had been wounded earlier in the fight with the *Lawrence*, received a second wound and had to be carried below; his first lieutenant, John Garland, was mortally wounded. Dozens of others fell as well. The *Niagara*'s port broadside smashed into the *Lady Prevost*, doing similar execution there. Perry's bold maneuver had completely reversed the tide of battle. Already weakened by the long battle with the *Lawrence*, the British were staggered by this new assault. Within minutes, both of the British big ships struck their flags, the *Queen Charlotte* first, then the *Detroit*.[72] Two of the smaller ships struck as well. Two others tried to escape, but they were chased down by the American gunboats and captured. In less than fifteen minutes Perry had completely reversed the battle and turned defeat into victory.

—

The butcher's bill was sobering. Some 123 Americans had been killed or wounded—21 percent of Perry's total complement of the nine ships. On Perry's *Lawrence*, the losses were particularly horrific. Out of just over 150 men on board the *Lawrence*, 83 of them were on the casualty list, a loss rate of 55 percent.* In the days of the Roman legions, when a unit lost 10 percent of its force, it was said to be "decimated." The Romans didn't even have a word for losing 55 percent. British losses were worse; a total of 134 were killed or wounded out of a smaller complement of men—a loss rate of 30 percent. On five of the six British vessels, both the captain and the first officer were killed or wounded.[73]

Ironically, Jesse Elliott was the first American officer to board the surrendered *Detroit* after the battle. Rowed over from the small gunboat *Somers*, he climbed up the side of the British flagship and at once slipped and fell in the gore that covered the deck, smearing his uniform coat with blood. The first sight that met his eyes was a surreal one. Barclay had brought a black bear on board the *Detroit* as a mascot, and now in the aftermath of battle, the bear was wandering about the deck lapping up the blood. Elliott found the wounded Barclay below, where Barclay offered Elliott his sword. Elliott refused it, knowing that the honor belonged to Perry, but he did take the *Detroit*'s flag and carry it with him over to the *Niagara*.[74]

Perry's first reaction on seeing the blood-covered Elliott climb onto the deck of the *Niagara* was to ask him if he was badly wounded. Assured that he was not, Perry was so euphoric due to the sudden reversal of fortune

* Of the ninety-six American casualties on board the *Lawrence*, thirty-seven suffered from splinter wounds, twenty-five from compound fractures, and ten from contusions. Surgeon's Mate Parsons performed six amputations on board—none of the six survived.

that he greeted Elliott enthusiastically, thanking him for the important part he had played in the victory. Others listening nearby wondered at the warmness of Perry's welcome and may have exchanged covert glances.

The end of battle did not mark the end of labor. The wounded, both friend and foe, had to be cared for, and the battered vessels had to be made secure and seaworthy. And, of course, General Harrison must be told. The whole point of the battle, after all, was to regain control of Lake Erie so that with logistical support restored, Harrison's army could take the offensive against the British and their Indian allies. Perry had promised Harrison that he would "dispatch an express to you the moment the issue of our contest with the enemy is known." Now, therefore, he used the back of an old envelope to write a quick note to Harrison: "Dear General, We have met the enemy and they are ours: Two ships, two Brigs, one Schooner, and one Sloop. Yours with great respect and esteem, O. H. Perry." Later, Perry would write a longer official report for the secretary of the navy. He took some time in preparing it, and no doubt he expected that his official report would be printed in the papers and be widely read. It never occurred to him that it was the short note to Harrison that would become immortal.[75]

In a carefully scripted naval minuet that was centuries old, the officers of each surrendered vessel came on board to offer their swords in token of formal surrender. With Elliott back on board the *Niagara*, Perry returned to the battered *Lawrence* to conduct this ceremony. Following the prescribed protocol, the British officers each offered their compliments to Perry on his victory, then tendered their swords to him hilt first. Perry fulfilled his part of the prescribed code, remarking in each case that the officer should keep his sword since he had distinguished it by making so gallant a defense.[76]

Another tradition of the sea was that in his formal report, the commanding officer should name all those who had performed well during the battle. Being "named in dispatches" not only confirmed one's public honor but was the surest and swiftest path to promotion. Just as he had refused all the tendered swords, so, too, was Perry suitably generous in his report. "Those officers and Men, who were immediately under my observation, evinced the greatest gallantry," he wrote, and he mentioned several by name, including Yarnall, Forrest, and Taylor. But what to do about Elliott? In his description of the battle, Perry finessed the role played (or not played) by the *Niagara*: "At half past two, the wind springing up, Capt. Elliott was enabled to bring his vessel, the Niagara, gallantly into close action." Of course, the report having already mentioned that the battle had begun at noon, it was clear that between noon and half past two the *Niagara* was somewhere other than in "close action." Perry also wrote that when he went personally on board the *Niagara*, that ship was "very little injured." Any veteran of naval combat would be able to read between the lines. But then Perry included this: "Of Capt. Elliott, already so well known to the Government, it would almost be superfluous to speak. In this action he evinced his characteristic bravery and judgment; and, since the close of the action, has given me the most able and essential assistance." Thus did Perry hope to avoid any unpleasantness about the role that Elliott had chosen to play in the battle.[77]

Meanwhile, there was a war to fight. Within a week Perry began to transfer Harrison's army first to South Bass Island, then to Middle Sister Island, and finally to Fort Malden, which the British abandoned as soon as they learned of Perry's victory. Perry then accompanied Harrison's army during its pursuit of the retreating British, and he was a spectator and volunteer aide to Harrison at the Battle of the Thames (October 5, 1813), which shattered what remained of the British army in Upper Canada. In that same battle, Tecumseh himself was killed, and with him died the dream of a great western Indian confederation.*

—

Perry's triumph was complete, but there was a bitter epilogue. In the immediate aftermath of the fight, Perry believed that Elliott lamented his behavior during the battle. Perry later claimed that Elliott admitted to him

---

* After the battle, the commander of the Kentucky militia, Colonel Richard Johnson, claimed that he had personally killed Tecumseh, and the fame he gained as a result helped make him presidential candidate Martin Van Buren's running mate in 1836. The losing presidential candidate that year was Johnson's commander at the Battle of the Thames, William Henry Harrison, who turned the tables on Van Buren four years later and became president in 1841.

that he "had missed the fairest opportunity of distinguishing himself that ever man had." If it was not quite an apology, Perry took it as one. Because the end result had proved so positive, he chose to overlook Elliott's performance during the battle. When Elliott wrote to ask him to comment "in candor" on Elliott's role in the battle, Perry responded generously: "It affords me great pleasure that I have it in my power to assure you that the conduct of yourself, officers and crew, was such as to meet my warmest approbation." Elliott promptly saw to it that Perry's letter was published.[78]

Of course, whatever Perry might say officially, everyone in the fleet had witnessed the conduct of the *Niagara* under Elliott's command. Even while the battle was being fought, the men on the *Lawrence* were muttering about it to themselves and to each other. Wounded men brought down into the cockpit of the *Lawrence* complained bitterly, even as the surgeon bound their wounds, that the *Niagara* was deliberately staying out of the battle, leaving the *Lawrence* to bear the full burden of the fight unsupported. Afterward, talk inevitably spread: first inside the fleet, and then in the towns and forts ringing the lake, and eventually in the public press. Perry told his friends to stop it. He believed that public controversy would sully the American victory. "Honor enough had been gained," he insisted. And perhaps the controversy would have died in whispered rumors if Elliott himself had not insisted on bringing it up.[79]

Elliott heard the continued mutterings and found them intolerable. Having once been the hero of Lake Erie himself, he could not bear that this sobriquet was now being applied to Perry and that, in practically the same breath, his own conduct was found wanting. His reaction was to become defensive and to blame the rumors on Perry's refusal to give him the credit he deserved. He was angered further when Congress promoted Perry to captain with his commission backdated to September 10, 1813, while Elliott's reward was merely to assume command of the squadron on Lake Erie—where, of course, there was no longer an enemy for him to fight. One factor in Elliott's resentment may have been that while Elliott himself had started his career late and scratched his way to official notice, Perry, the captain's son, had benefited from family influence. Eventually Elliott came to believe that he should get at least equal credit for the victory, and he argued selfishly that the officers and men of the *Lawrence* should not share in the prize money because, after all, the *Lawrence* had struck its flag. On at least one occasion, Elliott went so far as to declare that it would have been better if the British had won, just to prove that Perry did not deserve the victory.[80]

Lieutenant William B. Shubrick warned Elliott in a friendly way that Perry held Elliott's reputation in his hands, and "the least you and your friends can say . . . the better for you." It was good advice, but it elicited the opposite reaction. Instead of remaining quiet and being grateful for Perry's restraint, Elliott wrote Perry a challenging letter. "The wrongs I have suffered are many," Elliott wrote, thus setting a tone of wounded victim. "I am at a loss to know how it was possible you could have made such representations." Elliott all but ordered Perry to stop making "base, false, and malicious reports," especially "in the society of the ladies or that of young navy officers."[81]

It was now clear to Perry that since Elliott was going to make the issue public anyway, it was time to have it out. He prepared eleven specific charges against Elliott and submitted them to the navy secretary for a court-martial. He also wrote to Elliott to inform him of the charges, addressing him in language that seemed calculated to provoke a duel, call-

After the victory on Lake Erie, Congress ordered that medals be struck to honor both Perry and his second in command, Master Commandant Jesse Duncan Elliott, whose medal is shown here. Jealous that Perry received most of the public credit for the victory, Elliott began a campaign to elevate himself and discredit his senior. (U.S. Navy)

ing Elliott "impudent as well as base" and referring to his "unmanly conduct" during the battle. Stung by Perry's letter, Elliott did challenge Perry
to a duel, but Perry scornfully rejected it because, he said, Elliott was no
gentleman.[82]

It never came to a duel, nor to a court-martial. James Monroe, who
succeeded Madison in the White House, wanted no airing of the Navy's
dirty laundry at such a time, and the court-martial charges were simply
filed away without action.* The bickering over the prize money continued
a while longer. Eventually Congress approved the sum of $260,000, which
was divided up in the traditional way, with the greatest portions going to
those at the top.† Accordingly, the largest amount went to the overall theater commander, Isaac Chauncey at Sackett's Harbor, who never came
within two hundred miles of the battle, but who nevertheless got $12,750.
Perry and Elliott got $7,140 each. The other officers throughout the fleet
each received between $1,214 and $2,295, and the individual sailors (including the militia volunteers) got $214.89, paltry by comparison, but a sub-
stantial sum in 1818.[83]

After the war was over, Perry got command of a frigate, the brand-new
forty-four-gun *Java*, named in honor of *Old Ironsides'* second great victory,
and he took her on a Mediterranean cruise in 1816–17. Two years later, during a diplomatic expedition up the Orinoco River in Venezuela, he caught
yellow fever, and after battling the disease for a week, he died on his thirty-

---

* The feud between Perry and Elliott became an issue for historians as well. Two of the most distinguished of America's naval historians, James Fenimore Cooper and Alfred Thayer Mahan, took
opposite sides. Writing thirty years after the battle, Cooper took Elliott's side, arguing that Perry's
orders compelled Elliott to hold his position in the line of battle and insisting that Elliott's arrival
with the trailing gunboats was as important to the eventual American victory as Perry's breaking
the British line. Mahan drew exactly the opposite conclusion, pointing out that Perry's orders
required every captain to follow the movements of the *Lawrence* (which Elliott failed to do) and noting that Perry had used Nelson's phrasing at Trafalgar in declaring that no captain could do very
wrong if he placed his ship alongside that of the enemy (which Elliott also failed to do). On balance, Mahan makes the more convincing argument. See James Fenimore Cooper, *The Battle of Lake
Erie* (Cooperstown, NY: H. & E. Phinney, 1843), and Alfred Thayer Mahan, *Sea Power in Its Relations
to the War of 1812* (Boston: Little, Brown, 1918).

† Congress appropriated $255,000 in general prize money, plus an additional $5,000 for Perry.

fourth birthday. Perry's youngest brother, Alex, who had survived the battle on Lake Erie unscathed, died three years later, at the age of twenty-two,
while trying to save the life of a drowning sailor.

Elliott lived for another quarter century, but he remained a "stormy
petrel."[84] In 1820 he played a key role in provoking a duel between James
Barron (of the *Chesapeake-Leopard* affair) and Stephen Decatur (who had
supported Perry in the feud with Elliott). The origin of the duel was a stu-
pid quarrel that probably would have been settled amicably but for Elliott's
poisonous influence. As it was, both men fell wounded, Decatur mortally
so. Perry and Decatur were the two most distinguished public heroes of
the War of 1812, and Decatur's death only one year after Perry's left a great
void in Navy leadership. As for Elliott, he disgracefully fled the scene of the
duel rather than stay by the wounded Barron. In spite of that, Elliott was
later promoted to captain, and eventually he commanded both the West
Indies Squadron (1829–32) and the Mediterranean Squadron (1835–38).

The Treaty of Ghent, which brought an end to the war in 1815, essentially restored the status quo between the United States and Britain without resolving most of the issues that had led to war in the first place. The
British continued to insist that they had the right to impress British-born
sailors from American ships at sea, although since the war in Europe had
ended with Napoleon's defeat, they gave up the practice of doing so. Likewise, the British did not accept America's broad definition of neutral
rights, but once again the return of peace to Europe meant that America
no longer occupied its precarious neutrality, making the issue moot.

On one issue, however, there was a clear resolution. Perry's victory on
Lake Erie, which made possible Harrison's victory at the Battle of the
Thames, convinced the British to drop their demand for an independent
Indian federation in the Northwest. The way was clear for the westward
expansion of the United States.

—

Eighty years after the Battle of Lake Erie, a young American historian
named Frederick Jackson Turner presented a paper at the Columbian
Exposition in Chicago in which he argued that the presence of a proximate

frontier played a decisive role in defining America's culture, values, and character. Though Turner had (and still has) his critics, it is self-evident that the conquest, settlement, and defense of the frontier were critical in American history. But the mastery of the frontier was due not only to pioneers in buckskin or stalwart settlers carving farms out of the wilderness; it was possible in the first place because of the victory of Oliver Hazard Perry's small naval squadron over its British counterpart on September 10, 1813. With only fifteen vessels involved, most of them small gunboats, it was not a large engagement, but it had enormous strategic significance. An entire British squadron was captured intact; the command of Lake Erie shifted in one day—indeed, in a single maneuver—from Britain to America, and when it did, the momentum in the war for the Northwest changed as well. For the United States, the Battle of Lake Erie was a Lilliputian Trafalgar fought on fresh water, with consequences every bit as profound for America's future as Trafalgar was for Britain's survival. Perry's victory secured the northwestern frontier for the United States.

Moreover, the Battle of Lake Erie marked the pinnacle, for Americans at least, of a type of naval warfare that had been evolving for most of two centuries. Perry won the Battle of Lake Erie with wooden-hulled, square-rigged sailing vessels that would have been familiar to Sir Francis Drake or even Christopher Columbus. Perry and his men maneuvered their craft by manipulating a complex network of lines and sails, and they fought by working smooth-bore muzzle-loading iron guns that had to be manhandled about the deck by brute force. The men who served them required relatively little expertise. Both Perry and Barclay fought with almost as many soldiers as sailors on board their vessels, yet their men fought valiantly and stubbornly. For their part, the officers adhered to a professional culture that was centuries old and which was dominated by a code of behavior in which public honor was at least as important as private conduct. And yet, in terms of both technology and culture, the Battle of Lake Erie was a template of naval combat that was already passing. Six years earlier, Robert Fulton had successfully tested a steam-powered vessel on the Hudson River.

[PART TWO]

IRON, STEAM,
AND NATIONAL UNION

—

The Battle of Hampton Roads
March 8-9, 1862

IF THE MASTERY OF THE FRONTIER WAS THE NATION'S FIRST GREAT challenge, the second, and arguably its most traumatic, was the need to resolve the question of its own character as a democratic republic. Westward expansion eventually forced the nation's leaders to confront the question of whether slavery, too, should be allowed to expand. The Northwest Ordinance of 1787 had banned slavery from the territory that was later secured by Perry's victory in 1813, and consequently both Indiana (1816) and Illinois (1818) came into the Union as free states. But both Mississippi (1817) and Alabama (1819) entered as slave states. In 1819, the year Perry died of yellow fever, the territory of Missouri applied for admission. Since there were already several thousand black slaves working the rich bottomlands of the Missouri River, it naturally sought admission as a slave state. During the congressional debate, however, Representative James Talmadge of New York rose to offer an amendment that would make slavery illegal in Missouri as a condition of its admission. Southerners were first horrified, then outraged. Despite the small number of slaves in Missouri, the stakes were enormous because the passage of Talmadge's amendment would establish the precedent that Congress could restrict the growth of slavery in the American West.

The abolition of slavery was never the central issue in this dispute. Rather, what split the country in half was an argument over the expansion of slavery into the West. If slavery could not expand, southerners believed, it could not survive. Without new lands to bring under cultivation, the natural increase of the slave population would eventually create a society where there were more slaves than there was work for them to do. The price of slaves would plummet; their idleness would provoke an intolerable social crisis. The South therefore insisted that slavery must be allowed to spread: first into the western territories beyond the Mississippi River, and eventually southward as well, as the United States acquired part of Mexico and some of the islands of the Caribbean. A majority in the North insisted just as strongly that slavery should be restricted to the states where it already existed.

Over the next four decades, this argument was marked by occasional agreements and compromises (one of which allowed Missouri to become a slave state in 1821), but it was never resolved. Worse, from the southern point of view, the growth of northern political power seemed to foreshadow a time when the South would be unable to control, or even influence, the debate. In 1812 the War Hawks of the South and West had held the balance of political power in America, but by midcentury that power had shifted to the North and the Northwest. When in 1860 Abraham Lincoln was elected president—without a single vote from the deep South—on a platform of preventing slavery from expanding at all, southerners could read the writing on the wall. Without waiting to see what policies this new president might adopt, seven southern states took the extraordinary step of seceding from the Union to form their own confederation.

The ensuing Civil War changed the nation. In part this was due to the triumph of Lincoln's vision of permanent union over the southern concept of state sovereignty. But in part, too, it was a product of the war itself. Each side fielded armies of up to a hundred thousand men—more than thirty times larger than Harrison's army at the Battle of the Thames—and those armies had to be organized, transported, supplied, and fed. Before the war was over, more than three and a half million men would serve in uniform on one side or the other. Meeting the demands of such a large-scale war required the full capacity of a unified nation with a complex and integrated bureaucracy. Whatever its theoretical commitment to state sovereignty, the Confederacy as well as the Union had to deal with this reality, and both sides did so by imposing conscription and martial law on the states. It is one of the many ironies of history that the South's decision to secede and fight a war of independence generated far more sweeping changes in southern society and culture and was far more destructive of "State rights" than would have been the case if southerners had simply acquiesced to Lincoln's election.

Eventual Union success in the Civil War was due primarily to the sacrifices of the soldiers on the ground, who bore the brunt of battle and gave their lives profligately in the conviction that the Union was worth dying for, as well as to the administration that sustained them through four years

THE BATTLE OF HAMPTON ROADS

of war. But the Union war effort was aided significantly by northern naval superiority, which was nowhere showcased more poignantly than in the timely arrival in Hampton Roads, Virginia, of the USS *Monitor* on the night of March 8, 1862, literally in the nick of time to neutralize the offensive potential of the Confederate ironclad *Virginia*.

—

THE DARK, SQUAT OBJECT that crept menacingly out of the Elizabeth River early on the morning of March 8, 1862, looked nothing at all like the elegant vessels of Perry's or Barclay's squadrons on Lake Erie. For one thing, the Confederate States Ship *Virginia* boasted no masts or spars, nor sails of any kind. The black smoke emerging from its single stack amidships marked it as a steam-powered vessel. Somewhere deep inside that dark hull, coal-fed fires transformed water into steam, which drove pistons that turned a crankshaft attached to a seventeen-foot bronze propeller. The only visible evidence of all this internal activity, besides the black smoke, was the roiling brown water astern, a V-shaped wake that spread slowly across the placid surface of the roadstead. To add to the menacing, even sinister aspect of this grotesque craft, its entire superstructure was coated with iron plate, four inches of it, bolted on top of nearly two feet of oak and pine, the rounded heads of the bolts giving its skin a knobby appearance.

For all that, the most ominous aspect of this odd craft was that not a single human figure was in sight. No sailor clung to the absent rigging; no officer walked its weather deck; if there were men, stripped to the waist, hunching over its guns and ready for combat, they were not visible from the outside. Indeed, to those observing it for the first time—including more than 250 U.S. Navy officers and men who would perish at its hands that day—this object seemed hardly a vessel at all, and as if in testimony to that, the quartermaster on one of the Union warships in the roadstead announced its appearance by declaring, "That *thing* is a-comin' down." One Union officer likened it to a creature: "The water hisses & boils with indignation as like some huge slimy reptile she slowly emerges from her loathsome lair." But to most of the hundreds of observers watching from the shoreline, this smoke-belching, iron-plated "thing" was neither vessel nor creature but a machine: a giant, self-propelled, armored engine of war.[1]

Inside that engine of war, directing its movements, was sixty-one-year-old Franklin Buchanan, who had been a naval officer for most of his life. Buchanan had joined the Navy in the last days of the War of 1812, and his first sea service had been as a midshipman on board the frigate *Java,* where his commanding officer and first role model had been Oliver Hazard Perry. By 1862 Buchanan had accumulated nearly fifty years of active naval service, including a role as the founding superintendent of the Naval Academy at Annapolis (where the superintendent's house is named for him) and a tour as the flag captain under Matthew C. Perry (Oliver's brother) during that officer's mission to open Japan to Western trade in 1853–54.[2]

As a Marylander, Buchanan had been horrified by the outbreak of hostilities, and he had resigned his commission in the conviction that his own state would soon secede and join the Confederacy. But Maryland did not secede, and almost at once Buchanan regretted his decision. Somewhat sheepishly, he tried to recall his resignation. The Union secretary of the navy, Gideon Welles, would have none of it and responded curtly: "By direction of the president, your name has been stricken from the rolls of the Navy."[3] Angry at such cavalier treatment (as he saw it), Buchanan retired to his country estate on Maryland's eastern shore, where he nursed his anger and disappointment for two more months, growing more truculent by the day at what he considered the Lincoln administration's highhanded behavior. In the end he decided that he could not remain idle while others fought the great war of his generation. In July, only days after the Confederate victory at Bull Run, he left his Maryland home and made his way surreptitiously across the James River to Virginia to offer his services to the Confederacy.

The Confederate secretary of the navy, Stephen Mallory, chose Buchanan to command the *Virginia* because he believed the Marylander had the perfect combination of realism and boldness. "The *Virginia* is a novelty," Mallory wrote in his letter of appointment. It "is untried, and its powers unknown, and the Department does not give specific orders as to her attack on the enemy." But Mallory also made it clear that he hoped for great things from this experimental vessel and that he expected Buchanan to seize the initiative. "Action—prompt and successful action—now could be of serious importance to our cause," Mallory wrote. If Mallory wanted action, Buchanan was just the man for the job. One of the *Virginia*'s officers, after hearing Buchanan's initial address to the crew, described him as "a typical product of the old-time quarterdeck, as indomitably courageous as Nelson, and just as arbitrary."[4]

Buchanan wasted no time. The *Virginia* got under way for its first sea trial as an ironclad on the morning of March 8, 1862. Technically the ship was not yet finished; the shields for its broadside gunports had not been installed, and the engine had never been tested. But Buchanan was a man in a hurry. When the *Virginia* left its berth in the Gosport Navy Yard and eased slowly down the Elizabeth River escorted by a few small gunboats, only two men on board, besides Buchanan himself, knew that this was no trial run. Buchanan had decided that the run across the width of Hampton Roads was enough of a trial for the ship's questionable engine plant. Assuming that the engines could get him there, he planned to steer his experimental craft directly at the enemy. As the *Virginia* left the river's mouth and moved into Hampton Roads, Buchanan ordered the helm over, and slowly, ever so slowly, the prow of the great ironclad swung to port until it was aimed directly at the two Union warships anchored off Newport News Point.

Buchanan and the *Virginia* were about to make history.

———

If the appearance of the *Virginia* in Hampton Roads marked a milestone in naval warfare, the Civil War, in which it fought, was itself a milestone in defining the character of the nation. The country's regional differences were already manifest when Perry won his signal victory on Lake Erie in 1813. The War Hawks of the South and West had looked disdainfully on those (mostly from New England) who had opposed the War of 1812, and many in New England suspected that the War Hawks had motives of their own for promoting an invasion of Canada. In the years since then, however, the issues had changed, and the balance of political power had shifted. The sectional squabble over the admission of Missouri proved to be only the first of a series of disputes over the rights of slaveholders in the West. After the American victory in the war with Mexico (1846–48), the nation almost broke apart over the question of whether slavery would be allowed in the territories annexed after the war. A few years later, the dispute over slavery in Kansas actually led to the spilling of blood.

At the same time, continuing immigration and closer mercantile connections between the mid-Atlantic states and the Old Northwest had increased the relative strength of the northern states within the national government. Southerners, such as the former War Hawk John C. Calhoun, who had championed the consolidation of national power in the central government because they assumed that the southern states would always dominate that government, began to perceive as early as the 1830s that this was no longer likely. Threatened with the reality of the North's new political influence, they constructed a dramatically different interpretation of republican government, asserting that national authority was subordinate to and dependent on the states, rather than the other way around. With Lincoln's election in 1860, southern leaders realized that they had lost control, and they took the bold step of declaring themselves out of the Union.[5]

Like the American declaration of war on England in 1812, the secession of the South was a bold, even reckless step, and like that earlier declaration, it was based on several false assumptions. The first of these was the South's overestimation of its own economic leverage. Southerners believed (or at least they asserted) that the agricultural products of the southern states were so vital to the world's economy that a cotton-hungry planet would side with the South in order to ensure continued access to its goods. When Lincoln declared a blockade of Confederate ports a week after Fort Sumter, the Richmond *Examiner* editorialized that such a declaration was fatuous because, according to the *Examiner*, the world needed the South more than the South needed the world. "If the world respects the blockade," the *Examiner* declared, "all of mankind, civilized and savage, must suffer for the necessities of life; for all consume or use cotton, tobacco, rice and other of our agricultural products; and if those products be excluded from the markets of the world, the supply will be so deficient that universal want and privation will ensue, and starvation often occur throughout every State and country and continent of the world, and in every isle of the ocean." Instead, of course, the nations of the world found other sources for their cotton, tobacco, and rice, and it was the Confederacy that suffered "want and privation," if not actual "starvation," for lack of access to the world's markets.[6]

The South's second great error was to underestimate northern determination. Southerners could not believe that northern shopkeepers and tradesmen would willingly shed their blood to compel the southern states to remain in the Union against their will. The South's image of the North, grounded in four decades of sectional feuding and stereotyping, was that of a money-grubbing secular society where notions of honor, self-sacrifice, and courage simply did not exist. The "fire-eaters" who pushed hardest for secession in the crisis winter of 1860–61 publicly offered to drink every drop of blood spilled in a southern war for independence.[7] Such offers drew cheers and laughter from southern audiences, who understood clearly what was being implied: that northern men did not have the stomach for war, and when confronted by the united resolve of a defiant South, they would necessarily acquiesce in a peaceful, and bloodless, separation. That assumption, too, proved spectacularly misplaced. Over the next four years, northern shopkeepers and tradesmen as well as mechanics, clerks, teachers, farmers, lawyers, and others—350,000 in all—laid down their lives to preserve the Union.

And finally, the South underestimated the vast potential of the North's own economic powerhouse. In this case, southerners were misled not just by their conviction that agriculture trumped industry but by a historical phenomenon that caught almost everyone by surprise, for the Civil War turned out to be two things at the same time: both the world's last old-fashioned war *and* the world's first modern war. It was a war of galloping cavalry charges and open-field infantry attacks; a war in which regimental flags had a talismanic, almost religious, significance; a war where military orders were frequently subscribed (as Perry had ended his note to Harrison) "Yours with great respect and esteem." But if such elements harkened back to the past, other aspects of the war foreshadowed the future, for the Civil War was also a conflict of mass conscript armies armed with rifled muskets; of rapid troop movements by railroad; of instantaneous communication by telegraph; and, in its final phase, of both trench warfare and the kind of violence against society best exemplified by Sherman's famous march to the sea. It was, in short, a total war sustained by the mass production of standardized arms, uniforms, tents, and even rations.

The war marked a revolution in naval warfare as well. That revolution was already evident even before the war began in April 1861, as the graceful frigates and sloops of the Age of Sail gave way during the 1840s and '50s to coal-fired steamships. Many resisted the change. Coal was filthy; its ubiquitous dust permeated everything on board, making it impossible to maintain the kind of spit-and-polish cleanliness that had long defined successful command at sea. Moreover, while the wind was free, coal was expensive, and it was not available everywhere. A reliance on coal made warships operating thousands of miles from home dependent on foreign ports for fuel. In consequence, steam warships in the 1850s were often called "auxiliary steamers," and they carried a complete set of masts and spars so that they could navigate from place to place under sail. Propellers were generally two-bladed rather than four-bladed so that when a ship was under sail, the propeller could be fixed in a vertical position to reduce its drag on the water. Many steamships had hinged crankshafts so that the propeller could be lifted out of the water altogether; others had hinged smokestacks that could be lowered to the deck. Practicality as well as tradition led naval architects to design steamships that still looked as much as possible like the ships that had fought on Lake Erie.

Naval gunnery was changing, too. Naval guns still loaded from the muzzle, but by 1861 the guns had grown so large that their capacity was no longer measured by the weight of the shot (e.g., thirty-two-pounders) but by the diameter of the muzzle (e.g., seven inches). And once war began, the pace of change accelerated. Naval guns grew from seven inches to nine inches to eleven inches and finally to fifteen inches—guns so large they dwarfed the human figures that served them. Before the war was over, the Union Navy forged a twenty-inch gun that weighed over ten tons, and though it was never deployed in battle, it was larger than the biggest naval guns of World War II. Moreover, not only were these guns bigger, but many of them were rifled—that is, they had grooves cut in a corkscrew pattern inside the barrel that put a spin on the projectile, enabling it to keep a true trajectory for a much longer distance. And the projectiles they fired were more often than not explosive shells rather than solid shot.[8]

In addition to these bigger and more dangerous naval guns, there were entirely new devices, including what Federal sailors called "infernal machines," by which they meant underwater torpedoes or mines, as well as the first submarine that successfully (albeit at the cost of its own destruction) sank an enemy warship.* Above all, the war at sea featured the emergence of armored warships, commonly called "ironclads," vessels so different from Perry's majestic brigs on Lake Erie as to be virtually unrecognizable as warships. In this contest, metal would count almost as much as mettle, and in a contest where the weapons of war required the application of industrial productivity, the Union states had an overwhelming advantage over their southern counterparts.

Yet the North did not immediately take advantage of its overwhelming industrial superiority. Part of the reason was that for once the U.S. Navy found itself in the unfamiliar position of being the dominant naval power and, consistent with the inherent conservatism of the superior power, its initial instinct was to rely on the time-tested weapons of naval warfare. Lincoln's first order for the Navy was to announce a blockade of the southern coast. Blockade was a traditional wartime tool of maritime powers, though historically the great powers had used it not so much to stifle trade as to confine the enemy battle fleet in its own ports. Throughout the Napoleonic Wars, Britain had successfully maintained a blockade of the French Navy for most of two decades. In the Civil War, the U.S. Navy did not have to worry about keeping a Confederate battle fleet bottled up, because for all practical purposes the Confederacy had no navy. Instead,

---

* That vessel was the famous Confederate submarine *Hunley*, which sank the USS *Housatonic* off Charleston Harbor on February 17, 1864, but which herself perished in attempting to return to port.

the goal of the Union blockade of the Confederacy was much more ambitious: to close all of the ports and harbors along the coast, literally stopping all trade. In Lincoln's words, it was "to prevent entrance and exit of vessels from the ports aforesaid."[9]

Such a goal was easier to proclaim than to achieve. The Confederacy claimed a coastline of some thirty-five hundred miles, and the U.S. Navy had fewer than ninety warships. On the other hand, the North did not need cutting-edge technology or warships of innovative design to execute its blockade strategy. Indeed, almost any vessel—or at least any *steam* vessel (for sailing ships proved to be inefficient on blockade duty)—would suit. The Navy Department therefore went on a buying spree, purchasing steam merchant vessels, reinforcing their decks so that they could carry the weight of naval guns, and then sending them down to serve on the blockade. By 1864 the U.S. Navy boasted a ship's list of over four hundred such vessels, and over six hundred ships altogether.

The Confederacy could not hope to match these numbers, nor did it try. Just as the Union adopted the traditional strategy of superior naval powers, the Confederacy adopted the kind of naval strategy traditionally employed by weaker naval powers, a naval policy nearly identical to the one pursued by the United States in 1812 for its war against Britain: it would rely on its armies to master the war on land, conduct a war on commerce against Union merchant ships, and defend the coast by relying on shore fortifications supported by a few cutting-edge naval weapons.

If southerners did not conceive of the land war as "a mere matter of marching," as some of the War Hawks had proclaimed in 1812, they did harbor great confidence in the superiority of their land armies, a confidence that seemed to be well founded after several of the early land engagements resulted in Confederate victories before Union numerical and industrial superiority began to dominate. At sea, the idea of commerce raiding was particularly appealing because it would hit the Yankees where southerners believed it would hurt them most: in their pocketbooks. To execute such a policy, the Confederacy sent agents to Europe to purchase a handful of fast raiders. This eventually resulted in the acquisition of the *Alabama*, *Florida*, and *Shenandoah*, vessels that collectively destroyed more than 150 American merchant ships and provoked a near-panic among the bankers and businessmen of the North's Atlantic seaboard.

The protection of the southern coast proved more difficult. In those places where the Confederates were able to occupy existing forts built in the 1830s and '40s by the Army Corps of Engineers, such as Fort Sumter in Charleston Harbor or Fort Morgan at the entrance to Mobile Bay, they were able to fend off repeated naval assaults. But where they had to depend instead on fortifications thrown up since the onset of war, such as at Hatteras Inlet in North Carolina or Port Royal in South Carolina, the Union Navy generally had its way, blasting those dirt and log defenses into surrender within a matter of hours. To prevent Union domination of the coastline, Confederate navy secretary Stephen R. Mallory hoped to supplement the coastal forts by acquiring a few ships whose defensive characteristics were such that they could stand up to a whole squadron of conventional Union warships. "Knowing that the enemy could build one hundred ships to one of our own," he wrote his wife, "my policy has been to make such ships so strong and invulnerable as would compensate for the inequality of numbers." In a word, he wanted ironclads. As early as May 8, less than a month after Fort Sumter, Mallory urged the Confederate Congress (which had not yet moved from Montgomery to Richmond) to authorize the construction of an ironclad warship. "I regard the possession of an iron-armored ship, as a matter of the first necessity," he wrote. "Such a vessel at this time could traverse the entire coast of the United States, prevent all blockades, and encounter, with a fair prospect of success, their entire Navy."[10]

The concept of iron-armored warships was not a new one. Robert Fulton had designed and built a self-powered floating battery (which he called *Demologos*) for the defense of New York Harbor at the end of the War of 1812, though it never saw action. In 1854 the United States had experimented with a similar craft, the *Stevens Battery*, but it was still unfinished in 1861 and had design flaws that made it unlikely that it would ever be completed. In 1857 the French had initiated a program to build ten ironclad warships, thus stealing a nautical march (to use a mixed metaphor) on their British rivals, and the first of them, called *Gloire*, had been launched in 1859. Inspired (or, rather, provoked) by the French to reciprocate, the British had also begun construction of an armored warship.* Mallory's first thought was to try to buy the *Gloire* from the French outright. The French refused, however, not only because they were unwilling to relinquish the jewel of their fleet but also because it would be an obvious violation of neutrality. If Mallory wanted armored warships for his new navy, he would have to find a way to build them at home.

His problem was that the Confederacy lacked the facilities (what today would be called the industrial infrastructure) necessary to build such a vessel from scratch quickly. The design, fabrication, and construction of the engine plant alone was likely to take a year or more. Mallory therefore sought a shortcut, and he found one thanks mainly to the Federal commander of the Gosport Navy Yard near Norfolk, Virginia, Commodore Charles McCauley. Only days after Confederates fired the first shot of the war at Fort Sumter in Charleston Harbor and Virginia seceded from the Union, McCauley feared that a noisy mob of citizens outside the Navy Yard gate might try to storm the place. On April 20, 1861, he ordered that the yard be evacuated. Not only was his decision premature, but the evacuation was poorly coordinated and incompletely performed. Though McCauley ordered his men to destroy whatever could not be carried away, much of value was left behind, including repair facilities, machine shops, a huge granite dry dock, and the partially burned hull of the steam frigate *Merrimack*.

Months later, long after the *Merrimack* had been transformed into the ironclad *Virginia* and won its first dramatic victory, an argument emerged over who deserved the credit for planning and building the South's first ironclad. One candidate was a lieutenant in the Confederate Navy named John Mercer Brooke. On June 3, 1861, Brooke met with Mallory in Richmond to urge the construction of an iron-plated warship, and a week later he submitted a sketch of a casemate ironclad. For technical advice about the feasi-

---

* Unlike the French *Gloire*, which was protected by iron armor bolted over a wooden frame, the British *Warrior* was built entirely of iron. The *Warrior* remains in honorary commission today and is moored at Portsmouth near HMS *Victory*, Nelson's flagship at Trafalgar.

bility of the concept, Mallory sent for Chief Engineer William P. Williamson and Naval Constructor John L. Porter. Porter is the other contender for credit as the designer of the CSS *Virginia*. He had no idea why Mallory had summoned him, but he had been thinking about an ironclad warship independently, and when he traveled to Richmond he brought with him a design of his own for an ironclad warship. When he arrived there on June 23, he was surprised and pleased to discover that building an armored warship was the very project Mallory had in mind. In fact, Brooke's drawing and Porter's model were strikingly similar. They both featured an iron fort or casemate with angled walls (Brooke's at a forty-five-degree angle, Porter's at forty degrees), built atop a flat-bottomed hull. (After tests ashore, the walls of the casemate were eventually constructed at a thirty-six-degree angle.) The principal difference was that in Porter's model the casemate covered the entire hull, whereas in Brooke's plan both the ship's pointed prow and its rounded stern extended beyond the casemate, partly to prevent the bow wave from washing up on the armored shield and partly to increase buoyancy. Porter agreed that this was a desirable feature, and he volunteered to turn the rough sketch into a finished design.[11]*

Both men, along with Chief Engineer Williamson, then headed back to Norfolk to see if the hull of the partially destroyed *Merrimack*, which had been raised from the bottom of the Elizabeth River and placed in the masonry dry dock, would suit as a platform on which to construct their ironclad. Williamson thought it would, though both Brooke and Porter were dubious. They had each envisioned a flat-bottomed vessel. With some justification they feared that using the *Merrimack*'s V-shaped hull would give the ship too great a draft for operations in coastal waters. Nevertheless, they allowed themselves to be convinced, since, as they put it in their letter to Mallory, "it would appear that this is our only chance to get a suitable vessel in a short time."[12]

---

* For more than a quarter of a century afterward—indeed, until the day they died—Brooke and Porter quarreled about which of them deserved credit for the design of the CSS *Virginia*. In 1887 they each wrote articles for *Century* magazine emphasizing the centrality of his own role and disparaging that of the other.

By mid-July the work was under way. Porter supervised the refit as carpenters cut away the charred timbers on the *Merrimack* and began to erect a frame for the casemate. Williamson focused on repairing the cranky engines. Brooke designed the rifled guns that would make up the ship's armament, and he took charge of procuring the iron plate that would constitute its armor shield.

In the end, it was the iron armor that proved to be the bottleneck. Tests conducted in October proved that two-inch iron plate was dramatically more effective than one-inch plate, even several layers of it. But there was only one facility in all of the Confederacy capable of rolling two-inch plate (the Tredegar Iron Works in Richmond), and covering the *Virginia's* casemate with two layers of two-inch iron plate would require nearly eight hundred tons of iron. There was simply not that much iron available in all of Virginia. Brooke scavenged scrap iron, old smoothbore cannon, even tools, all of which was melted down into iron plate, but he still came up short. To make up the difference, the Confederacy began ripping up hundreds of miles of its own railroads, a measure of both its industrial weakness and its desperation.* Even with crews working around the clock, production was limited and frustratingly slow. By October only two tons of the two-inch iron armor had reached Gosport, and the last of it did not arrive until February 1862. The Confederacy had begun with a considerable head start in the arms race to construct an ironclad warship, but as delay followed delay, the window of opportunity was swiftly closing.[13]

Mallory agonized over every delay, and he had to play referee when Brooke and Porter quarreled over proposed changes in the design. Weary of the squabbling, Mallory sent Lieutenant Catesby ap Roger Jones to Gosport in November to take charge of the project and eventually to become the ship's executive officer. Jones had an impressive pedigree: he was the son of Roger Jones (the *ap* in his name was Welsh for "son of"),

---

* The Confederate Navy and southern railroads competed for scarce iron throughout the war. In January 1863 the Confederate Congress passed legislation that authorized the Navy to seize excess iron from railroads, but state governors protested and put so many roadblocks in the way that the Navy remained desperately short of iron.

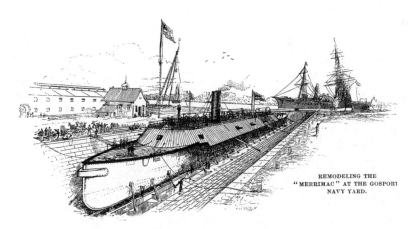

REMODELING THE
"MERRIMAC" AT THE GOSPORT
NAVY YARD.

After being raised from the bottom of the Elizabeth River, the USS *Merrimack* was placed in a stone dry dock at the Gosport Navy Yard and converted into the ironclad CSS *Virginia*. Note the iron ram positioned on the bow. (Ned Bradford, ed., *Battles and Leaders of the Civil War*)

who had been the Army's adjutant general, and he was the nephew of Thomas ap Catesby Jones, who had commanded the U.S. naval squadron in the Battle for New Orleans during the War of 1812. Moreover, Jones himself was a competent professional, and events would prove him to have been a good choice. But to command the ship, Mallory wanted a more senior officer, someone who would be aggressive enough to take full advantage of the vessel's presumed capabilities. Such a disproportionate amount of the Confederacy's naval resources was being committed to this project that it was crucial to have just the right man in command lest the vessel's capabilities be squandered. Mallory wanted a sea warrior, and he chose sixty-one-year-old Captain Franklin Buchanan.

—

One hundred miles away in Washington, officials had known for some time what the Confederates were up to in Norfolk. The Union's navy secretary, Gideon Welles, had even obtained a copy of Mallory's May 8 letter to the Confederate Congress claiming that one rebel ironclad vessel could "encounter, with a fair prospect of success," the entire U.S. Navy. At first

Welles did not take this boast seriously, his skepticism fed by the reaction of most of his senior naval officers, who scoffed at the notion. But all through May and June, news of the rebel activity in Norfolk continued to reach him. In the middle of the nineteenth century there was no such thing as industrial secrecy, and Welles knew almost as soon as Mallory did when the *Merrimack*'s hull was raised, when it was placed in dry dock, and when workmen began to reconfigure its superstructure. Southern newspapers proved a particularly valuable source of information and kept Welles up to date on the ship's progress, even publishing the results of the ordnance testing against one- and two-inch iron plate.[14]

By the end of June Welles decided that the Union Navy needed to develop a counterweapon, and on July 4 he asked Congress for an appropriation of $1.5 million to construct three experimental ironclad warships. To determine appropriate designs for these craft, that same legislation authorized the creation of an Ironclad Board consisting of three serving naval officers, all of them captains. The bill worked its way through Congress with unusual speed, and President Lincoln signed it on August 4. Three days later Welles issued a public solicitation of designs for an American ironclad warship. Like Perry and Barclay on Lake Erie, Welles and Mallory were engaged in a naval arms race for the control of a strategically critical body of water.[15]

Despite that, events continued with measured progress in Washington. Fifteen proposals were submitted to the Ironclad Board, though only two of them received serious attention. One was a gunboat designed by Samuel Pook that was submitted by an enthusiastic entrepreneur named Cornelius Bushnell; the other was for a more or less conventional frigate with iron plating. The Navy captains on the Ironclad Board, all veterans of the sailing era, were skeptical. Both designs called for the proposed vessels to carry a huge amount of iron plate above the waterline, and some board members openly expressed doubts that either ship would float. This is when Bushnell began to play a crucial if curious role. Bushnell had a lot invested (both financially as well as personally) in getting a contract, so he decided to verify his design with the man who he had been told was the nation's most gifted expert on maritime engineering: the Swedish-born immigrant John Ericsson. Visiting Ericsson at his New York residence, Bushnell asked him to calculate the buoyancy of the two vessels under consideration. Ericsson did so, assuring Bushnell rather quickly that both ships would indeed float. But then Ericsson asked Bushnell if, as long as he was there, he would like to see a "floating battery" that Ericsson himself had designed, and the inventor brought out a model of a flat-bottomed vessel whose salient feature was a rotating cylinder in the middle of its flat deck. Bushnell saw at once the potential of such a vessel, and he asked if he could show it to Welles. Ericsson agreed.[16]

Bushnell went straight to Welles's home in Hartford, Connecticut, where he declared somewhat melodramatically that "the country was safe because I had found a battery which would make us master of the situation as far as the ocean was concerned." Welles urged him to present the model to the Ironclad Board, but Bushnell did more than that. He got William H. Seward to write him a letter of introduction to Abraham Lincoln, and he took Ericsson's model straight to the White House. Among his many other interests, Lincoln was fond of gadgets. Years earlier, when he had still been a prairie lawyer, he had obtained a patent for a device to float river steamers over sand bars, and during the war he was a frequent visitor to the Washington Navy Yard, where he liked to observe ordnance tests. Intrigued by Ericsson's model, he agreed to accompany Bushnell to the next meeting of the Ironclad Board. At that meeting (on September 13), the members of the board remained skeptical, but Lincoln made his feelings known in a characteristic way, remarking: "All I have to say is what the girl said when she put her foot into stocking: 'It strikes me there's something in it.'"[17]

Even with that encouragement, the members of the board hesitated. They recalled that Ericsson had designed the screw sloop *Princeton* back in 1844, and rather unfairly they connected him with the explosion of one of the *Princeton*'s big guns during a cruise on the Potomac, an accident that had killed the secretaries of state and war, among others. Bushnell protested that the gun that had exploded was Robert F. Stockton's Peace-

maker, not Ericsson's Oregon Gun, but the captains remained unmoved.*
Charles Henry Davis was weary of Bushnell's impassioned advocacy; he
suggested that Bushnell "take the little thing [the model] home and wor-
ship it."[18]

Bushnell decided that the only man who could convince these skeptics
of the little ship's technical feasibility was Ericsson himself. But Bushnell
also knew that Ericsson would be less than eager to appear before the Navy
captains as a supplicant. With some justification, the Swedish inventor
believed that he had been ill treated by the Navy ever since the 1844 incident on the *Princeton*, and he had resolved long ago never again to set foot
in Washington. Aware of this, Bushnell was not completely honest about
the reception the model had received in Washington. He told Ericsson that
the board members had been impressed by the "genius" of the design but
that one member had asked a few technical questions that Bushnell had
not been able to answer. "Well," Ericsson replied, "I'll go—I'll go tonight."
"From that moment," Bushnell wrote later, "I knew that the success of the
affair was assured."[19]

Not quite. Both Bushnell and Welles knew that if the captains on the
Ironclad Board greeted Ericsson coolly, the touchy inventor was likely to
withdraw in a huff. Aware that time was running out, Welles urged Commodore Joseph Smith, the board's chairman, to give the inventor a fair and
cordial hearing. Even then, the meeting was nearly disastrous. Ericsson was
prepared for compliments, not criticism. He bristled from the start, but
the mood in the room turned when, in responding to a question about the
vessel's likely stability in a seaway, Ericsson became so involved in the
answer that he delivered a lengthy and technically detailed dissertation
that left the board members both silenced and impressed.

Impressed, but not yet convinced. It required another presentation in
Welles's office to satisfy the board members. At the end of that meeting,
Ericsson declared that his ship could be built in ninety days. Welles asked

* The Ericsson-designed Oregon gun did not explode, though because of the failure of Stockton's
Peacemaker, the Navy never fired it again. It sits now just inside the main gate at the U.S. Naval
Academy in Annapolis.

him how much it would cost. "Two hundred and seventy-five thousand dollars," Ericsson answered at once—only a fraction of the appropriation Welles had available. Welles then turned to face the board members and asked them one by one if a contract should be granted. Receiving an affirmative from each, Welles told Ericsson to get started; a contract would be forthcoming.[20] It was the fifteenth of September. Down in Norfolk, Confederates had already raised the *Merrimack*, cut away its charred scantlings, and redesigned and reconfigured it as an ironclad. On the other hand, the Tredegar Iron Works had only that month begun to produce the first sections of two-inch iron plate for the vessel's armor shield. The arms race was still winnable, but only if Ericsson could make good on his promise to build the ship in ninety days.*

Ericsson subcontracted various parts of the ship to other companies (something his Confederate counterparts could not do), but he personally supervised the critical components: the engines, the assembly of the hull, and in particular the novel revolving turret. This, indeed, was the key design feature of Ericsson's battery: twenty-one feet across and eight feet high, the turret was constructed of eight layers of overlapping one-inch iron plate, and it revolved on a spindle driven by a small steam engine. Inside that turret were only two guns—the ship's entire armament—but they were large-caliber guns, and because the turret could revolve, they could be pointed in any direction independent of the ship's heading. Workers began construction on October 25, and the vessel was launched ninety-three days later. At the launching, Ericsson was vindicated, and his critics silenced, when it floated with exactly the draft that he had calculated.

For the command of this unusual vessel, Welles chose forty-three-year-old Lieutenant John L. Worden of New York, a twenty-seven-year Navy veteran. Unlike Buchanan, Worden did not have a reputation as an aggres-

---

* In addition to Ericsson's *Monitor*, the Ironclad Board also approved two other designs: the Samuel Pook–designed *Galena*, which proved a great disappointment, and the armored frigate *New Ironsides*, which performed satisfactorily if unspectacularly as the flagship of the South Atlantic Blockading Squadron.

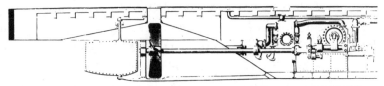

1. AFT SECTION. LONGITUDINAL PLAN THROUGH THE CENTER LINE OF THE ORIGINAL MONITOR.

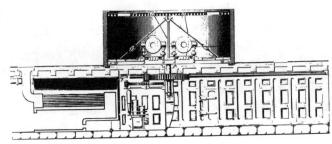

2. CENTRAL SECTION, SAME PLAN.

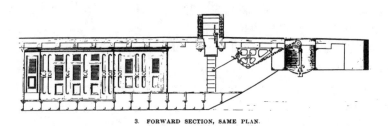

3. FORWARD SECTION, SAME PLAN.

This schematic drawing of the USS *Monitor* is based on John Ericsson's original plan. Note the four-bladed propeller in the top (rear) section, the horizontal gear that turned the turret in the center drawing, and at bottom, the ladder to the pilothouse and the anchor well. (Ned Bradford, ed., *Battles and Leaders of the Civil War*)

sive sea warrior—most of his active-duty service had been spent ashore in the Naval Observatory. But perhaps Welles felt that he owed Worden something. During the Fort Sumter crisis, Welles had sent him to carry secret orders to the commander of Fort Pickens near Pensacola. Worden had completed the assignment, successfully delivering the orders to the post's commanding officer, but by the time he was ready to return to Washington, the first shots of the war had been fired at Fort Sumter. Trusting to fate, Worden nevertheless bought a rail ticket north. He was arrested almost at once by Confederate authorities in Alabama and held as a prisoner for seven months before he was released on November 1 due to his failing health. After a month's sick leave, Worden received orders on January 12 to report to the Brooklyn Navy Yard to take command of the *Monitor*. In an unconscious echo of the orders Mallory prepared for Buchanan, Commodore Smith, who headed Welles's Ironclad Board, wrote Worden, "This vessel is an experiment. I believe you are the right sort of officer to put in command of her."[21]

In receipt of these orders, Worden immediately went down to the Navy Yard to view the famous Ericsson Battery, which Ericsson now decided should be called *Monitor*. Worden was less than overwhelmed by his first glimpse of the strange little craft, and he acknowledged his orders by cautiously expressing the hope that "she may prove a success." "At all events," he added gamely, "I am quite willing to be an agent in testing her capabilities." If Worden withheld judgment about the *Monitor*, the crew of that little vessel was equally uncertain about their new commander. Worden's health was still precarious when he reported aboard his new command on January 16, and he did not make much of an impression on the crew. He was thin, pale, and (in the opinion of at least one member of the wardroom) "effeminate looking." But Worden's appearance belied a fierce determination. For the next month, "everything was hurry and confusion" on the *Monitor* as Worden oversaw all the thousands of tiny details necessary to a ship's commissioning. The vessel was afloat, but it was not yet finished. As the final touches were added to the berthing spaces and officer's cabins, supplies of all kinds, from dishware to chamber pots, were loaded on board, including powder and shot for the vessel's two eleven-inch Dahlgren guns.[22]

Since the ship had only two guns, both Ericsson and Worden wanted the biggest-caliber guns they could get. Indeed, Ericsson had specifically requested that the *Monitor* be armed with new twelve-inch guns, but none were available. He therefore had to settle for two eleven-inch guns "borrowed" from other vessels in New York Harbor. Those guns came with a stipulation that no more than fifteen pounds of powder could be used for any single charge, a legacy of the explosion of Stockton's Peacemaker on the *Princeton* nearly twenty years before. If time had allowed, Worden might have been allowed to proof the guns by firing successive rounds from each one using progressively larger charges until it was clear that the weapon could bear the strain of larger loads without fracturing. But there was no time for such niceties in the current crisis.

On February 27 (the same day that the *Merrimack* was put into commission as the *Virginia* in Gosport), the *Monitor* embarked on its first sea trial. It was nearly disastrous. The engines worked well enough, driving the ironclad through the water at a respectable seven or eight knots, but the helmsman called out that the ship would not answer the rudder. The ship's great weight created such a powerful forward momentum that the tiller ropes connecting the wheel to the rudder had no effect. The *Monitor* ran back and forth across New York Harbor "like a drunken man on a side walk," as one crewman recalled, finally slamming into the Brooklyn dock near the city gas works with a jarring collision. Ignominiously, it had to be towed back to its berth in the Navy Yard. Notified of the problem, Ericsson came on board, went below, and began to tinker with the lines and pulleys that transferred orders from the wheel to the rudder. By multiplying the ratio, he soon fixed the problem. But this incident reminded Worden that, as Smith had warned him, "this vessel is an experiment."[23]

Departure was postponed for a day due to the weather, but on March 6 the *Monitor* left the Brooklyn Navy Yard bound for Hampton Roads. The journey itself was an adventure. In addition to relying on its own engines, the *Monitor* was also under tow, and it had an escort of two gunboats. Despite the predictions of the skeptics, the *Monitor* rode the water well, and the first day out, no new problems were identified. The engines clanked along satisfactorily, and from the top of the *Monitor's* turret (the only part of the vessel where a man might stand while the ship was under way) Worden watched the tow line dipping in and out of the water between his vessel and the tug four hundred feet dead ahead. Off to each side were the escorting gunboats; more distantly, he could see sailing vessels running in and out of New York. So far, the ironclad was performing magnificently.[24]

This was certainly good news to the fifty-seven men who made up the *Monitor*'s crew, all of whom were volunteers. Rather than accept men arbitrarily assigned to him from the receiving ships in the harbor, Worden had asked for volunteers, and he was gratified when more men volunteered than he needed. But if the men were enthusiastic and patriotic, they were also mostly inexperienced. The ship's executive officer, Samuel Dana Greene, was only twenty-one and just three years out of the Academy. Its paymaster was so innocent that he asked Worden if it was really necessary for him to buy a uniform: couldn't he just continue to wear his civilian clothes on board? Besides Worden himself, only the ship's chief engineer, thirty-four-year-old Alban Stimers, was a veteran of long experience, and he was on board mainly to observe and report on how the *Monitor* functioned at sea. Of the ship's crew of fifty-seven, only nine had sufficient experience to be rated as ordinary seamen.[25]

Now that they were at sea, they discovered that living and working in the semisubmerged world of the *Monitor* was relatively comfortable— much more comfortable, one sailor wrote, than the receiving ship *North Carolina* had been. So far, it seemed, duty in an ironclad was not too bad. The only drawbacks seemed to be that the inside temperature was either too cold or, once the heat from the boilers was tapped, too hot, and the interior lighting was so dim below decks that it was difficult to see. Most compartments had small waterproof windows in the overhead to admit some natural light, but it remained dark in the narrow passageways, and when the ship was buttoned up for combat, it would be almost pitch black.[26]

The good weather did not last. On the second day out, the barometer dropped and the wind increased. Heavy waves washed over the *Monitor*'s flat deck, foaming and sloshing against the turret. The officers in their staterooms looked up through the glass windows to see green water overhead. Save for the turret, the ship was, in effect, under water. From the tug, only the *Monitor*'s turret was visible above the waves, and occasionally even that was obscured by the rolling seas. Those seas also affected the ship's movement, especially under tow. Twenty-seven-year veteran that he was, Worden nevertheless felt the cold prickly sweat and rising nausea of seasickness. He had not fully recovered from his seven months in captivity, and the confined spaces, the hot-oil smell from the engine, and the motion of an iron ship under tow sent him rushing to the top of the turret, where the bracing wind and sea spray provided only partial relief.

Despite his personal misery, his own health was not Worden's greatest worry. Ericsson had designed the *Monitor*'s turret so that it rested on a smooth brass ring embedded in the deck. He had calculated that the weight of the 120-ton turret would press so securely on this ring that it would create a perfect waterproof seal. But just prior to the vessel's departure from New York, Stimers had placed a "plaited hemp rope" between the turret and the deck in order to provide what he thought would be a more secure seal. Now, as the weather worsened, water began to work its way through this hempen seal, and soon water was dripping—and then cascading—down into the berthing spaces. The men below were now not only seasick but soaked, and Worden allowed his fellow sufferers to join him atop the ship's turret. There they lay flat on their backs atop the iron grating, shielded from the worst of the sea spray by a canvas tarpaulin.[27]

Then at 4:00 the ventilating fans in the engine room stopped working. So much water had sloshed down the blower pipes that the leather belts driving the blowers had stretched and lost their purchase on the pulleys. Smoke built up in the engine room, and sailors fought their way out coughing and wheezing. Rushing in to try to solve the problem, Stimers succumbed to the smoke and gas. He had to be dragged out unconscious and taken to the top of the now-crowded turret top. Without a fire in the boiler, the pumps would not work, and Worden ordered the crew to man the hand pumps. The men went to work with a will, but the hand pumps were not powerful enough to force water all the way from the bilge to the top of the turret, which was the ship's only opening to the outside. Water began to build up below, and Worden ordered the ship's flag to be hoisted upside down as a signal of distress. In such a sea, however, there was nothing the escorting gunboats could do. Eventually, only the easing of the storm saved the ship. That allowed the engineers to restart the engines and reengage the pumps.[28]

The next day was March 8—a fateful day in American naval history. At noon Worden sighted Cape Henry at the northern entrance to Chesapeake Bay, and a few hours later, as the land crept closer, those on board the *Monitor* began to hear "heavy firing in the distance," which led to intense speculation. Some thought it was only the guns of Fort Monroe "at practice," but Worden feared that the *Merrimack* had at last come out and that he was too late. He ordered the ship cleared for action and asked for maximum speed. In spite of his eagerness, however, the ship would not be hurried. "Our iron hull crept slowly on," one officer wrote home, "& the monotonous clank, clank, clank of the engine betokened no increase of its speed." It was evening by the time the *Monitor* and its escorts entered Chesapeake Bay, and full dark before it entered the roadstead. The towline was cast off and a pilot came on board. From him, Worden learned that the *Merrimack* had indeed come out that day, and that it had all but destroyed the Union fleet. Worden directed the pilot to put the *Monitor* alongside the *Roanoke*, the flagship of the Union squadron. Not until he was alongside did Worden learn the scope of the disaster that had been wrought that day by the rebel ironclad.[29]

—

Measured in terms of lives lost, the fighting in Hampton Roads on March 8, 1862, marked the worst defeat in the history of the United States Navy until the Japanese attack on Pearl Harbor eighty years later. Unlike that later attack, however, there had been no stealth in the assault by the CSS *Virginia* against the Union Navy's wooden ships in Hampton Roads. Cheered on by a crowd of spectators lining the shore, Buchanan ordered the *Virginia* to steam boldly out of the Elizabeth River in the bright sunlight of a spring morning, black smoke billowing from its single stack, and head directly toward its quarry: the USS *Cumberland* and USS *Congress*, waiting at anchor off Newport News Point. Between them, those two Union vessels, both of them sailing ships, mounted a total of seventy guns to the *Virginia*'s ten, but such a comparison, pertinent in the days of Perry and Barclay, was largely irrelevant now.

Officially the *Virginia* was rated as a "ram." A fifteen-hundred-pound cast iron prow had been bolted onto the ship's bow just below the waterline, and though it protruded only a few feet from the ship's stem, it made the ship itself, as well as its guns, a potentially lethal weapon. Buchanan's plan was to steam his vessel directly at the *Cumberland* and drive that cast iron prow into the *Cumberland*'s wooden hull. He targeted that ship first because, although it had fewer guns than the *Congress*, the *Cumberland*'s guns were larger and included two ten-inch pivot guns. Buchanan feared (incorrectly, as it happened) that these guns might be rifled, and since large-caliber rifled guns were the only ones likely to prove capable of penetrating the *Virginia*'s iron shield, the *Cumberland* had to be dispatched first. The risk was that such a direct attack would enable the *Cumberland* to "cap the T" of the *Virginia* as it approached: that is, the *Cumberland* would be able to fire several broadsides at the *Virginia* during its lengthy transit, while the *Virginia* would be able to answer only with its one bow gun, a seven-inch Brooke-designed rifle.

The *Virginia*'s straining engines were able to propel the great ship through the water at only about five knots, so the men on both sides had plenty of time to consider the pending encounter. Whatever they felt internally, outwardly they displayed confidence and a grim determination. Men stood quietly at their posts, some out of a sense of duty, some out of patriotism, some simply because their pride would not let them do otherwise. On the *Virginia*, one officer noted "the pale and determined countenances of the gun crews as they stood motionless at their posts, with set lips unsmiling." But in at least some cases—if not most—that stoic demeanor belied a deep apprehension. The third assistant engineer, Eugenius Jack, recalled that he felt "no little anxiety" and was "a little weak kneed" as the *Virginia* closed its foe. For most of the gunners and firemen on the *Virginia*, this would be their first combat on a ship of war. The majority of them had been recruited from army units nearby, and the slow journey down the Elizabeth River was their total seagoing experience. Jack no doubt spoke for many when he noted in his memoirs, "There are few men who do not feel some symptoms of fear when going into battle; pride has kept many a man's face to the foe, when his heart would turn it away."[30]

Similarly on the *Cumberland*, Lieutenant Thomas Selfridge, who commanded the ship's first division, recalled that the men waited at their guns

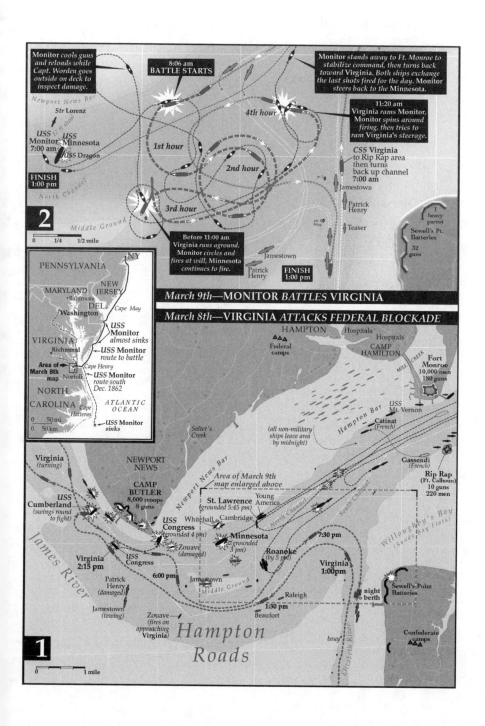

"cool, grim, silent, and determined." If they were appalled by the grotesque iron-plated war machine steaming slowly toward them, they took comfort, as soldiers and sailors have done throughout the history of organized war, in the proximity of their messmates. That bond gave them a collective strength that masked their individual uncertainties. Selfridge wrote that they felt "the mutual dependence upon each other arising from long association."[31]

What was unique about this engagement was not merely that it pitted steam against sail, or even iron against wood, but that it marked a confrontation between men *on* a ship and men *in* a ship. On the Union warships the sailors stood by their guns and sighted along the barrels much as Perry's or Barclay's men had done on Lake Erie. From the weather deck on the *Cumberland* or the *Congress* they had a clear view of the "thing" that was slowly approaching them. Inside the *Virginia*, on the other hand, most of the men had to guess at what was happening outside their iron shell. The gunners tried to peer out the narrow gunports, but the view was constricted, and the officers availed themselves of the privileges of rank to take all the best vantage points. Down below there was no view at all. In the darkened fireroom, E. A. Jack recalled that "the suspense was awful." He could track the slow-motion approach of the *Virginia* toward its quarry only in his mind's eye, and he knew that the battle had begun only when he heard "the dull reports of the enemies artillery, and an occasional sharp crack and tremor of the ship told that we had been struck." But whether those shots striking the shield had penetrated to the gun deck, he did not know. Then he heard "the sharp reports of our own guns," and soon afterward "there came a tremor throughout the ship and I was nearly thrown from the coal bucket upon which I was sitting." The *Virginia* had rammed the *Cumberland* in its starboard side, punching its fifteen-hundred-pound ram deep within the wooden hull of its foe. Surely such a blow would be mortal, Jack thought. "The cracking and breaking of her timbers told full well how fatal to her that collision was."[32]

The sounds and sensations that reached the men inside the *Virginia* only hinted at the destruction that was taking place aboard the *Cumberland*. While the shells from the *Cumberland* glanced harmlessly off the *Virginia*'s iron casemate, the *Virginia*'s bow rifle caused horrible execution on the deck of the *Cumberland* even before the fatal collision. The second shot fired by the *Virginia* exploded in the midst of a gun crew that was urgently reloading the *Cumberland*'s forward ten-inch pivot. The explosion dismounted the gun and killed every man in its crew except the gun captain, who lost both of his arms.

On board the *Virginia*, the gun crews reloaded. Lieutenant Charles Simms, captain of the bow gun, called out, "Sponge!" and the sponge man, Charles Dunbar, leaped over the breeching tackle and thrust his head out through the gunport to obey. A U.S. Marine on the *Cumberland* who had been watching the gunport for just such an opportunity squeezed his trigger, and Dunbar fell back into the *Virginia* shot through the head.[33]

When the *Virginia*'s iron prow struck the *Cumberland*, men on both ships were knocked from their feet. Water poured in through the gaping hole in the *Cumberland*'s side. Even then, with the ship literally sinking beneath them and the dead and dying all about, the men on the *Cumberland* dragged the dead to the unengaged side of the ship and returned to

The CSS *Virginia* drives its iron prow deep into the starboard bow of the USS *Cumberland* in this line drawing, first published by *Century* magazine at the end of the nineteenth century. The *Virginia*'s rampage on March 8, 1862, marked the worst defeat for the U.S. Navy until the Japanese attack on Pearl Harbor some eighty years later. (Ned Bradford, ed., *Battles and Leaders of the Civil War*)

their guns, loading and firing as fast as they could. Because the forward magazine had flooded, powder and shell had to be manhandled from the after magazine, but the guns kept firing. Nevertheless, it was clear that the *Cumberland* was mortally wounded. A junior officer recalled, "The once clean and beautiful deck was slippery with blood, blackened with powder and looked like a slaughter house." Even as the gunners continued to work the big guns, the ship began to settle beneath them.[34]

The men on the *Virginia* had little time to savor their victory. For a few anxious moments it seemed likely that the *Cumberland* would take her assassin down with her. The *Virginia's* ram had plunged so deeply into the *Cumberland* that, although Buchanan had immediately ordered all astern, the ironclad remained embedded in the side of its sinking victim. Water began to rush through the *Virginia's* forward gunports into the casemate, and the deck of the big ironclad canted forward alarmingly. The two ships began to settle in tandem until the James River current swung the *Virginia's* stern slowly to starboard, and the resulting torque on the ship's ram caused a section of it to break off. With that, the *Virginia* was able to extricate itself from its mortally wounded foe and back away.

The *Cumberland* continued to settle, more swiftly now as tons of water rushed in through the gaping wound in its side, though the men on board continued to serve the guns as long as they were above water. With the decks awash, the sailors finally abandoned their guns; those who could swim plunged into the water on the landward side and made their way to shore as best they could. Only now did it become evident that carrying the wounded below decks had been a terrible error. There was no time to bring them back up to the weather deck, and dozens of wounded men drowned below decks as the *Cumberland* settled bow first, its stern rising briefly before the ship settled on the bottom of Hampton Roads, the tips of its masts still showing above the surface with the vessel's commissioning pennant still flying.* On Perry's *Lawrence* back in 1813, some 96 of the 159 men on board had been

---

* Selfridge later claimed that he returned to the *Cumberland* that evening and rescued the ship's flag, which was still flying at the mizzen. According to his memoirs, he hid it ashore, but when he returned for it later, it was gone.

killed or wounded, but "only" 22 of them had been killed outright. On the *Cumberland*, more than five times as many were killed: 121 out of 376. Ashore, Lieutenant Selfridge looked back aghast at the scene of disaster. That night, he admitted in his memoirs, he "sobbed like a child."[35]

Buchanan was not done yet. Sea warrior that he was, his goal was to destroy the entire Federal squadron, and the *Congress* was next. Because the James River current had pushed the *Virginia*'s stern downstream, its bow was now pointing upriver. Buchanan therefore had to conn his balky vessel upriver to gain sea room before executing a slow 180-degree turn to port to reenter Hampton Roads. The *Virginia* was so heavy and unmanageable that it took nearly forty minutes, with its keel scraping bottom most of the way, to execute the turn. At first the sailors watching from the *Congress* thought the *Virginia* was fleeing upriver, and they began to cheer, but the cheers died on their lips as the heavy ironclad continued its slow turn to port and then steadied on a course directly toward them.

The destruction of the *Cumberland* had uncorked the blockade of the James River, allowing the gunboats of the Confederate James River squadron to steam downriver and join the fight, though they made little difference. A Federal shell fired from the shore ripped through the boiler of the CSS *Patrick Henry* early in the battle, scalding four men to death and sending it out of the fight. The single gun on the CSS *Raleigh* slipped from its carriage and became useless. But if these conventional warships proved easy meat for the Federal gunners, every sailor on the *Congress* had witnessed the *Virginia*'s destruction of the *Cumberland*, and they could no longer doubt the seriousness of the menace it represented.

There were actually two captains on board the *Congress* that day, both of them named Smith. Lieutenant William Smith had been formally detached from command, though he remained on board as a volunteer while effective command was executed by Lieutenant Joseph Smith Jr. The two men were no relation to each other, though the latter, coincidentally, was the son of the Joseph Smith who had chaired Welles's Ironclad Board. Having witnessed the *Virginia*'s easy conquest of the *Cumberland*, he saw at once that his own ship had no hope of standing up to the rebel ironclad, and he ordered the anchor slipped, raised the jib, and steered his vessel into shoal water, where the *Merrimack* (as the Federals continued to call it) could not follow.

Aground on the seventeen-foot shoal, the *Congress* was safe from ramming, but not from the *Virginia*'s guns. Buchanan carefully maneuvered his ship so that he could hammer away at the *Congress* from a distance of less than two hundred yards, close enough to ensure efficient and devastating fire. Hard aground, the *Congress* could not maneuver to bring its broadside to bear, and it could employ only its two stern guns. Those two guns fired away defiantly but uselessly, until the stern of the *Congress* was so utterly wrecked by the *Virginia*'s constant pounding that they could no longer be served. The *Congress* was now helpless, a passive target absorbing punishment. Scores died, including young Joe Smith Jr., who was virtually decapitated by a shell fragment. It was evident that surrender was the only humane and sensible option, and the burden of that decision fell on the ship's executive officer, Lieutenant Austin Pendergrast. A few minutes before 4:00, the *Congress*'s flag fluttered down.[36]

The guns ceased firing, and a strange silence settled over the roadstead. Buchanan and most of the *Virginia*'s officers left the acrid casemate and climbed up to stand on the upper deck. From there, Buchanan ordered Lieutenant William H. Parker in the gunboat *Beaufort* to go alongside the *Congress* and accept its formal surrender. He instructed Parker to bring the officers and the wounded aboard the *Virginia* and allow the able-bodied men to escape to shore. Then he was to set the *Congress* afire. Fifty-year veteran that he was, Buchanan was a sailor of the old school. At this moment he very likely envisioned a scene similar to the one that had taken place aboard the *Lawrence* in 1813, when British officers in full dress uniform had come on board to offer their swords to Perry. Perhaps afterward Buchanan would invite the captain of the *Congress* to accompany him to his cabin for a glass of sherry. It was even possible that Buchanan's brother might join them, for McKean Buchanan had remained loyal to the Union, and Franklin Buchanan knew that his brother was serving on the *Congress* as that ship's paymaster.

If Buchanan envisioned such a scenario, it evaporated almost at once. When Parker's vessel bumped alongside the *Congress*, Pendergrast offered him a ship's cutlass; somewhat annoyed, Parker told him to go get his officer's sword. Much more seriously, Federal soldiers of the 20th Indiana regiment on the nearby shore opened fire on Parker's gunboat as it lay alongside the grounded *Congress*. Parker later claimed that while he was under fire from the soldiers on shore, three bullets passed through his clothes, his cap was shot off, and he was wounded in the knee. Outraged at this violation of the traditions of sea warfare, Parker insisted that Pendergrast order the soldiers to stop firing. But even if Pendergrast had been willing to do so, he had no authority over Army soldiers, who in any case were not impressed by the traditions of the sea, whatever they might be. When a Federal lieutenant ashore tried to stop the shooting, Brigadier General Joseph K. Mansfield overruled him. "I know the d——d ship has surrendered," he growled, "but we haven't." Meanwhile on board the *Congress*, Pendergrast urged Parker to hoist a white flag to prevent his crew from being shot to pieces. Parker refused. He would be damned before he would surrender his ship to a gaggle of soldiers. He sheered off and steamed out of range.[37]

Watching all this from the *Virginia*, Buchanan could not understand why his orders were not being carried out. The *Congress* was flying a white flag of surrender, yet the enemy continued to fire on officers who were attempting to take possession of a surrendered prize. Furious, he exclaimed to no one in particular: "That ship must be burned!" His young aide, Bob Minor, volunteered to take a ship's boat over to the *Congress* and set it afire, and Buchanan agreed. Minor put out in the only ship's boat that had not been destroyed in the fight, and, to make sure there was no misunderstanding, he raised a white flag of truce. But the boat was no sooner under way when more shots from shore drove it back, one of the shots wounding young Minor. Buchanan was now beside himself with fury. "She's firing on our white flag!" he sputtered. From the exposed roof of the *Virginia*'s casemate, he put a rifle to his shoulder and fired a shot toward the offending infantry on shore. Unsurprisingly, they at once fired back, and soon Buchanan slumped to the deck, shot through the groin.*

---

* Though Buchanan was certain that he was struck by a bullet fired from the shore, a Marine corporal on board the *Cumberland* later claimed that he had fired the shot, and even received a medal for it.

Very well—if the perfidious Yankees were going to ignore the rules of war, he decided, they must pay the consequences. Once he had been carried below, Buchanan tersely ordered the *Virginia* to reopen fire on the grounded and helpless *Congress*.[38]

Each side felt the fury of violated honor. To the Confederates, the Yankees were the guilty party, since they had fired on a white flag while officers attempted to take possession of a lawful prize. To the Federals, the Confederates were at fault, since they now opened fire on a grounded vessel full of helpless men, a vessel that was flying not one but two white flags of surrender. This was where the time-honored traditions of the Age of Sail collided with the realities of total war in a mechanized age. For the rest of the war, and for decades afterward, each side would point an accusing finger at the other to charge that in Hampton Roads on March 8, 1862, the traditional rules of naval warfare—indeed, the very ideals of chivalry and humanity—were sacrificed to a new template of modern war: a mechanized war without rules, without restraint, without mercy, and without honor.

The *Virginia* fired three deliberate rounds of "hot shot" into the grounded hull of the *Congress*. Iron shot was heated on grates in the ship's furnace, rolled out into iron buckets, and carried up to the gun deck. There it was carefully loaded into the muzzles of guns that had been previously prepared to receive them by placing wads of wet hemp on top of the powder so that the heated shot would not prematurely ignite the charge. When the heated iron balls struck the dry, sun-baked wood of the *Congress*'s hull, they kindled the sailor's worst enemy: fire. As the fire spread, small boats ferried the surviving crew of the *Congress* to shore as fast as they could. Those who could swim leaped over the side and struck out on their own. The dead, and many of the wounded, had to be left behind. Soon the *Congress* was burning briskly, the flames running up its rigging and lighting up the roadstead, and at last the firing ceased, though the *Congress* continued to burn through the twilight and into the evening. One hundred and ten of the ship's 434 men had been killed outright, and another ten died that evening—more than 27 percent of the ship's complement.[39]

The *Virginia* had suffered relatively little. Two men had been killed and a score wounded, though only Buchanan and Minor were wounded seriously. A few, such as Charles Dunbar, had been hit by musket balls aimed through the gunports by Marines on board the *Cumberland*; others had suffered concussions when shells crashed against the outside of the armor shield while they were leaning against it. The ship's smokestack was riddled with holes, the anchor had been shot away, and the casemate was pocked with indentations, but otherwise the vessel was intact and ready to fight again. There were still two hours of daylight left and three more Union warships in the roadstead. But it had been a long day. The crew was exhausted, and the pilots were reluctant to maneuver the deep-draft *Virginia* in a confined roadstead with a falling tide and growing darkness.

The USS *Congress*, set ablaze by hot shot from the *Virginia*, burns briskly as the crew abandons ship. One hundred and twenty men died on board the *Congress* on March 8. (Ned Bradford, ed., *Battles and Leaders of the Civil War*)

After exchanging long-range fire with the grounded *Minnesota* for about an hour, Jones, with Buchanan's agreement, directed the *Virginia* to an anchorage off Sewall's Point on the south side of the roadstead, from which point it could renew the attack the next day. After all, the *Minnesota* would still be there tomorrow.[40]

The *Congress* was still burning at midnight, the flames reflecting dramatically off the inky waters of the roadstead, when the *Monitor* tied up alongside the *Roanoke*. As the new arrivals watched, the flames reached the ship's magazine, and the USS *Congress* exploded in a giant fireball.

━

Dawn on March 9 revealed a scene of devastation. The *Cumberland*'s topmasts, with the blue commissioning pennant still flying, jutted above the surface of the water off Newport News Point, while nearby the blackened ribs of the *Congress* protruded from the sea, which was littered with bits and pieces of the ship's wreckage. In addition, the Federals had lost two small transports and one schooner in the fighting, and most of the Federal ships that had survived were damaged. The *Minnesota* had been struck a dozen times and was fast aground on the seventeen-foot shoal; beyond it, more than halfway to Point Comfort, the *St. Lawrence* was also aground. Only the *Roanoke* found relative safety under the guns of Fort Monroe.

News of the disaster in Hampton Roads had been telegraphed to Washington, where it provoked a state of near panic. Secretary of War Stanton in particular feared that the *Merrimack* (as he called it) would steam out of Hampton Roads to attack the cities of the eastern seaboard one by one, starting with Washington. During the emergency cabinet meeting that Lincoln called that morning, Stanton repeatedly jumped up from his chair and rushed over to the windows, looking downriver to see if the *Merrimack* was even then on its way to bombard Washington.[41]

On board the *Virginia*, Buchanan knew that such a scenario was impossible. The *Virginia* was simply not seaworthy enough to survive in the open water of Chesapeake Bay, much less the Atlantic Ocean, and her draft was too deep to allow her to ascend the Potomac to Washington in any case. Still, he was determined to finish the job begun the day before by destroying the rest of the Union squadron in Hampton Roads, starting with the grounded *Minnesota*. That would not only clear the Federal Navy from the roadstead, it would make it difficult, if not impossible, for the Federals to maintain their foothold on the Virginia coast at Fort Monroe. Indeed, though Buchanan could not have known it, his victory in Hampton Roads threatened to overturn the entire grand strategy of the Union Army commander, Major General George B. McClellan. That officer had been waiting all winter to transport his army to the Virginia peninsula by sea for a thrust at Richmond in a campaign that he hoped and believed would end the war. Now McClellan had to rethink his plans. "The performances of the *Merrimac*," he wrote, "places a new aspect on everything, & may very probably change my whole plan of campaign." Just as Harrison's campaign in 1813 had depended on the control of Lake

Erie, so now did McClellan's campaign depend on the control of Hampton Roads.[42]

Alas for him, Buchanan's wound was a serious one; the bullet that struck him down had grazed the femoral artery, and for a while it was feared that the sixty-one-year-old sea warrior would not survive. Clearly he could no longer exercise command of the *Virginia*, a duty that now fell to his executive officer, Catesby Jones. Even so, Buchanan was reluctant to abandon his command. The code of the sea, he believed, required him to stay on board and share victory or defeat with his officers and crew. Despite that, the ship's surgeon convinced him that it was his duty to go ashore, if not for his own well-being, then because the captain's cabin would be needed to treat others who might fall wounded in the renewed contest. Buchanan grudgingly agreed, and soon he and young Bob Minor were being rowed to the naval hospital in Norfolk.[43]

After bidding Godspeed to Buchanan, Jones made a quick inspection of the *Virginia*, rowing around the anchored vessel in the ship's one surviving boat. There were a number of dramatic dents in the ship's armor but none that threatened the integrity of the shield. Apparently this inspection failed to reveal to Jones that most of the ship's bow ram had broken off after the collision with the *Cumberland*. The flanges of the ram remained bolted to the hull, and Jones concluded that the ram itself had merely been twisted out of shape rather than sundered. Back on board, he ordered the engineers to get up steam. There was work to be done.

Like Buchanan, Jones was a veteran of the prewar U.S. Navy, though his twenty-five years of service were only about half that of his predecessor. If Buchanan was a sailor of the old school, Jones was a member of the new class of "scientific officers." He had spent much of his career in the Hydrography Office and in the Bureau of Ordnance, where he had been an assistant to John A. Dahlgren, the man who had designed the big guns inside the *Monitor*'s turret. In that respect Jones had more in common with John Worden, who had spent much of his career in the Naval Observatory, than he did with the old sea dog Franklin Buchanan. Thus, two men of science, each in command of a warship on the cutting edge of naval technology, represented a new generation of naval officers, grounded in engineering, metallurgy, and ordnance, as they squared off against one another in the confined waters of Hampton Roads.

Unaware as yet of the *Monitor*'s presence, Jones ordered the *Virginia* to get under way at about 7:00 A.M. He directed it first toward the northeast in the general direction of Fort Monroe until it reached the main ship channel. Then he ordered the helm over, and the great ship swung to port and began to close on the *Minnesota*, approaching the grounded frigate from its stern, where only a few of its guns could be brought to bear. During the approach, Jones stood atop the *Virginia*'s casemate with the ship's gunnery officer, Hunter Davidson. Off to the south he could see dozens of small craft filled with the curious who had come out to witness what they were sure would be the final destruction of the Federal fleet. Many of them waved hats or handkerchiefs as tokens of support. To the north was the looming presence of Fort Monroe, its ramparts lined with equally curious, though far less confident, spectators wearing Union blue.

After the *Virginia* turned into the ship channel, Jones focused his attention on the grounded *Minnesota*. He could see a few tugs around her apparently trying to pull her off the shoal into deep water, but as the morning fog lifted and the range closed, he noted that there was something else there, too. He could not quite make it out. It appeared to be a large water tank on a raft, though it seemed unlikely that the *Minnesota* was taking on fresh water. Perhaps the *Minnesota*'s boiler had been removed for repair, though that, too, seemed unlikely. Davidson ventured the hopeful notion that it was a raft and that the *Minnesota*'s crew was abandoning ship. Whatever it was, it was screening the *Minnesota* from the *Virginia*. Only when it moved away under its own power did Jones realize that this was the Ericsson Battery that he had heard of, and that this day's fighting might be somewhat different from that of the day before.[44]

For his part, Worden knew exactly what the *Virginia* was from the moment it materialized out of the morning fog. The previous night, after hearing a detailed report of the day's slaughter from John Marston, captain of the *Roanoke*, Worden had been astonished to be handed an order from Welles dated three days before directing him "to proceed immediately to Washington with his vessel." But Marston also had in hand another telegram from Welles authorizing him to use his "best judgment" about the disposition of the vessels in Hampton Roads, and after discussing the situation, Marston and Worden decided that the *Monitor* should stay. An hour before midnight Worden conned the *Monitor* from the *Roanoke* to the grounded and wounded *Minnesota*. On board the *Minnesota*, the news that the Union ironclad had come alongside produced a surge of hope. But most of those who peered over the railing to look down at the odd little craft relapsed into despondency. Much smaller than the *Virginia* to begin with, its profile was such that with only the twenty-one-foot-wide turret showing above the water, it seemed a pitiable little vessel by comparison. Although the *Minnesota's* captain, Gersham Van Brunt, later insisted that the *Monitor's* arrival led all on board to feel that "we had a friend that would stand by us in our hour of trial," at the time he sustained little hope that this ludicrous little vessel could do anything to prevent the *Merrimack* from completing its campaign of destruction.[45]

Once alongside the *Minnesota*, Worden made sure that everything was ready for battle, and having done that, there was nothing to do but wait. He did not sleep—it was already 2:00 A.M., and dawn was less than four hours away. Instead, he remained atop the turret with his twenty-one-year-old executive officer, Samuel Greene, discussing the forthcoming battle and watching for the appearance of the rebel ironclad. The hands were ordered to sleep by their battle stations, though (as one recalled) "no one slept." Indeed, few, if any, had slept at all since leaving New York three days before. Several times during the night, false alarms kept the crew of the *Monitor* on edge, until finally just past dawn, as the fog lifted, they could make out the dark blur of the rebel ironclad off Sewell's Point. Only when the *Virginia* made its turn into the ship channel and began to close the *Minnesota* did Worden order his own vessel to get under way. As the lines were cast off, Van Brunt shouted across to Worden: "If I cannot lighten my ship off [the shoal] I shall destroy her."

"I will stand by you to the last," Worden called back.

Morosely, Van Brunt replied: "No Sir, you cannot help me."[46]

As had been the case the day before, the shoreline was lined with spectators. The local geography conspired to turn the roadstead into a natural
amphitheater, and the weather cooperated as well: the fog lifted like a curtain going up, and the sun shone down to light the stage. Most of the spectators on both sides expected the *Virginia* to continue its track of
destruction. Even after the spectators became aware of the presence of the
Monitor, they (like Van Brunt) had trouble believing that it would make
much of a difference.

Worden's plan was to close to point-blank range before opening with
his two eleven-inch guns. Climbing down from the roof of the turret, he
watched as the gun crew hoisted a 165-pound shot into the muzzle of one
of the big Dahlgren guns. "Send them that with our compliments, my
lads," he told them. Then, leaving the management of the big guns to his
young executive officer, he climbed down through the hatch into the ship's
semisubmerged hull and went forward to take his position in the pilothouse, a small boxlike projection forward of the turret. There he directed
the helmsman to steer a course to close the approaching enemy ironclad.[47]

Worden's battle station was unique for a ship's commanding officer.
Confined within a tiny space only thirty-two inches wide and forty-two
inches front to back—a space he shared with both the pilot and the helmsman—he had a letterbox view of the world, since his only window was a
narrow slit only seven-eighths of an inch wide. Moreover, because Worden
had to peer through nine inches of armor, his vertical field of vision was so
limited he could not even see the bow of his own ship. Unlike Perry, who
had walked his open quarterdeck with the wind in his hair, and unlike
Buchanan (and now Jones), who could walk the length of the *Virginia*'s 170-
foot-long gundeck, Worden was a virtual prisoner in his little metal box.[48]

Most of his crew shared that sense of confinement. "Everybody was
shut in," one officer recalled. As they went into battle for the first time, the
men inside the *Monitor*, like those inside the *Virginia*, had a strange sense
of isolation and detachment. With the hatches closed tightly over the glass
windows in the deck, only "a few straggling rays of light found their way
from the top of the tower [turret] to the depths below," the ship's paymaster, William F. Keeler, recalled. In the half-light provided by the lanterns, it

was also profoundly silent but for the steady clanking of the engines. The fact that the ship's hull was already submerged and that it was made of iron impressed all on board with the notion that a breech anywhere in the ship's armor would send them all immediately to the bottom with little chance to escape. Just as E. A. Jack had done on the *Virginia*, Keeler examined his emotions as his vessel steamed forward into battle. "I experienced a peculiar sensation," he wrote later to his wife. "I do not think it was fear, but it was different from anything I ever knew before. We were enclosed in what we supposed to be impenetrable armour—we knew that a powerful foe was about to meet us—ours was an untried experiment & our enemy's first fire might make it a coffin for us all." And like Jack, Keeler was conscious of being strangely separated from the real world outside the ironclad where the sun was shining. "We knew not how soon the attack would commence, or from what direction it would come." And then, again echoing Jack, he wrote: "The suspense was awful."[49]

The *Virginia* fired first. At about 8:30 Lieutenant Simms pulled the lanyard on the *Virginia*'s seven-inch Brooke rifle in the bow and sent a shell not at the *Monitor* but toward the grounded *Minnesota*, more than a mile and a half away. The first shot passed through the *Minnesota*'s rigging; the second exploded inside the tug *Dragon*, which lay alongside. The *Monitor*'s guns remained silent. Worden was determined to get as close as possible before firing. Communication between the gun turret and the pilothouse had to take place by messenger, and Greene passed a message to Worden asking if he could open fire. "Tell Mr. Greene not to fire until I give the word," was Worden's calm reply. As the *Virginia* continued to fire on the hapless *Minnesota*, Worden ran the *Monitor* to within a mere fifty yards of the *Virginia* before stopping its engines and giving the order: "Commence firing!" Greene pulled the lanyard, and a 165-pound wrought iron ball, propelled by fifteen pounds of black power, smashed into the side of the *Virginia*'s casemate with what one of the *Virginia*'s officers called "a resounding wham." The *Virginia* shuddered from the concussion, but its armored walls remained intact. Now it was the *Virginia*'s turn, as shells from its nine-inch Dahlgrens and seven-inch rifles struck flush on the face of the *Monitor*'s turret.[50]

Up to that moment no one (besides the ever-confident Ericsson) was sure if the eight layers of one-inch iron plate on the *Monitor*'s turret would repel shot effectively or if the concussion of a well-aimed shot would knock the turret off its spindle. Inside the crowded turret, Greene and the twenty-one others both felt and heard the jarring impact, and they could see the bulge that one shell made in the turret's wall. Alarmed, Greene pointed out the bulge to the chief engineer, Alban Stimers. Stimers was technically a passenger on the *Monitor*, since his role was to assess the fighting capabilities of the new vessel for the Navy. Moreover, engineers were outside the regular chain of command in the Civil War Navy, and although the twenty-one-year-old Greene was the ship's executive officer, the thirty-four-year-old Stimers was not overly impressed by that fact. Almost like a schoolmaster instructing a particularly slow student, he asked Greene if the shot had come through the armor.

"No," Greene replied, "but it made a big dent."

"A big dent!" Stimers exclaimed. "Of course it made a big dent—that is just what we expected. What do you care about that so long as it keeps out the shot?"

Despite Stimers's irreverent tone, Greene took comfort from the answer. "Oh, it's all right then," he replied. With that, the men handling the guns in the turret breathed out, and their sense of confidence rose perceptibly.[51]

As soon as it was evident that his guns had little effect on the *Monitor*, Jones decided to ignore it and concentrate his fire on the grounded *Minnesota*. But the pilots on the *Virginia* insisted that they were unable to take him any closer to the *Minnesota* for fear of running aground, and, in any case, Worden kept interposing his little craft between the *Virginia* and its prey. Both ironclads had trouble elevating their guns, and as a result they fired by ricochet: the shells skipping across the water like stones across a pond, kicking up great geysers at each ricochet en route to the target. With the *Monitor* in his line of fire, Jones had little choice but to accept battle with the interloper.

The ships circled each other, firing as fast as the gunners could load. The *Virginia* fired faster and with more guns, but the *Monitor*'s guns not only were larger, they also fired solid shot, which was better devised for punching through armor plate. Because Confederate authorities had expected to meet only wooden warships, the *Virginia* had mostly shells in her magazine. Inside both ships, the air filled with smoke and the nearly constant sound of guns firing, of shot and shell smashing against unyielding iron plate, and shouted orders. On the *Virginia*, the orders became a mantra: "Sponge. Load. Fire." Rivulets of sweat ran down the backs of the gunners, making tracks through the black powder grime, as they executed these orders inside their casemate, unable to see or evaluate the effect of their labor. "Powder smoke filled the entire ship," recalled one officer, "so that we could see but a short distance and its acrid fumes made breathing difficult." Another described the scene more poetically: "The noise of the crackling, roaring fires, escaping steam, and the loud labored pulsations of the engines, together with the roar of battle above and the thud and vibrations of the huge masses of iron which were hurled against us, produced a

The two ironclads target each other at point-blank range during the height of the battle on March 9. Note the square pilothouse on the bow of the *Monitor*, where John Worden watched the battle through its narrow slit. The *Virginia*'s deck is depicted as being awash in this drawing, though the reduction in its draft after firing off tons of heavy ordnance later exposed its deck and rendered it vulnerable to a well-aimed shot at the waterline. (Ned Bradford, ed., *Battles and Leaders of the Civil War*)

scene and sound to be compared only with the poet's picture of the lower regions."[52]

On the *Monitor*, the loading of the twin Dahlgrens required a lengthy process. First the turret had to be rotated away from the foe to protect the gun crew, then the guns had to be swabbed out, and a sack containing a premeasured fifteen pounds of black powder had to be loaded and rammed home. Then the 165-pound shot had to be hoisted to the muzzle and seated home against the powder. The gunnery officer fixed a primer filled with fulminate of mercury over the vent as the turret rotated back to face the foe. When the enemy target rotated back into view, the gunner pulled the lanyard, tripping a hammer down on the primer and exploding the black powder. The two big Dahlgrens could not be fired simultaneously because the heavy iron gunport shields on the turret both swung inward, toward each other, instead of off to the sides, and there was insufficient space between the gunports to accommodate both of them at once. These factors dramatically reduced the *Monitor*'s rate of fire, but if it fired less frequently, each shot was more than twice the weight of the shells coming from the *Virginia*. A few of these 165-pound shots dented the *Virginia*'s armor plate so badly that the twenty-four-inch wooden backing cracked and bent inward, throwing splinters across the deck. The Confederates feared that repeated such blows on a single spot would eventually break down the ship's shield. But the gears on the *Monitor*'s turret engine had rusted during the trip down from New York, and it proved almost impossible to stop the turret exactly on target. Instead, Greene had to fire the guns on the fly as the turret swept past the target.[53]

Another missed opportunity on the *Monitor* was the regulation that limited the gunners to using no more than fifteen pounds of powder per charge. Afterward, tests made it evident that if Worden had increased the charge to twenty-five or thirty pounds, the shot from his eleven-inch guns would almost certainly have penetrated the *Virginia*'s casemate. But the guns on the *Monitor* had never been proofed beyond fifteen pounds, and Worden knew that if one of his guns exploded from being overloaded, it would not only instantly kill everyone inside the turret but disable and perhaps destroy his own vessel. In such a case the *Virginia* would have its way with the rest of the Union forces in the roadstead.[54]

While Worden maneuvered the *Monitor* from the pilothouse based on his tiny letterbox view of the world, Greene and the gunners in the turret did not have even that restricted view. With the ship constantly maneuvering and the turret continually rotating, it did not take long for the men in the turret to lose their bearings entirely. "How does the *Virginia* bear?" Greene would call out to one of the messengers, and soon the answer came back, shouted up through the hatch: "On the starboard beam," or "On the port quarter." But Greene had no idea where the starboard beam was. White markings had been painted on the hull below the turret to indicate port and starboard, but they became obscured almost immediately once the fighting started. All he could do was continue to load the big guns as fast as he could and fire them whenever the *Virginia*'s armored walls came into view through the gun ports. It was a particularly detached and impersonal sort of warfare. The officers and men who fed the *Monitor*'s engines

This panoramic view of the Battle of Hampton Roads shows how the contestants dueled in a kind of natural amphitheater with the troops on shore and the sailors on the ships in the foreground hanging on the outcome. (U.S. Army)

in the darkened areas below decks, those who controlled its movements, and those who worked its guns each operated in discrete confined spaces cut off not only from one another but from the world generally.[55]

After more than an hour, it became evident that the *Virginia*'s smaller guns, firing mainly shell, were unlikely to overcome the *Monitor*'s heavy iron armor. When Jones noted that one of his gun crews had stopped firing, he asked its officer, Lieutenant John Eggleston, why his crew was standing at ease. "Why, our powder is very precious," Eggleston answered. "After two hours of incessant firing I find that I can do her [the *Monitor*] about as much damage by snapping my thumb at her every two minutes and a half."[56] Accepting this reality, Jones decided to try to ram the *Monitor*, unaware that most of the *Virginia*'s ram was still inside the *Cumberland*.

Maneuvering the unwieldy *Virginia* with its twenty-two-foot draft in the confined spaces of Hampton Roads was difficult in the best of circumstances, and while trying to find sea room to make a run at the *Monitor*, Jones and everyone else on board felt it when the big ship suddenly lurched to a halt. It had run fast aground. Under the circumstances this was more than bad luck; it could very well be fatal. The *Virginia* could not maneuver to bring its guns to bear, and with its lighter draft the *Monitor* could take a position on her quarter and pound her at close range with round after round. Jones had to get his ship back into deep water. He ordered his chief engineer, Ashton Ramsay, to give him full power. The engines strained and the ship's huge two-bladed propeller churned up the mud furiously, but the vessel did not move. Jones then ordered Ramsay to tie down the safety valves and let the steam pressure build up past the limits of both safety and prudence until finally with a shudder the *Virginia* pushed itself into deep water.[57]

This brush with disaster did not deter Jones from his determination to ram the little *Monitor*, and somehow he managed to get the much larger *Virginia* into ramming position. He drove his ship into the side of the Union ironclad, striking it a glancing blow that knocked the men inside the *Monitor* off their feet, but the blow had struck the *Monitor*'s five-foot-thick armor belt, and as a result it did more damage to the stern of the *Vir-*

ginia than it did to the *Monitor*. Ramsay reported that the collision had started a leak forward, and only now did Jones realize that at least part of the *Virginia*'s ram was gone. The pumps could handle the leak, Ramsay told him, but it was clear that ramming was not a viable tactic. The gunnery duel continued.

On board the *Virginia*, Lieutenant Davidson ordered some of the gunners to arm themselves with Springfield rifles and try to aim shots in through the *Monitor*'s gunports as the two vessels passed. One young enlisted man named Richard Curtis positioned himself accordingly and peered out a gunport, only to see the mouth of an eleven-inch Dahlgren gun "looking me squarely in the face." His companion yelled, "Look out Curtis!" and the two men ducked back just as the gun fired, barely missing the open gunport in the *Virginia*.[58]

Soon the supply of ammunition began to run down on both ships. This dangerously affected the trim of the *Virginia*. Each broadside from four nine-inch Dahlgren guns lightened the ship by more than 350 pounds. In an hour, the *Virginia* shot away more than seven thousand pounds. Combined with the shot and shell it had fired away the day before, plus the loss of its fifteen-hundred-pound ram, the *Virginia* was now more than five tons lighter than it had been when it began its maiden voyage the day before. Since its armored shield extended only a few inches below the waterline, there was a real threat that as the *Virginia* became lighter its vulnerable lower hull might become exposed.

On the *Monitor*, the expenditure of ammunition was less critical—its armor belt extended several feet below the waterline. But once the ready ammunition in the turret had been expended, more had to be brought up from below, and the only communication between the gun turret and the lower hull was through a single hatch. In order to bring up more ammunition, it was necessary to freeze the turret in place so that the access hatch in the floor of the turret lined up with the one in the ship's deck. During this evolution, the ship would not be able to fire its guns, and Worden ordered the *Monitor* to steam off toward Fort Monroe into shallow water, where the *Virginia* could not follow. While the crew manhandled the powder and shot up from the ship's magazine—which Greene described as "a slow and tedious operation"—Worden left his post in the pilothouse and, making his way up through the turret, climbed out onto the exposed deck to inspect the damage done by the enemy's shells. He was gratified, and no doubt relieved, to see that the only evidence of the severe pounding it had received was a number of perfectly smooth dents in the turret's armor plate.[59]

The moment the *Monitor* steamed away to replenish its ammunition, Jones returned his attention to the *Minnesota*. The distance—still over a mile—was great, but the *Virginia*'s marksmanship was excellent. The first shot hit the *Minnesota* amidships, passed through the engineers' berthing spaces, and exploded in the boatswains' mess, igniting some stored gunpowder and setting the ship on fire. In return, Van Brunt ordered a full broadside, a storm of shot and shell that he later claimed "would have blown out of the water any timber-built ship in the world," but which had no more effect on the *Virginia* than "so many pebblestones thrown by a child." Once again Van Brunt worried that his command would be destroyed. After consulting with his officers, he made preparations to abandon ship and destroy it to prevent it from being taken by the rebels.[60]

His concern was premature. Within less than twenty minutes, the *Monitor* was back in the fight, once again interposing itself between the *Virginia* and the *Minnesota*. The captains on both ships each sought to find a weakness in the other. The *Monitor* had not been built as a ram, but Worden nonetheless decided to try to ram his prow into the stern of the *Virginia*, hoping to disable its rudder. For his part, Jones considered boarding, and volunteers talked about jamming a wedge between the *Monitor*'s turret and its deck or throwing hand grenades through the roof of the turret, which, like the overhead on the *Virginia*, was composed of railroad rails spaced a few inches apart. Such bold efforts proved impossible to execute, however, and Jones told his gunners to concentrate their fire on the *Monitor*'s small pilothouse, where Worden watched the fight through his narrow viewing slit.[61]

Soon afterward, the fight reached a decisive moment when a shell from one of the *Virginia*'s guns exploded square on the face of the pilothouse while Worden was looking out through the slit. A "flash of light" lit up the tiny pilothouse and filled it with smoke. Worden staggered backward, his hands to his face. "My eyes," he cried out. "I am blind."[62]

The ship's paymaster and surgeon manhandled Worden down from the pilothouse and laid him on the deck of the passageway. The paymaster remembered that "blood was running from his face which was blackened with powder." The wound was not fatal, but clearly Worden could no longer exercise command. He sent for Greene and formally relinquished command to him. "Do what you think best," he told him. "I cannot see, but do not mind me. Save the *Minnesota* if you can."[63]

Greene had never been in combat before, and his first decision was an instinctive one. He ordered the helm over and took the *Monitor* out of the fight. For the second time that morning, the Union ironclad steamed off into shoal water. But once Greene had an opportunity to assess the situation and talk with the other officers, it was clear that his duty was to renew the fight. Leaving the direction of the guns in the turret to Stimers, he took up his new post in the pilothouse. The shell that had blinded Worden had bent one of the pilothouse's four iron posts, but the little structure was still standing. From it, Greene ordered the helmsman to take the *Monitor* back into the fray. From the moment Worden was wounded to the moment the *Monitor* returned to the fight, about half an hour had passed.[64]

On board the *Virginia* there was celebration when the *Monitor* withdrew from the fight, and Jones at once turned his attention back to the *Minnesota*. But it was now nearly noon, and the tide was on the ebb. The pilots told Jones they could not get the ship any closer to the *Minnesota* than it already was; in fact, they warned that the falling tide might make it impossible for the *Virginia* to get back over the bar at the mouth of the Elizabeth River, stranding her in the roadstead with no access to repair facilities, ammunition, or fuel. In addition, there was the fact that the *Virginia*'s lightened draft had increased her vulnerability by exposing her lightly armored hull below the waterline. Resupplying the ship with coal and ordnance would not only make her more battleworthy but also increase the draft, restoring the ship's armor protection. After consulting with his officers, Jones decided to return to port. Just as the *Monitor* was returning to the fight, the *Virginia* steamed slowly back to the Elizabeth River to receive a hero's welcome.

Astonishingly, despite the hours of close combat and the tons of ordnance the two vessels had hurled at each other, no one had been killed in this epic confrontation. Both sides claimed victory. Confederates noted that the *Monitor* had retired from the scene of combat first; Unionists insisted that when the *Monitor* returned to the fight, it was the *Virginia* that fled. The argument lasted beyond the war and into the postwar years. "If the *Monitor* was a victor," a survivor of the *Virginia*'s crew asked rhetorically fifty years later, "what prevented her from pursuing the *Merrimack* and destroying her?"[65] He and others pointed out that the *Virginia* subsequently reappeared at the mouth of the Elizabeth River, challenging the *Monitor* to renew the combat, but that the *Monitor* ignored her and remained by the wooden vessels of the squadron. The reason for this was that the Lincoln administration was simply unwilling to risk the *Monitor* in another round.

The officers and men on the *Monitor* chafed at being thus tethered. Paymaster Keeler opined, "The fact is the Government is getting to regard the *Monitor* in pretty much the same light as an over careful housewife regards her ancient china Set—too valuable to lose, too useful to keep as a relic, yet anxious that all shall know what she owns and that she can use it when the occasion demands."[66] Somewhat defensively, Union veterans explained that the *Monitor*'s job was to protect the *Minnesota*, which it did. If the *Virginia* really wanted to renew the fight, why didn't it come out into the roadstead to threaten the Union squadron? Eventually both sides grudgingly decided to call the battle a draw, and so it has been described in most history books ever since.

Such arguments illustrate both the continued partisanship between the sections and the importance of a warrior's code among naval combatants. In reality, deciding which ship left the scene first, or even which vessel "won" the fight, is no more historically valuable than deciding whether North Carolinians or Virginians ascended further up the slope of Cemetery Ridge at Gettysburg. The more important question is how the action of March 9 affected the campaign. And in answering that question, it is clear that the little *Monitor*'s timely arrival effectively neutralized the offensive potential of the *Virginia* and preserved Union control of Hampton Roads. The Federal Navy remained in the roadstead after March 9, and

This photograph of the *Monitor*'s turret, taken after the battle, shows some of the battle scars from its fight with the *Virginia*, including large dents in the turret just left of the empty gun port. Note, too, that the pilothouse has now been protected by sloping sides. The two men at right are William Flye and Albert Campbell, two of the ship's officers. (Mariners' Museum)

McClellan's long-planned peninsular campaign went ahead as scheduled. Moreover, the Union Navy remained in Hampton Roads for the duration of the war. When in the spring of 1864 Ulysses S. Grant sought to outflank Lee's defenses in Virginia, he took advantage of the Union possession of Hampton Roads to send a force (the Army of the James) to Richmond's back door. That winter, when the Confederacy sent delegates to talk with Lincoln to discuss a possible end to the war, they met on board a Federal vessel anchored safely and securely in Hampton Roads.

By then, both the *Virginia* and the *Monitor* had departed the historical stage. When McClellan's troops advanced up the Virginia peninsula in the summer of 1862, the Confederates were forced to evacuate Norfolk. Because the *Virginia* could neither ascend the James River nor survive without its base, Confederate leaders felt compelled to destroy it to prevent it from falling into the hands of their enemies. On May 12, two months and three days after its epic fight with the *Monitor*, the *Virginia*'s own crew did what Federal guns could not. Behind Craney Island on the west bank of the Elizabeth River, a massive explosion broke the mighty *Virginia* into pieces. Then the surviving pieces were destroyed in subsequent explosions. Eventually its anchor and a piece of its crankshaft were recovered and are now on display outside the Confederate Museum in Richmond. The rest of it lies buried, presumably forever, in the landfill west of the river's mouth.

The *Monitor* lived only seven months more. En route to Charleston, South Carolina, under tow, it encountered a storm off Cape Hatteras, that graveyard of the Atlantic, and in a deadly reprise of its experience off the New Jersey coast, water worked its way through the seal between the turret and the deck, and sea spray inundated the blower pipes, putting out the engines and making the pumps unworkable. This time, however, the storm did not abate, and on the last day of the year, the *Monitor* sank in 240 feet of water seventeen miles off the coast, taking sixteen men down with her. The wreckage was discovered in 1973, and since then various parts of it have been recovered. In August 2002 a team of U.S. Navy divers and National Oceanic and Atmospheric Administration scientists raised the 120-ton turret and its two Dahlgren guns, and these, along with the engine, crankshaft, and propeller, are on exhibit at the Mariners' Museum in Newport News, only a few miles from the site of its 1862 battle with the *Virginia*.

Franklin Buchanan survived his wound. Promoted to the rank of full admiral (the only Confederate naval officer ever to bear that rank), he assumed command of the rebel squadron in Mobile Bay in 1863, where he oversaw the construction of the ironclad *Tennessee*, which he took as his flagship. On August 5, 1864, the day that Farragut "damned the torpedoes," he fought a hopeless action at close range against Farragut's entire Union squadron until his vessel was overwhelmed. Again wounded, this time he was compelled to surrender his ship and was taken prisoner.

Catesby Jones did not get to keep command of the *Virginia*. Supplanted by the more senior Josiah Tattnall, he escaped the painful humiliation of

ordering the ship's destruction. Jones subsequently commanded the Confederate naval facility at Columbus, Georgia, where his principal duty was
to supervise the manufacture of naval guns, including the guns that made
up the battery on Buchanan's doomed *Tennessee*.

John Worden, too, survived the battle. Eventually he recovered his sight
and was restored to active duty. He commanded the monitor *Montauk* in
operations against Charleston in 1863 and finished the war as a captain.
After the war, he was promoted to rear admiral and served for five years
(1869–74) as superintendent of the Naval Academy, where the drill field is
named for him. On Friday afternoons in good weather, midshipmen to
this day march past Buchanan House en route to Worden Field.

As for the young Samuel Dana Greene, who commanded the *Monitor*
during the brief period of fighting after Worden was injured, he spent the
rest of his life defending himself from the charge that instead of continuing the fight, he initially fled the scene before bringing the *Monitor* back to
renew the duel. Although Worden supported Greene without reservation,
Greene suffered—almost physically—from the whispered imputations of

Neither the *Virginia* nor the *Monitor* survived the year. The *Virginia* was destroyed by her
own crew in May when the Confederates had to evacuate Norfolk, and the *Monitor*, depicted
here in a contemporary drawing, went down in a storm off Cape Hatteras in December. (U.S.
Naval Institute)

others. In 1884, when he was asked to write a short article for *Century* magazine's "Battles and Leaders" series, Greene described his role in the battle in some detail, providing the best view we now have of what happened inside the *Monitor*'s turret during the fight with the *Virginia*. He wrote the article out in longhand, addressed and mailed it, then returned to his office in the Portsmouth Navy Yard, put a gun to his head, and took his own life. As one authority notes: "His death is perhaps the only fatality directly attributable to the battle of March 9, 1862."[67]

The *Monitor*'s success against the *Virginia* led to a severe case of "monitor fever" in the Union states. Gideon Welles in particular decided that the *Monitor* was a kind of "magic bullet" and ordered the construction of ten more. Eventually the United States constructed scores of monitors of various sizes and design, including the *Montauk*, which Worden commanded off Charleston. The Confederacy, too, tried to replicate the success of the *Virginia*, but the lack of the needed industrial support system made this largely an exercise in frustration. Confederate authorities began construction on a total of fifty-two ironclads, and they succeeded in completing, or nearly completing, thirty-one of them. But most of these had to be destroyed by their builders before they ever fired a shot when Yankee armies captured their bases. Only a half dozen Confederate ironclads ever saw combat.

After the Battle of Hampton Roads, writers and pundits fell over one another in predicting that the advent of ironclad warships in Hampton Roads marked not merely a milestone but the passing of one era and the beginning of another. And more than a few mourned the transition. The writer Nathaniel Hawthorne, who visited Hampton Roads a few weeks after the battle and went on board the *Monitor*, was one such. Describing the *Monitor* as looking like a "giant rat trap," he predicted that its very existence proved that "all the pomp and splendor of naval warfare are gone by." Men would no longer be warriors of the sea, he wrote, but rather servants of insentient machines. No more would personal bravery and calculated audacity decide the outcome of battles.

"Human strife is to be transferred from the heart and personality of man into cunning contrivances of machinery, which by-the-by, will fight out our wars with only the clank and smash of iron, strewing the field with broken engines but damaging nobody's little finger except by accident."[68]

Such predictions were premature. Warfare remained very much a human activity, and death and dismemberment would remain its cost and consequence. Nor did armored ships mark so clearly the end of one era or the beginning of another. Iron plate, after all, is not the same thing as a steel hull, and it would be twenty-one years before the U.S. Navy commissioned its first steel-hulled warship. After an initial enthusiasm for armored ships in the years following the Civil War, by the turn of the century it became evident that no amount of armor, even several feet of it, could fully protect a vessel from the larger and heavier naval guns that were being built at the same time. Then, too, heavy armor made ships not only slow but also prodigious consumers of fuel. To save weight, warship designers began placing armor around only the most vulnerable parts of warships, such as the engine and the magazine. Eventually even this became superfluous, and armor plating was scaled back further until by the end of the twentieth century it had all but disappeared. Iron-armored they may have been, but the Confederate ram *Virginia* and the Union *Monitor* were not the lineal grandparents of modern steel warships.

Those two vessels did, however, significantly redefine the character of naval combat. The officers and sailors in either vessel would not have felt terribly out of place in a World War I submarine, and even if they would not know what to make of the vast array of electronics in a modern combat information center, at least they could intuit the feeling of being a part of a complex machine of war. For it was not in the technology of armor plate or solid shot that the duel in Hampton Roads showed the path to the future, but in the roles played by the officers and men who fed the fires, manned the guns, and fought one another in the world's first battle between floating, self-propelled machines of war.

PART THREE

ARMORED CRUISERS AND EMPIRE

The Battle of Manila Bay
May 1, 1898

IN THE THIRD OF A CENTURY BETWEEN THE END OF THE CIVIL WAR in 1865 and the American declaration of war against Spain in 1898, the United States was transformed. Even as the nation struggled painfully through the period of broken pledges and sectional resentment that history has labeled Reconstruction, it also strengthened its hold on the North American continent, strapping it together with railroads and telegraph wires and stamping out the last resistance from the native tribes. At the same time, American industry became a force of historic proportions. Triggered in part by the mass production of war matériel from 1861 to 1865, fueled by new developments in engineering and metallurgy, and fed by a cheap labor pool of immigrants, the United States became an economic and industrial powerhouse by the 1890s, establishing the foundation that would eventually make it the most powerful nation on earth. If the rest of the world failed to take sufficient note of this historic phenomenon, it was in part because until the very end of the century the transformative significance of these developments was not immediately evident beyond America's insulating and protecting oceans.

The U.S. Navy did not keep pace with the economic and industrial explosion. The fleet of ironclad monitors was placed in ordinary (what later generations would call "mothballs"); the blockade fleet, composed of mostly converted merchantmen, was sold off; the fast cruisers, designed to hunt down rebel raiders such as the *Shenandoah* and the *Alabama*, were scrapped. By the 1880s the United States Navy consisted of little more than a handful of antique steamers—museum pieces by the standard of most European navies—all of them fully equipped with masts and sails for their day-to-day work of "showing the flag" on distant station patrols. In his 1880s short story "The Canterville Ghost," Oscar Wilde provoked a knowing chuckle from his British audience when his central character contradicted an American who declared that her country had no ruins or curiosities. "No ruins! No curiosities!" the ghost exclaimed. "You have your Navy and your manners."[1]

For Americans, however, there seemed to be little reason to pour public money into a revitalized Navy, for unlike Oscar Wilde's England, the
United States had no proximate enemies unless one counted the western
Indians (who would not have been impressed by American battleships in
any case), nor did it have overseas colonies to protect. To most Americans,
the small, antiquated U.S. Navy of the 1870s and '80s seemed perfectly ade-
quate to the limited task assigned to it. Indeed, it is possible to argue that
there was little reason for the Navy to abandon its low profile even at the
end of the century, for in the 1890s there were still no perceivable threats
on, or even over, the horizon.

Change was coming nonetheless. It was evidenced in 1883 when Congress authorized the first three vessels of what would eventually become a
new generation of steam-and-steel warships: the "New Navy." The very
next year, Stephen B. Luce founded the U.S. Naval War College at Newport, Rhode Island, and hired an otherwise undistinguished naval officer
named Alfred Thayer Mahan to lecture there. At the end of the decade,
Mahan published his collected lectures in book form as *The Influence of
Sea Power upon History, 1660–1783*. Citing Britain's domination of the Age
of Sail as his case study, Mahan declared that naval power was the principal instrument of national greatness and, by implication at least, suggested
how the United States, too, could achieve the status of great power. It was
the existence of a dominant battleship fleet, Mahan declared, that had
allowed Britain to secure control of the sea and thereby control not merely
three-quarters of the globe but also the trade routes and the colonial
empire that brought her wealth, power, and influence.[2]

The astonishing success of Mahan's book was more a matter of good
timing than keen insight. The same year that it was published, the U.S.
Census Bureau noted that there was no longer an area in the western
United States that could properly be designated as "the frontier." Not only
did this prompt young Frederick Turner to offer his interpretive essay
about the wellsprings of the American character at the 1893 Columbian
Exposition in Chicago, it also foreshadowed a turning point in America's
role in the world by implying, at least, that the United States might now
begin to look outward, beyond its protecting oceans, to find a broader out-

let and a bigger stage for its national energy. Mahan's essay thus provided a credible rationale for the program of U.S. naval expansion that was already under way. At the same time, it provided a justification for Europeans to compete in what amounted to a naval arms race—a competition that would last into the next century and play a role in the catastrophe that engulfed Europe in 1914.

It is entirely possible that the United States would have built its "New Navy" even without the influence of Mahan's book, for at the end of the nineteenth century, the United States was a nation emerging from its awkward teenage years: a bit gawky still—its clothes a bit too short at the wrists and ankles—but bursting with the strength and power of imminent adulthood. At the end of the decade, the United States found employment for its new steam-and-steel warships by fighting what Secretary of State John Hay famously called a "splendid little war" against the fading Spanish Empire. It was a war with broad implications and historic significance, for it thrust the United States into the ranks of great powers and thereby signaled a dramatic sea change for both the United States, and for the world. Though the conflict was ostensibly rooted in American concern about Spanish misrule in Cuba, the milestone naval engagement of this war in the age of the battleship was one that involved no battleships at all and which took place almost exactly halfway around the world from Cuba, in a remote bay that most Americans had never even heard of.

—

O N   T H E   N I G H T of April 30, 1898, a column of six American warships, trailed by three small support vessels, steamed purposefully toward the three-mile-wide gap of water that marked the entrance to Manila Bay in the Spanish Philippines. The U.S. ships were all but invisible from the shore. They had recently been repainted, their peacetime white covered by a wartime gray-green so that they would blend with the sea, and they were running blacked out, each vessel burning only a single fantail light that was carefully screened by baffles to ensure that it showed only from directly astern, thus allowing the ships to follow one another single file through the unfamiliar waters of the channel. The lead vessel was the

5,870-ton protected (that is, partially armored) cruiser USS *Olympia*, and on its open bridge wing Commodore George Dewey peered into the dark waters ahead. At age sixty, Dewey was of medium stature with a compact but no longer trim figure, looking much like a man who was entirely comfortable with himself. His pale brown hair was graying at the temples, and except for a rather spectacular walrus mustache, he was clean-shaven above the constricting stock of his white uniform. His face was dominated by a slightly hooked nose and a high forehead on which rested a pillbox-shaped officer's cap, its brim decorated with the gold "scrambled eggs" of his rank. As usual, however, his expression was unreadable; like the surface of the water around him, he projected placidity and calmness.

Indeed, there was little that appeared warlike in this tableau. When the new moon broke through the patchy clouds overhead, it left a bright sheen on the calm water, though Lieutenant C. G. Culkins recalled that in the distance, "dancing pillars of cloud, pulsating with tropical lightning," provided dramatic backlighting. As the *Olympia* turned into the channel between the dark headlands, high "volcanic peaks densely covered with tropical foliage" jutted out from the water on both sides. Late as it was, there were a large number of sailors topside. At 10:40 the word had quietly been passed for the men to stand to the guns, and they stood now at their battle stations, happy to be there not only because of the excitement of impending action but because it was "oppressively hot" below decks; "the ship," one officer recalled, "was like a furnace." Or at least it was until around eleven, when a light shower passed over the column of warships, cooling the air but also dampening the white duck uniforms of the men, though, as one recalled, "nobody noticed such trifles."[3]

Behind the *Olympia*, the other ships of the American Asiatic Squadron followed at regular intervals. They were all relatively new: built not of wood or iron but of steel, an alloy that was stronger and lighter than raw iron, and their coal-fired steam engine plants powered not only the screw propellers that drove them through the water but also the onboard electrical generators that lit the passageways below decks so that lanterns were no longer necessary. The oldest of the ships was the *Boston*, launched in 1884 (the same year that Luce had founded the War College), one of a trio of small cruisers all named for American cities—*Atlanta, Boston,* and *Chicago*—which, along with their consort, the dispatch vessel *Dolphin,* had come to be known as the "ABCD ships." Commissioned in the late 1880s, they had been the first ships of an American naval revival that had continued through the nineties and turned the United States from a third-rate naval power into, if not quite a first-rate power, then at least a top-tier second-rate power. Though the *Boston* still bore masts and spars, giving it the silhouette of a sailing ship, it was designed to operate as a steamer, and it boasted a powerful battery of rifled guns, including two eight-inch guns and a half dozen six-inch guns.

The newest and largest of the ships was the *Olympia,* which led the column, and on whose bridge Commodore Dewey stood watching the

The cruiser USS *Boston,* one of the ships in Dewey's squadron at Manila Bay, was also one of the first vessels of the "New Navy" begun during the 1880s. With its sister ships *Atlanta* and *Chicago,* and the dispatch vessel *Dolphin,* it was part of the "Squadron of Evolution," often referred to as the "ABCD ships." Note that despite its steel construction, it still carried a full suit of sails, and it carried most of its guns in broadside. (U.S. Navy)

approaching headlands. Commissioned only three years before, in February 1895, the *Olympia*'s battery was even more impressive than that of the *Boston*: it carried a quartet of eight-inch guns, which, in testimony to the continuing influence of John Ericsson's design for the *Monitor*, were mounted in two gun turrets (one fore and one aft), plus ten more five-inch guns carried in broadside, as well as twenty-one small-caliber "quick-firing" guns. The *Olympia* had a top speed of twenty-one knots, three times as fast as any Civil War monitor, though it was making only about eight knots now as it slipped into the channel between the southern headland to starboard and the dark bulk of Corregidor Island to port, which looked to one sailor "like a huge ill-moulded grave."[4]

There were two entrances into Manila Bay, and Dewey had selected the wider of them—Boca Grande—primarily to maximize the range from the Spanish shore batteries. Dewey had received reports that the Spanish had sown mines in the channel, but he was skeptical. He knew that mooring contact mines in the deep water of the Boca Grande Channel would be difficult in any case, and he doubted that the Spaniards had either the time or the expertise to do it effectively. Even if there were mines in the channel, he believed the tropical waters of Manila Bay would render most of them inoperable, and he suspected that all the reports he had received about mines were part of an elaborate ruse by the Spanish to discourage him from forcing the entrance to the bay.[5]

On the other hand, the threat from the Spanish shore batteries was very real. Dewey knew that the Spanish had several 5.9-inch guns on Corregidor, as well as 4.7-inch guns on the smaller islands in the channel: El Fraile to starboard and Caballo to port. He had no intention of stopping to shoot it out with them; his goal was to get past them into the bay and seek out the Spanish naval squadron. In making this determination he was not only thinking of Mahan's declaration that the primary object of any naval campaign must be the enemy's main battle fleet but also recalling his own experience more than thirty years before, when as a young midshipman during the Civil War he had served under David Glasgow Farragut in that officer's dramatic run up the Mississippi River. Just as Farragut had run

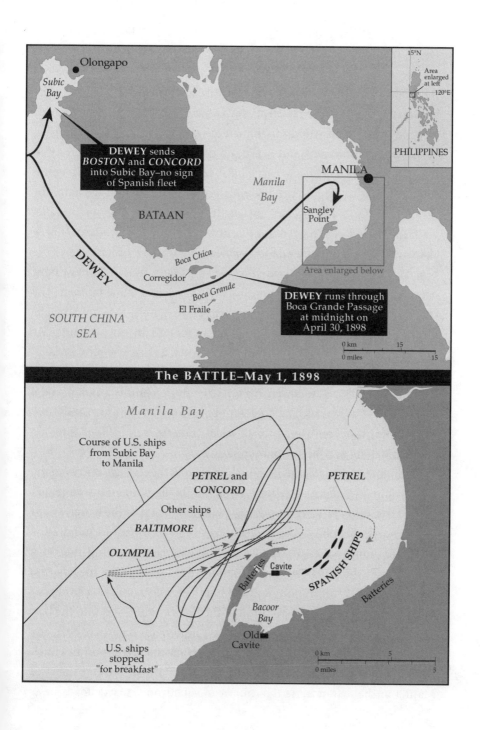

Olongapo

Subic
Bay

15°N

Area
enlarged
at left

120°E

PHILIPPINES

DEWEY sends
BOSTON and *CONCORD*
into Subic Bay–no sign
of Spanish fleet

MANILA

*Manila
Bay*

BATAAN

Sangley
Point

Area enlarged below

DEWEY

Boca Chica

Corregidor

Boca Grande

El Fraile

DEWEY runs through
Boca Grande Passage
at midnight on
April 30, 1898

SOUTH CHINA
SEA

0 km   15

0 miles   15

The BATTLE–May 1, 1898

Manila Bay

Course of U.S. ships
from Subic Bay
to Manila

PETREL and
CONCORD

PETREL

Other ships

BALTIMORE

OLYMPIA

Batteries

Cavite

SPANISH SHIPS

Batteries

*Bacoor
Bay*

Old
Cavite

U.S. ships
stopped
"for breakfast"

0 km   5

0 miles   5

past Forts Jackson and St. Philip to capture New Orleans, so now did Dewey intend to run past El Fraile and Caballo into Manila Bay.[6]

The narrow part of the channel was now at hand; it was just before midnight when the *Olympia* came abreast of Corregidor. "That was the hardest part," one sailor recalled, "not knowing which moment a mine or torpedo would send you through the deck above." As the island slid past, "men held their breaths and hearts almost stood still." But there was no sign of life ashore. Dewey may have begun to wonder if his entire squadron might slip into the bay undetected, and he passed the word for the crew to stand down. Then, just as the *Olympia* was passing El Fraile, which appeared as a "jagged lump" only half a mile to starboard, Dewey changed course from due east to northeast by north in order to enter the bay. The *Olympia*'s stern swung toward El Fraile, and its fantail light became visible to the watchers on shore. At almost the same moment, the soot in the stack of one of the support vessels caught fire and a bright plume of flame shot up into the night, a beacon to anyone watching. At once a light from El Fraile blinked out a signal, a response blinked back from Corregidor, and a signal rocket streaked skyward. An orange stab of flame on El Fraile was followed in a few seconds by a muffled thump, and a shell whistled overhead. The crew raced back to man the guns, and there was a moment of confusion in the dark as running men collided into one another, "falling over hoses, ammunition, etc."[7]

Behind the *Olympia*, the *Boston*, the *Concord*, the *Raleigh*, and even the supply ship *McCulloch* all returned fire, but the flagship's guns remained silent. Dewey was looking ahead. His goal was to get past the batteries and into the bay, where he would find the Spanish naval squadron and destroy it. Consequently, the gun duel with the batteries guarding the Boca Grande was short. The El Fraile battery fired only three rounds; the Americans fired "only about 8 or 10 shots." By 1:00 A.M., all the ships of the American squadron were through the Boca Grande and into the bay. The Americans had found no evidence of mines, nor had there been any other resistance beyond those three shots from the battery on El Fraile. Dewey pointed the *Olympia* toward the faint glow of the city lights of Manila in the distance. As the American squadron cruised slowly eastward, "the white glow on the northeast broke into bright points of electric light, marking the avenues of Manila." The fox was inside the henhouse. Somewhere on the broad surface of that bay, perhaps under the glow of those lights from the city, was the Spanish fleet of Rear Admiral Don Patricio Montojo y Pasaron, and with the day's first light, Dewey intended to find it and sink it.[8]

Dewey passed the word to his flag captain, Charles Gridley, to have the crew stand down from general quarters and get some rest. If the day unfolded as he planned, the men would need all the rest they could get. Dewey, however, remained on the open bridge wing, his face impassive. But that public demeanor was a pose; his orders were terse and brusque, and his unsmiling visage concealed roiling emotions. At 4:00 A.M., with the eastern sky beginning to brighten, a steward appeared at his elbow with a cup of coffee. Dewey brought it to his lips and sipped. When the bitter caffeinated liquid hit his stomach, he turned and vomited violently on the spotless deck of the *Olympia*.[9]

—

The sequence of events that brought Dewey's squadron to Manila Bay at midnight on April 30, 1898, had begun a quarter of a century earlier and half a world away. By the middle of the nineteenth century, the enormous Spanish Empire in the Western Hemisphere, an expanse of territory that dwarfed the Roman Empire at its height, had all but disappeared. One by one, pieces of that empire had been stripped away as they secured their independence, cheered on by Americans who saw in these revolutions Latin versions of their own struggle to break free of a colonial power. For the Spanish it was a cruel and painful process. It was a Spanish tradition that their American empire had been a gift from God for the Reconquista, the military campaign that in 1492 had driven the forces of Islam from their toehold in Europe. Was it mere coincidence that in the very year of that victory Christopher Columbus had sailed under Spanish colors to "discover" the New World? Yet four hundred years later the gift was all but gone. Of all that vast territory, only Cuba and nearby Puerto Rico were left. Though Cuba was a profitable colony, it was more for pride than greed

that the Spanish clung to it, dubbing it "the Ever-Faithful Isle" and resisting sporadic revolutionary outbreaks.

American interest in Cuba was more than a century old. Up to the time
of the Civil War, one element of that concern had been the ambition of
southerners to acquire Cuba as a new slave state to balance the growing
power of the free states in the North. In 1848, at the end of the war with
Mexico, President Polk had tried to buy the island from Spain for $100
million, but Spain was not interested. Another element of the American
concern was strategic; the location of Cuba, corking as it did the bottle of
the Gulf of Mexico, made it of great interest to American strategic planners. In 1854 these twin interests combined when, in Ostend, Belgium, a
trio of American diplomats announced what amounted to an ultimatum.
They declared that Cuba was a natural part of the United States and that if
Spain did not agree to sell it, the United States would be justified in seizing
it. "The Union can never enjoy repose," these Americans declared, "nor
possess reliable security, as long as Cuba is not embraced within its boundaries." The United States subsequently disavowed the Ostend Manifesto,
however, and southern hopes for a slave state in Cuba died with the Civil
War.[10]

While the United States struggled through the Reconstruction years
after the Civil War, Spain survived a long and wasting revolution in Cuba
that was subsequently named the Ten Years' War (1868–78). When not distracted by their own internal problems, Americans watched with interest,
and often with open sympathy, for the rebel cause. A few American citizens
did more than sympathize. Motivated by ideology, by profit, or simply by
the romance of it all, these sympathizers, known as filibusters, smuggled
weapons to the *insurrectos* and even volunteered their own services. In the
middle of the Ten Years' War, in 1873, the Spanish navy stopped and
searched a chartered steamer named *Virginius* that was headed for Cuba
under the American flag. Its captain was a former U.S. naval officer named
Joseph Fry, the crew was a mixed group of Americans and Cubans, and the
cargo consisted of arms that were certainly intended for the Cuban rebels.
Though the men were unquestionably filibusters, it would have been hard
to make an ironclad case against them, for their vessel was still on the high

seas when it was intercepted. Nevertheless, the Spanish conducted a quick trial, condemned the officers and crew of the *Virginius* to death, and shot fifty-three of them before the protests of a British official halted the executions.

It might have led to war. President Grant sought to make a statement of sorts by ordering a concentration of the U.S. fleet at Key West, though there is no indication he intended any more than that. Instead, the U.S. State Department obtained an apology from the Spanish, who also agreed to pay an indemnity. The fact that the United States was then wallowing in the worst financial crisis of the postwar years—the so-called Panic of '73—may have muted American outrage. Still, it was sobering to some when the attempted mobilization of the fleet betrayed the weakness of the U.S. Navy in the 1870s. The monitors, called out of mothballs, were so crank and unseaworthy that they were a greater threat to their own crews than to any potential enemy. In short, the *Virginius* episode demonstrated that in 1873 the United States lacked the capability to express its outrage, even against a tired and fading empire such as Spain.[11]

That was no longer true in 1895, when a second round of revolutionary activity broke out in Cuba. By then, Luce had founded the War College, Mahan had published his book, and the United States had begun building the steam-and-steel ships of the "New Navy." That very year, in fact, the United States launched the USS *Olympia*, the newest vessel of its expanding fleet. It was not that the United States had any particular opponent in mind when it constructed this "New Navy," just a vague sense that the time had come for the United States to possess a war fleet worthy of a great nation. After all, the possession of modern weapons would give America options that were otherwise not available in a diplomatic crisis. A few skeptics noted that great-power status brought dangers as well as options, but they were largely ignored.

The renewed insurrection in Cuba was led by the poet José Martí, who quickly became its first martyr, and by two gifted field generals, Antonio Maceo and Maximo Gomez, who focused their campaign on the sources of Spanish wealth in Cuba, especially the sugar mills and tobacco fields. By 1896, the scorched-earth policy of these rebel generals had caused so much damage to the Cuban economy that Spanish authorities turned to the ruthless Lieutenant General Valeriano Weyler y Nicolau to bring order to the island. Weyler had served as a Spanish observer during the American Civil War and was a great admirer of William T. Sherman. He responded to the destructive tactics of the rebels by adopting a hard-line policy of his own designed to deprive the rebel armies of the wherewithal to continue the fight. In order to protect loyal Cubans from the rebels, Weyler relocated (or concentrated) them into armed camps, a policy remarkably similar to the "strategic hamlet" program adopted by Americans during the Vietnam War seventy years later. Overcrowded and often unsanitary, these camps spawned both hunger and disease, and the term "concentration camp" took on a very negative connotation. Outside the camps, the rebels took or destroyed whatever of value they could find that was unprotected. The Spanish controlled the cities and the harbors, the rebels controlled the countryside, and the people of Cuba suffered.[12]

Americans professed to be shocked by the brutality of the conflict. The major urban newspapers, especially the big New York dailies controlled by William Randolph Hearst and Joseph Pulitzer, vied with one another to present horror stories of destruction and brutality. In almost every case, the Spanish were portrayed as the principal instigators of violence and the rebels as victimized patriots. A representative example is the report filed by a *New York World* correspondent in May 1896:

> The horrors of a barbarous struggle for the extermination of the native population are witnessed in all parts of the country. Blood on the roadsides, blood on the fields, blood on the doorsteps, blood, blood, blood! The old, the young, the weak, the crippled, all are butchered without mercy. There is scarcely a hamlet that has not witnessed the dreadful work. Is there no nation wise enough, brave enough to aid this smitten land?[13]

Recognizing that Weyler's tactics not only failed to suppress the rebellion but also produced bad publicity, Spain's rulers dropped the *reconcentrado* policy and replaced Weyler with the moderate Ramón Blanco. It was too late. The momentum of outrage combined with Spain's tendency to brush off U.S. complaints, all of it fueled by the nearly hysterical popular press, had created a climate in which war became almost irresistible. Under these circumstances, another incident like the *Virginius* episode would very likely have far different consequences.[14]

Though the Spanish-American War is commonly associated with the presidency of William McKinley, who was elected in 1896 over the populist William Jennings Bryan, the new American president dreaded the prospect of war and found the mounting martial drumbeat a distraction from his primary goal of ensuring the continued prosperity of the nation's business interests. Though his predecessor in the White House had suspended courtesy visits by U.S. Navy warships to Cuban ports for fear of inciting a negative reaction, McKinley decided to renew them. In January he responded to a request from the U.S. consul general in Havana, Fitzhugh Lee (Robert

The USS *Maine* at anchor in Havana Harbor in February 1898. Though the *Maine* bore tall masts, they were more for observation than locomotion. In fact, the sails for the *Maine* were never delivered, and she operated as a steamship throughout her short career. Note the forward gun turret placed off the centerline on the starboard side. (*Century*, November 1898)

E. Lee's nephew) to send the second-class battleship USS *Maine* to Havana Harbor.[15]

The *Maine* was America's first "modern" battleship, and as evidence of its transitional status, it incorporated a hodgepodge of design features. Like Perry's *Lawrence,* it boasted a full set of masts and spars, though the sails for those spars were never delivered and throughout its short history it operated as a steam vessel. Like Buchanan's *Virginia* (*Merrimack*), it was equipped with a forward ram, and like Worden's *Monitor*, its main battery was housed in revolving armored gun turrets. But the *Maine* had a curiously unbalanced appearance. Its two main turrets were offset from the centerline: the forward turret overhung the starboard side, and the after turret was cantilevered over the port side. The idea was to allow the ten-inch guns of its main battery to fire both forward and aft, but the result was disharmonious, and only an especially proud captain ever would have called it a beautiful ship.[16]

Captain Charles Sigsbee was the *Maine*'s captain, and whether or not he thought his ship beautiful, he was very much aware of the sensitivity of his assignment. Even after bringing the *Maine* safely to anchor in Havana Harbor at midmorning on January 25, 1898, he kept the ship on alert, with one-quarter of the crew on duty around the clock and two of the ship's four boilers on line. Publicly, however, he carried on as if his presence in Havana Harbor were nothing more than a routine port visit. He greeted dignitaries on board and gave them tours of the ship; he allowed officers (though not the men) shore liberty; and Sigsbee himself attended a bull-fight in Havana as the guest of Blanco's deputy, Major General Julian González Parrado. He later wrote that he "had but one wish" and that was "to be friendly to the Spanish authorities as required by my orders."[17]

Meanwhile, McKinley became the center of a new crisis when the Spanish minister in the United States, Enrique Dupuy de Lôme, wrote an indiscreet private letter to a friend who happened to be the editor of a Havana newspaper. A worker in the editor's office who was sympathetic to the rebels stole the letter and passed it on to others who made sure that it landed eventually on the desk of William Randolph Hearst. It was published on the front page of the *New York Journal* on February 9. In that missive, de Lôme referred to the new American president as "weak and a bidder for the admiration of the crowd." He was, de Lôme concluded, a "common politician." It was a pretty astute analysis, but diplomats of foreign governments are not supposed to say such things. De Lôme resigned and Spain apologized, but the damage had been done.[18]

Six days later the *Maine* blew up in Havana Harbor.

—

In the crisis mentality of February 1898, it is not surprising that Americans assumed as a matter of course that the Spanish had somehow managed to detonate a mine or some other "infernal machine" under the *Maine* and destroy it, killing some 260 American officers and men in the process. The penny press in America reached a crescendo of outrage about Spanish perfidy, encouraging most Americans to assume that the Spanish had deliberately destroyed the American ship and murdered most of its crew. Even those who doubted that Spain was complicit in the destruction of the *Maine* insisted that the Spanish were nevertheless responsible because they had failed to ensure the *Maine*'s security. And even if none of that was true, there was still the lingering resentment of Spain's repressive regime in Cuba and the accumulated sympathy of Americans for the suffering of the Cuban people. In the end, angry Americans justified hostilities against Spain by arguing that its repressive regime in Cuba, by itself, was sufficient grounds for war.* The influential Vermont senator Redfield Proctor soberly described Spain's administration in Cuba as "the worst misgovernment of which I ever had knowledge."[19]

Calm reflection (something few seemed interested in at the time) would have suggested that of all the possible causes of the *Maine* disaster, a deliberate attack by Spanish agents was the least likely explanation. After all, the destruction of the *Maine* was an even greater disaster for the Span-

---

* In much the same way, the advocates of an American invasion of Iraq in 2003 argued that even if Iraq was not complicit in the September 11, 2001, attack on the World Trade Center and the Pentagon, the wickedness of Saddam Hussein, by itself, was sufficient reason for war. The difference was that in 1898 a belligerent Congress pushed war on a reluctant president, while in 2003 a president determined on war secured a congressional resolution despite widespread doubts.

ish than it was for Americans, for it resulted in a major international crisis at a time when Spain already had its hands full. Indeed, if any group had a motive to destroy the *Maine* and thereby widen the rift between the United States and Spain, it was the Cuban *insurrectos*, whose tactics were certainly consistent with such an act.

In fact, neither the Spanish nor the rebels were responsible. Though an early postwar investigation initially confirmed that the *Maine* had been destroyed by an external explosion, the most thorough postwar analysis demonstrates convincingly that it was the victim of an internal accident: a smoldering fire in the forward coal bunker that flared up suddenly and ignited the magazine for the ship's six-inch guns. Coal was a volatile fuel, and it was not uncommon for small fires deep inside the fuel pile to burn for hours or even days, undetectable from the outside until they burst into flame. A team of U.S. Navy analysts headed by Admiral Hyman Rickover concluded in 1975 that "the characteristics of the damage [to the *Maine*] are consistent with a large internal explosion" and that "there is no evidence that a mine destroyed the *Maine*."[20]

In this case, however, it was not the actual cause of the explosion that mattered but the perceived one. The destruction of the *Maine* provoked a national outcry, including public pleas such as "Remember the Maine!" which was often rhymed with "And to hell with Spain!" McKinley was determined not to be stampeded by the popular sentiment—"I don't propose to be swept off my feet," he told a Republican senator—but he lacked the courage or commitment to stand against the tide of public opinion. In the end, the outbreak of the Spanish-American War took place not only because many sought it but also because too few made any serious effort to oppose or prevent it. Those who saw war as unwise or unnecessary kept quiet, out of either diffidence or a fear of being ostracized by the groundswell of public opinion, whereas those who sought war did so loudly and publicly. In addition, many Americans were enthusiastic about war in 1898 because an entire generation of young men, raised on stories of the Civil War, had not seen a war in their lifetime. Someone who was twenty-two years old in 1898 had been born in 1876, the year Reconstruction ended. Many feared they would miss out on the kind of great adventure that had defined the lives of their forebears. Recalling the time years later, Carl Sandburg wrote, "I was going along with millions of other Americans who were *about ready for a war*." Like the attack on Pearl Harbor in 1941 or the destruction of the World Trade Center towers in 2001, the sinking of the *Maine* was such a traumatic national event that Americans felt it necessary to strike out and strike back.[21]

Thanks to the recent expansion of the Navy, they could. In 1884, the year that Luce opened the doors of the Naval War College at Newport, the United States had possessed no battleships at all and its appropriation for the Navy had totaled just over $10.5 million. Five years later, Secretary of the Navy Benjamin Franklin Tracy called for the construction of an American fleet of twenty battleships and sixty cruisers, and the next year the Navy's budget topped $25.5 million. In March 1898, in the wake of the *Maine* crisis, Congress passed a supplementary national defense bill authorizing an additional $50 million, and by the end of the year naval appropriations had reached $144.5 million, a staggering sum at a time when the entire national budget did not exceed $450 million. When the supplementary appropriations bill unanimously passed the House, the former Confederate cavalry general Joe Wheeler, now a Democratic congressman from Alabama, greeted the vote with a ringing rebel yell that echoed through the House chamber.[22]

McKinley continued to hope that war could be avoided. When he offered a long-awaited speech to Congress in April, he reviewed the frustrating history of U.S.-Spanish relations over Cuba but stopped short of asking for a declaration of war. Instead he requested the authority "to use military and naval forces . . . as may be necessary." Congress dutifully granted McKinley his request, but a week later the legislative branch demonstrated that it was on the verge of seizing control of American policy from the executive when it passed a joint resolution declaring that Cuba was an independent country, demanding that Spain leave the island at once, and directing McKinley to use the nation's naval and military forces to enforce these pronouncements. This piece of legislation also con-

tained the self-denying Teller Amendment, in which the United States for-
swore any territorial concessions in Cuba.[23]*

Unwilling to be made entirely superfluous, McKinley three days later
issued a call for 125,000 volunteers, and three days after that he requested a
formal declaration of war backdated to April 21. That same day, Navy secretary John D. Long telegraphed Dewey in Hong Kong: "War has commenced between the United States and Spain. Proceed at once to
Philippine Islands."[24]

—

That George Dewey was in Hong Kong to receive that historic message was
due, at least in part, to the influence of the brash young assistant secretary
of the Navy, Theodore Roosevelt. The relationship between Long, the dig-
nified fifty-nine-year-old Navy secretary, and his hyperkinetic thirty-nine-
year-old assistant was a curious one. Long looked upon the antics of his
young assistant with an avuncular tolerance, going so far as to acknowledge that since his own tendencies were innately cautious, it was perhaps a
good thing that Roosevelt was there to prod him. Long, it appears, found
Roosevelt amusing, even entertaining.[25] Thus encouraged (or at least not
discouraged), Roosevelt frequently took liberties with his office, acting
more in conformance with his own perceptions of what America ought to
be doing than with administration policy. Even as McKinley worked to
prevent or postpone a clash with Spain, Roosevelt acted as if war were a
settled fact, and he did whatever he could to make it so. When Roosevelt
learned that the steady and temperate John A. Howell was in line for the
command of the Asiatic fleet, he urged Dewey, whom Roosevelt considered more of a warrior than Howell, to use whatever influence he could to
obtain the position for himself. Thus prodded, Dewey, who was originally

---

* Many Americans began to regret passage of the Teller Amendment almost at once. Congressmen
who had voted for it in the enthusiasm of the moment repented their vote, insisting that they had
supported it, in the words of Albert Beveridge, "in a moment of impulsive but mistaken generosity." The subsequent Platt Amendment, inserted into the 1901 Cuban constitution, effectively repu-
diated the Teller Amendment by declaring that the United States could intervene in Cuba any time
Cuba's "security and stability" were imperiled.

from Vermont, visited the powerful Vermont senator Redfield Proctor, who lobbied Secretary Long on Dewey's behalf.[26]*

Officially, at least, Dewey's orders said nothing about a possible war with Spain. He was to perform the traditional tasks of the American squadron in the Far East: guard the interests of U.S. merchants, protect Western missionaries, keep an eye on the state of affairs in Korea (or Corea, as it was often spelled then), and otherwise stay out of the way of the great-power rivalries along the China coast. Those rivalries had reached new heights with the German seizure of Kiau Chau Bay. The European powers at the turn of the nineteenth century acted toward China the way American settlers treated the Western frontier: as unoccupied territory available to anyone willful enough to claim it and strong enough to defend it. The British, French, and Portuguese, and now the Germans, had all grabbed chunks of the Chinese coast to use as naval bases and/or commercial ports, and while the Chinese mostly resented it, they were too disorganized and too weak to do anything about it. The fact that the United States did not assert a claim of its own in China was less out of consideration for Chinese sensibilities than an acknowledgment of the relatively minor role that America played in world affairs in the waning years of the nineteenth century. That, however, was about to change.

Dewey made the usual round of formal calls on local rulers and officials. He visited the emperor of Japan, who greeted him in full military dress surrounded, as Dewey recalled in his autobiography, by an anxious group of "court chamberlains, gentlemen in waiting, etc." In many ways it was a measure of how much Japan had changed in the forty-five years since Matthew Perry's first visit there in 1853. Then Japan had been an

---

* Secretary Long denied that Proctor, Roosevelt, or anyone else, for that matter, had had any influence on his decision. In his diary, Long wrote on October 9, 1898, that while he had received the usual letters of support on behalf of both candidates, those letters "had no weight at all" and that he made up his mind to appoint Dewey "before the receipt of any of them." Perhaps. But Long's pique at being manipulated is evident in his decision to withhold from Dewey the rank of rear admiral, which was traditional for the commander of the Asian Squadron. Instead, Dewey took command as a commodore and did not receive his promotion to admiral until after his victory in Manila Bay.

exotic regime of such mystery that no man was permitted even to look upon the face of the emperor; now Dewey found it "but little different from . . . any court of Europe." Indeed, much like the United States, Japan was a country on the cusp of becoming a major naval power. It had defeated China in a naval war in 1895, and the first two modern Japanese battleships were even then under construction in British naval yards; the delivery of these ships would make Japan a major player in the Asian balance of power.[27]

But even as Dewey fulfilled the traditional functions of American squadron commanders abroad, he remained acutely aware of the possibility of imminent war with Spain. He knew full well what was expected of him: the minute war was declared, he was to steam to the Philippines and destroy the Spanish naval squadron there. Though the Philippines had nothing whatsoever to do with the independence of Cuba, it was a central tenet of Admiral Mahan's famous doctrine that the sea was a seamless cloth—or as Mahan himself dubbed it, "a great common"—and that the existence of an enemy fleet anywhere on its surface was a threat to sea control. As early as 1895, officers at the Naval War College in Newport, where Mahan had developed his theories of naval warfare, were drafting plans calling for the U.S. Asiatic Squadron to attack the Philippines in case of war with Spain. The first blow for Cuban independence, therefore, would take place eleven thousand miles away in the principal harbor of the Spanish Philippines.[28]

In considering such an attack, Dewey confronted logistical problems as perplexing in their own way as those Perry had encountered on Lake Erie. For one thing, none of his ships had a complete supply of ammunition, a commodity not easily found seven thousand miles from the nearest U.S. naval base. Before he had left the United States, Dewey had urged Navy authorities to forward ammunition to him as quickly as possible, but despite the near-hysterical tone of the public press, peacetime lethargy dominated in the Bureau of Ordnance. Navy officials shook their heads and declared they could not guarantee a speedy delivery of ammunition because commercial shippers quite reasonably refused to carry Navy powder and shells as cargo. That meant that Dewey would have to wait until the USS *Charleston*, then under repair, was ready for a Pacific crossing. Demonstrating that Roosevelt had chosen a kindred spirit for the command, Dewey overcame these obstacles and convinced the department to use the gunboat *Concord*, which was at Mare Island Navy Yard in San Francisco Bay, to carry the ammunition. He even visited the *Concord* personally to cajole its skipper into cramming as much powder and shell on board as possible. As a result, the *Concord* arrived in Yokohama on February 9 (the same day the de Lôme letter was printed in New York), and Dewey took thirty-five tons of ammunition on board the *Olympia* the next day. To supply the rest of the squadron, Dewey eagerly anticipated the arrival of the cruiser USS *Baltimore*, which carried a second load of ammunition.[29]

Dewey's next task was to concentrate the fleet. When he arrived in Japan in January, the handful of ships belonging to what was rather grandly titled the American Asiatic Squadron was scattered all over the western Pacific: in Korea, in Japan, and along the China coast. If it came to war, as Dewey surely expected, this would not do. Consistent with the Mahanian prescription that fleet concentration was the key to victory, Dewey sent out orders for all the vessels to concentrate at Hong Kong, and as soon as he loaded the ammunition brought by the *Concord*, he set out with the *Olympia* and *Concord* for the British crown colony on the South China coast.

News of the destruction of the *Maine* was waiting for Dewey when the *Olympia* arrived at Hong Kong on February 17. All over the harbor, the ships of a dozen nations had lowered their flags to half staff in recognition of the disaster, and throughout the following days, boats plied back and forth across the harbor as representatives of the various squadrons delivered the formal condolences of their nations to the American visitors. Much like the international response to the September 11, 2001, disaster, the world reaction in 1998 was "horrified amazement at such an act."[30]

Meanwhile, other U.S. vessels arrived to augment Dewey's squadron, including the veteran cruiser *Boston*, a dozen years old now but armed with eight-inch guns, and the newer but smaller *Raleigh*, with six-inch guns. Most welcome of all was the *Baltimore*, another eight-inch-gun cruiser that originally had been dispatched as a replacement for the

Olympia but which in the new circumstances would join the American squadron as a reinforcement. Equally important, the *Baltimore* brought with it enough ammunition to bring the ships of the squadron up to about 60 percent of capacity. This was probably sufficient even for a large-scale battle, but Dewey's awareness that his ships did not have a full complement of ammunition and that there was no source of resupply closer than California remained a nagging worry in the back of his mind.

The most serious of Dewey's logistical problems concerned fuel. The Americans had no naval bases in the Far East and were therefore dependent on the hospitality of the Japanese at Yokohama or the British at Hong Kong. In the case of war, even those bases would be closed to them, since international law forbade neutrals from allowing belligerents to operate from their ports and harbors. Lacking an American naval base in the Far East, Dewey's steam-powered ships would have no place where they could recoal. The solution, though not a perfect one, was somehow to acquire a number of coal ships, or colliers, to provide floating logistic support. Dewey cabled Secretary Long for permission to purchase both coal and a collier to carry it. Long approved the request and suggested that Dewey might purchase the British *Nanshan*, due any day in Hong Kong with a cargo of Welsh coal. Dewey did so, and he also purchased the British revenue cutter *McCulloch* and the small supply ship *Zafiro*. All three vessels became U.S. auxiliary warships, but although Dewey put a U.S. Navy officer and four signalmen on board each vessel, he kept their original English crews and registered the ships as merchant vessels so that they would not have to leave Hong Kong with the rest of the squadron when war was declared. To sustain the deception, Dewey filed papers listing Guam in the Spanish Ladrones as their official home port, an island that was then so remote it was, as Dewey said, "almost a mythical country."[31]

Dewey also had to resolve some personnel problems within the officer corps. Two of Dewey's senior officers, Captain Charles V. Gridley of the *Olympia* and Captain Frank Wildes of the *Boston*, were due to rotate back to the States. Both men begged Dewey to be allowed to stay with their commands until after the fight. Having spent a lifetime in a peacetime navy, neither wanted to miss the one chance they were likely to have for martial glory. Dewey was sympathetic; he allowed Gridley to stay in command of the *Olympia* despite his precarious health, and he asked Captain Benjamin P. Lamberton, who had orders to take command of the *Boston*, if he would instead accept an appointment as chief of staff on the flagship. Finally, there was the problem of what to do with the old monitor *Monocacy*, relic of a former age. Aware that the *Monocacy* would be of little value in a fight with the Spanish, Dewey decided to leave it in Shanghai under a skeleton crew, and he distributed the rest of the men to fill out the crews of his other ships, bringing her skipper, C. P. Rees, onto the *Olympia* as the flagship's executive officer. Another addition to the *Olympia*'s wardroom was Joseph L. Stickney, a Naval Academy graduate who had resigned his commission to become a journalist. He asked Dewey for permission to accompany the squadron into battle. Dewey not only agreed, he made Stickney a volunteer aide, and Stickney was therefore present on the bridge of the *Olympia* throughout the campaign, making him an early embedded journalist.

Dewey had already completed most of these dispositions when he received a cablegram from Roosevelt that confirmed most of his decisions: "Order the squadron, except for *Monocacy*, to Hong Kong. Keep full of coal. In the event declaration of war Spain, your duty will be to see that the Spanish squadron does not leave the Asiatic coast, and then offensive operations in Philippine Islands. Keep *Olympia* until further orders."[32]

Dewey labored daily to ensure that the assembled squadron was ready for combat. He had the ships scraped and painted, covering their traditional peacetime white with an equally traditional drab gray-green that the sailors called "war colors" and which the Spanish later referred to as "wet moon color." When Lamberton arrived in Hong Kong aboard the small steamer *China*, he had been out of touch with unfolding events during the long Pacific crossing. As he peered ahead into Hong Kong Harbor through a lifting fog and saw the American squadron at anchor, he cried out to a fellow passenger: "They're gray! They're gray! That means war!"[33]

All of these preparations had to be conducted in the open; there were no secrets in the roadstead at British Hong Kong. Most of the British openly sided with their American cousins, but despite that sympathy, international law compelled the British to ask Dewey to leave as soon as the United States became a formal belligerent. On April 24 Dewey received a formal message from the governor general of Hong Kong, Major General Wilsone Black, who notified him that he would have to stop taking on coal and stores in Hong Kong and leave port by four the next afternoon, though in a private note, Black confided: "God knows, my dear Commodore, that it breaks my heart to send you this notification."[34]

By this time, the Americans had completed most of their preparations and Dewey had already decided to quit Hong Kong and take his fleet to Mirs Bay, some thirty miles up the coast. Mirs Bay was indisputably Chinese territory, but in 1898 the notion of Chinese sovereignty was little more than an abstraction. Dewey believed—correctly, as it proved—that he could anchor his squadron there without fear of "international complication."[35] The same day he received Black's notice, therefore, Dewey sent his four smaller ships to Mirs Bay and planned to follow them the next day with the rest of the squadron. He used the extra day to complete the scraping and painting of the *Baltimore* and to make engine repairs on the *Raleigh*. Ensign Harry Chadwick would be left behind with the chartered tug *Fame* to accept delivery of a new circulating pump for the *Raleigh* and to bring the latest information about the Spanish squadron in the Philippines. That night, one of the British regiments hosted the American officers at a farewell dinner, and afterward one British officer remarked lugubriously: "A very fine set of fellows, but unhappily we shall never see them again." At ten the next morning, six hours in advance of the British deadline, the American squadron steamed slowly out of Hong Kong harbor as British sailors manned the side in a gesture of silent support, and patients on the British hospital ship offered up three rousing cheers, which were answered by the Americans.[36]

Safely anchored in Mirs Bay, Dewey ordered that the ammunition brought by the *Baltimore* be distributed to the ships of the squadron, and he kept the crews busy day and night preparing for battle. A few of the ships were shorthanded. Like most nineteenth-century navies, the U.S. Navy accepted sailors of virtually any nationality. In addition to native-born Americans, about 20 percent of the crew consisted of Englishmen,

Irishmen, Frenchmen, Chinese, and others. On the eve of the departure from Hong Kong, a handful of these foreign nationals had disappeared. The rest, however, worked with a will. They tore off the decorative gilt woodwork and threw it over the side so that wooden splinters would not add to the casualties, though on the *Olympia*, Dewey merely ordered the woodwork covered with canvas and splinter nets. Sailors also kept busy constructing makeshift barricades of iron to protect the ammunition hoists and draping chains over the sides to add another layer of "armor" to otherwise unarmored areas. In the midst of all this activity, on April 27 officers on the *Olympia* saw the little tug *Fame* enter Mirs Bay at top speed, its whistle blowing shrilly, and soon a grinning Ensign Chadwick was on the quarterdeck delivering a cablegram from Secretary Long: "War has commenced between the United States and Spain. Proceed at once to Philippine Islands. Commence operations at once, particularly against the Spanish fleet. You must capture vessels or destroy. Use utmost endeavors."[37]

Even without the two references to acting "at once," Dewey planned to waste no time. He ordered the signal for "all captains," and within the hour he was meeting with his senior officers. He gave no fiery speeches such as those offered by Perry and Buchanan before their battles. Instead he explained the squadron's mission quietly and dispassionately, and after a businesslike meeting he dismissed them to their ships. At 2:00 that same afternoon the nine vessels of the American Asiatic Squadron hoisted their anchors and shaped a course for the Philippine Islands.

Six hundred and thirty miles to the south, Rear Admiral Don Patricio Montojo y Pasaron was contemplating his alternatives, none of which looked particularly good. Montojo had been in the Spanish navy for forty-seven years, having obtained his commission three years before Dewey had entered the Naval Academy at Annapolis. He was a proud man who loved his country, but he was sufficiently realistic to appreciate that his aging squadron of two small cruisers and five gunboats had virtually no chance against the newer, bigger, and faster American warships. From the start, therefore, it was evident to him that his role was not so much to win as it was to lose honorably, and if possible heroically. Three years earlier, in contemplating a war with the United States, the Spanish governor general of Cuba had declared that "honor is more important than success," and that could well have stood as Montojo's motto.[38]

Unlike Dewey, Montojo had a secure base from which to operate, and that should have given him a significant advantage, but no one in the Spanish chain of command, from the governor general on down, seemed willing to undertake the kind of energetic measures necessary to prepare for the coming fight. The correspondence from the Ministry of Marine and the governor general was characterized more by banal generalities than realistic planning. They proclaimed their confidence that Montojo would do his best without ever suggesting what that might involve. Typical of such documents was a broadside penned by the archbishop of Manila that was intended to inspire resistance to the pending American attack. He referred to the United States as a country "without a history" whose leaders were men of "insolence and defamation, cowardice and cynicism." Such a country dared to send "a squadron manned by foreigners, possessing neither instruction nor discipline . . . with the ruffianly intention of robbing us" and forcing Protestantism on a Catholic population. Such swaggering fatuousness not only failed to inspire resistance, it gave the Americans increased determination, since a copy of it found its way to Hong Kong and eventually to Dewey, who had it read aloud on board each of the American vessels during the transit from Mirs Bay, provoking predictable vows of revenge.[39]

Montojo was equally complicit in the general malaise, offering little guidance to his subordinates beyond a general instruction to "do everything possible to guard the honor of the flag and the navy." Whether from conviction or fatalism, the Spanish leadership clung to the notion that the old values of personal bravery and heroic behavior would be sufficient to overcome the technological advantages of America's "New Navy."[40]

Even if the Spanish had been more focused in their preparations, it would probably have made little difference, for Montojo's ships were hopelessly overmatched. His newest and biggest vessel was the 3,500-ton cruiser

Reina Cristina, whose six 6.2-inch guns were the largest in the Spanish squadron, but which could be easily outranged by the eight-inch guns on the *Olympia, Boston,* and *Baltimore.* Montojo's second largest ship was the much older 3,260-ton *Castilla,* which was built partly of wood, had no armor, and had ancient engines that had broken down completely. Her carved and gilded woodwork gleamed in the sunlight, but she was, in fact, no more than a floating battery that had to be towed from place to place. The rest of his squadron consisted of five small gunboats of just over a thousand tons each, none of which had a gun larger than 4.7 inches.*

Early on, Montojo concluded that if he had any chance at all, it was to fight the Americans from the protected anchorage at Subic Bay, some thirty miles up the coast from Manila.† As war clouds gathered following the explosion of the *Maine* in February, he ordered that four 5.9-inch guns originally intended for Sangley Point near the Cavite Navy Yard in Manila Bay be sent instead to Subic Bay and installed there to provide support for the fleet in case the Americans attacked. He placed this crucial duty in the hands of Captain Julio Del Rio, but, having given the orders, he did not bother to follow up on them or exercise any personal oversight, and predictably the work lagged. On the very day that Dewey left Hong Kong for Mirs Bay, Montojo took his own squadron to sea, steaming out the Boca Grande and then turning north along the coast of Bataan for the anchorage at Subic Bay, the *Castilla* towed by the transport *Manila.* En route, the *Castilla* began taking on water through her propeller-shaft bearing, and her crew had to fill the bearing with cement. That stopped the leak, but it also ensured that her engines would never work again.[41]

When Montojo arrived at Subic Bay he learned "with much disgust"

---

* After the battle was over, American journalists and some naval officers tried hard to suggest that the opposing squadrons had been roughly equal in strength; a few even declared that the Spanish squadron had been superior. Most such efforts involved adding the guns of Spanish shore batteries to the enemy total, or counting as part of Montojo's squadron any vessel that might have been used for hostile purposes if it had been armed. But three stark facts demonstrate the disparity between the opposing squadrons: Dewey's oldest ship was newer than Montojo's newest ship, Dewey's slowest ship was faster than Montojo's fastest ship, and while the Spanish had no gun afloat larger than 6.2 inches, the Americans had three cruisers that carried eight-inch guns.

† This harbor, now the site of a major U.S. Navy base, was then called Subig Bay.

that none of the four guns he had sent there had been mounted and that no mines had been laid. Very little at all, it seemed to him, had been done to prepare for the coming fight. For a few hours he nursed the hope that it might still be possible to complete the work before the Americans arrived, but the very next day he learned that the Americans had left the China coast and were already en route. Confronted with this reality, Montojo called a council of war on board the *Reina Cristina,* where to a man his captains voted to return to Manila Bay and fight the Americans there. It is a measure of Spanish fatalism that the decisive argument in this discussion was that the water in Manila Bay was shallower than it was at Subic, so when the Spanish ships were sunk, the crewmen would have a better chance of surviving. With such logic ruling the day, Montojo resignedly led his squadron back to Manila Bay, where it arrived late on April 29, one day ahead of the Americans.[42]

At Manila, Montojo assessed his few remaining options. One—undoubtedly his best—was to anchor his fleet under the walls of the city of Manila. A sprawling metropolis of some three hundred thousand, Manila sat on a coastal plain where the Pasig River flowed into the bay, and it was well fortified on both its landward and seaward sides by fifty-foot-thick masonry walls thirty to forty feet high. Atop those walls were a total of 226 heavy guns. Most of them were old muzzle-loaders of little practical use against modern ordnance, but there were also four 9.4-inch rifled guns, two of which faced the bay. They were the biggest guns in the theater and could outrange even the eight-inch guns of the Americans. If Montojo wanted to even the odds between his ornate but elderly cruisers and Dewey's more modern armored ships, his best bet was to anchor under the guns of the city. But that would mean that overshots from the American fleet would land in the city itself, with the result that hundreds, maybe thousands, of civilians would die. Montojo, therefore, rejected the idea. "I refused to have our ships near the city of Manila," he wrote, "because, far from defending it, this would provoke the enemy to bombard the plaza."[43]

Montojo's second option was to fight a battle of maneuver with the Americans. But there was no hope that this ploy would be successful: the *Castilla* could not move at all, and even the fastest of the Spanish ships was slower than the slowest American vessel. His only remaining option, then, was to fight from anchor, and if he could not (or would not) do so from Manila, his only other chance was to anchor his fleet near the Cavite Navy Yard, on the southern edge of the bay, where two 5.9-inch guns and one 4.7-inch rifle could add their weight to the coming fight, though only one of the 5.9-inch guns faced the bay.

Montojo anchored his seven ships in the traditional line-ahead formation stretching out in a gentle curve from Sangley Point, which enclosed Bacoor Bay on the southern shore of Manila Bay. He moored several lighters filled with sand alongside the immobile *Castilla* to give that unarmored vessel some protection, ordered the topmasts taken down, removed the ship's boats, had the anchors buoyed, and all in all prepared his doomed command for combat. As he made these preparations, the telegraph brought the news that the Americans had stopped to look into Subic Bay and, finding nothing there, had shaped a course for Manila. The day passed with no further news, but then at midnight Montojo heard the sound of gunfire from the Boca Grande as Dewey's squadron ran into the bay. It would be only a matter of hours now. "I directed all the artillery to be loaded, and all the sailors and soldiers to go to their stations for battle."[44]

—

It was 5:00 A.M. and the sun was rising above the hills behind Manila when the American cruisers arrived off the city. Dewey had not moved from his position on the *Olympia*'s starboard bridge wing, and as he surveyed the waterfront, it was evident even without the reports from the lookouts that the Spanish fleet was not there. The Manila batteries opened fire from long range, most of the shots falling well short, though one of the shells from a 9.4-inch gun landed directly in the wake of the *Olympia* as it steamed past. *Boston* and *Concord* replied with two eight-inch shells each, which landed near the Spanish batteries, but it was little more than a gesture, since Manila was not Dewey's target, and in any case he wanted to husband his ammunition. As the sun spread its light across the "misty haze" of the bay, lookouts on the *Olympia* spotted "a line of gray and white vessels" four miles to the south anchored in "an irregular crescent" off Sangley Point, near Cavite Navy Yard. Dewey immediately ordered the *Olympia* to turn toward them and increase speed to eight knots. The *Baltimore, Raleigh, Concord, Petrel,* and *Boston* all followed in the *Olympia*'s wake, large battle flags flying from every masthead, and with bands playing patriotic airs on at least two of the ships. The three transports remained behind, beyond range of the Spanish guns, but close enough to tow crippled ships out of the battle line if necessary.[45]

Dewey's battle plan was a simple one. The *Olympia* would lead the American warships past the Spanish vessels, each firing in turn, and then it would circle back to pass the enemy again on the other tack. He was determined to come as close to the Spanish as he could without running aground. He remained concerned about his squadron's limited ammunition and wanted to make sure that every shot counted. The Americans had

Dewey's flagship, the protected cruiser USS *Olympia*, presents an imposing façade as it steams toward the camera during firing exercises. Note the officers on the open bridge wings and the conning officer at the top of the ladder. (U.S. Navy)

a chart of the bay, and it showed plenty of deep water up to within two thousand yards of the Spanish position, but Dewey was taking no chances. From the *Olympia*'s bluff bow, a leadsman regularly hurled a weighted line out in front of the ship, reeled it in after it struck bottom, and called out the depth of water under the hull.[46]

At a few minutes past five, the Spanish battery on Sangley Point opened fire, though the shots fell well short. The Spanish had a virtually unlimited supply of ammunition and could afford to be wasteful. Dewey held his fire. Still attired in his dress white uniform, the constricting collar buttoned up to the chin, Dewey was the very picture of stoicism, though others on the *Olympia* had made pragmatic adjustments to their clothing. The gunners had stripped to the waist in the tropical heat, and they stood silent in the tension-filled run-up to battle. One participant recalled that there was no sound but for the steady *chunk, chunk, chunk* of the engines and "the monotonous voice of the leadsman." Down below, in the engine room, the stokers fed the fires, ignorant of what was happening topside except for infrequent updates shouted down to them by thoughtful sailors. They had been allowed a break at 4:30 A.M., but once the action began they would remain "shut up" in their "little hole" until the battle was over.[47]

At about 5:15 the Spanish ships opened fire, the 6.2-inch guns of the *Reina Cristina* throwing up large plumes of water in front of *Olympia*, the shells landing closer now, but still well short. The American ships remained silent for another fifteen minutes—a passage of time that seemed like hours to the waiting gunners. Finally at about 5:40, with the two fleets nearly parallel to one another and about five thousand yards apart (two and a half nautical miles), Dewey turned to the *Olympia*'s captain and said laconically: "You may fire when ready, Gridley." Gridley passed the order, and the eight-inch guns of the *Olympia*'s forward turret spoke. Immediately the guns on every U.S. ship opened as well. A witness on the *Olympia* recalled that the Americans poured out "such a rapid hail of projectiles" that it seemed to him that "the Spanish ships staggered under the shock." Down below in the *Olympia*'s engine room, the stokers were aware that the battle had been joined at last. "We could tell when our guns opened fire by the way the ship shook," recalled stoker Charles H.

Twitchell. "We could scarcely stand on our feet, the vibration was so great. ... The ship shook so fearfully that the soot and cinders poured down on us in clouds."[48]

Like the battles on Lake Erie and at Hampton Roads, the Battle of Manila Bay was a gun duel. Neither mines nor torpedoes played any important role in the fight, nor did any of the opposing warships get close enough to ram one another. Early in the battle, two small vessels came out from behind the main Spanish battle line, and one of them steamed toward the *Olympia* with apparent hostile intent. The Americans concluded that it was a torpedo boat bent on a suicide mission. A hailstorm of American shells sank it, and the other vessel turned back and ran itself aground near Sangley Point.* Except for that, both sides relied exclusively on gunfire. The American ships cruised slowly past the Spanish battle line, the guns of the port side battery firing as fast as the gunners could load them, both sides firing at will.

When the entire fleet had passed, Dewey ordered the *Olympia* to make a 180-degree turn to port and retrace the same course back again, this time a little closer to the target and with the starboard batteries firing. His plan was to run back and forth in a figure-eight pattern in front of the Spanish fleet, moving closer at each pass and firing alternately from the port and starboard batteries until the Spanish surrendered or were destroyed. The noise was tremendous, and visibility was soon significantly limited due to the clouds of smoke that roiled up from the opposing battle lines. Both sides were using black powder, which generated great clouds of white smoke. That, mingled with the black smoke from the funnels of the American ships and the mist of the morning fog, enshrouded the scene of battle with a smoglike haze. From a range of nearly two miles, it was hard to tell what effect, if any, the guns were having. Near misses sent geysers of water onto the decks of the American vessels, overhead wires and signal halyards

---

* After the battle, a British businessman claimed ownership of the wreck of the small boat that beached itself near Sangley Point and insisted that it had merely been trying to get out of the way of the fighting by running to Manila. Most Americans, however, continued to insist that it, or its consort, or both had been Spanish torpedo boats.

were sheared, and a few shells actually struck the American ships, though none of them found a vital target.[49]

For the most part, the Spanish remained anchored in their stationary battle line. At one point, Montojo's flagship, the *Reina Cristina*, made a short-lived effort to come out and attack the Americans, more, perhaps, for the sake of honor than because it promised any tactical advantage. But as soon as the *Reina Cristina* moved from its anchorage, it became the target of every gun in the American squadron and was battered by a number of hits, including one from an eight-inch shell that tore through the vessel bow to stern, killing a score of men and wrecking the ship's steering gear. Afire in two places, the *Cristina* ran aground off Sangley Point, and Montojo shifted his flag to the *Isla de Cuba*.

Showing no concern for the scarcity of ammunition, the American gunners loaded and fired as fast as they could. The routine of firing the big

A contemporary drawing of the Battle of Manila Bay with Dewey's *Olympia* heading a column of American warships. It is followed by (in order) the *Baltimore, Boston, Raleigh, Concord,* and *Petrel.* Compare this depiction with the image of the French and British ships in the Battle of the Capes in the Prologue (p. 13). Though the technology is significantly different, both battles featured the traditional line-ahead formation. (*Harper's New Monthly Magazine,* December 1898)

naval guns had changed a bit in the three and a half decades since Hampton Roads. One change was that the guns were now loaded at the breech rather than at the muzzle. After each round, it was the responsibility of the gun captain to unlock and throw open the breech block. He then stood aside while others washed off "the powder residue from breech block and the bore" and shoved another round of shell and powder into the chamber. The second captain then closed and locked the breech "with a heavy clang," put in a new primer, and reported the gun ready. But at this point, the routine reverted to the time-honored practice of navies past. As a contemporary noted, "each gun was loaded and fired independently," and it was up to each gun captain to select a target, determine the range, aim, and fire his weapon.

As in the Age of Sail, the gun captains at Manila Bay leaned over the gun barrel, sighting with the naked eye. The difference was that now they sighted on a target that was as much as two miles or more away. Determining the range to the target was a matter of sighting on cross bearings while glancing at a chart. Though the target was motionless, the U.S. ships were under way, and as a result each gun captain had to wait for the target to pass across his line of vision. At the same time, the American ships were also rising and falling as they responded to the gentle swell in the bay, and the target therefore swam before the gunner's eyes, moving up and down as well as right to left. As each gun captain watched and waited for the right moment, he called out a series of orders to the men of the gun crew, who trained the gun to the right or left using a series of hand wheels connected to gears. "Right!" he would call out as the target moved across his line of sight, then perhaps as the result of a slight shift in the helm of his own vessel, he would shout, "Left!" Finally, when "the line of sight strikes the target," the gun captain would jump aside and yank the lock string in his hand. At once there was "a thunderous crash" and a great "stifling cloud of smoke," and the gun's recoil sent it flying backward "as if it were a projectile itself." But thanks to a hydraulic cylinder, it quickly slowed and stopped, and the whole process started over again as the gun captain flung open the breech block to receive the next round.[50]

It is not surprising that American marksmanship was terrible.* One American officer admitted candidly that "in the early part of the action, our firing was wild." Lacking any more effective way to determine the range or aim the guns except by line of sight, hitting a target at five thousand yards was more a matter of luck than skill. The fact was that the range of the naval guns had outstripped the ability of the gunners to put their ordnance on target. On Lake Erie, and especially at Hampton Roads, the gunners had fired into targets so close they could hardly miss, even with smooth-bore iron cannon. On Manila Bay, the rifled steel guns dramatically increased the range, but without any way to coordinate the fire or put the guns on target, most of the shots flew high or wide. Moreover, firing by ricochet, skipping the shells across the surface of the water as the ironclads had done at Hampton Roads, was no longer practical; a gunnery officer on the *Olympia* noted that although direct hits were difficult, "ricochet effects were worthless." He recalled a sense of "exasperation" as he noted "a large percentage of misses from our well-aimed guns."[51]

It was hot work—literally as well as figuratively. The men at the guns had stripped off their shirts even before the action had begun, and they fought now with their heads bound up in water-soaked towels. Those who served in the steel-jacketed gun turrets, where the air was stagnant and the heat all but unbearable, stripped to their undershorts, a few keeping on only their shoes to prevent their feet from burning on the hot deckplate. Down below in the engine room, where the temperature neared two hundred degrees, it was so "unbearably fierce at times," one stoker recalled, that "our hands and wrists would seem on fire, and we had to plunge them in water." The oppressive conditions did not stifle enthusiasm. On the *Raleigh*, a junior officer went down into the fireroom to check on the stokers and found the men singing "There'll Be a Hot Time in the Old Town Tonight"

---

* Postwar analysis showed just how awful American marksmanship was. Out of 9,500 shells fired by ships of the American squadron, only 123 of them actually hit a Spanish vessel, an efficiency of about 1.3 percent. The best record was achieved by the largest guns. Of 405 shells fired by the eight-inch rifles on the three big American cruisers, 16 of them (nearly 4 percent) found their target. Spanish marksmanship, however, was even worse.

as they worked. On the *Olympia*, however, three of the stokers passed out from the heat and had to be hoisted unconscious up to the deck.[52]

After the third pass, the Americans had come to within two thousand yards (one nautical mile) of the Spanish battle line. From this range, the American guns should have been doing serious damage, and in fact they were. But that was not immediately evident to the knot of senior officers watching from the bridge of the *Olympia*. As one of them reported later, "At that distance in a smooth sea, we ought to have made a large percentage of hits; yet, so far as we could judge, we had not sensibly crippled the foe."[53]

Though Dewey's stoic expression never changed, he was growing increasingly worried. If the Spanish fleet remained intact after the Americans fired off all their ammunition, it would not matter if his own ships remained substantially unhurt; he would have to abandon the contest and withdraw. The *Olympia* had been hit five times already, one shell striking the hull just below the bridge where Dewey was standing, though by fate or by chance none of those shells had done any serious damage. But Dewey did not know the condition of the other vessels in the American squadron. As far as he knew, they had suffered grievous casualties, and the Spanish ships continued to fire defiantly. One American officer noted that "the Spanish ensigns still flew and their broadsides still thundered." An American sailor wrote simply that "they fought

Coal heavers in the *Olympia*'s fire room stoke the engines during the battle in a drawing labeled "The Unseen Heroes on a War Ship." On the *Raleigh*, an officer checking on the stokers during the battle found them singing "There'll Be a Hot Time in the Old Town Tonight" as they worked. (Adelbert Dewey, *Life and Letters of Admiral Dewey*)

like beasts at bay." By the time the American ships began their fifth pass, just after 7:00 A.M., there were still "no visible signs of the execution wrought by our guns."[54]

Then at 7:35, after two hours of battle, Gridley approached Dewey with a startling piece of information. He had just been informed that the *Olympia* had only fifteen rounds of five-inch ammunition left. Fifteen rounds could be fired away in a matter of minutes. The *Olympia* would still have her four big guns, but without the five-inch guns, its rate of fire would fall off dramatically. And if the five-inch ammunition was so badly depleted, how long before the eight-inch ammunition began to run out? This was the scenario Dewey had feared most. His ships would be out of ammunition, with no way of getting any more, in the face of a still-defiant

This "Kodak snap" of Dewey on the bridge of the *Olympia* during the Battle of Manila Bay captures his stoic demeanor. An officer on the bridge commented on Dewey's "grave vigilance of expression" during the fight. (Murat Halstead, *Life and Achievements of Admiral Dewey*)

Spanish fleet possessed of unlimited quantities of ammunition and ready for battle. He would be helpless. "It was a most anxious moment for me," he later recalled. "So far as I could see, the Spanish squadron was as intact as ours. I had reason to believe that their supply [of ammunition] was as ample as ours was limited." He saw no option but to call off the fight and withdraw out of range in order to redistribute ammunition among the ships and perhaps reassess the situation. He ordered the fleet to "withdraw from action."[55]

The *Olympia* turned away from the roiling smoke and led the American squadron off toward the center of the bay. Though he retained his characteristic impassive expression, his mood was dark. A volunteer officer on the bridge wrote later: "I do not exaggerate in the least when I say that as we hauled off into the bay, the gloom on the bridge of the *Olympia* was thicker than a London fog in November." Ironically, while the mood on the bridge reflected disappointment and despondency, the men at the guns were upbeat and optimistic. The embedded journalist, Acting Lieutenant Joseph Stickney, while making the rounds of the ship, was stopped frequently by the smoke-blackened gunners, who wanted to know why they were breaking off the action. Not wanting to depress their obviously high morale, he told them that "we were merely hauling off for breakfast." When Stickney returned to the bridge and reported what he had said to Dewey, the commodore replied that he could give any reason he wanted except the real one.[56]

But Dewey's dark mood soon improved. Once the fleet had hauled off and some of the battle smoke lifted, it became evident that the Spanish fleet had been considerably damaged after all. He could see flames rising from both of the Spanish cruisers, and occasional muffled explosions aboard both ships indicated that they had been badly hurt, perhaps fatally so. Then Dewey got even better news. It turned out that the previous report about the scarcity of ammunition had been in error. It was not that there were only fifteen rounds left; rather, only fifteen rounds had been expended! There was plenty of ammunition left, more than enough to continue the battle and finish off the Spanish fleet. Dewey needn't have broken off the battle at all, for he was clearly winning. Having done so, however, he now issued the order for the crews to go to breakfast and for commanding officers to report their casualties. He still did not know how much damage his own squadron had suffered.[57]

As the American captains came aboard, one by one, they reported the absence of any casualties. Most of them offered this information diffidently, even apologetically. Raised in the age of wooden ships and iron men, they had become accustomed to the notion that the heroism of a ship's crew could be measured by its butcher's bill of killed and wounded. Perry's victory on Lake Erie had been particularly glorious in part because the casualties had been so heavy. Now each of Dewey's captains reported that they had suffered no fatalities—none at all—and no serious damage to their ships. The ship that had suffered the most damage was the *Baltimore*. Montojo had incorrectly identified her as a battleship and had ordered his gunners to concentrate on her. In consequence she had been hit six times, though not seriously. Indeed, the hand of Providence seemed to have guided the flight of some of the shells. In one case, a five-inch armor-piercing shell had passed through two groups of sailors on the *Baltimore* without hitting any of them, struck a steel beam, and was deflected upward through a hatch cover, hitting the recoil cylinder of the port six-inch gun. Then it fell to the deck, where it spun like a top before it finally skittered over the side, all without exploding. The *Boston* had been hit four times, and one 6.2-inch shell had exploded in the officers' wardroom, but since the room had been unoccupied at the time, there had been no injuries.[58]

It was all right, then. The ships of the American squadron were uninjured, there was plenty of ammunition on hand, and the Spanish fleet was seriously damaged. As soon as the men had a chance to grab something to eat, Dewey could renew the action and finish the job. The sailors munched away happily, though many of them passed up the opportunity to eat in order to grab a few moments of sleep. The breakfast laid out by the stewards in a corner of the officers' wardroom went largely untouched. One reason, perhaps, was that the sardines, canned beef, and hardtack lay on the same table as the surgeon's knives, saws, and probes, since the wardroom served as the surgeon's cockpit during battle stations. All this time, fires continued to burn out of control on the Spanish ships, and even from a dozen miles away, the men on the American vessels could hear "frequent explosions" from deep inside the hulls of their adversaries.[59]

The second round of fighting began at 11:15. By now there was no doubt left about the outcome. The *Baltimore* led the American battle line, which closed to within less than two thousand yards to finish off the badly crippled Spanish vessels, all but a few of which had retired behind Sangley Point. Spanish fire was slow, irregular, and inaccurate, and the few vessels still able to resist at all fired only about a dozen shells while being pounded by the American warships.

If American casualties were minimal, Spanish casualties were horrific. The grounded *Reina Cristina* was hit seventy times, and out of a complement of 493 men, some 330 were either dead or missing and another 90 had been wounded—a casualty rate of over 80 percent. The unarmored *Castilla*, her wooden hull still painted peacetime white, burned out of control. The *Don Antonio de Ulloa* continued to fight until she sank at her moorings, colors still flying. The shore batteries, too, were soon silenced, and white flags were raised above their parapets. By noon it was all over: white flags flew above the batteries ashore, and virtually all the Spanish vessels were on fire or sinking.[60]

Dewey sent the *Petrel* into Bacoor Bay to secure the prizes. The *Petrel* was the only American vessel with a shallow enough draft to enter the bay, and there were a few anxious moments as the little gunboat ran into the bay unsupported. Her commander, Lieutenant Edward M. Hughes, sent the ship's two whaleboats inshore to round up the few undamaged small boats as prizes and set fire to the abandoned hulks that were not already burning. There was no resistance, and Hughes signaled the main fleet: "The enemy has surrendered."[61]

After that, the *Olympia, Baltimore,* and *Raleigh* steamed slowly northward for Manila, where the American ships dropped anchor off the city as if they were making a routine port visit. The heavy guns of the city's battery, which had kept up a desultory fire all morning, were now silent. Dewey dropped anchor well inside their effective range and sent Consul O. F. Williams ashore to inform the Spanish governor general that any fire

The wreckage of the Spanish cruiser *Reina Christina* after the battle. The Spanish fleet was utterly wrecked during the fight, and several ships went down with their guns firing and flags still flying. (Photograph by Frank R. Roberson in Murat Halstead, *Life and Achievements of Admiral Dewey*)

against American vessels from those guns would compel Dewey to bombard the city. The governor agreed at once to a cease-fire.[62]

Once it was evident that the shooting was over, curious civilians began to gather along the waterfront to stare at the American warships that had humbled their navy. As the sun set and the late afternoon breezes cooled the tropical air, the crowd grew. The *Olympia*'s band assembled on the ship's foredeck and began to play. A witness recalled that "the ramparts were filled with a gaily dressed throng eagerly listening to the strains of 'La Paloma' and other Spanish airs which were being played for their benefit." As the music wafted over the city, the Spanish colonel who commanded the city's batteries, denied by the governor's orders a chance to fire his guns in defense of the city, locked the door to his office and shot himself in the head.[63]

The American victory was complete. Indeed, it was the most complete naval victory in the history of the nation, more complete even than Perry's on Lake Erie eighty-five years earlier. This time Dewey had not only destroyed the enemy fleet but suffered virtually no casualties in doing so, aside from a few men lightly wounded on the *Baltimore*. And like Perry, Dewey was eager to communicate the news of his victory. He asked the Spanish if he could use the submarine telegraph cable from Manila to Hong Kong to report the outcome of the battle. Understandably, perhaps, the Spanish refused. Dewey therefore ordered the *Zafiro* to drag the bottom of the bay, find the telegraph cable, and cut it, thus isolating Manila from the outside world. At the same time, perhaps in unconscious imitation of Perry's message to William Henry Harrison, he penned a quick note to Secretary Long that he had "engaged the enemy and destroyed the following vessels," naming the eleven ships sunk in the action. He was pleased to be able to add: "The squadron is uninjured. Few men slightly wounded." The only note of concern was his urgent request to "send immediately from San Francisco [a] fast steamer with ammunition." He entrusted the note to the captain of the *McCulloch*, who steamed off to Hong Kong, from where it could be communicated to Washington. The *McCulloch* returned six days later with the news that Dewey had been promoted to the rank of rear admiral.[64]

As the master of Manila Bay, Dewey was also the master of Manila itself, though the Spanish flag continued to fly over the walled city. But having destroyed the Spanish fleet and gained control of the bay, what was he to do next? The justification for attacking the Spanish fleet in Manila Bay in the first place had been to fulfill the Mahanian doctrine that a nation's first objective in war was to seize command of the sea by defeating its opponent's main battle fleet. Montojo's little squadron was not Spain's main battle fleet, but as long as it existed, it posed at least a theoretical threat to American naval supremacy. Having now accomplished his mission, Dewey might have decided simply to steam away, though where he might go was problematic, for neutral ports were still closed to him as long as the war lasted. Months later, in the midst of a national debate about the Philippines and their future, one witness claimed to have overheard President McKinley mutter: "If Dewey had just sailed away when he smashed that Spanish fleet, what a lot of trouble he would have saved us." That McKinley ever uttered such words is doubtful. Still, the comment suggests that the most important thing about Dewey's victory was not that it had demolished a small Spanish squadron and thereby secured a kind of theoretical American command of the sea, but that it opened the door for a reconsideration of America's role in the Far East.[65]

George Dewey in the uniform of a full admiral. Dewey's decisions in the wake of his victory in Manila Bay had far-reaching consequences. (U.S. Navy)

Though this was an issue of the greatest national significance, it did not become a matter of national debate until after many of the critical decisions had already been made. The first was Dewey's decision to remain in Manila Bay after the battle and effectively blockade the city. His decision was partly pragmatic; since the United States and Spain were still at war and neutral ports were still closed to him, there was literally no place for him to go. But in addition to that, Dewey believed that at some level his victory had made him, and by extension the United States, responsible for the Philippines, or at least for the security of Manila Bay. In his autobiography, he noted that his first thoughts after the battle were to ensure that "American supremacy and military discipline must take the place of chaos." He therefore sent parties ashore to assume control of the Cavite Navy Yard; he assigned all foreign ships to designated anchorages in the bay; and although he allowed warships of other powers to enter the bay (ostensibly to check on the well being of their foreign nationals in the city), he made it clear that they did so at his sufferance. He even sent to Washington for "one or two battleships" to intimidate any foreign government that might be tempted to take advantage of the volatile environment to expand its own interests. And most importantly, he requested the dispatch of an army of occupation.[66]

Dewey's request for an occupying force was crucial, for it fundamentally changed the nature of his original mission. Moreover, his request seems to have sprung not from any real or perceived chaos in Manila itself but from Dewey's own notion that, having conquered Manila, the United States was somehow entitled to possess it. Commander Nathan Sargent, who later wrote the semiofficial version of the campaign, wrote that his commander's "fortunate isolation" in Manila Bay was a blessing because it "forced the Navy Department to leave matters to his discretion." Reflecting the operational commander's traditional view of the relationship between political and military authority, Sargent asserted that "governments rarely recognize the fact that their agents at a distance, if at all worthy of confidence, are infinitely better capable of forming correct judgments in emergencies than the home authorities probably thousands of miles away; yet the temptation to interfere is ever strong and can rarely be resisted." Whatever the merits of such a view, there was no direct cable connection to Washington, and so it was left to Dewey to make the initial decisions about the future status of the Philippines in general and Manila Bay in particular, and among them was his decision to send for an army of occupation. Once that decision was made, much of what followed appears as inevitable.[67]

Of course, McKinley did not have to accede to Dewey's request. The president later claimed that "when the Philippines dropped into our laps, I confess I did not know what to do with them." He even claimed that he had no idea where they were. "I could not have told where those darned islands were within 2000 miles," he wrote. When news of Dewey's victory arrived, he had to look up the location on a globe. But once he received Dewey's request for an army of occupation, it seemed to him, as it did to Dewey, that the United States bore some responsibility to fill the power vacuum that Dewey's victory had created. Without a great deal of thought about the long-term political consequences, the president acceded to Dewey's request and ordered four thousand soldiers to Manila under the command of Brigadier General Wesley Merritt.[68]

While these decisions were being made, news arrived in Washington of a second spectacular naval victory over the Spanish. On July 3, U.S. naval forces virtually annihilated Spain's Atlantic Fleet off Santiago de Cuba. In even less time than it had taken Dewey to destroy Montojo's squadron in Manila Bay, the combined forces of Rear Admiral William T. Sampson and Rear Admiral Winfield Scott Schley destroyed all six ships of Admiral Pascual Cervera's fleet as they attempted to escape the Bay of Santiago, where they had been trapped. Besides losing four cruisers and two destroyers, the Spanish also lost 300 men killed, 150 wounded, and more than 1,800 taken prisoner, including Cervera himself; American casualties totaled a single man killed and another wounded. Spain still had the ships of its Home Squadron, which were even then steaming eastward across the Mediterranean for the Suez Canal, presumably en route to the Philippines. But the news of Cervera's disaster led Spain's leaders to recall them and accept the inevitable. Two weeks later, on July 18, they asked for a cease-fire.[69]

That same day, the first elements of an American army of occupation went ashore south of Manila. Just as the Spanish request for an armistice marked a change in the course of the war, the arrival of American troops in the Philippines dramatically changed the political circumstances in those islands. If it was a stretch to explain Dewey's attack on the Spanish fleet in Manila Bay as an essential part of a war to liberate Cuba, it was even more difficult to explain why an American army of occupation in Manila had anything at all to do with the liberation of Cuba. The arrival of American ground troops was questioned not only by the Spanish but also by a twenty-nine-year-old Filipino named Emilio Aguinaldo, who had arrived at the Cavite Navy Yard two months earlier on board an American steamer from Singapore. Before the outbreak of the war, Aguinaldo had led a resistance movement in the Philippines known as the Katipunan. Though he liked to present himself as a freedom fighter in the mold of George Washington, he was in fact an individual with a keen eye for the main chance. In 1897 he had accepted a substantial monetary payment from the Spanish to go into exile. He later claimed that he had accepted the offer in return for Spanish promises of reform, but his enemies asserted that he simply took a bribe. Now he returned to the Philippines with the expectation of filling the vacuum of authority created by Dewey's victory.[70]

Almost at once Aguinaldo sought an audience with Dewey. There is no record of their conversation, and different versions emerged over time, but for the moment they agreed to cooperate in the effort to drive the Spanish from Manila, each very likely believing that he was using the other. Dewey agreed to supply Aguinaldo with arms, and Aguinaldo agreed to cooperate in the American siege of the city. Within days, however, Aguinaldo declared himself ruler of the Philippines, and on June 23 he proclaimed the establishment of the "First Republic of the Philippines" and issued a call for local elections. A week later, the first elements of an American army of occupation arrived. Now, instead of a vacuum of authority, there were two authorities—three, if one counted the Spanish, whose days were clearly numbered.[71]

Dewey's decision to accept and even encourage the cooperation of Aguinaldo's irregulars in the siege of Manila gave the Filipino nationalist a certain legitimacy. Aguinaldo himself later claimed that Dewey had at least implied that in exchange for this help, the United States would recognize Philippine independence. It is unlikely that Dewey made any such pledge, but it is also easy to see how Aguinaldo might have assumed it. In any case, Aguinaldo's troops virtually surrounded Manila, and when Merritt's soldiers arrived, the erstwhile allies cooperated to the extent of agreeing upon zones of responsibility.

As American soldiers and Filipino nationalists closed in on Manila, the Spanish in the city became terrified that Aguinaldo's natives would break in and pillage the city. Like Hull at Detroit in 1812, they feared a massacre by their foe's undisciplined allies more than they feared the ignominy of surrender. In secret negotiations with the Americans, they agreed to a kind of charade in which the Americans would launch a realistic-looking assault that would allow the city's defenders to surrender to them with their honor intact. The Spanish agreed to this only on the condition that the Americans agreed to keep Aguinaldo's forces outside the walls, a condition the Americans accepted. This charade was carried out in the second week of May, and the city "fell" to the Americans. Soon afterward news arrived that an armistice ending the war had been signed.[72]

That same day Dewey wired Washington for a clarification of American policy. Now that Manila was in American hands, how should the United States deal with the nationalists who had claimed their independence? The answer came back four days later in a cablegram from the War Department declaring that "insurgents and all others must recognize the military occupation and authority of the United States."[73]

—

Spain's request for an armistice was an admission of defeat. National pride had prevented the Spanish from surrendering to American demands without a fight, but the destruction of both her Pacific and Atlantic fleets compelled her to ask the French government to act as intermediary in arranging a cease-fire. Spanish authorities knew that it meant the loss of Cuba—and Puerto Rico, too, since the Americans made that a condition of a cease-fire. But the armistice agreement left the future of the Philippines unresolved. The Americans would continue to occupy Manila during the treaty negotiations in Paris in which the political future of the Philippines would be decided.

That fact triggered a national debate in America about what role, if any, the United States should play in the future of the Philippine archipelago. Naval authorities wanted an American port facility in the islands, preferably at Subic Bay, where Montojo had hoped in vain to conduct his defense of the islands. Possession of such a port would give the U.S. Navy the ability to operate in the Far East without depending on the hospitality of either the Japanese or the British. Some, such as Theodore Roosevelt, who had resigned his position as assistant secretary of the Navy to serve as the lieutenant colonel of a cavalry regiment in Cuba, believed the United States had a right to take the entire archipelago by right of conquest. Roosevelt's former boss, Secretary Long, eventually came to agree that the United States should take possession of the Philippines, but for very different reasons. "To abandon the Philippine Islands," he wrote in his diary, "is to return them to Spain," a country that had already demonstrated its incapacity for just stewardship by its tyrannical behavior in Cuba. Long's conclusion was that "our whole affair should be to Americanize and civilize them [the Filipinos] by the introduction of American institutions."[74]

Other Americans recoiled at the idea that their country, founded on the principle of self-government, should embrace imperialism. Wasn't colonialism exactly what the Founding Fathers had rebelled against? Hadn't the United States gone to war in the first place to relieve Cuba of the burden of colonialism? Was the United States now simply to replace Spain as the colonial master of the Philippines? Eventually those who found American imperialism distasteful rallied around William Jennings Bryan, the Democratic presidential nominee in 1900, who made it the centerpiece of his campaign.

In Paris, the U.S. claim to the Philippines derived from a variety of pressures. The Navy continued to press for a coaling station and naval base. But taking only part of the Philippines struck many as awkward. If the United States took only Subic Bay, or even all of Luzon, what was to be done with the rest of the archipelago? Most Americans agreed with Secretary Long that returning it to Spain was unacceptable. Both Japan and Germany informally expressed a willingness to step in and occupy the islands, but the United States viewed both of those nations as rivals in the Pacific. A few suggested that the Philippines, like Cuba, should become independent, though most Americans regarded the Filipinos as "not ready" for independence. After agonizing over these various options, McKinley finally decided that the only responsible position for the United States was to assume responsibility for the entire archipelago in the name of "duty and humanity." Indeed, the president suggested that American annexation of the Philippines was somehow fated, an inevitable outcome of circumstances that were beyond his control. "The march of events rules and overrules human action," he wrote. The war had brought "new duties and responsibilities" to the country, and it was time for the United States to step up and accept those responsibilities "as becomes a great nation."[75]

Having virtually no bargaining position left, Spain reluctantly but necessarily acceded to the American demands, accepting a $20 million payment as a balm for the loss of its overseas empire. The treaty was signed in November 1898, and although some Americans continued to argue that imperialism was inappropriate for a democracy, Bryan's defeat at the polls two years later by an even wider margin than in 1896 effectively ended the anti-imperialist movement.

The fighting in the Philippines, however, was not over. Only days after the American occupation of Manila, Aguinaldo's army began erecting fortifications facing the city. General Merritt negotiated a temporary truce in exchange for vague promises of American "beneficence." But Merritt soon left to take part in the negotiations in Paris and was replaced in command by Brigadier General Elwell S. Otis.* In December McKinley ordered Otis to carry out "the actual occupation and administration of the entire group of the Philippine Islands," in order to achieve what the president called the "benevolent assimilation" of the archipelago, "substituting the mild sway of justice and right for arbitrary rule." Aguinaldo recognized at once that assimilation, however benevolent, left no room for him, and the result was that open warfare broke out on February 4, 1899, between the U.S. troops in the Philippines and Aguinaldo's ragtag army of nationalists.[76]

While theoretically sympathetic to the principle of self-government, McKinley was disinclined to grant it to a people who resisted America's helping hand. To him, and to most Americans, Aguinaldo was not George Washington, he was Geronimo. "It is not a good time for the liberator to submit important questions concerning liberty and government to the liberated," McKinley declared, "while they are engaged in shooting down their rescuers." For the next three years, therefore, the United States fought a bloody and increasingly vicious war to suppress the Philippine independence movement and secure its outpost in the Far East.[77]

It was an ugly little war, one in which the putative rules of combat gradually gave way before the realities of fighting an elusive enemy that depended in part on guerilla tactics. For all the outrage Americans had felt toward General Weyler ("the Butcher") in Cuba, American troops in the Philippines soon adopted tactics that were nearly identical. Moreover, given the prevailing racist character of American society in that era of Jim

---

* Otis was subsequently replaced by Brigadier General Arthur MacArthur, who had won a Medal of Honor on Missionary Ridge in the Civil War and was the father of Douglas MacArthur. It was Arthur MacArthur who presided over much of the subsequent fighting with the Filipino insurrectionists.

U.S. Army soldiers battle Filipino *insurrectos* outside Manila. The long and bloody war of pacification in the Philippines lasted far longer, and claimed far more lives, than the war against the Spanish. (Photograph by Frank R. Roberson in Murat Halstead, *Life and Achievements of Admiral Dewey*)

Crow, it is not surprising that American soldiers in the Philippines routinely referred to their darker-skinned opponents as "niggers" and seldom accorded them the rights of a belligerent.* Indeed, the United States prosecuted the war with a thoroughness and vehemence that often outstripped Weyler's. In southern Luzon, the United States gathered the loyal population into concentration camps (called "zones of protection"), where thousands died of disease, and U.S. forces conducted lengthy sweeps through the countryside that denuded whole islands of both crops and villages. On the island of Samar, Major W. L. T. Waller of the Marines sought to turn the island into a "howling wilderness" and ordered his men to regard every male over ten years old as an enemy combatant.[78]

News of such tactics did not go unnoticed in the United States. The *Philadelphia Ledger* noted the irony that "the same policy" pursued by

---

* During the insurrection, Americans also began to refer to the Filipino opponents as "gooks." Subsequently U.S. forces applied that term to the rebels in Nicaragua, to Pacific islanders in World War II, and to Korean and Vietnamese soldiers in those wars.

Weyler in Cuba was now "adopted and pursued as the policy of the United States." The less restrained *New York Evening Journal* expressed its outrage at Waller's conduct on Samar with a headline that shouted: "Kill All: Major Waller Ordered to Massacre the Filipinos." As Max Boot has noted, "the Philippine War was a rude awakening for those Americans who imagined their country to be morally superior to the sordid Europeans."[79]

The U.S. Navy played a crucial role in the war, ferrying troops from island to island, interdicting supplies of the rebel bands (mainly rice boats), and intercepting arms shipments. Inevitably in this guerilla war, U.S. Navy vessels sometimes opened fire on the wrong target. In September 1901 a pro-American rally brought a thousand or more Filipinos to a public meeting. The commanding officer of the U.S. gunboat *Arayat*, unaware of the planned event, opened fire on the crowd.[80]

Though such events made pacification more difficult, U.S. forces eventually triumphed not only by overwhelming the Filipinos with firepower but also by engaging in what later generations would call "nation building"—constructing roads, schools, and hospitals. It was, as Brian Linn has pointed out, a different kind of war for Americans, one in which "army officers would have to devote at least as much attention to civic projects, public works, government, and education as they would to military operations." Though no one knew it at the time, it was a template for many of America's twentieth-century—and twenty-first-century—wars.[81]

The Philippine War (or Philippine Insurrection, as it is often labeled) lasted over three years, cost over forty-two hundred American deaths (more than eleven times the number killed in the war with Spain), and ended officially on July 4, 1902, though sporadic resistance continued for decades, and indeed never ended completely.

—

The assertion that Dewey's victory at Manila Bay in 1898 marked a turning point in American history is hardly novel. To some it was a "metamorphosis" or "rite of passage." Others noted that it plunged America "into the maelstrom of world politics," even "into the role of superpower and conqueror." Redfield Proctor, the Vermont senator who had urged Dewey's appointment, declared, "It is almost a creation or a new birth." Observers in Europe also noted its significance. Writing in the *Frankfurter Zeitung*, a German editorialized that Dewey's victory marked "a new epoch in history, not only for the United States, but likewise for Europe," since in consequence "the United States now reaches beyond the American continent, and claims its share in the conduct of the world's affairs." More than a few in that racist age saw it as a victory of Anglo-Saxon superiority over the weaker races of the world. Henry Cabot Lodge declared confidently that the American triumph marked the final victory of Englishmen, Dutchmen, and their American descendants over the ruins of the empire of Philip II. To him, there was a direct historical link between the defeat of the Spanish Armada in 1588 and Dewey's victory in 1898. Spain collapsed, in Lodge's worldview, because it was "unfit" and "for the unfit among nations there is no pity." That same year, Rudyard Kipling published his poetic plea to America to take up "the white man's burden" by bringing the enlightenment of Western values to the darker races.[82]

Even those Americans who questioned such explanations saw in Dewey's victory a new opportunity for America to reassert its role as a "city on a hill"—a model for the less enlightened. If democracy by example was not enough, Americans now accepted the notion that it was justifiable to use force to extend the blessings of democracy to others. McKinley himself defended the American occupation of the Philippines as an altruistic act, declaring that in later years, the Filipinos would "bless the American republic because it emancipated and redeemed their fatherland." Like a father who knows best, McKinley predicted, in essence, "You'll thank us later."[83]

The final peace treaty negotiated in Paris gave the United States not only the Philippines and Puerto Rico but also Guam in the Ladrones (Marianas) and tiny Wake Island, halfway between Guam and Midway (which was also a U.S. possession, having been acquired by purchase in 1867). Separately but simultaneously, the United States decided to annex the Kingdom of Hawaii. McKinley had submitted a treaty for Hawaiian annexation before the war, but he had not pushed it in Congress. It was the war that made annexation a matter of urgency. Three days after Dewey's victory, a new annexation bill was introduced in the House. McKinley came out openly and enthusiastically for it in June, and it passed both houses of Congress within weeks by more than a two-to-one margin.[84]

No longer would U.S. Navy forces in the Far East have to operate seven thousand miles from a friendly port. From Hawaii to Midway, Wake, Guam, and finally the Philippines, the United States now possessed a string of islands that stretched across the Pacific Ocean like beads on a string—or, more appropriately perhaps, like stepping stones—to support America's commercial and naval presence in the Far East. Of course, those possessions brought new responsibilities as well as new opportunities. American occupation of the Philippines extended the nation's territorial responsibilities some seven thousand miles westward. It not only gave the United States a presence in the Far East, it made the United States a Pacific power.

—

The war liberated Cuba from Spain, but that war-torn island became "independent" only in the most nominal sense. Though the Teller Amendment to the declaration of war had prohibited the United States from acquiring Cuba for itself, another amendment—the 1901 Platt Amendment, which was inserted into the Cuban constitution—gave the United States the right and the responsibility to intervene in Cuba whenever, in the view of the American government, it was appropriate to do so. The initial U.S. occupation of Cuba ended in 1902, but American forces continued to intervene periodically. In 1906 an American "army of pacification" arrived to suppress another rebellion, and it remained there until 1909. Other interventions occurred with some regularity until the introduction of Franklin Roosevelt's Good Neighbor Policy in 1934.

In addition to the acquisition of an overseas "empire," another consequence of the astonishing success of the U.S. Navy in the Spanish-American War was that it prompted a dramatic increase in the size of the fleet. On December 7, 1900, a month after McKinley's reelection victory at the polls, the government invited bids from contractors for the construction of five new battleships and six new armored cruisers, a force that would more than double the size of the Navy. All of the new ships would be significantly larger than the ships of the existing fleet. It was, as a contemporary noted proudly, "the largest single addition to our armored ships ever advertised for at one time."[85]

McKinley never lived to see it. He was shaking hands in a receiving line in Buffalo, New York, in September 1901 when an anarchist named Leon Czolgosz stepped forward and fired two shots into his chest. The mortally wounded president lingered for over a week before he died, leaving the office to his new vice president, Theodore Roosevelt, who presided over the subsequent naval expansion and who dispatched the so-called Great White Fleet on its global circumnavigation five years later.

As for Dewey, his great popularity after the victory in Manila Bay led to a short-lived "Dewey for president" boom. But the stoic and phlegmatic naval officer made a poor candidate, and the boomlet soon faded. Dewey lived out the rest of his professional career as chairman of the prestigious but only modestly influential General Board of the Navy. In the end, Dewey's place in history—his fifteen minutes of fame, to employ the modern euphemism—depended on a single event, and the phrase most closely associated with him is the not-quite-heroic command he gave to the *Olympia*'s captain on the morning of May 1: "You may fire when ready, Gridley."

The man to whom those words were addressed, Captain Charles V. Gridley, having lived to participate in a great naval battle, surrendered command of the *Olympia* and started home soon afterward. He never made it. The ill health that had plagued him for months, exacerbated perhaps by the pressure of recent events, claimed his life before he made it as far as Japan.

Montojo returned to Spain to face a court-martial. Accused of dereliction of duty, the wounded veteran argued that his squadron had been defeated not because of any failure on his part or that of his men, but because they were simply overmatched by Dewey's newer and larger force. At Montojo's request, Dewey wrote a lengthy letter acknowledging that Montojo had fought bravely, as befitted the great Spanish Navy, but he stopped short of admitting that the American force had been vastly superior. That, after all, would demean his own accomplishment. It probably didn't matter, because someone needed to take the fall for the humiliation of Spain's once proud navy. Montojo was found guilty and expelled from the service.

Though some scholars have attempted to suggest that American imperialism in the Pacific and the Caribbean was the product of a deliberate conspiracy by industrialists and expansionists who sought to turn the United States into an empire, a more likely explanation is that the Battle of Manila Bay triggered a sequence of events that led all the participants down a road that few had foreseen and for which even fewer were prepared. For most Americans, the rhetoric of 1898 was real; to them liberating Cuba was a noble and unselfish goal. But in the process of achieving it, forces were unleashed that led the United States into an entirely new chapter of its national history. Sympathy for Cuban rebels had led to war; Mahan's theories of naval supremacy had led Dewey to Manila Bay; the destruction of Montojo's fleet had created a vacuum of authority in the Philippines; America's decision to fill that vacuum led to a brutal war of conquest. In the end, the United States emerged from the war as an acknowledged world power. Given America's circumstances, this moment would surely have come sooner or later even if Dewey had never steamed into Manila Bay. But as it happened, his victory there was the milestone event that signaled this turning point in American and world history. The United States was a world power, a status from which there would be no retreat.

The Spanish-American War, and the Battle of Manila Bay in particular, marked not only the advent of an American empire in territorial terms, but also the first manifestation of American efforts to remake the world in accordance with its notion of what constituted proper government. In that respect, it marked a critical redefinition of America's place in the world and an appropriate beginning to what subsequent historians would label "the American century." As the London *Times* put it four weeks after Dewey's victory: "This war must in any event effect a profound change in the whole attitude and policy of the United States. In future America will play a part in the general affairs of the world such as she has never played before."[86]

[PART FOUR]

NAVAL AVIATION
AND WORLD WAR

The Battle of Midway
June 4, 1942

IF DEWEY'S VICTORY IN MANILA BAY SIGNALED AMERICA'S debut as a world power, U.S. participation in the Great War of 1914–18 confirmed it. Shocked by the German policy of unrestricted submarine warfare, the United States entered the war in 1917 just as the original combatants were exhausting themselves. As a result, not only did the United States avoid the massive casualties endured by the other combatants in the bloody fighting on the Western Front from 1914 to 1917, it also tipped the balance of forces at just the right moment to help determine the outcome. American industrial capacity played a significant role by producing the cargo ships, transports, and escorts, in both record time and record numbers, to overcome the German U-boat menace. This might have marked the moment when the United States emerged as a preeminent—even dominant—world power. But it proved to be a false dawn. Americans in 1918 were not yet ready to don the mantle (and the responsibility) of world power, a fact signaled by the Senate's rejection of both the Versailles Treaty and membership in the League of Nations.

During the two decades of peace between the world wars, the United States was only partly successful in remaining detached from international disputes. The United States objected when Japan invaded Manchuria in 1931, but not strenuously. Guided by popular skepticism about overseas entanglements after the anticlimactic results of World War I, the government declared only that it would not recognize the puppet regime that the Japanese established there. Undeterred by such legal niceties, Japan invaded China six years later, in 1937. This time the United States objected more vigorously, especially after the American theater-going public viewed newsreels of Japanese atrocities in China, including the virtual destruction of the city of Nanking, an event known then, and ever since, as "the rape of Nanking." Though U.S. protests grew more pointed through the 1930s, they fell short of specific threats. The United States had fought its war with Spain in 1898 in protest of Spanish misrule in Cuba, and it declared war against Germany in 1917 due in part to what Americans perceived as inhumane conduct by that country, but the notion that the United States should police the bad behavior of other nations was not yet a majority view.

Meanwhile, the Second World War began in Europe. After a six-month "Phony War," the German blitzkrieg swept across Belgium and France in the spring of 1940, completing in a few months what German armies had failed to do in four years during the First World War. Japan's leaders saw opportunity in these circumstances, and soon after the fall of France, the Japanese occupied French Indochina. This time the protest of the United States was more than pro forma. The Franklin Roosevelt administration notified the Japanese that unless they evacuated Indochina and showed a willingness to discuss (at least) their position in China, the United States would halt the sale of oil to Japan.

This was a serious threat, for the United States—at that time a petroleum-exporting country—was Japan's primary source of oil. The American threat exposed Japan's dependence on foreign oil and provoked a national crisis within the government. To the Japanese, the choice seemed to be either to do what the Americans demanded in return for the privilege of buying their oil or to maintain the nation's dignity and sovereignty by finding an alternative source of oil. To the Japanese, this was no choice at all. As it happened, there was another source nearby in the oil-rich islands of the Dutch East Indies. Moreover, the Dutch East Indies—like French Indochina—had become a political orphan since the Netherlands, too, had fallen to the German war machine. Japanese conquest of these islands would go a long way toward making Japan energy-independent.

The problem was that the American Philippines lay directly astride the line of supply and communication between the Dutch East Indies and the Japanese homeland. Though the Americans might not interfere with Japanese tankers carrying the lifeblood of Japanese industry from Java, Borneo, and Sumatra to Japan, the point was that they could. Therefore, to obtain an alternative source of oil and to secure the supply route for that oil, the Japanese would have to control the Philippines—and that meant war with the United States. The logic was irresistible. After a series of fruitless negotiations, the Japanese made the final decision for war in November 1941. They would strike preemptively at the American battleship fleet in Hawaii in accordance with the Mahanian dictum that success in war derived from the destruction of the enemy's main battle fleet.

In general, the Japanese were delighted with the results of their attack; not only was the American battleship fleet virtually destroyed in Pearl Harbor on December 7, 1941, but the attacking Japanese aircraft carriers escaped without even being detected, much less damaged or destroyed. As it happened, however, the Japanese attack had missed an important element of the American order of battle, for by chance the American aircraft carriers were not in port on that historic and infamous December 7. At the time, the Japanese much regretted that they had missed an opportunity to destroy the American carriers as well as the battleships . . . but not as much as they would regret it later.

—

A T DAWN ON MAY 28, 1942, the American aircraft carrier *Yorktown* (hull number CV-5), trailing a ten-mile-long oil slick, limped into Pearl Harbor under its own power after a three-thousand-mile trek across the Pacific. The *Yorktown* was returning from the Battle of the Coral Sea, the first naval engagement in history in which all of the casualties and all of the damage—to both fleets—had been inflicted by carrier-based airplanes rather than by naval gunfire. It was the first naval battle in which the opposing fleets never actually sighted each other. The *Yorktown* had received a near-mortal wound in that battle when a Japanese Val dive-bomber had penetrated the umbrella of American fighter planes overhead to drop a 551-pound semi-armor-piercing bomb onto her wooden flight deck. The bomb had smashed through the deck and exploded deep inside the ship, killing or wounding sixty-six men and starting fires that spread quickly despite the efforts by damage control teams to contain them.[1]

The *Yorktown* had survived, but her consort, the *Lexington* (CV-2), had not. Hit by two torpedoes and three bombs, the *Lexington* suffered a huge secondary internal explosion that compelled her captain to order abandon ship. The loss of the *Lexington* was a heavy blow to the Americans, for it left the United States with only three carriers in the Pacific theater. Indeed, the Japanese thought there were only two, for they believed the damage they had inflicted on the *Yorktown* would also be fatal. Instead, the wounded flattop made it safely back to Pearl Harbor, where blocks were set up in Dry Dock Number One to receive her.

The *Yorktown* crept into dry dock at 6:45 that morning, and almost at once some fourteen hundred workers swarmed over her. The dockyard workers labored with a purpose and intensity that suggested that every minute counted. They worked throughout the day and into the growing darkness. Though only a dozen miles away in Honolulu the city was blacked out ("as dark as the inside of a derby hat," in one officer's phrase), Pearl Harbor was lit up by giant floodlights as workers labored on through the night. Pushed to make quick fixes rather than permanent repairs, the men did not bother with blueprints or plans. They cut plywood templates on board to match the gaping holes, sent the templates ashore to be duplicated in steel, then welded or bolted the patches into place. Deep inside the ship, work parties shored up sagging bulkheads instead of replacing them. No one even bothered with fresh paint.[2]

The work was still under way when the valves were opened to refill the dry dock on the morning of the twenty-ninth, and men were still working—the bright points of light from their acetylene torches visible from shore—when the big carrier moved out into the ship channel at 9:00 A.M. on May 30, barely forty-eight hours after her arrival. The two other American carriers in the Pacific, *Hornet* and *Enterprise*, had departed Pearl Harbor two days before, the same morning that the *Yorktown* had gone into dry dock, and now the *Yorktown* was heading for a rendezvous with them at a predetermined point 325 miles north of the tiny atoll of Midway, a location designated somewhat hopefully as "Point Luck."[3]

Despite the jury-rigged repairs, the *Yorktown* was an imposing sight as she headed out to sea: at 809 feet long and displacing 19,800 tons, she was three times longer and four times heavier than Dewey's *Olympia*. Both her size and her silhouette would have utterly confounded Dewey and his contemporaries. Even the imaginative John Ericsson would have been impressed, for no fewer than eight of Ericsson's *Monitor*s, sitting side by side in pairs, would have fit comfortably on the *Yorktown*'s flight deck. That deck, essentially a floating landing strip, was overlooked by an incongruous "island": essentially a five-story building that jutted up on her starboard side and which served as both the ship's bridge and airport tower.

The *Yorktown* carried a respectable battery of eight five-inch guns, four quad-mounted 1.1-inch pom-pom guns, an array of .50-caliber machine guns, and newly installed twenty-millimeter Oerlikon antiaircraft guns. But all of that was secondary to her principal weapon. Though her flight deck was empty now, once she was well out to sea she would take on board an impressive array of fighting aircraft: Wildcat fighter planes, Devastator torpedo bombers, and Dauntless dive-bombers. Ever since the Battle of the Capes more than a century and a half earlier, when the opposing forces had engaged at a half cable's length (one hundred yards), the range between naval combatants had been growing. In the Battle of Hampton Roads, the *Virginia* had fired at the grounded *Minnesota* from a mile away; Dewey had engaged Montojo in Manila Bay from two and a half miles, but the bombers on the *Yorktown* could deliver their ordnance onto a target more than two hundred miles away. The effective range of the fleet's strike arm had grown so long that navies could now engage—as they had in the Coral Sea—without ever sighting each other.[4]

The furious repairs conducted aboard the *Yorktown*, and its urgent orders back to sea, were a direct consequence of one of the best-kept secrets of the war. In the basement of the Fourteenth Naval District Headquarters building at Pearl Harbor, a team of cryptanalysts, or code breakers, known to the few who were even aware of it as "Hypo" (the British phonetic designation for the letter *H*, referring to Hawaii), worked to penetrate the coded Japanese radio signals. Headed by Lieutenant Commander Joseph J. Rochefort, the men of Hypo spent their days (and often their nights) reading encoded Japanese messages and attempting to winkle some useful intelligence out of them. It was a task requiring patience and perseverance as well as instinct and insight.

The Japanese operational code, known as JN-25, consisted of forty-five thousand five-digit number groups, each of which represented a word or a phrase. Thus the messages the American cryptanalysts read might look something like this:

29845 87463 14975 27406 38591 19393
93755 29573 57144 38048 29485 11844

Aware that the Americans would try to penetrate the meaning of these coded numbers, the Japanese inserted random number groups throughout their messages to confuse the code breakers. The Japanese were confident that their code was sufficiently complex that no one could break it, or at least that no one could break it quickly enough to gain a tactical advantage.[5]

Rochefort and his Hypo team worked frantically to crack the Japanese messages. In part their dedication derived from the nagging anxiety that if only they had been given access to the JN-25 intelligence before December 7, they might have been able to predict the Pearl Harbor attack. Instead, that information was confined to the team at Corregidor (the team known as "Cast") and not shared with Hypo. Now that Rochefort's team had access, they kept long hours in their sunless offices looking for repeats or patterns in the five-digit number sets. In time, they were able to "read" every fourth or fifth number group and guess at its meaning. That enabled them to make a reasonable guess at the subject of the messages. Most of those messages were routine and altogether unhelpful. The Hypo cryptanalysts might labor for hours over what looked like an important message only to determine that it was a report on the weather in Hokkaido two days before. With a sigh, they would push the message aside and start on the next one. It was not just a matter of finding familiar number groups and "translating" the message; a key element to code-breaking success was gaining an understanding of Japanese character and culture, which might offer insight into the meaning of the messages.[6]

In all their work, the overriding goal of the men who worked in Hypo was to find and track the "Nagumo Force," the six-carrier strike force of Vice Admiral Chuichi Nagumo, which had conducted the attack on Pearl Harbor on December 7 and which they referred to by its Japanese designation as the "Kido Butai." Repeatedly they asked one another, or some-times muttered aloud to themselves, "Where is the Kido Butai?" The answer to that question often indicated where the next Japanese blow was likely to fall.[7]

Their diligence paid off. In April, Rochefort had been able to tell Nimitz about a Japanese plan to attack the allied base at Port Moresby, on the south coast of New Guinea, in time for Nimitz to send the *Yorktown* and the *Lexington* to the Coral Sea. The Japanese thrust had been turned back, though that American success had come at a heavy cost due to the loss of the *Lexington* and the severe damage that had been inflicted on the *Yorktown*. Then, even before the Battle of the Coral Sea was over, Rochefort and his team achieved another breakthrough. The Japanese, Rochefort reported, were about to launch an even bigger operation, one that involved most of their fleet, including the Kido Butai. The attack would take place in early June, and the target, Rochefort declared, was the tiny atoll of Midway.

The number of individuals who were privy to the fact that Rochefort's team was reading the Japanese code was very small, and not all of them were convinced that Rochefort had interpreted the messages correctly. In Washington, the head of the Code and Signal Section (Op-20-G), Captain John Redman, questioned Rochefort's analysis. His doubt fueled the con-cern of the chief of naval operations, Admiral Ernest J. King, that the next Japanese operation would be against the American West Coast. If Rochefort was wrong and the Japanese hit the American mainland, there would be hell to pay. Was he absolutely sure?

He was. Indeed, he was a little annoyed by the reluctance of some offi-cials to accept his analysis. So to convince the skeptics, his men devised a scheme. The messages they had been tracking identified the targets of the next Japanese offensive as AK and AF. There was no dispute that AK referred to the Aleutian Islands, but to confirm the identity of AF, Rochefort's men sent a message to the garrison at Midway by submarine cable asking that they send back a radio message in the clear—that is, uncoded—stating that their salt water evaporator had broken down and that they were running short of drinking water. Sure enough, two days after this bogus report hit the airwaves, an intercepted Japanese message reported that AF was short of drinking water. Rochefort had his smoking gun: beyond any doubt, the target of the next Japanese offensive was Midway.[8]

One of America's stepping stones across the Pacific to the Philippines, Midway was a circular coral reef embracing an enclosed lagoon. On the southern edge of that lagoon, two small sandy islands barely broke the sur-

Midway Atoll from the air. The island in the foreground is Eastern Island, which contained the airfield, completed only four months before the Japanese attack. Beyond it is the appropriately named Sand Island. The dredged ship channel into the central lagoon ran between the two islands, and a secondary channel can be discerned running from the lagoon to the landing dock on Eastern Island. (U.S. Navy)

face of the sea; the larger island, appropriately named Sand Island, was less than two miles long. It was a barren outpost populated principally by gooney birds, whose ritual mating dance was virtually the only interesting thing on either island. Indeed, Midway had no value whatsoever but for its location. It was, quite literally, a thousand miles from anywhere: 1,100 miles to the southeast was Oahu and the American naval base at Pearl Harbor, and 1,130 miles to the southwest was Wake Island, captured by the Japanese in the early days of the war. So remote was it that there is no record of its having been "discovered" until 1859. The United States established a coaling station there two years after the Civil War, and two years after that, in 1869, the Navy began dredging a channel to provide access to the atoll's inner lagoon, though the project ran out of money before the channel could be completed.

Five years after the war with Spain, in 1903, President Theodore Roosevelt placed Midway under the control of the Navy Department, and that same year the United States established a telegraph cable station on Sand Island. The outpost was further developed in the 1930s when Pan American Airlines used it as a seaplane base for its transpacific Clippers and even built a small hotel there for its passengers. In 1940, with the Second World War already under way in Europe, the Navy finally completed the channel into the central lagoon, providing a safe anchorage for deep-water ships, and the next year, only four months before the Japanese attack on Pearl Harbor, the Navy completed an airfield on the smaller island, Eastern Island. Even with these improvements, however, Midway was not a post of great strategic significance. And yet in the late spring of 1942 it became the focus of arguably the most important naval battle of the Second World War, and one of the pivotal battles of American history.[9]

It was not the atoll or its airstrip that made Midway the target of the Kido Butai and much of the rest of the Imperial Japanese Navy. It was the Japanese determination to finish the job they had begun in December by luring the American carriers out from their naval base at Pearl Harbor and sinking them in deep water, where they would be beyond recovery. Midway would be the bait. The Japanese plan was to attack the American base at Midway with carrier-based airplanes, and when the American carriers sortied from Pearl Harbor to meet the challenge, they would steam into a carefully prepared trap. With the destruction of the American carriers, the Japanese would then be free to consolidate their conquests in the Southwest Pacific—including the Philippines and the oil-rich islands of the Dutch East Indies—and draw upon the resources of their new empire for economic self-sufficiency.[10]

The news from Hypo that the Japanese planned to launch a major operation directed at the capture of Midway was an intelligence coup of the first order for the Americans, but it also created a dilemma for the commander of the U.S. Pacific Fleet, Admiral Chester Nimitz. Though he was only fifty-seven, Nimitz had snow white hair, and behind his back his young staffers took to calling him "Cottontail." The nickname belied Nimitz's personality, however, for there was nothing cuddly or frivolous about the American commander, who had been on the job only since the first of the year. Nimitz's German ancestry and his Texas hill country upbringing gave him a cool, calculating, and undemonstrative demeanor. One officer who knew him well described him as "coldly impersonal." His steady hand on the helm had helped to restore confidence after the disaster of the December 7 attack, though his inspiring competence could not completely mask the precarious situation of the American fleet in the early spring of 1942.[11]

The "fleet" Nimitz had inherited consisted of a score or so of submarines and a few aircraft carriers, plus the cruisers and destroyers that had survived the Pearl Harbor attack. Nimitz himself came from the submarine community, and he immediately sent out the handful of American submarines to conduct offensive operations. It is a measure of how much the world had changed in twenty-five years that although the United States had professed horror at the German use of unrestricted submarine warfare in 1917, the first U.S. Navy operational order of the Second World War was to "begin unrestricted submarine warfare against Japan." Early in the war, however, the U.S. submarines performed indifferently, mainly because their Mark 14 torpedoes did not work properly, though this was not discovered until later. In the meantime, sub skippers had to endure the frustration of risking their command and their lives in order to line up for a shot, and then watch while their torpedoes either failed to explode or ran too deep. When they reported these malfunctions up the chain of command, many of those in the Bureau of Ordnance who read their reports assumed unfairly that the commanding officers were making excuses for having missed the target. Not until the end of 1942 did sufficient evidence accumulate to provoke a change in torpedo design.[12]

The carriers, too, had a disappointing debut. Though the *Enterprise* (CV-6) and the *Hornet* (CV-8) executed a dramatic, headline-grabbing raid on Tokyo in April by the Army Air Corps planes of Colonel James Doolittle, that raid had been designed principally to boost morale, and elsewhere there was little to cheer about. In the first five months of the war, the United States lost the *Langley* (CV-1), the *Lexington* (CV-2), and the use of the *Saratoga* (CV-3), which was hit and badly damaged by a Japanese submarine whose torpedoes worked only too well. That left Nimitz with only the *Enterprise* and *Hornet* plus the damaged *Yorktown*. All the battleships, of course, were either under repair or still at the bottom of Pearl Harbor.*

Under these circumstances, many commanders would have been satisfied to remain on the defensive—to wait until America's superior industrial capacity produced a new armada of ships and planes—before seeking a fight with the enemy. After all, the Japanese navy—especially the six carriers of the Nagumo Force, the Kido Butai—had been running rampant in the western Pacific since December, gobbling up new possessions and sinking any foe foolish enough to stand in their way. Nagumo's carriers operated freely, striking at targets from Ceylon in the Indian Ocean to the Gilberts in the southern Pacific, from the Kuriles in the north to the Solomons in the south, roaming at will across a gigantic expanse of ocean without serious opposition. Only in the Coral Sea northeast of Australia had the Japanese been checked, and that had come about principally because Nimitz had trusted the information Rochefort had provided.[13]

---

* The United States had three other carriers: the *Ranger* (CV-4) and the *Essex* (CV-9) were in the Atlantic, and the *Wasp* (CV-7) was on its way from the Atlantic to the Pacific, though it would arrive too late to participate in the Battle of Midway. Once it was repaired, the *Saratoga* (CV-3) also headed for Hawaii, but like the *Wasp*, it would arrive only after the battle was over.

Nimitz had already decided to trust Rochefort again and to oppose the attack on Midway with everything he had. Such a decision may seem logical in retrospect, but given the disparity of forces available to each side, it was a significant gamble. If the United States lost its few remaining carriers in the fight for Midway, there would be little between Nagumo's powerful striking force and the West Coast of the United States. Was Midway with its gooney birds worth such a risk? Nimitz thought it was. He calculated that the advance knowledge provided by Rochefort's code breakers considerably evened the odds. Moreover, the scheduled return of the *Saratoga* and the arrival of the *Wasp* from the Atlantic would give him a backup battle force even if everything went wrong.

But Nimitz did not expect everything to go wrong. He expected to complete emergency repairs on the *Yorktown* and get all three of his carriers to sea before the Japanese arrived, thereby throwing a wrench into their plans. Instead of being surprised by the Japanese, he would surprise them and send at least some of their carriers to the bottom. Nimitz was no Texas gambler; he did not throw the dice thoughtlessly. Behind those cool blue eyes was the calculating mind of a man who weighed the odds carefully and made plans accordingly. He expected to win.[14]

Nimitz recalled the *Hornet* and *Enterprise* to Pearl Harbor and issued orders that the *Yorktown* go into immediate dry dock when it arrived to undergo emergency repairs. He scheduled a staff meeting for May 25, three days before the *Yorktown*'s expected arrival, to plan the details of the operation. He wanted Rochefort there to explain what he knew—or what he thought he knew. The senior brass assembled at the designated hour, but Rochefort was late. For half an hour, the commanding officer of the Pacific Fleet and his entire staff waited impatiently for a lieutenant commander. When Rochefort finally showed up, he apologized for being late and, handing Nimitz a sheaf of papers, said that the documents would explain everything. They did. Rochefort had been delayed because his team had been busy decrypting a series of recently intercepted Japanese messages dated five days earlier. As Nimitz looked them over, he saw that they not only confirmed that Midway was the target, they included "the strength of the attack and the composition of the attack forces," and even "such things as where the Japanese carriers would be when they launched their planes, degrees and distance from Midway, and the hour and the minutes."[15]

A few skeptics worried that it might be a trick—the information was too complete. But Rochefort was certain of its genuineness. "I could not understand why there should be any doubt," he later insisted. Nimitz agreed. The only thing he did not know was how many carriers the Japanese would have. If they sent all six carriers of the Kido Butai, the American carriers would be outnumbered two to one, even assuming the *Yorktown* could be patched up in time. But Rochefort predicted there would be only four carriers in the Japanese strike force. "Why not six?" Nimitz asked him. Rochefort replied that the message traffic mentioned only Carrier Divisions 1 and 2, which suggested that the two Japanese carriers that had fought in the Coral Sea—*Shokaku* and *Zuikaku*, the newest and biggest of the enemy's carriers—had returned to Japan for repair. He did not think they would be involved in the forthcoming operation. But whether the Japanese had four carriers or six, Nimitz planned to make a fight of it regardless. After all, Midway itself would be an element of the fight—its airfield made it a kind of unsinkable aircraft carrier, which, along with the three American carriers, would make it an even fight against four Japanese carriers. And even if there were six enemy carriers, Nimitz calculated that American advance knowledge of the Japanese intention was enough to even the odds.[16]

There was still the problem of who would command. As theater commander, Nimitz himself would remain at his headquarters in Pearl Harbor. To command the carrier force at sea, he needed a steady and thoughtful carrier officer, a man who knew when to take a chance and how big a chance to take. The logical man was Vice Admiral William F. "Bull" Halsey, the best-known and most aggressive of America's carrier admirals. But Halsey had come down with a severe case of shingles, a horribly painful skin disease that would keep him hospitalized for weeks. Devastated that he would miss the forthcoming operation, Halsey had no choice but to accept his fate, and he recommended that the commander of his cruiser-destroyer force, Rear Admiral Raymond A. Spruance, assume temporary command of the carrier division consisting of the *Enterprise* and *Hornet*.

The recommendation was controversial, for Spruance was not a carrier man. He was, in the Navy's lingo, a "black shoe" admiral: a surface warrior who had spent his career in destroyers, cruisers, and battleships. How could he be expected to know what to do in a carrier battle? Nimitz, however, thought the suggestion was inspired, for Spruance was a man very much in the Nimitz mold: quiet and undemonstrative in his behavior, but calculating and bold in his decision making.[17]

Spruance would not be the senior man afloat. That responsibility fell to a rear admiral with the quintessentially American name of Frank Jack Fletcher, who not only was senior to Spruance but also had commanded the American carriers in the Battle of the Coral Sea. This was the source of another problem, however, for Fletcher's performance in the Coral Sea had come under criticism in some quarters. Admiral King, the no-nonsense chief of naval operations in Washington, thought that Fletcher had been

The three senior American commanders at Midway: Admiral Chester Nimitz (in pith helmet) talks with Raymond Spruance, commander of Task Force 16 that included the carriers *Hornet* and *Enterprise*; right: Frank Jack Fletcher who commanded Task Force 17 that included the *Yorktown*. (U.S. Navy)

insufficiently aggressive in that fight and urged Nimitz to replace him. Concerned, Nimitz called Fletcher in for a conversation and quizzed him about his operations in the Coral Sea. At the end of the conversation, he decided that King's criticism was both unfounded and unfair. Fletcher, Nimitz wrote to King, was "an excellent, seagoing, fighting naval officer" and just the man Nimitz wanted in command.[18]

Of course, Fletcher could not go to sea until the *Yorktown* was repaired, and Nimitz had no intention of keeping the *Enterprise* and *Hornet* waiting around for her. On May 28, therefore, even as the *Yorktown* eased into dry dock, the two undamaged American carriers left Pearl Harbor as Task Force 16, with the *Enterprise* flying the flag of Rear Admiral Raymond Spruance. Fletcher would exercise overall command when all three carriers operated together, but meanwhile Spruance, the "black shoe" admiral, would command two-thirds of America's carrier force in the Pacific.

Nimitz's orders to both Fletcher and Spruance suggested a lot about the commanding officer's philosophy of combat: "In carrying out the task assigned," Nimitz wrote, "you will be governed by the principle of calculated risk." He didn't need to point out that the decision to fight for Midway in the first place was already a calculated risk. Privately, he urged both task group commanders to do as much damage as they could to the enemy carriers without unduly risking their own. It was an assignment that required delicate judgment and, in Nimitz's words, "delicate timing." After all, the Japanese would have overwhelming superiority since they were sending more than 150 warships against only 26. On paper it looked hopeless.[19]

But battles are not won or lost on paper.

—

As the *Yorktown* turned north outside Pearl Harbor, it was surrounded by an escort of two cruisers and five destroyers, which formed a circular screen to provide both antisubmarine and antiair protection. For three hundred years and more, war fleets had gone to battle in a column—the line-ahead formation. But by 1942 the aircraft carrier had emerged as so critical a component of naval warfare that the standard formation was now a circle with smaller warships arranged around the one essential fighting platform of modern navies.

Once the task force (designated Task Force 17) was well on its way, with Oahu only a smudge on the southern horizon, Fletcher ordered the formation to turn into the wind to take aboard the carrier's air wing. Though wind direction had been crucial to Oliver Hazard Perry on Lake Erie, it had been largely irrelevant to the combatants in Hampton Roads and Manila Bay. Now the wind mattered once again, because in order for a carrier's planes to take off or land on its relatively short deck, it was necessary to maximize the relative wind speed across that deck from fore to aft. During the ensuing battle, and indeed throughout the Pacific War, the carriers of both navies had to turn into the wind in order to launch or recover airplanes.

The *Yorktown*'s air wing was commanded by Lieutenant Commander Oscar Pederson, who was concerned that he would not be taking his regular command into battle. The *Yorktown*'s air wing had suffered heavy losses during the fight in the Coral Sea—the *Yorktown* and the *Lexington* had lost a total of sixty-six planes in that fight, over 40 percent of their full complement—and as a result, Pederson now had a disproportionate number of rookies in his command. A few veterans from other squadrons made up a valuable cadre of experienced pilots, but most of those who flew in to land on the *Yorktown* that May 30 were relative novices, many of them straight out of flight school. Worse, at least in the opinion of some, the squadrons bore unit designations that did not even identify them as belonging to the *Yorktown*. In short, the *Yorktown*'s air wing was something of a lash-up.[20]

There is no such thing as a routine carrier landing. Approaching a landing platform that was itself moving at between twenty and thirty knots, the pilots dropped their landing gear, lowered their flaps, and throttled down to just above stalling speed. As they maneuvered, they kept one eye on the landing signal officer (LSO), who stood near the stern with large colored paddles in his hands. If a plane came in too fast or too high, if it was not lined up properly, or if the deck was not yet cleared from the previous landing, the plane got a "wave-off" from the LSO, and the pilot gunned the throttle to pull out of his glide and go around for another approach. If the LSO swept his paddles downward, giving the OK, the pilot throttled back the engine and dropped his plane down jarringly onto the carrier's wooden deck, where it sped forward at sixty or seventy knots toward the crash barrier that guarded the parked aircraft on the bow, until a hook hanging from the plane's fuselage caught one of several wires stretched across the carrier's deck. The wire arrested the plane's forward progress and brought it safely, if rather abruptly, to a stop. Crewmen on board the ship then rushed out to disengage the wire and directed the pilot to taxi forward beyond the crash barrier to clear the landing area for the next plane. Once forward, the plane's wings folded back like those of a sleeping dove to conserve space on the crowded deck, and eventually it was lowered by a giant elevator to the hangar deck below.

It was an inherently dangerous activity. Indeed, landing on an aircraft carrier was very likely the most dangerous noncombat activity in war; even a veteran pilot had to focus all his skills on the difficult job of bringing his airplane to a safe landing on a moving platform only eighty feet wide.

The fighters came in first. Lieutenant Commander John S. "Jimmy" Thach led the twenty-seven planes that made up the squadron that was designated as VF-3. The *V* simply referred to aircraft, the *F* stood for fighter, and the *3* indicated that the squadron belonged to the *Saratoga* (CV-3), though it had been hastily patched together from what was available. At least the squadron had relatively new airplanes: the F4F-4 Wildcats that Thach and his men flew were a singular improvement over the stubby, slow (and appropriately named) F2A-3 Buffalos that some of them had flown previously. It would soon become evident that even these newer Wildcats were no match for the nimble Japanese Zeros, but the Buffalos had been virtual sitting ducks. A veteran pilot reported bitterly that the Buffalo "is not a combat aeroplane. . . . Any commander that orders pilots out for combat in an F2A-3 [Buffalo] should consider the pilot as lost before leaving the ground."[21]

Thach was more worried about the inexperience of his young pilots. They had been taught how to fly, but only a few of them had ever fired their guns in earnest, and "they knew practically nothing about fighter tactics." In addition, though all of them had made at least one carrier landing in training, "none of them had landed a Wildcat aboard a carrier." Thach and his executive officer, Lieutenant Commander Don Lovelace, had done what they could to instruct and encourage their young pilots in the few days they had with them before flying out to the *Yorktown*, but there was no real substitute for experience. Lovelace was one of the few who did have experience, which was why he had postponed his orders to rotate back to the States and take command of his own squadron in order to stay with VF-3.[22]

Lovelace's wingman, a fresh young ensign named Robert Evans, had so little flight experience that Lovelace told him to follow him closely in the landing pattern and to copy his movements. Lovelace brought his Wildcat in for a clean landing and taxied safely beyond the crash barrier. But Evans brought his plane in too high and missed the wire; it bounced once, floated over the barrier, and crashed directly on top of Lovelace's plane. Ensign Evans survived, but Commander Lovelace became the first mortal casualty of the Battle of Midway.* There was no time to stop and contemplate this tragedy; other planes were already circling into the pattern. After extricating Lovelace's body from the wreckage, both wrecked planes were unceremoniously shoved over the side, and landing operations continued.[23]

Once all the fighters were aboard (twenty-five now instead of twenty-seven), the next to land were the thirteen TBD-1 Devastator torpedo bombers of VT-3 (*T* for torpedo). These planes were designed to be ship-killers. When armed for combat, the Devastators each carried a single twenty-two-hundred-pound Mark 13 torpedo slung under the fuselage. Because of that, they were relatively slow and subsequently vulnerable both to fighter attack and to antiair fire. They had a theoretical maximum speed of just over 200 mph, but in practice they seldom topped 160 mph, and cruised at just over 100 mph.[24] The Japanese Zero fighters that assailed them topped out at better than 330 mph. Moreover, to launch their large and cumbersome weapons, the Devastators had to approach their intended targets low and slow, flying just fifteen or twenty feet above the

---

* Lovelace was more likely the second mortal casualty of the campaign since a Dauntless dive-bomber from the *Hornet* on antisubmarine patrol had failed to return the day before, and its pilot had been declared missing. No trace of the plane was ever found.

surface, and throttling back to about eighty knots before releasing their torpedoes. To be effective, therefore, the American torpedo bombers needed the protection of Thach's fighters while they made their attack run. Even then, it took nerves of steel to fly a Devastator into its target, and as much nerve to man the rear-seat machine gun, sitting backward and fending off enemy fighters while the pilot lined up for a shot.*

After all of the torpedo bombers landed safely and without incident, the dive-bombers came in. The *Yorktown* had two squadrons of dive-bombers: thirty-seven planes divided into two squadrons labeled VB-3 (*B* for bomber) and VS-5 (*S* for scouting). The planes in both squadrons were relatively new SBD-3 Dauntless dive-bombers, which their pilots called either "the beast" or "the barge." Despite these unheroic nicknames, the Dauntless constituted the principal strike arm of the American carrier force. They could attack an enemy more than two hundred miles away, flying down out of the sun from twenty thousand feet to drop either a single thousand-pound bomb or one five-hundred-pound bomb and two hundred-pound bombs. The bombs were gravity-guided, so doctrine called for the pilot to fly nearly straight down at a seventy-degree angle toward the target, then release a bomb so that it plunged downward on that same trajectory before the pilot pulled out of his dive. No wonder they were called "hell divers." Like the Devastator, the Dauntless had a two-man crew: a pilot in front and a gunner/radioman in the rear seat who handled a twin-barreled .30-caliber machine gun. Even with that rear-seat gunner, however, the Dauntless was most effective when it was accompanied by Wildcats so that the pilots could focus on their targets rather than on dodging enemy fighters.[25]

By late afternoon, the *Yorktown* had taken seventy-seven airplanes on board, and Task Force 17 resumed its northward course. A patched-up ship and a patched-together air wing escorted by seven survivors of the Pearl Harbor attack all headed north at twenty-four knots toward Point Luck.

---

* Technically, the TBD-1 had a crew of three, with a bombardier occupying the middle seat. But when the plane was armed to carry torpedoes, a bombardier was just excess baggage, and during the Battle of Midway, the Devastators flew with two-man crews.

There, some 325 miles north of Midway, they would rendezvous with the two American carriers of Task Force 16 to lie in wait for the Japanese fleet.

—

The same day that the *Yorktown* had limped into Pearl Harbor, the Japanese First Mobile Strike Force—the Kido Butai—got under way from its anchorage in Hiroshima Bay on southern Honshu and steamed out the Bungo Strait to begin its long trek across the Pacific to Midway. As Rochefort had predicted, the Japanese strike force included four carriers, not six. The *Shokaku* and *Zuikaku*, Japan's newest carriers, stayed behind. The *Shokaku* had been seriously damaged in the Coral Sea by three bomb hits that had bent her deck plates so badly that she could not launch or recover airplanes. Repairing them would take time, though if the Japanese had been willing to jury-rig the repairs on the *Shokaku* the way the Americans did on the *Yorktown*, they might have made her serviceable in time to operate with the fleet. The *Zuikaku* had not been harmed at all in the Coral Sea, but she had lost most of the planes from her air wing and, more importantly, many of her veteran pilots. Rather than go to sea with a reorganized or undermanned air wing (like *Yorktown*), she, too, stayed behind. The Japanese would have occasion to reconsider and regret these decisions later, but at the time it hardly seemed to matter. According to Japanese estimates, the Americans had only two carriers, and surely four Japanese carriers would be more than a match for them, especially considering that the Japanese would have the element of surprise on their side—or so they believed.[26]

Nagumo's four carriers had a significantly different look than their American counterparts. For one thing, two of them—the flagship *Akagi* and the *Kaga*—had been constructed on top of battle cruiser and battleship hulls and were therefore significantly larger, each of them displacing more than forty thousand tons. That circumstance also gave them a distinctive profile, since their flight decks, instead of being integral to the hull, were built on top of stiltlike structural supports and were consequently high off the water, a fact that, combined with their heavy hulls, made them slower than most frontline warships—the *Kaga* had a top speed of only twenty-seven knots. In addition, their "islands" were comparatively tiny. Nagumo's other two carriers, the *Soryu* and *Hiryu*, were both slightly smaller and faster, having been built from the keel up as carriers. Among them the four carriers of Nagumo's command carried a total of some 249 aircraft, and as they moved out into the broad Pacific they were surrounded by a substantial screen of heavy cruisers, light cruisers, and destroyers.[27]

As this armada put to sea, cheered on by men in the small fishing boats bobbing offshore, the morale of the officers and sailors was sky high. And why not? They had been masters of the western Pacific for more than half a year. They had literally conquered an empire, grabbing the Philippines from the Americans; Borneo, Sumatra, and Java from the Dutch; Singapore and Malaysia from the British. These conquests were critical to Japanese grand strategy. They had gone to war in the first place to secure a reliable source of raw materials for Japan's burgeoning industry—foodstuffs, iron, and especially the oil that was essential to Japan's economy—launching a knockout blow at America's battle fleet in Pearl Harbor to buy the time necessary to establish and consolidate their Pacific empire.

As it happened, however, the offensive potential of the American fleet had not been destroyed at Pearl Harbor, for the American carriers were still out there. The Japanese thought they had sunk four of them. They had, in fact, sunk two—the *Langley* and the *Lexington*—but the Japanese also listed both the *Saratoga* and *Yorktown* as sunk in their battle damage estimates. Of course that still left two more, or possibly three, and Admiral Isoroku Yamamoto, commander in chief of the combined fleet, was determined to finish them off. At a strategy planning session in early April, a spokesman for Yamamoto declared, "In the last analysis, the success or failure of our entire strategy in the Pacific will be determined by whether or not we succeed in destroying the United States fleet, more particularly its carrier task forces."[28] So determined was Yamamoto to finish off the remnants of the American fleet that he threatened to resign if his plan for an attack on Midway was not accepted. The bluff—if it was a bluff—worked. In early April the Japanese committed formally to an all-out attack on Midway in order to lure out and destroy the American carriers. The dramatic raid by Doolittle's bombers over Tokyo two weeks later added a sense of urgency to the planning, for that raid nominally threatened the life of the emperor and embarrassed the Imperial Japanese Navy.

In planning the Midway operation, however, the Japanese made two fundamental errors that in the end proved fatal. First, they lost focus on their primary objective. The whole point of the operation was to destroy the American carriers using Midway as bait. But in the planning process, the occupation of Midway as an advanced outpost, or even as a preliminary step to an invasion of Hawaii, grew more and more prominent until the tail began to wag the dog. Those in charge of the landing operation insisted that the landings had to be made in the first week of June in order to take advantage of a full moon, which would allow night operations. That factor then drove the rest of the planning until the landing, as much as the battle against the carriers, emerged as a primary goal of the operation.[29]

Second, the plan that finally emerged was overly complex, and it completely ignored the Mahanian doctrine that to achieve sea control, a nation should keep its main battle fleet concentrated. Though the Japanese had overwhelming naval superiority, they planned to divide their forces into no fewer than ten battle groups for the coming operation and, even worse, to deploy them so distant from one another that they would not be able to provide mutual support. One example of this was the notion that a simultaneous attack on several of the Aleutian Islands would somehow distract and confuse the Americans. The Japanese planned to commit four battle groups to American positions in the Aleutians: the islands of Attu and Kiska at the far end of Alaska's long tail, and Dutch Harbor, the small U.S. naval base nearly a thousand miles further east. The force assigned to Dutch Harbor included one full-sized carrier and one light carrier, which, if they had accompanied the Nagumo Force instead, might have changed the outcome of the battle for Midway.*

---

* Most sources describe both of the carriers the Japanese committed to the Aleutian campaign as light carriers, but the larger of the two, the *Junyo*, carried forty-five airplanes, nearly as many as the carriers of the Kido Butai (fifty-three). The second carrier assigned to the Northern Group was the *Ryujo*, which carried thirty-seven planes.

Five other, much larger naval groups would focus on Midway, but they would not operate together. Appropriately, the Kido Butai, with Nagumo's four carriers plus two battleships and a screen of cruisers and destroyers, would lead the attack. More than five hundred miles behind, beyond not only gun range but also the range of combat aircraft, Yamamoto himself would command the main body of seven battleships, including the brand-new and enormous *Yamato*, at seventy thousand tons the biggest warship on the planet, as well as a substantial screen that included another light carrier. In addition to separating the main body from the strike force, Yamamoto's decision to command the operation from his flagship was ill-considered, since in order to achieve surprise, his battle group, like all the others, would have to operate under radio silence at least until the battle began. If he had remained at Saipan or even in Japan, he could have sent out or forwarded an unlimited number of radio orders without fear of disclosing the location of any of his forces. At sea, however, he had to maintain radio silence for fear of giving away his own position. Too distant to support Nagumo and not distant enough to provide him with either orders or information, he might as well have stayed at home.*

Separate from both these substantial armadas, two more groups were devoted to the invasion of Midway itself. Vice Admiral Nobutake Kondo commanded the invasion force, which consisted of two more battleships and seven heavy cruisers. That force was to cover the transport group, carrying the five-thousand-man landing force, and its support group. Finally, there was a tenth element, consisting of the Japanese submarines whose job it would be to track the sortie of the Americans from Pearl Harbor and, after reporting their location, inflict as much damage on them as possible before the Japanese carriers and battleships closed in to finish them off. It was an elegant plan, rather like a complicated piece of origami. But

---

* Hugh Bicheno (*Midway* [2004], pp. 73–77) postulates that the complexity of the Japanese plan may have had less to do with strategy than with political rivalry between the Japanese army and navy. He suggests that Yamamoto may have gone to sea in the *Yamato* not so much to support Nagumo as to be able to claim a naval victory afterward and return to Tokyo with sufficient prestige to unseat Tojo's army-dominated government. It is an interesting speculation, but since Yamamoto was killed in 1943 (in yet another application of American code breaking) we will never know.

such elegance was superfluous given Japan's overwhelming numerical and operational superiority.

This should have become evident during the war games held in early May aboard Yamamoto's flagship, the giant *Yamato*. On one occasion during those exercises, as officers gamed the forthcoming attack on a giant tabletop, the umpire ruled that attacking American bombers made nine hits on the Japanese carriers and sank two of them. But Rear Admiral Matome Ukagi, who was overseeing the games, overruled the umpire and declared that the carriers had been only slightly damaged. The games resumed, and the outcome "proved" the viability of the war plan. In part Ukagi's decision was a measure of the disdain the Japanese had for American military prowess. In part, too, it was a classic example of "victory disease": the kind of overconfidence that follows remarkable success. That overconfidence led the Japanese to make a series of assumptions about the coming battle that proved far too optimistic. They assumed that the Americans would be caught by surprise; that the American carriers would not sortie out of Pearl Harbor until after the attack on Midway had begun; that the Japanese submarines would find them and track them; that the torpedo bombers of the Kido Butai would attack and sink them; and that if there were any survivors, the ships of Yamamoto's main body would close in and finish them off with gunfire. In the event, every one of these assumptions proved false.[30]

It began to go wrong almost at once. The first glitch was the failure of the Japanese to confirm that the American carriers were, in fact, still in Pearl Harbor. To obtain this intelligence, they had planned to send long-range patrol planes over the American base for a visual sighting on May 30. In a coordinated plan code-named Operation K, two Emily seaplanes from Jaluit Atoll in the Marshall Islands would fly 1,700 miles eastward to make a landing in the protected lagoon of French Frigate Shoals, an unoccupied outpost 450 miles west of Oahu. There they would rendezvous with Japanese submarines, which would refuel them for the round trip to Oahu. After confirming that the American flattops were still in port, they would land again at French Frigate Shoals to refuel for the return trip back to Jaluit. But when the Japanese subs poked their periscopes up at French

Frigate Shoals on May 29, they found three American warships already anchored there and evidence that the Americans were using the lagoon for their own seaplane base. So the reconnaissance mission was scrapped.[31] Had it been completed, the Japanese would have discovered that all three American carriers had already left Pearl Harbor.*

The next thing to go wrong was that the Japanese submarines that were supposed to be in place between Oahu and Midway to monitor the departure of the American carriers from Pearl Harbor did not get into position until June 2, by which time the American carriers had already passed northward to Point Luck. As a result of these failures, the surface forces of the Imperial Japanese Navy steamed eastward in nine battle groups, unaware that their principal quarry had already flown the coop. During their approach to Midway, Japanese eyes would be focused southward toward Pearl Harbor, from which direction they expected the U.S. carriers to appear. Instead the U.S. carriers were already in position 325 miles north of Midway in the last place—quite literally, as it turned out—that the Japanese would look for them.

—

The battle of Midway began at 8:00 A.M. on June 3, when planes from the Japanese carrier *Junyo* and the light carrier *Ryujo* struck at Dutch Harbor, the American naval base in Alaska. It was not a heavy blow. Many of the attacking airplanes failed to find the target, and in the event only nine bombers and three fighters got through the cloud cover to pound the naval base there. A follow-up attack focused on several of the American destroyers offshore, though the attackers made no hits. The American surface force, which Nimitz had posted nearby under Rear Admiral R. A. Theobald, was hampered by heavy fog and unable to locate the Japanese strike force, which retired westward at noon. The damage it had inflicted

* The failure of Operation K was due in part to the fact that the Japanese had tried this trick before. In early March they had refueled two Emilys at French Frigate Shoals and those planes had then flown to Hawaii to drop a few bombs on Pearl Harbor. The raid not only failed to do any damage to the American base but revealed both the Emily's long-range capability and the usefulness of French Frigate Shoals as a seaplane base, which was why Nimitz had sent vessels there.

on Dutch Harbor was significant but not permanent, and although the Japanese did subsequently occupy both Attu and Kiska, those islands offered no particular strategic advantage and mainly created a hardship duty for the Japanese occupying force. All in all, it was a pretty understated beginning to one of the greatest naval battles in history. The most significant aspect of this action was that it kept the *Junyo*, the *Ryujo*, and their ninety aircraft away from the battle that was about to begin for Midway itself.

That same June 3, the four carriers of the Kido Butai were steaming eastward through a heavy fog that was so thick, the ships of the Japanese task force could not see one another. Nagumo's carriers had to sound their foghorns at regular intervals to avoid collision. On one hand, this was a stroke of luck, for it hid the Japanese ships from the prying eyes of American search planes, but on the other hand it also prevented Nagumo from sending out his own scout planes. Steaming through a literal "fog of war," Nagumo maintained radio silence, sounded his foghorns, and continued eastward, confident that the Americans had no idea of his approach.

But if the Americans had not yet spotted any of the Japanese forces converging on them, they were very much aware of them. Armed with Rochefort's estimates, Nimitz had not only sent his carriers north of Midway to Point Luck, he had dramatically reinforced Midway itself. By June 3, the atoll was host to 115 planes of all types—more than on any carrier—though many of those planes were not front-line combat aircraft. Indeed, even as Japanese planes struck at Dutch Harbor and Nagumo's fleet plowed eastward through the fog, long-range search planes from Midway were already in the air conducting patrols to the north and west. Nagumo's force remained fog-enshrouded and undiscovered, but at 9:00 in the morning on that June 3, a long-range PBY Catalina seaplane nearly seven hundred miles west of Midway was about to make its turn toward home when the pilot, Ensign Jewell "Jack" Reid, spotted "some specks on the horizon." At first he thought it might be dirt on the windshield, but as he squinted forward and the range closed, he saw that they were, indeed, ships—many ships. At 9:25 he sent a message back to Midway: "Sighted main body." He then circled around behind the ships, staying low to avoid detection, and slipped up behind them before sending a more complete report: eleven ships, including one small carrier, two battleships, and several cruisers, were headed due east at nineteen knots. Then he got the hell out of there.[32]

It was not, in fact, the main body that Reid had sighted, but Kondo's invasion force of two battleships, seven cruisers, and a score of transport ships—Reid was simply mistaken about the carrier. The actual main body, consisting of Yamamoto's battleships, was at least three hundred miles further north, and Nagumo's carriers—the real target—were more than six hundred miles to the northeast, still fog-enshrouded. Still, the news electrified the Americans on Midway, for it proved that whatever the source of Nimitz's intelligence information, it was remarkably accurate, for here, indeed, was an enemy fleet approaching the atoll, exactly as forecast.

Ensign Jack Reid (sitting on the wheel strut) and his crew pose alongside their PBY long-range reconnaissance aircraft. It was Reid who first spotted the approaching Japanese armada on June 3, 1942. (U.S. Navy)

Nimitz, too, heard the report. He monitored the entire battle from his headquarters by listening in on the radio net. He did not want to interfere in the decision making of his operational commanders, but neither did he want them to go off half cocked. Aware of the whole picture provided him by Rochefort, he knew that what Ensign Reid had spotted was not the main body. He therefore sent a message of his own to Midway: "That is not, repeat not, the enemy striking force."[33] The unstated subtext of the message was: *Have patience. This is not our principal target.*

Perhaps not. But it was still a target. Among the reinforcements that Nimitz had sent out to Midway during the buildup was a squadron of Army B-17s, the four-engine, high-level bomber that would soon gain fame in Europe as the "Flying Fortress." The Army commander on Oahu had been reluctant to send them off to remote Midway, but Nimitz had worked his charm—and a bit of dissimulation—to get his way. Now with Reid's sighting, nine of those B-17s took off from Midway and flew westward toward the reported coordinates. They found Kondo's force that afternoon, and each plane dropped four six-hundred-pound bombs from high altitude. The Japanese ships twisted and turned under the rain of bombs, which exploded when they hit the water. The flash of the explosions, followed by the giant plumes of water they generated and the black smoke from the Japanese ships as they made high-speed turns, all looked pretty spectacular from ten thousand feet. Making accurate assessments of damage under such conditions is difficult enough, and it was especially difficult for Army pilots unaccustomed to bombing ships at sea. The pilots reported that they had made five hits and five near misses; a Japanese battleship, they reported, was on fire and sinking.[34]

In fact, the Army bombers had made no hits at all. Still, the reports encouraged Rear Admiral P. N. L. Bellinger, who commanded the patrol craft on Midway, to try his hand. The only plane in his arsenal that could reach so distant a target was the Catalina PBY, a large, fat-bodied, twin-engine seaplane generally used for long-range reconnaissance. Bellinger had four of them equipped with jury-rigged torpedo racks and torpedoes, and he dispatched them toward Kondo's force for a night attack. As one authority has suggested, this was an idea "straight out of a comic strip," but it illustrated the can-do attitude of the American defenders and their willingness to improvise. Remarkably, the American PBYs not only found the enemy at 1:30 A.M., they launched their torpedoes by moonlight and actually scored a hit on the Japanese transport *Akebono Maru,* which suffered twenty-four mortal casualties and significant damage, though effective damage control by her crew not only managed to keep her afloat but enabled her to maintain her place in the convoy.[35]

The long-range attacks by Army B-17s and Navy PBYs on June 3 did nothing to slow down the approach of the various elements of the Japanese armada. But they proved that the Americans were on the alert and aware that an enemy force was approaching. There seemed to be no reason any longer for the Japanese to maintain radio silence. Kondo reported the attack on his force to Yamamoto by radio, but the Japanese commander in chief did not forward the news to Nagumo. Perhaps he assumed that Nagumo had heard the reports himself, but as it happens, the vice admiral did not. So despite these early forays by Midway-based aircraft against the invasion force, Nagumo continued to steam toward Midway with the Kido Butai, convinced that the Americans were unaware of his approach.

Meanwhile, more than two hundred miles to the east, at the coordinates the Americans had designated as Point Luck, the three American carriers steamed quietly in circles, maintaining radio silence but listening intently to the radio net in hopes of hearing a report that would reveal the location of the Kido Butai from one of the American scout planes out of Midway.

—

In the full darkness that still covered the Pacific an hour before dawn on the fourth of June, more than a hundred airplane engines sputtered and then roared into life on the elevated flight decks of Chuichi Nagumo's four carriers. Altogether, Nagumo had some 249 combat aircraft at his disposal, divided evenly among bombers, torpedo planes, and fighters. Plane for plane, his aircraft were better than those of the Americans—in particular, the Mitsubishi Type 0 (Zero) fighter was both faster and more maneuverable than the American F4F-4 Wildcat. Nagumo's torpedo bombers, too, were not only faster than their American counterparts, they carried a vastly superior torpedo. The greatest difference, however, was that because Japanese planes carried much less armor than the American planes, they had a significantly longer range. Of course, this benefit came with a price: without armor, not only were the planes more vulnerable, but when the Japanese lost a plane, they often lost the pilot as well.[36]

Nagumo's plan was to send roughly half of his force of bombers and fighters to assault Midway to soften it up for the invasion, while he retained the other half (and his best pilots) in reserve in case his scouts sighted any American surface ships. Once Midway itself was neutralized, the invasion force could close on the atoll and take possession of it while Nagumo searched for the American carriers. The first wave of 108 airplanes (thirty-six fighters, thirty-six bombers, and thirty-six torpedo planes) would take off at 4:30, a half hour before dawn.

Simultaneously, Nagumo planned to launch seven search planes to scour the area for surface ships. This was merely precautionary, since he was pretty sure he knew where the American carriers were: in their base at Pearl Harbor. That assumption was one reason his plan called for only a single-phase search—that is, one airplane to each quadrant—rather than a double-phase search in which two planes, departing twenty minutes or so apart, scoured the same area. Moreover, only two of the seven scout planes he committed to this mission came from his carriers. Nagumo disliked using combat planes for scouting missions; to him it was like using a warrior as a spy. He preferred to use the floatplanes off his accompanying cruisers. Each of the Japanese heavy cruisers carried one or two long-range floatplanes (that is, seaplanes) that could be launched by catapult off the cruiser's fantail, then recovered after they landed in the water by winching them back aboard with a crane.[37]

The easiest way to envision the various search areas that Nagumo's staff assigned to these reconnaissance planes is to imagine the Kido Butai at the center of a clock face. Nagumo wanted his planes to search all the quadrants east of the Kido Butai from 12:00 (due north) to 6:00 (due south). Each plane was assigned a search area that was a pie-shaped wedge three hundred miles long and sixty miles wide, roughly corresponding to an "hour" on this imaginary clock face. The search planes would fly out along one edge of that wedge, fly sixty miles counterclockwise along its circumference, then fly the three hundred miles back. The two carrier-based planes would cover the critical area to the south where Nagumo thought the Americans were most likely to be discovered (at roughly 5:00 and 6:00 on the clock face), a single short-range plane of the cruiser *Haruna* would cover the least promising area to the north (at 1:00), and two planes each from the heavy cruisers *Chikuma* and *Tone* would cover the area due east of the Kido Butai corresponding to the quadrants from 2:00 to 4:00.

The American carriers were at approximately 3:00—due east.

At 4:30 A.M. floodlights on all four carriers illuminated the flight decks of the Japanese carriers as the air officer waved a white flag, and Nagumo's bombers and fighters rolled off the deck and into the air on schedule, their wing lights tracing their liftoff in the predawn darkness. Instead of sending full deckloads from two carriers, Nagumo sent half loads from all four. Even as they formed up into one enormous formation and flew southward—an awesome sight in the growing light—the crews were already bringing up the rest of the fighters and torpedo planes from the hangar deck to stand by. Meanwhile, the scout planes were also ready to launch—or nearly so.[38]

By far the strangest aspect of the Battle of Midway is the story of the Japanese scout planes—particularly scout plane number 4 from the cruiser *Tone*. According to plan, the *Tone*'s two floatplanes were to be shot off her catapult at 4:30, at the same time that the Midway attack force was being launched. But that didn't happen. Various reasons have been advanced for the delay—problems with the catapult, engine trouble on the floatplanes, perhaps both—but whatever the cause, the second of *Tone*'s floatplanes did not depart on its mission until 5:00. As Mitsuo Fuchida wrote in his memoir of the battle, "The delay in launching *Tone*'s planes sowed a seed which bore fatal fruit for the Japanese in the ensuing naval action."[39]

Timing is crucial in war. In 1781 de Grasse's arrival at the Chesapeake Bay just a day after Lord Hood sped off to the north was decisive in deciding the outcome of the Yorktown campaign; Barclay's untimely arrival off Put-in-Bay in 1813 when Perry's brigs were over the bar but still unarmed was nearly disastrous; the *Monitor*'s arrival in Hampton Roads in 1862 literally in the nick of time to thwart the *Virginia* seemed providential. All of those examples highlight the significance of timing in war, much of it entirely fortuitous. But none of them matches the extraordinary coincidence that the one airplane that suffered a critical half-hour delay in its departure was the one assigned to search the precise quadrant due east of the Japanese strike force where the American carriers lay in wait.

There, at Point Luck, the men on board the twenty-six American ships of Task Forces 16 and 17 were keyed up and waiting impatiently for news of the enemy carriers. None waited more impatiently than Frank Jack Fletcher and Raymond Spruance. They had agreed in advance that their best chance was to strike at the Kido Butai with everything they had as soon as they discovered its location, for they knew that whichever side got in the first blow would have a huge advantage. The two American task forces operated under strict radio silence, but they communicated with each other by blinker signal. They also listened in on the radio traffic from Midway and Pearl Harbor to keep up with unfolding events—they heard, for example, the reported results of the B-17 attack on the Japanese invasion force the day before—but so far there was no news of Nagumo's carriers.

At 4:20 that morning, ten minutes ahead of the Japanese, Fletcher launched a "security search" to patrol the area north of Point Luck out to one hundred miles. The planes had been gone about an hour when the *Yorktown* intercepted a report from Lieutenant Howard P. Ady, who was flying a PBY out of Midway and sent out the galvanizing report: "Carrier bearing three two zero [from Midway], distance one eight zero." Staff officers on the *Yorktown* quickly leaned over the chart: at a point 320 degrees from Midway (just west of due north) and 180 miles out from that atoll, they made a small X on the chart. It was just over two hundred miles west of their own position—almost, but not quite, within striking range.[40]

Though Fletcher still believed the best idea was to hit first and to hit hard, two factors stayed his hand. The first was that the report indicated only one carrier. The Americans did not know if the Kido Butai was operating as a unit, or even how many carriers the Japanese might have.

Rochefort had predicted four, but there still might be five, or even six. Where were the others? Then there was the range, over two hundred miles, beyond the capability of the American torpedo bombers.

Fifteen minutes later (at 5:45) the *Yorktown* intercepted another message, sent out in plain English by an excited PBY pilot: "Many airplanes headed Midway bearing three one five." That meant Nagumo had launched his attack on Midway. Swiftly calculating the time it would take for those airplanes to complete their mission and return, Fletcher wondered if a delay in launching his own strike would enable him not only to close the range but also to catch the Japanese carriers while they were in the process of recovering the planes returning from that strike. So while the deck crew spotted the planes on the flight deck and the pilots waited impatiently in the ready room, Fletcher decided to hold off until he received further information.[41]

It came in twenty minutes later from the reliable Lieutenant Ady: "Two carriers and battleships bearing three two zero degrees, distance one eight zero, course one three five, speed twenty five." With this report, Fletcher now knew that there were at least two enemy carriers and two battleships within maximum striking range. It was a worthwhile target. Then, too, further delay might squander the opportunity. After all, the longer he waited, the more likely it was that a Japanese patrol plane might find him and he would lose the element of surprise. (At that moment, approximately 5:50, the tardy floatplane from *Tone* was about halfway out its search leg, heading directly toward the American carriers.) On the other hand, Fletcher needed to recover the search planes that he had sent northward that morning, and he still hoped to catch Nagumo at sixes and sevens while the Japanese carriers were recovering aircraft. Fletcher decided to hedge his bets. At 6:07 he blinkered a message to Spruance in the *Enterprise:* "Proceed southwesterly and attack enemy carriers when definitely located. I will follow as soon as planes recovered." Meanwhile, he would hold the *Yorktown's* air wing "in reserve pending receipt of information on additional enemy carriers."[42]

Over on the *Enterprise,* Spruance was ready. His volatile and impulsive chief of staff, Captain Miles Browning, had been urging an immediate strike since the first sighting, never mind the range. Now unleashed by Fletcher, Spruance did not hedge his bets; he decided to launch everything he had in the hope of inflicting an early knockout. He would keep only a handful of fighters for combat air patrol to protect the task force. Everything else would go into the air at once for an all-out attack on the enemy carriers. At 6:16 the klaxon on the *Enterprise* sounded general quarters, and a voice over the 1MC intercom system announced: "Pilots, man your aircraft."[43]

Taking off from a carrier is no more routine than landing on one. Though the carrier flight decks were over eight hundred feet long, the aft portion of the deck was crowded with airplanes, most of them already manned and with their engines running. The first planes to lift off, there-

The planes of Eugene Lindsay's VT-6 on the flight deck of USS *Enterprise* on the morning of June 4. The 1,220-pound Mark 13 torpedoes can be seen slung under the fuselage of the foremost planes. Only four of the planes shown here returned from the strike against the Kido Butai. (U.S. Navy)

fore, had only about four hundred feet of runway to get airborne. The *Yorktown* had hydraulic catapults that were theoretically capable of accelerating the planes to nearly a hundred miles per hour within a hundred feet of deck space. But it was a jarring and not always reliable system. The catapults shot the planes forward at full thrust from a dead start ("a real kick in the butt," as one pilot recalled), then the boost tailed off as the hydraulic container lost pressure. The result was often a "cold cat shot" that failed to get the plane airborne. Because of that, there were no such catapult takeoffs on June 4; the planes got airborne on their own.[44]

Soon after receiving Fletcher's order, Spruance ordered his two big carriers to turn into the wind and increase speed to twenty-five knots. The wind that day was light, only about five knots, and it was blowing directly toward the enemy, which meant that the carriers had to turn *away* from their objective in order to launch; even then the light winds made takeoff difficult. The pilots kept their wheel brakes on and revved their engines. Then, at a signal from the flight deck officer, the lead pilot released the brake and gave his engine maximum throttle. At exactly 7:00 A.M. the first planes on the *Enterprise* rumbled forward into the wind, picked up speed, and lifted off. Two minutes later the first plane from the *Hornet* also took to the air.[45]

The fighters went first, then the dive-bombers—half of them armed with thousand-pound bombs, half with five-hundred-pound bombs—then the torpedo planes. It took about an hour to launch all 119 planes of the strike force. Those that launched first circled above the task force until the others could join the formation. Just over halfway through the launch cycle, at about 7:30, Spruance was handed a report that a long-range enemy floatplane had been spotted. The fighter control director, Lieutenant Commander Leonard "Ham" Dow, vectored several fighters toward it, but the enemy plane disappeared into the clouds. This, of course, was the long-delayed scout plane from *Tone*, and the Americans had to suspect that it would report their position. It was too late now to rethink the decision to attack. Presumably the enemy carriers would have to maintain course and speed in order to recover the planes they had sent to Midway. So the launching continued, and when all 119 planes were formed up, the entire formation flew off westward toward the intercept point that had been calculated by extrapolating the enemy's course and speed from the last sighting. As soon as the last plane was airborne, Spruance reversed course in order to close the enemy as quickly as possible. The decision to launch at this distance meant that some of the planes might easily run out of fuel on the return trip. Spruance's maneuvering also took him out of visual distance from the *Yorktown* and Task Force 17. From this point on in the battle, the two American task forces operated independently.[46]

While Fletcher wrestled with his options and Spruance turned his carriers into the wind to launch his air wing, the 108 planes of the Japanese strike force were closing in on Midway. The defenders were ready for them. Historians have paid a lot of attention to the importance of decrypted intelligence in the Battle of Midway, and rightly so, but less attention has been paid to another critical source of American intelligence, and that was that the Americans had radar—on each of their carriers as well as at Midway—and the Japanese did not. The radar station on Midway picked up the signal of the approaching enemy planes ninety miles out, and the Marine Corps pilots based on Midway—most of them flying old F2A-3 Buffalos—immediately took off, climbed to fourteen thousand feet, and headed out in the direction of the approaching enemy to intercept them. Afterward the rest of the planes on the island also took off. The scout planes and heavy bombers not already dispatched on combat missions were ordered to fly south simply to get out of the way. The principal objective of the Japanese air strike at Midway was to eliminate the threat from Midway's airfield, but by 6:00 A.M. there were no planes left on the ground at Midway for the Japanese to target. The last to leave was an old PBY that took off and lumbered southward just as the Japanese were coming in from the north.[47]

Forty miles out, the Marine fighter pilots spotted the approaching Japanese planes flying below them in six nine-plane V formations. Because the Japanese expected to catch the American planes just taking off, the Zero fighter pilots were looking down and were surprised when the

Marines swooped down on them from fourteen thousand feet, sending half a dozen enemy bombers down in flames. The Marines' good fortune did not last. Despite the skill and determination of the pilots, the F2A-3 Buffalos they flew were easy meat for the Japanese Zeros. One by one the American planes were shot from the sky, and the rest of the Japanese bombers flew through the intercept to complete their mission.[48]

They were hugely disappointed, however, to find that the runways on Eastern Island were bare. They hit the base power plant, blew up the fuel tanks and hangars, and did as much damage as they could, but because the American airplanes had been removed from harm's way, it was evident that the attack had not eliminated Midway as a threat to the approaching invasion force. En route back to the carriers, at 7:00 A.M., the Japanese flight commander, Lieutenant Joichi Tomonaga, reported: "There is need for a second attack." At that precise moment, though none of the Japanese

Smoke from a burning oil tank hit by the Japanese during their air raid on Midway fails to impress the gooney birds in the foreground. (U.S. Navy)

decision makers knew it, the first planes were lifting off from the *Enterprise* and *Hornet* to attack the Japanese carriers.[49]

Tomonaga's report gave Nagumo something to think about. He already had the other half of his air wing spotted on the decks of his carriers. But they were armed with antiship weapons: torpedoes and armor-piercing bombs. To launch a second attack on Midway, those planes would have to be rearmed. While he thought about it, the bugle call for air raid sounded on board his flagship.[50] The attack was not by planes from the American carriers—it would take them two more hours to reach the intercept point—it was more land-based bombers from Midway. This time it was four Army twin-engine B-26 bombers that had been rigged to carry torpedoes, and six Navy TBF torpedo bombers.* The Japanese Zeros swarmed down on them and shot down seven of them even as three others managed to launch their torpedoes. None of those torpedoes scored a hit, however, and the three surviving planes headed back toward Midway. It was another American failure, as fruitless as the B-17 attack the day before, though more costly to the attackers. But the attack had an impact on the battle nevertheless, for it very likely helped Nagumo decide that a second strike on Midway was indeed necessary, since these planes had obviously come from Midway's airfield. A few minutes later Nagumo ordered that the planes already spotted on the flight decks of his four carriers be rearmed with explosive ordnance for a second strike on Midway.

That work was well under way when, sometime after 7:30, the tardy floatplane from the *Tone* finally made a report: "Ten ships, apparently enemy, sighted. Bearing zero one zero, distant two four zero from Midway. Course one five zero, speed more than twenty knots." This was, of course, Spruance's Task Force 16, which consisted of seventeen warships, including two carriers, but apparently distance and cloud cover obscured the size and character of Spruance's command. Like the officers on *Yorktown*, the

---

* The TBF Avenger was similar to the TBD Devastator except that it was made by Grumman Aircraft rather than by Douglas, and it carried its torpedo inside the fuselage rather than slung underneath, which made the Avenger slightly more aerodynamic. Though the Avenger proved effective later in the war, it had no more luck at Midway than the Devastator.

bridge team on the *Akagi* immediately bent over the chart. A quick trian-
gulation showed that the enemy ships were less than two hundred miles
away, already within range of the Japanese attack planes. Nagumo immediately suspended the rearming of the planes and ordered the thirty-six torpedo planes that he had ready to "prepare to carry out attacks on enemy
fleet units." Before he committed himself, however, he needed more information. To the pilot of the *Tone*'s search plane pilot he radioed: "Ascertain
ship types and maintain contact." For a few precious and irrecoverable
moments the entire Japanese strike force was frozen in suspension while
Nagumo waited for the answer.[51]

It came ten minutes later: "Enemy ships are five cruisers and five
destroyers." Nagumo breathed out. Cruisers and destroyers could safely be
ignored until Midway was dispatched. He ordered work to resume at once
on the changeover from torpedoes to bombs for a second strike on Midway. That order proved difficult to execute, however, because during the
next thirty minutes the Kido Butai was attacked three times by more
planes from Midway. The first attack came from Army B-17s bombing
from high altitude. Bombs fell all around the *Hiryu* and the *Soryu*, sending
up great plumes of water, but none of them scored a hit, though once
again the pilots reported severe damage to both carriers.

Then, almost immediately afterward, sixteen Marine Corps dive-
bombers attacked. All but three of the pilots in this group were rookies;
none of them had ever flown a Dauntless before or had practiced dive-
bombing. Their only training had been in "glide bombing," which called
for a descent toward the target at a modest thirty-degree angle. Because of
that, the commanding officer, Major Lofton "Joe" Henderson, "decided to
use a glide bombing attack." Starting from eight thousand feet, the
Marines power-glided down to four hundred feet before releasing their
bombs. The Zeros were all over them, shooting down exactly half of the
planes, including Henderson's, and riddling the others with bullet holes
(one managed to return to Midway with no fewer than 210 holes in its
fuselage). Rookies though they were, the Marines pressed the attack and
released their bombs. The *Hiryu* all but disappeared in water spouts from
the bomb explosions, but when the water settled, it was steaming along as

before. Once again, despite determination and sacrifice, the Americans had made no hits.[52]

Finally, a dozen antiquated Marine Corps Vindicators tried their hand. The aged fabric-covered Vindicators (which their pilots dismissively referred to as either "Vibrators" or "Wind Indicators") fared no better. Two were splashed by the Zeros, two more were damaged, and none scored a hit. Thus between 8:10 and 8:30 the carriers of the Kido Butai survived unscathed three separate attacks by Midway-based bombers. The only advantage gained by the Americans in these otherwise futile attacks was that the armament shift from armor-piercing to explosive ordnance on Japanese aircraft was slowed by the violent maneuvering of the carriers.[53]

In the midst of the last of these attacks, the *Tone*'s search plane radioed a correction—or rather an addition. Apparently the clouds had cleared sufficiently to give him a better look at Spruance's command: He now reported: "Enemy force accompanied by what appears to be aircraft carrier bringing up the rear." A carrier! That changed everything. Or maybe not. After all, the report indicated that it "appears to be" a carrier. Nagumo had little time to contemplate his response to this news, for by now the planes from his own strike on Midway were returning, and they would need clear decks on which to land. An immediate decision was necessary. Nagumo had thirty-six torpedo planes armed and ready to go against the American carrier, but if he sent them now, they would have to attack without fighter cover, and during the last half hour he had just witnessed the futility of air attacks made without fighter cover on his own carriers. Assuming there was time, it would be better to send off a coordinated attack. Rear Admiral Tamon Yamaguchi, the eager commander of the Second Carrier Division, had the temerity to offer unsolicited advice by blinker: "Consider it advisable to launch attack force immediately." But Nagumo would not be rushed. He also did not want to do things by halves. He made his decision: instead of launching a partial attack at once, he would strike the planes that were then on deck back down to the hangar deck, recover the planes returning from Midway, rearm and refuel the entire wing, and then send a full coordinated air strike toward the American position.[54]

By the time he made this decision, it was 8:30; the planes from the *Hornet* and *Enterprise* had been in the air for an hour and a half.

—

Among the fifty-eight planes launched from the *Hornet* that morning were the fifteen torpedo bombers of VT-8, led by Lieutenant Commander John C. "Jack" Waldron, a twenty-one-year Navy veteran from South Dakota who was particularly proud of being one-eighth Sioux. Waldron was eager to tangle with the enemy. He had argued for an earlier launch that would catch the Japanese by surprise, and he had been disappointed when he was told to wait. He was even more disappointed when the *Hornet*'s captain, Marc "Pete" Mitscher, decided that the Wildcats of the *Hornet*'s fighter squadron (VF-8) would accompany the dive-bombers rather than the torpedo planes. The rationale was that because the Wildcats could not climb as effectively as the Zeros, it was better for them to come in high so that they could fly down on the Zeros, rather than have to struggle up from low altitude.[55]

Waldron claimed to have a "sixth sense" that was a product of his Indian heritage, and that sixth sense was at work that morning, for he was convinced that the coordinates of the Japanese carriers given at the briefing that morning were in error. He believed that instead of continuing south, the Japanese carriers would turn north as soon as they learned there were American carriers in the area. On his way to his aircraft he stopped Ensign George Gay, the squadron navigator, and told

Lieutenant Commander Jack Waldron, who had a gut feeling about the location of the Japanese carriers, poses in front of his TBD-1 Devastator torpedo bomber. Every plane of Waldron's VT-8 squadron was lost in the ensuing strike. (U.S. Navy)

him that "the Japs will not be going toward Midway. . . . The Group commander [Commander Stanhope Ring] is going to take the whole bunch down there. I'm going more to the north. . . . Don't think I'm lost. Just track me so that if anything happens to me the boys can count on you to bring them back."[56]

Ring took the *Hornet's* bombers almost due west; Lieutenant Commander Wade McClusky, with the *Enterprise* bombers, flew a more southerly course. Neither Ring nor McClusky, however, found the Japanese carriers where they were supposed to be. Ring actually passed well north of the Kido Butai and, concluding that the enemy must be closing Midway, he turned south. McClusky was well south of the target, but, unaware of that, he commenced a standard search patrol, boxing the compass in gradually expanding circles while searching the horizon. But Jack Waldron, leading the *Hornet's* torpedo bombers, followed his gut and split the difference, flying, as it turned out, directly toward the enemy. At 9:20 he found the Kido Butai.[57]

Approaching at fifteen hundred feet, Waldron was awestruck by the sight of the Japanese fleet spread out before him, but his seat-of-the-pants navigation apparently had been too good, for he could see no other American planes in the vicinity. Although Waldron didn't know it, there *were* other American planes nearby: Nearly four miles straight up, Lieutenant James S. Gray's squadron of Wildcats from the *Enterprise* was circling over the Japanese fleet at twenty-two thousand feet, waiting for the arrival of the dive-bombers. At such vertical distances, however, Gray was as ignorant of Waldron's presence as Waldron was of Gray's. All Waldron could see were Japanese ships—lots of them. At the back of the formation, Ensign Gay had a clear view. "The first capital ship I recognized was a carrier—the *Soryu*. Then I made out the *Kaga* and the *Akagi*. There was another carrier further on, and screening ships all over the damned ocean." Waldron concluded that there was no use waiting for support. He broke radio silence to announce: "We will go in. We won't turn back. Former strategy [coordination with the dive-bombers] cannot be used. We will attack. Good luck." Gray might have swooped down to assist, but the planes from the *Enterprise* and *Hornet* were using different radio frequencies, and Gray never heard the call.[58]

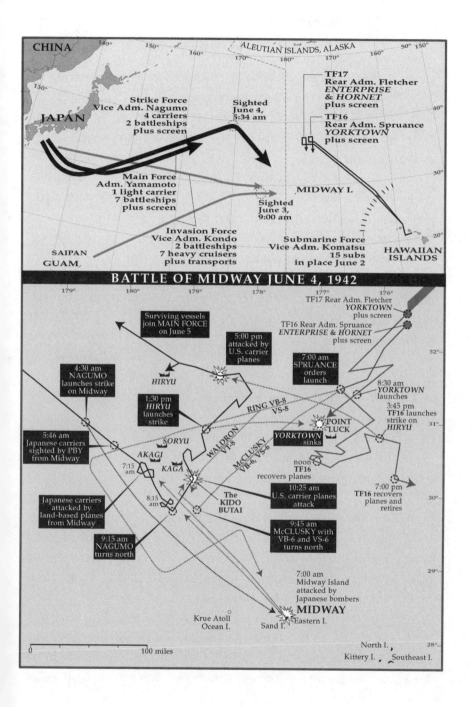

CHINA

ALEUTIAN ISLANDS, ALASKA

JAPAN

Strike Force
Vice Adm. Nagumo
4 carriers
2 battleships
plus screen

Sighted
June 4,
5:34 am

TF17
Rear Adm. Fletcher
ENTERPRISE
& *HORNET*
plus screen

TF16
Rear Adm. Spruance
YORKTOWN
plus screen

Main Force
Adm. Yamamoto
1 light carrier
7 battleships
plus screen

MIDWAY I.

Sighted
June 3,
9:00 am

Invasion Force
Vice Adm. Kondo
2 battleships
7 heavy cruisers
plus transports

Submarine Force
Vice Adm. Komatsu
15 subs
in place June 2

SAIPAN
GUAM

HAWAIIAN
ISLANDS

BATTLE OF MIDWAY JUNE 4, 1942

TF17 Rear Adm. Fletcher
YORKTOWN
plus screen

TF16 Rear Adm. Spruance
ENTERPRISE & HORNET
plus screen

Surviving vessels
join MAIN FORCE
on June 5

5:00 pm
attacked by
U.S. carrier
planes

7:00 am
SPRUANCE
orders
launch

4:30 am
NAGUMO
launches strike
on Midway

HIRYU

8:30 am
YORKTOWN
launches

1:30 pm
HIRYU
launches
strike

RING VB-8
VS-8

3:45 pm
TF16 launches
strike on
HIRYU

5:46 am
Japanese carriers
sighted by PBY
from Midway

SORYU

WALDRON
VT-8

POINT
LUCK

AKAGI

7:15
am

KAGA

McCLUSKY
VB-6, VS-6

YORKTOWN
sinks

noon
TF16
recovers planes

7:00 pm
TF16 recovers
planes and
retires

Japanese carriers
attacked by
land-based planes
from Midway

8:15
am

The
KIDO
BUTAI

10:25 am
U.S. carrier planes
attack

9:15 am
NAGUMO
turns north

9:45 am
McCLUSKY with
VB-6 and VS-6
turns north

7:00 am
Midway Island
attacked by
Japanese bombers

Krue Atoll
Ocean I.

MIDWAY

Sand I. Eastern I.

0   100 miles

North I.

Kittery I.   Southeast I.

Waldron led his squadron toward the carrier in the middle of the enemy formation, and as he did so the Japanese fighters swarmed to the attack. At once, the swift Zeroes began to score hits. Swooping in from astern, the faster and more nimble Zeros savaged the slow and level-flying torpedo bombers. One torpedo bomber went down, then two. "Zeros were coming in from all angles and from both sides at once," Gay recalled. "They would come in from abeam, pass each other just over our heads, and turn around to make another attack." The Zeros focused on the lead planes and worked their way back. Waldron's plane was one of the first to go down. As the last plane in the formation, Gay managed to get closer than most. Since the target carrier was swinging its bow toward him to comb any torpedoes that might be launched, Gay looped out to starboard to try an approach on its port bow. Bullets from the Zeros and from intense antiair fire riddled his plane; he could hear and feel bullets smacking into the armored back of his pilot's seat, and several smashed through the instrument panel in front of him. Bullets struck his leg and his left hand; his gunner slumped dead in the seat behind him. At eight hundred yards he triggered the electrical release to launch his torpedo. Nothing happened. Since he had been shot through the left hand, he shifted hands and tried to launch the torpedo manually with his right hand, but when he yanked on the manual release cable, it pulled out of the instrument panel. He had done everything he could to launch the torpedo, but he couldn't tell if it had dropped or not. In any case, there was no more he could do here. He banked sharply left to get out of there as fast as he could.[59]

It was not fast enough. The Zeros had backed off when Gay had flown inside the envelope of the fleet's antiair fire, but now they returned, and a twenty-millimeter cannon shell took out his left rudder control. As the plane careened toward the water, Gay tried to hold it level for a crash landing. He hit the water hard but managed to scramble out of the sinking plane before it went down. Inflating his life vest, he covered his head with the seat cushion from the bombardier's middle seat to avoid being strafed. Peeking out from under it, he could see several Zeros overhead but no American torpedo planes. Though he didn't know it yet, he was the only survivor from VT-8, and none of them had scored a hit on any of the Japanese ships.[60]

The rest of the planes from the *Hornet* never even found the Japanese task force. After flying 250 miles to the west, Ring turned south toward Midway, then east again, but, seeing nothing but empty sea below him, and low on gas, he decided to return to base. Most of the bombers in his squadron turned toward Midway; a handful made it back to the *Hornet*. The fighters who accompanied them mostly ran out of gas and had to ditch in the water.

Of course, there were still the planes from the *Enterprise*, and the next attack on the Kido Butai came from Lieutenant Commander Gene Lindsay's VT-6, approaching the Japanese carriers from astern. They, too, attacked without fighter cover. Patchy clouds and poor radio reception killed any hope of coordination with Gray's Wildcats; Lindsay's lumbering Devastators suffered nearly as much as Waldron's, and once again the Americans scored no hits.

By this time Fletcher had also unleashed the air group from the *Yorktown*, and it was the twelve Devastators of Lieutenant Commander Lance "Lem" Massey's VT-3 that struck next. The Zeros were ready and waiting, and they pounced on the new arrivals fourteen miles out. But unlike Waldron or Lindsay, Massey had fighter support: six Wildcats of Jimmy Thach's VF-3. As Ensign Gay watched, bobbing in his life vest in the middle of the Japanese task force, Massey's twelve torpedo planes pressed home their attack, dropping down to 150 feet to make their torpedo runs while Thach's fighters provided cover. Thach was angry that Fletcher had sent him off with only six of his twenty-five planes, keeping most of the fighters behind to protect the task force.* This was particularly bothersome because Thach had developed an innovative combat tactic—subsequently dubbed the "Thach weave"—that could be executed only when the Ameri-

---

* In addition to his uncertainty about the location and status of the rest of the Japanese carrier force, the fact that Fletcher had been criticized for not keeping enough fighters behind to protect the task force during the Battle of the Coral Sea may have influenced his decision to keep most of his fighters behind for combat air patrol (CAP).

can fighters maneuvered in groups of four. Six, Thach had pointed out angrily that morning, was not divisible by four! Still, he did the best he could with his half dozen planes, and in the process he demonstrated that innovative tactics could partially compensate for the Zero's superior speed and agility—but only partially.[61]

The Zeros streamed in on the American fighters from behind. At first Thach was surprised that the Japanese would send their fighters after him instead of concentrating on the torpedo bombers. Then he saw that "they ... were streaming in right past us and into the torpedo planes." Even though he had only six planes, Thach ordered his small squadron to begin the "weave" pattern they had practiced. The Wildcats opened up their formation, and as the Zeros streamed in from behind, one of the Wildcats in each pair turned inward, toward its wingman, to confront the Zeros nose to nose. It worked; a Zero exploded and went down. But the Zeros had the numbers, and they were savaging the American torpedo planes. Somewhat bitterly, Thach wrote in his after-action report that "six F4F-4 airplanes cannot prevent 20 or 30 Japanese VF from shooting our slow torpedo

planes." Lem Massey's plane was one of the first to be shot down. "It just exploded," Thach remembered. "The air was just like a bee hive" as the fighters turned and twisted while the surviving torpedo bombers tried to hold a steady course for the Japanese carriers.[62]

In the midst of the air battle, Thach's wingman, twenty-one-year-old Robert A. M. Dibb (called "Ram" due to his initials), called out: "There's a Zero on my tail." Thach made the inside maneuver of the weave pattern and came up face-to-face with the onrushing Zero. The two planes raced toward each other at

The commander of VF-3, the fighter squadron on the *Yorktown*, Lieutenant Commander John S. "Jimmy" Thach, in the cockpit of his F4F-4 Wildcat. (U.S. Navy)

full speed. "I was really angry then," Thach recalled. "I was mad because here's this poor wing man who'd never been in combat before . . . and a Zero was about to chew him to pieces. I probably should have decided to duck under this Zero, but I lost my temper a little bit, and I decided I'm going to keep my fire going into him and he's going to pull out." The two planes closed each other at a combined five hundred miles an hour. At the last possible second the Zero pulled up, and the two planes missed one another by a matter of feet. It was, Thach recalled, like playing chicken while shooting.[63]

Thach's fighters claimed several Zeros, but the Zeros claimed even more torpedo planes. Ten of Massey's fourteen torpedo planes were splashed, and their sacrifice was in vain. Although several managed to launch torpedoes, none of them found a target. Altogether, of the forty-one Devastator torpedo bombers that the Americans launched against the Japanese carriers that day, only four returned, and none scored a hit.[64]

All this time, the Japanese carriers had been maneuvering wildly to avoid the torpedoes in the water. The radical turns had slowed the work crews trying to complete the ordnance changeover from explosive bombs to armor-piercing bombs and torpedoes. Clad only in shorts and slippers, the Japanese crewmen had worked furiously to complete the changeover. Instead of taking the time to lower the removed ordnance back to the ship's magazine, they had laid much of it aside while they armed the bombers with antiship ordnance. Fuel lines snaked across wooden decks; a small gasoline truck drove from plane to plane to top off their tanks. Now the planes for the air strike against the American carriers were at last spotted on their flight decks, fueled and ready to go, their engines already turning over. With the elimination of the American torpedo planes, Nagumo gave the order for his carriers to turn into the wind. Within fifteen minutes—twenty at the most—Nagumo's strike group would be in the air. The first fighter planes were already rolling down the deck.

It is seldom possible to pick a precise moment when the course of history changes, but this was one such moment. At 10:20 A.M. on June 4, 1942, the Japanese were not only winning the Battle of Midway, they were winning the war. The carriers of the Kito Butai had survived seven separate air attacks without a scratch. Their superior attack planes were armed and ready on the flight deck—victory lay before them. The first fighter plane of the attack force had already lifted off, and others were accelerating toward the bow. Then Thach, looking out his windscreen, saw a glint high up in the sky where the sun caught the edge of a dark blue wingtip. And down they came. "It looked like a beautiful silver waterfall," Thach recalled, "those dive bombers coming down."[65]

On board Nagumo's flagship, the lookout screamed out a warning: "Hell divers!"[66]

Like the frustrated Dauntless pilots from the *Hornet*, the dive-bomber pilots from the *Enterprise*—two squadrons of thirty planes, all under Lieutenant Commander Wade McClusky—had found only empty ocean when they arrived at the coordinates given to them at the briefing that morning. While Commander Ring flew south with the bombers from *Hornet*, McClusky decided to go north. The need to maintain radio silence left this crucial decision up to him; because he was out of touch with his superiors, McClusky made his decision based on instinct, as Jack Waldron had done. His decision was fateful. As Nimitz wrote afterward in his battle report, "This was one of the most important decisions of the battle."[67]

Boxing the compass in a general search pattern, McClusky spotted a lone Japanese destroyer speeding northward at thirty knots. Though he did not know it, this was the *Arashi*, which had been dispatched to deal with a pesky American submarine (the *Nautilus*) that had briefly penetrated the Japanese screen and fired several torpedoes at the Japanese carriers. After forcing the *Nautilus* to dive and dropping several depth charges to keep it down, the *Arashi* was now speeding northward to rejoin the fleet. In a flash of insight, McClusky realized its intent, and drawing a mental line northward along its track, he led his thirty dive-bombers in that direction. Sure enough, just past 10:00 A.M., nearly three hours after lifting off from the *Enterprise*, McClusky found the Kido Butai. Twenty thousand feet below him, intermittently visible through patchy white clouds, was the enemy strike force: a dozen or more battleships, cruisers, and destroyers protecting two large carriers, with other ships filling up the ocean to the horizon and beyond. The two carriers below him were "maneuvering radically" to avoid the torpedoes that the unlucky U.S. torpedo bombers had managed to launch before being shot down. As stunning as that panoramic image was, what was even more astonishing was that there were no Japanese fighters over the strike force. All of the Zeros flying combat patrol over the carrier force had descended to low altitude to deal with the torpedo bombers. Gray's Wildcats, by then very low on fuel, had also departed. The skies were empty.[68]

Lieutenant Commander Clarence Wade McClusky, who commanded the dive-bombers from the *Enterprise*, shown here in a commander's uniform in a photo taken after the battle. (U.S. Navy)

Doctrine called for the lead squadron in McClusky's command (Earl Gallagher's VS-6) to bypass the first target and take on the more distant one, which was Nagumo's flagship *Akagi*. But in the excitement of the moment, both squadrons headed for the nearer *Kaga*. Unmolested by enemy fighters, the Dauntless pilots winged over into steep dives and flew almost straight down—like a "silver waterfall," in Thach's words—aiming along the "fore and aft line of the target" at the bright red sun painted prominently on the *Kaga*'s orange flight deck. McClusky held his dive to eighteen hundred feet before pulling the lever that released his bomb. With the *Kaga* maneuvering radically, that first bomb hit close alongside, as did the next two, but the fourth detonated among the planes spotted on the *Kaga*'s crowded flight deck and triggered a series of secondary explosions that turned the big carrier into a holocaust. Within seconds, two more bombs struck the wounded flattop, and within minutes the giant *Kaga* was a burning wreck.

Though most of his command had followed McClusky in his furious attack on the *Kaga*, Richard Best, commanding VB-6, had held back when it became evident that both squadrons were going after the same ship. When he was sure that the *Kaga* was mortally wounded, he led a small group of only five planes to attack the *Akagi*. It was enough. Best landed his own thousand-pound bomb directly on the *Akagi*'s flight deck near the forward elevator, and two other bombs hit on or near the ship's fantail. Fires enveloped Nagumo's flagship and triggered several secondary explosions. From his vantage point in his circling Wildcat, Thach thought he had never seen "such superb dive bombing. It looked like almost every bomb hit." The flames from the *Akagi* reached higher into the sky than the carrier was long, and at 880 feet, the *Akagi* was the longest carrier in the Japanese fleet.[69]

By coincidence, at almost the same moment that McClusky's pilots winged over to attack the *Kaga* and *Akagi*, the dive-bombers of Lieutenant Commander Max Leslie's VB-3 from *Yorktown* also arrived over the Kido Butai. Fletcher had delayed the takeoff of his strike force by an hour and a half, not only so that he could recover his scout planes but also to ensure that all the carriers of the Kido Butai had been located. Leslie's planes had flown a more direct route to the target, however, and therefore arrived over the Kido Butai only seconds after McClusky. Leslie himself could not deliver a bomb onto the inviting target he saw spread out below him, for his bomb had prematurely jettisoned en route when he had armed his electronic release trigger. The same thing had happened to three other planes of his command before Leslie had broken radio silence briefly to order his pilots to forget the electronic release and rely on the manual release. Though Leslie had lost his bomb, he was nevertheless determined to lead the attack. He picked out what he thought was the Japanese flagship but which was, in fact, her sister ship, the *Soryu*. Leslie noted that "its flight deck was covered with planes spotted aft." Those planes were warming up and ready to go, but they would never take off. Leslie circled the target once to give Lem Massey's torpedo bombers a chance to attack, but hearing Massey's frantic report that he was being overwhelmed by Zeros, he waited no longer. At 10:22, at virtually the same moment that McClusky's pilots began their dive on the *Kaga*, Leslie pushed his stick forward, putting his Dauntless into a steep dive.[70]

Though Leslie himself could only strafe the big flattop (at least until his guns jammed), the next plane, piloted by Lieutenant Paul "Lefty" Holmberg, landed its thousand-pound bomb square in the middle of the fully armed and refueled planes on the *Soryu*'s flight deck. Instantly the whole after part of the Japanese carrier was turned into a "flaming inferno." A Zero fighter, accelerating toward the bow for takeoff, was blown over the side by the force of the explosion. One by one, the other pilots of VB-3 landed their bombs on the flight deck or scored near misses that shook the giant carrier from stem to stern. Within minutes, the *Soryu*, like the *Kaga* and the *Akagi*, was transformed from a terrible weapon of war into a burn-

A dive-bomber's-eye view of the Japanese carrier *Soryu* taken by one of the planes of Max Leslie's VB-3 from *Yorktown* just prior to the attack, around 10:20 A.M. The *Soryu* has initiated a radical turn to starboard in the hope of throwing off the attacking dive-bombers. Note the rising sun painted on the forward part of the flight deck. (U.S. Navy)

ing wreck. It was so thoroughly shattered that the rest of Leslie's bombers shifted their target to what they thought was a light carrier acting as plane guard astern of the *Soryu* but which was actually a destroyer. On the Japanese carrier, Captain Ryusaku Yanagimoto continued to call out encouragement to his men, but he refused to leave the bridge, and eventually he went down with his ship, softly singing the Japanese national anthem.[71]

In less time than it takes to read about it, three of Nagumo's four carriers were utterly destroyed. The damage control teams never had a chance. A carrier might survive three, four, or even five bomb hits, but the first of the American bombs had set off dozens of secondary explosions as the bombs and torpedoes on the Japanese planes spotted on the deck cooked off one by one. One deck below, where ordnance had been hastily laid aside on the hangar decks during the rearming process, the flames found more fuel, and soon the entire hangar area was ablaze. Within minutes it was clear that all three carriers were lost. Yanagimoto was not the only commander who considered going down with his ship. Nagumo himself felt the sting of shame and failure. But his staff convinced him that he had duties yet to fulfill, and with some reluctance he allowed himself to be transferred to the cruiser *Nagara*. The Kido Butai, which had ruled the western Pacific for six months, had been reduced in five minutes to a single carrier.[72]

———

That single carrier, however, still posed a very real threat. Though Nagumo's plan for a coordinated strike by all four carriers had been interrupted in the most spectacular way by the onslaught of the American dive-bombers, some twenty-four planes (eighteen bombers and six fighters) lifted off *Hiryu* without interference, and by 11:00 they were winging their way toward the American carriers, though it is worth noting that this was a less potent strike force than the thirty-six planes Nagumo could have launched at 8:30, when he first heard that an American carrier was in the vicinity.

Once again, American radar proved invaluable. While the Japanese carrier crews learned of the American dive-bombing attack only as it was happening, the men on the *Yorktown*—the target of the *Hiryu*'s air

strike—learned of the approaching enemy bombers well in advance thanks
to the *Yorktown*'s CXAM radar. A few minutes before noon, radio electri-
cian V. M. Bennett reported "thirty to forty bogeys" approaching, forty-six
miles out on bearing two four zero. This advance warning gave Captain
Elliott Buckmaster the opportunity to prepare. Refueling was halted at
once, the auxiliary aviation fuel tank was dumped unceremoniously over
the side, the hoses were purged, and all watertight doors were locked down
and secured. In addition, the *Yorktown* launched a dozen Wildcat fighters,
and Lieutenant Commander Oscar Pederson, acting as fighter director,
vectored them out toward the incoming bombers.[73]

The American Wildcats intercepted the incoming enemy planes twenty
miles out. Their counterattack immediately broke up the attack formation,

The *Yorktown* under attack by planes from the *Hiryu*. A bomb has just exploded on the *York-*
town's flight deck, while to the right a Japanese bomber crashes into the sea. The black
clouds filling the sky are the result of antiaircraft fire from the *Yorktown*'s escorts. (U.S. Navy)

as the Japanese bombers were forced to maneuver individually. An air battle is fast-paced and confusing; it is virtually impossible to follow the action as individual planes roil about the sky, each seeking an advantage. As one observer remarked, the battle seemed to "roll" toward the task force.[74] As fighter director, Pederson sought to coordinate the action from the bridge of the *Yorktown* using the carrier's radar and the radio. He had to track two plots simultaneously: a search plot to keep track of incoming bogeys, and a fighter director board to keep track of his own air assets. He addressed the fighters individually with the *Yorktown*'s call sign, Scarlett. In the radio chatter, Pederson's directions mixed with the pilots' responses:

"All Scarlett planes keep a sharp lookout. . . ."

"Twenty bandits approaching 305. Thirty miles, large group of bandits."

"All Scarlett planes, bandits eight miles 255."

"This is Scarlett 19. Formation seems to be breaking up."

"O.K. Break 'em up."

"Tally ho!"[75]

One problem that manifested itself very soon was the relatively small size of the magazines on the American fighters. The F4F-4 version of the Wildcat carried six guns in its wings, but each gun had only 240 rounds of ammunition. In a frenzied dogfight, that could be used up very quickly. Since Pedersen was using the radio to direct the attack, pilots signaled ammunition and fuel problems by hand signals. "We'd fly by the bridge and shake our fist at them, that meant I'm low or out of ammunition," Thach recalled. "If you were low on gas, you could stick your hand out of the cockpit and rake it along the gas tank."[76] The *Yorktown*'s twelve Wildcats thinned out the number of approaching bombers, splashing several of them as well as bagging a few of the fighters, but it was evident almost at once that the *Yorktown* needed help from Spruance's carriers, and Pederson called for it:

"Red from Scarlett. We need some VFs."

"Scarlett from Red, repeat."

"Red from Scarlett, we need relief for our combat patrols, getting low on ammunition."

"Scarlett from Red, We are sending the Blue patrol to assist. . . . Blue patrol being launched now."

The CXAM radar also allowed Pederson to vector specific planes out to investigate specific radar contacts:

"Scarlett 19, investigate plane bearing 235. . . . Distance ten to twelve miles, altitude low. Go get 'em."

"O.K. Got him. Have bogey in sight. . . ."

The Wildcats splashed seven bombers before the attackers even came within anti-aircraft range of the task force. Then the cruisers and destroyers opened fire. Once the bombers entered the envelope of the antiair fire from the task force, the Wildcats peeled off, and, nearly out of gas as well as ammunition, they now needed a place to land. The Yorktown could not recover airplanes, for it was maneuvering to avoid bombs and torpedoes. Pederson had to advise his pilots to head for Spruance's carriers over the northern horizon; if they could not make it that far, they would have to ditch in the water. Even worse, Max Leslie's dive-bombers, returning from the strike on the Soryu, had to circle overhead, unable to land, and eventually they, too, had to seek the carriers of Task Force 16 or land in the water.[77]

Fierce antiair fire splashed three more Japanese bombers as they closed on the task force, but five planes got through and dropped their bombs. Two missed, but the next three all found their target. The first, tumbling in flight, hit the Yorktown "just abaft No. 2 elevator on the starboard side." It smashed through the flight deck and exploded on the hangar deck, where three planes caught fire, one of which was armed with a thousand-pound bomb. Quick action by the hangar deck officer triggered the sprinklers, and the fire was contained. The second bomb passed through both the flight deck and the hangar deck and exploded on level three, among the engine uptakes from the boilers. The Yorktown's speed immediately dropped to six knots, and twenty minutes later, at 12:40 P.M., the Yorktown was dead in the water. The third bomb also did damage, but it was the loss of the engines that was critical.[78]

The damage control crews immediately got to work. There was no sense of panic; the damage control parties simply went to work with a calm professionalism. The fifteen minutes of warning provided by the radar had made a world of difference. Fires were quickly contained, the holes in the deck were patched, and the boiler technicians worked to repair the uptakes on three of the boilers. Within ninety minutes the boilers were back on line, and ten minutes after that the engine room reported that the *Yorktown* could make twenty knots, enough to resume air operations.[79]

The *Yorktown*, it seemed, had survived yet again. Then, just ten minutes later, the *Yorktown*'s radar reported another set of bogeys inbound. This time it was ten torpedo planes and more fighters. Again the *Yorktown*'s fighters were scrambled, though since the *Yorktown* was making only about sixteen knots, several of the planes struggled to get into the air. Some were still in the process of taking off when the torpedo bombers began their attack run. A twenty-two-year-old ensign with the unlikely name of Milton Tootle IV had barely cleared the bow in his takeoff and did not even have time to manipulate the hand crank to wind up his landing

The *Yorktown*'s damage control team begins patching a hole in the big carrier's flight deck. Seventy minutes after being struck by three bombs, the *Yorktown* was again operational, launching and recovering aircraft. (U.S. Navy)

gear when he wheeled toward an attacking torpedo plane and shot it down with one long burst. When he pulled up, he was struck by the *Yorktown*'s own antiair fire and crashed into the sea. His whole flight lasted about sixty seconds, but he got his bogey.[80]

The leader of the Japanese torpedo planes was Lieutenant Joichi Tomonaga. Even before he left the *Hiryu*, he knew that he would not be coming back. The left wing fuel tank on his aircraft had been punctured during the Midway raid, and as a result, he had only enough gas for a one-way trip. He approached the *Yorktown* very low, almost at wave-top height. But Jimmy Thach spotted him and made a side approach. Thach fired several quick bursts, and Tomonaga's plane caught fire. Thach could see the ribs of the plane showing through the flames, and yet somehow Tomonaga kept his plane on course. "That devil still stayed up in the air," Thach later recalled in amazement, "until he dropped his torpedo." Tomonaga crashed into the sea, but his torpedo ran straight and true and struck the *Yorktown* flush on its port side.[81]

"It was a real WHACK," Ensign John "Jack" Crawford recalled. "You could feel it all through the ship. . . . I had the impression that the ship's hull buckled slightly."[82] Then, just moments later, another torpedo struck the carrier, also on the port side near frame 75. The lights blinked and went out as the ship lost power. Once again the *Yorktown* was dead in the water. Commander Clarence E. Aldrich, the damage control officer, reported that without power, none of the damage control equipment was working. The big flattop began to list over to port and continued to list until by 3:00 it reached twenty-six degrees. Men on the flight deck could barely keep their feet. Unable to make repairs and fearing that "the ship would capsize in a few minutes," Buckmaster ordered the crew to abandon ship.[83]

—

While the *Hiryu*'s bombers sought to dispatch the *Yorktown*, search planes from Spruance's Task Force 16 were looking for the *Hiryu*. At nearly the same moment that Tomonaga's torpedo slammed into the *Yorktown*, an American lieutenant with the patriotic name of Samuel Adams reported sighting one carrier, two battleships, and three cruisers heading due north, and he gave the coordinates. Immediately the *Enterprise* launched twenty-four bombers, half with thousand-pound bombs, half with five-hundred-pound bombs, but with no fighter escort since the fighters had their hands full over the *Yorktown*.

As these planes sped toward the *Hiryu*, the commander of that vessel, fifty-year-old Rear Admiral Tamon Yamaguchi, was planning a third attack on the Americans. Yamaguchi, who had completed two years of graduate study at Princeton just before the war, was by nature the most aggressive of the Japanese carrier commanders (he was the one who had urged Nagumo to make an immediate strike at 8:30 that morning), and despite the virtual destruction of three-fourths of the Japanese carrier force, he remained stubbornly optimistic. His bomber pilots reported that they had left one carrier dead in the water and on fire, and soon afterward his torpedo bombers reported that they had delivered a mortal blow to an apparently undamaged carrier that was still launching aircraft. Yamaguchi quite naturally assumed that his planes had struck and destroyed two different American carriers. By his reckoning, each side now had one carrier left, and he hoped that one more effective strike against that lone American carrier could still secure a victory for the Kido Butai. Because he had only fifteen planes left (five bombers, four torpedo planes, and six fighters), Yamaguchi planned to wait for dusk, both to give his pilots a much-needed rest and to catch the Americans by surprise. He would launch his third strike at 6:00.[84]

Instead, the American dive-bombers from the *Enterprise* arrived over the *Hiryu* at 5:00. The *Hiryu* at once began twisting and turning to throw off the attackers, and the first several American bombs fell harmlessly into the sea. But there were too many bombers, and the most daring of the American pilots held their dives until they were only a few hundred feet above the target before releasing their bombs. The first bomb that struck the *Hiryu* blew the forward elevator back against the ship's island and opened a huge crater in the flight deck. The almost giddy mood of the American pilots was evident in the recorded message traffic on the open radio net:

"That scared the hell out of me. I thought we weren't going to pull out."

"Your bomb really hit them on the fantail. Boy that's swell."

"Look at that Son-of-a-Bitch burn!"

"Hit the Son-of-a-Bitch again!"

"Those Japs are easy as shooting ducks in a rainbarrel."

"Gee, I wish I had just one more bomb."

"Tojo, you son-of-a-bitch, send out the rest and we'll get those too."[85]

Hit by four bombs, and enduring several secondary explosions, the *Hiryu* was a wreck. After heroic but hopeless damage control efforts, Yamaguchi, his hopes now utterly shattered, ordered abandon ship at 2:30 in the morning. Twenty minutes later, Yamamoto officially canceled the Midway operation.*

It was not quite over. Throughout the night there would be hundreds of individual stories of survival as sailors and airmen in the water tried to hang on while awaiting rescue, and there would be hundreds of other stories that would never be told, by those who were never found. There would be more attacks on disparate elements of the far-flung Japanese force as it retreated. Yet another American air strike sank one heavy cruiser and severely damaged another. But all that was epilogue. The outcome of the battle had been decided in the five minutes between 10:20 and 10:25 on the morning of June 4, when dive-bombers from the *Enterprise* and *Yorktown* screamed down out of the sun, at the precise moment when they would have maximum impact, to lay their bombs on the decks of three Japanese carriers. The *Soryu* and the *Kaga* went down that same evening. The *Akagi* stubbornly remained afloat and was scuttled by the Japanese at dawn the next day to prevent the Americans from claiming it as a prize. The *Hiryu* went down four hours later, its shattered wreck sent to the bottom by "friendly" torpedoes.

---

* Two groups of B-17 Flying Fortress bombers also participated in the attack on the *Hiryu*, though none of them scored a hit. Indeed, of the 322 bombs dropped by B-17s during the Battle of Midway, none of them struck a target. Despite this, newspapers at the time gave most of the credit for the U.S. victory at Midway to the Army bombers. The *New York Times*, for example, reported on June 9 that "the main damage to the Japanese fleet off Midway was inflicted by our land-based airplanes." The subsequent controversy led to more than one brawl between Army and Navy personnel ashore.

The Japanese carrier *Hiryu* dead in the water and burning on June 5. This photo, taken by a Japanese scout plane sent by Yamamoto to assay the damage to the *Hiryu*, shows the gaping hole in the *Hiryu*'s bow. (U.S. Navy)

As for the *Yorktown*, Captain Buckmaster toured the badly listing ship from the catwalk to the hangar deck to ensure that there were no more crewmen on board. He later wrote in his report that "by this time, the port side of the Hangar Deck was in the water." He had no thought of going down with his ship; to him such traditions were melodramatic nonsense. After one last look, he went over the stern, rappelling down a rope line to a small boat, which took him to the destroyer *Hammann* and then to the cruiser *Astoria,* where Fletcher was now flying his flag.[86]

But the *Yorktown* didn't roll over. Instead, it stabilized at twenty-six degrees, and Fletcher and Buckmaster decided to put a salvage team on board to see if it could still be saved. At first light (about when the Japanese were scuttling the *Akagi*) Buckmaster led a team of volunteers on board, and they worked all morning to stabilize the big ship. They put out the worst of the fires, and to compensate for the list to port, they dumped the charred planes over the side and cut away a five-inch gun mount from the port side, which disappointingly brought the ship back only to a twenty-four-degree list.

Then at 3:30 the salvage workers on board saw the wakes of four torpedoes headed directly for the *Yorktown*. There was nothing anyone could do; without power, the *Yorktown* was quite literally a sitting duck. The men on the destroyer *Hammann* alongside got ready to attack the submarine—for it could only be a submarine—by removing the safety forks from the depth charge racks. But before the *Hammann* could even get under way, a torpedo virtually cut her in half, and she immediately began to sink. Two other torpedoes hit the *Yorktown* amidships, this time on her starboard side. As the *Hammann* began to settle, her armed depth charges began to go off, concussing many of the men of her own crew who had abandoned ship and were struggling in the water. The force of the underwater explosions was so great that one survivor's pocket watch was flattened to "the thickness of a silver dollar."[87]

The *Yorktown* lists at 28 degrees as a salvage team attempts to save it. Note the ropes off the side used by the crew to abandon ship. The destroyer at right is USS *Balch*. (U.S. Navy)

Even then, the *Yorktown* refused to sink. Indeed, because the torpedoes had struck her starboard side, the damage reduced the list to seventeen degrees, though the ship was now very heavy in the water and the structural damage was massive. Sections of the flight deck crashed down through to the hangar deck as the ship began to break apart. The *Yorktown* stayed afloat through the night, but there seemed little chance now that it could be saved. Having used the last of its nine lives, it finally went down just before 5:00 A.M. on June 7.[88]

That dawn broke on a new world. History itself had tipped on the fulcrum of the Battle of Midway. The destruction of the Kido Butai ended the six-month period of Japanese domination in the western Pacific. The war would go on for another three years and two months as U.S. forces fought their way from Guadalcanal to the Philippines and from Tarawa to Iwo Jima and Okinawa. But in all of these engagements, it was American forces that were on the offensive. The period of Japanese expansion—of Japanese offensives—was over. As Mitsuo Fuchida stated after the war, "The catastrophe of Midway definitely marked the turning of the tide in the Pacific War, and thenceforward that tide bore Japan inexorably on toward final capitulation." But Midway did more than that. As former U.S. defense secretary James Schlesinger declared at a 2003 Midway Night dinner: "It was far more than the turning of the tide in the Pacific War. In a strategic sense, Midway represents one of the great turning points of world history." Victory at Midway enabled the United States and its allies to maintain at least the pretense of a Europe First strategy in the Second World War. It allowed the United States to send much-needed support to the British in North Africa, to commit more forces to the Battle of the Atlantic, and to increase supplies to the Soviet Red Army, which was carrying the brunt of the fight against Hitler's armed legions in Europe. Without the victory at Midway, it is at least conceivable that public opinion would have forced President Roosevelt to commit some of those assets to the Pacific instead. Secretary of State Henry Stimson noted that success at Midway meant that "we could reverse our rush of reinforcements to the West Coast and send back the forces that we had diverted from BOLERO [a projected early invasion of Europe]." Midway provided the sea change that allowed the allies to carry the war forward to victory not just in the Pacific but around the world.[89]

—

Midway was both the first step toward American victory in the Pacific War and a crucial element of Allied victory in World War II. But as Wellington said of Waterloo, it was a very near-run thing, for it came at a time when the United States did not yet have the matériel superiority that would eventually win the war, forcing Nimitz, Fletcher, and Spruance to rely instead on better intelligence, bold decision making, and more than a little luck. Nor did the American counteroffensive against Japan begin immediately after Midway. Before that could happen, American industry had to mass-produce the weapons of war that made possible both the Central Pacific Drive and eventually the landings in northern France on D-Day.

For a few brief days after the loss of the *Yorktown*, Nimitz had only two carriers at Pearl Harbor. The arrival of the *Saratoga* and *Wasp* doubled that number. Then in December, six months after the Battle of Midway, the newly constructed carriers began to arrive. The first of them was the *Essex*, namesake of its class. It was eight thousand tons larger and sixty-five feet longer than the *Yorktown*, and it boasted two improved catapults that could launch planes more quickly and with significantly less risk. Nine more Essex-class carriers followed. The second of them had been scheduled to bear the name *Bonhomme Richard* in honor of John Paul Jones's flagship in the American Revolution, but after Midway its name was changed to *Yorktown*, which is how it happened that both CV-5 and CV-10 bore the same name. That second *Yorktown*, nicknamed "The Fighting Lady," fought throughout the Pacific war and retired after a lengthy career. It is now open to visitors at Patriot's Point in Charleston Harbor, South Carolina.

After the ten Essex-class carriers came ten Ticonderoga-class carriers and then five Independence-class carriers. Every one of these twenty-five vessels was larger than any of the American carriers that fought at Midway, and taken together, they carried a total of more than two thousand combat aircraft. When Nimitz began the island-hopping campaign across the central Pacific in 1943, the carrier task force that accompanied the landing force grew to sixteen carriers, all of them under the command of the man who had commanded the *Hornet* at Midway: Captain (later Vice Admiral) Marc "Pete" Mitscher. And even as the Pacific War neared its culmination, American industry continued to churn out new weapons of war. By V-J Day in September, the United States Navy boasted an astonishing total of one hundred heavy, light, and escort carriers. It was an armada that would have been unimaginable in June 1942, and its very existence constituted a dramatic sea change not only in American history but in world history, for it evidenced the emergence of the U.S. Navy as the greatest sea force on the planet.

In February 1945, as U.S. Marines were going ashore on Iwo Jima, America's newest carrier, appropriately named the USS *Midway*, was launched at Newport News, Virginia. At 45,000 tons, it was more than twice the size of the *Yorktown* that had sunk at its namesake battle, and the *Midway*'s 1,000-foot flight deck carried an authorized complement of 137 aircraft, all of them bigger, faster, and capable of heavier payloads than anything flown by Jimmy Thach, Jack Waldron, or Wade McClusky. Fifteen years later, long after the Second World War was over, in September 1960, the United States launched the USS *Enterprise*. Here was another sea change, for the *Enterprise*, at 85,600 tons, was not only much larger, it was propelled by nuclear power, and the planes that were catapulted from its 1,100-foot-long flight deck were jets capable of delivering nuclear weapons.

By then, the world had changed again. Only six months after the Japanese surrender on board the U.S. battleship *Missouri*, Winston Churchill offered a subsequently famous speech in Fulton, Missouri, in which he declared that an "iron curtain" had descended across Europe. His declaration merely recognized a historical reality: that a postwar rivalry between the Soviet Union and the West had emerged from the ashes of World War II. In that conflict the United States assumed a global leadership position dramatically different from its traditional aloofness. This time it was not a false dawn: American industrial capacity and American leadership in World War II made the United States a global power, and there would be no retreat from either the burdens or the responsibilities of that status.

PART FIVE

MISSILE WARFARE AND THE AMERICAN IMPERIUM

Operation Praying Mantis
The Persian Gulf
April 18, 1988

THE COLD WAR WAS A PERIOD OF PUTATIVE WORLD PEACE punctuated by countless small wars—and some that were not so small. From Berlin to Cuba, Korea to Vietnam, the two superpowers focused much of their national energy—and their national treasure—on an effort to gain an advantage over the other, or at least to prevent the other from gaining an advantage. The weapons grew increasingly sophisticated and terrible as both sides developed nuclear capability as well as ever-larger rocket engines to increase warhead "throw weight" in a grisly calculation of mutual deterrence.

U.S. aircraft carriers more than doubled in size, from 45,000 tons to 96,000 tons, and the planes they carried were supersonic jets capable of carrying nuclear payloads. Submarines, too, became bigger, much quieter, and much, much deadlier. The advent of nuclear propulsion made possible extended sea-keeping capability for the nation's huge new carriers and especially for its ballistic-missile submarines—called boomers—which gave the Navy a role in strategic deterrence. By the 1960s a "triad" of Air Force bombers, land-based missiles in silos, and Polaris missiles housed in nuclear-powered submarines was supposed to provide a deterrent so convincing that the Soviets would fear to embark on the program of world conquest that most Americans believed was their ultimate goal.

Of all these technological changes, however, the one that marked the most dramatic milestone in the character of naval warfare was the revolution in electronic integration, communication, and missile capability developed toward the end of the twentieth century even as the Soviet Union was collapsing. That a revolution in warfare had taken place first became evident to the American public during the 1991 Gulf War when it watched with awe and admiration as U.S. ordnance fitted with television cameras took out Iraqi targets with astonishing precision. If subsequent investigation proved that not every strike was quite as precise as initially advertised, it was nevertheless a far cry from the gravity-guided bombs of World War II. Moreover, the integrated electronic infrastructure that made the delivery of these weapons possible marked a revolution as well. While a World War II naval aviator might nod in recognition at a nuclear-powered aircraft carrier even as he wondered at its size and puzzled over its propulsion plant, he would have been dumbfounded by his first look inside the combat information center on an AEGIS-equipped guided missile cruiser: a dark, air-conditioned room filled with banks of humming computers that linked air, surface, and even satellite assets together in a worldwide, real-time network.

For much of the Cold War, the important battlegrounds were in Europe (Berlin), Asia (Korea and Vietnam), and even Latin America (Cuba), but toward the end of the twentieth century the Middle East emerged as a region of special concern for the United States and for the U.S. Navy. Though the ancient empire of Persia officially changed its name to Iran in 1935, the body of water that marked its western boundary retained its former designation, and it was in the Persian Gulf that the post–Cold War U.S. Navy made its public debut.

The Persian Gulf is roughly twice the size of Lake Erie, and it washes the shores of eight countries: Iran, Iraq, Kuwait, Saudi Arabia, Bahrain, Qatar, Oman, and the United Arab Emirates. That, and the fact that it is the centerpiece of a region that possesses 80 percent of the world's proven oil reserves, made it one of the busiest waterways in the world by the 1980s. Every day dozens of tankers carrying millions of barrels of oil transited the length of the Gulf to pass into the Arabian Sea through the narrow Strait of Hormuz, heading for America, Europe, and especially Japan, which in the 1980s obtained nearly two-thirds of its oil from the Persian Gulf.

On April 18, 1988, in the last twilight days of the Cold War, the U.S. Navy provided a glimpse of the new template of naval warfare, and of America's apparent willingness to act as a world policeman, when it fought the largest naval battle since World War II in what was known officially as Operation Praying Mantis.

—

O N   T H E   E V E N I N G   of May 17, 1987, the USS *Stark*, an *Oliver Hazard Perry*–class frigate, was cruising in what was nearly the geographical center of the Persian Gulf, ninety miles northeast of Bahrain.

Poking along at three knots, the *Stark*'s mission was vague at best. While it was supposed to demonstrate American interest and concern in a part of the world that supplied much of the world's oil, it was also cruising through a war zone. For more than six years, ever since Iraq had invaded Iran in an attempt to expand its own tiny coastline at its neighbor's expense, Iran and Iraq had been engaged in a vicious war that showed no sign of ending. By 1987 the war had settled into a bloody stalemate and had spilled over into the waters of the Gulf, where Iraqi warplanes attacked shipping headed for Iranian ports, and Iranian gunboats attacked vessels that traded with Iraq. Although no U.S. vessels had been targeted so far, the ships of several neutral countries were being assaulted by both sides. Just that week the United States had pledged itself to begin protecting oil tankers from Kuwait, but as of May 17 it had not yet begun active patrols, and the *Stark*'s role was essentially one of showing the flag.

The *Stark* was a relatively new ship, built less than five years before as part of a program to develop a "low-cost, no-frills warship."[1] At only 3,600 tons, it was no larger than the ABC cruisers that had heralded the "New Navy" back in 1883 and considerably smaller than Dewey's *Olympia*. In theory a large number of such vessels would give the United States a greater worldwide presence than fewer larger (and therefore more expensive) warships. Because of the American concern with Soviet submarines, the *Stark*'s primary mission was antisubmarine warfare (ASW). It had a small landing deck and twin helicopter hangers aft, and its main battery consisted of a single seventy-six-millimeter (three-inch) rapid-fire gun amidships. It also had the ability to fire what the Navy called its standard missile (SM-1), which could be aimed at either surface or air targets and which had a range of some thirty miles. Most of the rest of the superstructure of the *Stark* was covered by an array of communications antenna and radar receivers: air search, surface search, and fire control systems. In conformance with its ASW mission, it also had a modern sonar system to detect and pursue Soviet submarines.*

---

* Although a vast improvement over World War II sonar systems, the hull-mounted SQS-56 sonar on the *Stark* was not very sophisticated compared to more advanced sonar systems available at the time. Irreverent American sailors referred to it dismissively as the "Helen Keller" sonar system.

The *Perry*-class frigates had numerous critics, who derisively called them "Kmart ships," noting that they had only one propeller, which made them both slower and less maneuverable than larger twin-screw warships. They were also relatively thin-skinned, having only five-eighths of an inch of aluminum alloy between the living spaces and the sea, and unlike Ericsson's *Monitor*, they had almost no armor. When operating beyond the range of friendly air cover, they could be vulnerable to air attack. They were not defenseless, however. The *Stark* could fire off clouds of aluminized plastic confetti, known as chaff, to confuse the radar of inbound missiles. And atop the helicopter hanger at the stern was an odd-looking contraption: a radar dome shaped like a giant beehive with a bundle of six gun barrels poking out of it. It was a Phalanx close-in weapons system (the acronym was CIWS, but

The *Oliver Hazard Perry*-class frigate USS *Stark* is shown soon after its commissioning in 1982. The small white beehive-shaped object above her twin helicopter hangers is the CIWS—the automated Gatling gun designed to shoot down incoming missiles. Note the extensive antennae forward. (U.S. Navy)

everyone pronounced it "C-WIZ"): a self-aiming, automated Gatling gun capable of throwing up a virtual wall of twenty-millimeter depleted-uranium rounds at the rate of three thousand per minute. Though useful only at short range, its purpose was to shoot down incoming missiles.

At a few minutes after 8:00 P.M. on that May 17, Lieutenant Basil Moncrief, who had the duty as tactical action officer (TAO) in the *Stark*'s combat information center (CIC), received a report from an airborne warning and control system (AWACS) airplane—essentially a flying radar station—that an Iraqi F-1 Mirage fighter had departed Shaibah Military Airport in southern Iraq and was "feet wet" over the Gulf, flying southward toward the *Stark*'s position. By itself, the report did not set off any alarms. Ever since the outbreak of the Iran-Iraq war six years earlier, there had been a lot of air traffic over the Gulf, most of it Iraqi. Almost routinely, Iraqi fighters and attack planes flew southward down the center of the Gulf— which Americans had begun to call "Mirage Alley"—then turned east toward the coast of Iran to launch their missiles in the general direction of Iran, or at shipping that was headed for Iran, before streaking home again. Just that morning an Iraqi jet had fired missiles into a Cypriot tanker in an Iranian port. By itself, therefore, the information that an Iraqi Mirage jet was flying south down the Gulf was unremarkable.

The *Stark*'s air search radar picked up the Iraqi plane at two hundred miles; it was keeping to the western side of the Gulf, well out of Iranian air space, and it was closing on the American frigate. At about 9:00 the *Stark*'s captain, a forty-four-year-old, sandy-haired career officer named Glenn Brindel, asked Moncrief for an update. The plane was then about seventy miles out and still closing. The petty officer manning the radar system asked if he should generate a standard warning message, but Moncrief hesitated. "No," he said. "Wait." During the past few months the *Stark* had experienced a number of close fly-bys, and he suspected that this was simply one more. Five minutes later, with the Iraqi jet less than fifty miles out, it turned sharply toward the *Stark*. Moncrief alerted Brindel, who directed Moncrief to send out a message on the international air distress frequency demanding identification: "Unknown aircraft, this is U.S. Navy warship on your 078 for twelve miles. Request you identify yourself."[2]

Even as this message hit the airwaves, the Iraqi pilot fired an Exocet AM39 air-to-surface missile. Launched at two thousand feet, the missile dropped quickly to sea level and then began streaking toward the *Stark*, only eight feet above the surface, at five hundred miles an hour. Within seconds, the Iraqi pilot fired a second missile, then turned abruptly northward and headed for home. The SPS-49 radar on the *Stark* did not detect the separation of the Exocet from the Mirage. If it had, Brindel could have ordered the deployment of the chaff or CIWS systems. The first notice of approaching disaster came not from the sophisticated sensors but from a lookout on the bridge, who spotted the Exocet when it was only a mile away, which gave the ship about four seconds' warning. A shout from the lookout led Brindel to order the *Stark* hard to starboard in order to unmask the CIWS system astern.[3]

Too late. At 9:09 the first missile slammed into the *Stark*'s port side just below the bridge. The warhead did not detonate, but it tore a ten-by-fifteen-foot hole in the ship's side, then disintegrated into a hundred pieces, the largest of which ripped through the crew's quarters, the ship's barber shop, and post office and lodged against the starboard side. The second missile struck thirty seconds later, and its warhead did explode, igniting fires that spread almost instantly through the crew's quarters. Seven men were thrown into the sea by the impact. Resting in the crew's quarters near where the first missile hit, Petty Officer Michael O'Keefe was thrown from his bunk onto the deck. Jumping to his feet, he dashed to the main hatch and pulled it open only to encounter a giant fireball. "That's when I knew we were in real trouble," he said later.[4]

Brindel ordered counterflooding on the starboard side to avoid capsizing and to keep the huge hole on the ship's port side above the waterline. The damage control teams performed heroically, fighting the fires all night, joined later by teams from the guided missile destroyers USS *Waddell* and USS *Conyngham*. The fires were so hot (eighteen hundred degrees) they melted the aluminum alloy of the ship's superstructure; water sprayed onto the fires turned into superheated steam that scalded the firefighters. A shortage of oxygen canisters, which allowed firefighters to breathe amid the heavy smoke, also retarded the crew's firefighting efforts. For several hours it was problematic whether they could keep the ship afloat. Not until the afternoon of the next day was it evident that the *Stark* would survive. The fire in the combat information center was not quenched until 5:00 P.M., nineteen hours after the attack. Assisted by a salvage tug, the *Stark* limped into Bahrain with thirty-seven dead on board.[5]

In keeping with the traditions of the sea, Brindel lost his job. A Navy investigation concluded that he had "failed to provide combat oriented leadership," and he was forced to resign. Many, both in and out of the Navy, acknowledged that the rules of engagement (ROE) under which Brindel had to operate had severely limited his options. Those rules authorized him to fight back "whenever hostile intent or a hostile act occurs." But "hostile intent" is impossible to know, and due to the failure of the ship's SPS-49 radar, it was not evident that a "hostile act" had occurred until four seconds before the missile struck, when the forward lookout

The *Stark* lists alarmingly to port after being struck by two Exocet air-to-surface missiles on May 17, 1987. Heroic damage control saved the ship from going down. (U.S. Navy)

shouted a warning. Brindel's critics suggested that he should have put the chaff and CIWS systems into automatic mode, or at least challenged the approaching fighter sooner than he did. His defenders insisted that if he had shot down the Mirage before it launched the missiles, he would have been cashiered for being too quick on the trigger. Whatever the merits of either argument, it is the merciless law of the sea that a captain accept responsibility for his ship's failure or success, and Brindel was no exception. Lieutenant Moncrief was also forced to resign.[6]

The Iraqis explained away the incident as a matter of mistaken identity and pilot error, which it almost certainly was, for Iraq had nothing to gain by alienating the United States, which was supporting its war against Iran. If some Americans doubted the sincerity of Iraq's apology, the Reagan administration accepted it because it wanted to maintain its pro-Iraqi stance. The disaster did provoke sharp questions from Congress and the press. The Senate voted ninety-one to five to delay the implementation of the American commitment to escort Kuwaiti tankers in the Gulf until the Reagan administration clarified its policy. In a rare criticism of his own party, Republican Senator Robert Dole of Kansas declared bluntly, "We need to rethink exactly what we are doing in the Persian Gulf." More pointedly, the *New York Times* editorialized that "the Administration . . . had no business sending ships sailing into harm's way without having thought [it] through." And *Newsweek* chimed in with an article entitled "A Questionable Policy," which asked, "What are the administration's goals in the gulf?"[7]

It was an important question, and over the next fourteen months it prompted a reevaluation of American foreign and defense policy. At the heart of the debate was a consideration of the readiness or willingness of the United States to accept the role of international peacekeeper in the Persian Gulf—or anywhere else, for that matter. The United States had played the role of peacekeeper before (President Truman had referred to the Korean War as a "police action"). But to some, American interests in the Persian Gulf were not clear, and many feared that the country was trying on the uniform of global policeman. Moreover, these considerations took place at a time when the first rumblings of an earthquake in the global balance of power were becoming evident. Within half a dozen years the Soviet Union—America's rival for forty years—would begin to fall apart, leaving the United States as the sole remaining superpower on earth. The collapse of the Soviet Union and the willingness of the United States to take on the responsibilities of what amounted to a maritime constabulary force marked a shift not only in U.S. policy but also in America's role in the world. It was, as one American sailor in the Persian Gulf declared, "a whole new ball game."[8]

The Persian Gulf became the focus of this policy reassessment because of two issues that, though technically unrelated, became entangled nonetheless, and drew the United States into the region with all the centripetal force of a whirlpool. One was America's Cold War rivalry with the Soviet Union, and the other was oil.

The need for oil—the mother's milk of modern industry—had led Japan to risk its empire in a war with the United States in 1941. In the United States, however, the availability of oil had never been a particular concern. Throughout the Second World War and into the early Cold War years, the United States had plenty of oil for its own use and even continued to export it abroad, selling it overseas as fast as it could be pumped out of the vast Spindletop oil fields in Texas. But in the winter of 1947–48 the expanding postwar economy—and the resulting spike in the domestic use of oil—led for the first time to shortages at home. The shortage was serious enough that for a while it seemed the United States might run out of heating oil just as winter set in. Newspapers recalled the coal strike of 1902, when Theodore Roosevelt had threatened to nationalize the mines to prevent families from freezing to death in their homes. In 1948 Truman was less draconian. He called for conservation, ordering the thermostats in government offices to be set back to sixty-eight degrees (as both Nixon and Carter would do during later energy scares), but he also released one million barrels of the U.S. Navy's strategic oil reserves for domestic use. For the first time both the United States and the U.S. Navy confronted the reality of their dependence on oil.[9]

That year also marked a turning point in the emerging relationship between the U.S. Navy and the countries bordering the oil-rich Persian Gulf. Even before the fuel crisis of 1948, the Navy had begun to buy oil from the Gulf region simply because it was cheaper there. Oil cost about $1.48 per barrel in the United States, but in the Persian Gulf it could be had for $1.05 a barrel from the Arab-American Oil Company (ARAMCO). The 1948 crisis increased U.S. Navy reliance on Persian Gulf oil, and Navy planners began to see the region as important to American interests. In consequence, they established Task Force 126 (U.S. Naval Forces, Persian Gulf), which initially consisted only of Navy oil tankers. Over time this force was augmented and renamed the Middle East Force, eventually becoming part of Central Command (CENTCOM) in 1983.[10]

It was clear at once that operating in the Persian Gulf posed special problems for the U.S. Navy, both politically and operationally. Politically, the absence of American naval bases in the region required the United States to develop relationships with states that bordered the Gulf. Eventually the United States negotiated basing rights with the tiny sheikdom of Bahrain, taking over the former British base at Jufair, and tried repeatedly to gain similar rights in Saudi Arabia, though the Saudis proved to be reluctant partners at best.

Operationally, there were two problems. The first was the weather. When the United States sent its first task force into the Gulf in the summer of 1948, the officers and crew were entirely unprepared for the relentless heat. With daytime temperatures topping 120 degrees, it was too hot to eat in the galley, and the sailors took their trays topside to sit at tables on the fantail, where at least there was a little breeze; it was impossible to shower, as the water in the pipes was literally scalding; and even sleeping was difficult because the nighttime temperature in the berthing spaces sometimes topped 115 degrees.[11]

The other operational problem was the peculiar geography of the Persian Gulf. It is so narrow, and large parts of it, especially on the eastern side, are so shallow, that it funnels all deep-draft ship traffic into a fairly narrow channel. Indeed, the geography of the Gulf region compelled the Navy's "blue water" fleet to adjust to the requirements and limitations of littoral warfare. The Gulf was (and is) a particularly unsatisfactory place for aircraft carriers to operate. In order to provide air cover for U.S. Navy surface units operating in the Gulf, therefore, American carriers stationed themselves south of the Strait of Hormuz in the Gulf of Oman—a location sailors immediately dubbed "Camel Station."*

Besides oil, the other factor in the American strategic equation in the early Cold War era was the constant, even obsessive, American concern about the Soviet Union. The overarching U.S. policy of containment, which required the United States to confront Soviet ambitions everywhere in the world, certainly included the Middle East, especially since that region's volatile politics and proven oil reserves made it both vulnerable and desirable. After World War II, the United States sought to bolster the stability of the Gulf region by cultivating close relations with Saudi Arabia and by backing Mohammed Reza Pahlavi, the shah of Iran, in what amounted to a coup to overthrow Iran's nationalist (and virulently anti-British) prime minister Mohammed Mossadegh.[12] In the early 1970s, in the wake of the American withdrawal from Vietnam and the British retreat from maintaining a military presence "east of Suez," President Richard Nixon sought to formalize U.S. relationships with both Saudi Arabia and Iran, which he referred to as "the twin pillars" of stability in the Gulf region.

While American interest in the Persian Gulf was firmly grounded in the rivalry of the Cold War, other issues were percolating beneath the surface. Arabs had long resented America's strong support for Israel, and during the 1970s anger at what some Arabs saw as American cultural imperialism contributed to a revival of Islamic fundamentalism. Unrest was particularly great in Iran because, even though he often proved resistant to American advice, the shah was nevertheless perceived as an American puppet. In addition, he squandered about a third of his country's entire budget buy-

---

* Conventional wisdom held that it was unwise to operate carriers in an area where they had limited sea room and were vulnerable to land-based air. For that reason, the United States had not sent carriers into the Persian Gulf since 1976, though in 1990 the United States did send two carrier groups into the Gulf as part of the buildup for Operation Desert Storm. By then, the term "Camel Station" had been dropped in favor of "Gonzo Station," which was an acronym for Gulf of Oman Northern Zone.

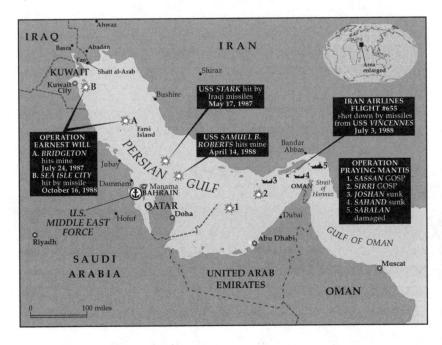

ing modern weaponry that was well beyond any realistic assessment of Iran's defense needs. In early 1979 the country exploded in anger, and the shah and his wife were forced to flee. The government collapsed, and what eventually filled the vacuum was a regime grounded in Islamic religious law and dominated by the Shiite ayatollah Ruhollah Khomeini. For the United States, the decisive event in this crisis was the seizure of the American embassy in Tehran by student supporters of the new regime. For more than a year, some fifty-two Americans, including eight Marines, were held as hostages in Tehran. Televised images of blindfolded American hostages and their gleeful, unrepentant captors infuriated the American public.*

---

* A popular song of the 1970s by a group called Tony Orlando and Dawn told of a man returning from prison who was unsure that his girl still wanted to see him. In the song, he writes her to suggest that if she wants him back, she should "tie a yellow ribbon 'round the old oak tree." The song inspired Americans to tie yellow ribbons around trees, light poles, and mailbox posts as symbols of their support for the hostages in Iran. A huge yellow ribbon was tied around the Super Dome in New Orleans for Super Bowl XV. Since then, a yellow ribbon has come to symbolize support for U.S. troops on overseas duty.

President Jimmy Carter used a State of the Union address to warn the Soviet Union (which sent troops into Afghanistan that same year) not to try to take advantage of the chaos in Iran. "An attempt by any outside force to gain control of the Persian Gulf region," he warned, "will be regarded as an assault on the vital interests of the United States." This statement, quickly labeled the Carter Doctrine, marked a revival of American commitment to international involvement that had waned significantly in the wake of the nation's unhappy experience in Vietnam. More significantly, it was a policy that, under Carter's successors, would go a long way toward establishing the United States as a kind of regional policeman.[13]

For Iraq, the 1979 revolution in Iran was both bad news and good news. Iraq was a secular state with a Shiite Muslim majority, but its government was dominated by Sunni Muslims. The elevation of a Shiite ayatollah in Tehran was therefore of considerable concern, especially if it encouraged Iraqi Shiites to look to Tehran rather than to Baghdad for leadership and inspiration. On the other hand, the revolution had separated Iran from its rich and powerful American patron and dramatically weakened its military forces, which were in a shambles after being purged of those who were not loyal to the new regime. In such circumstances, the new president of Iraq, Saddam Hussein, believed he saw an opportunity.

Since its creation as a British mandate after World War I, Iraq's most significant geographical deficiency was that except for a tiny toehold on the northern end of the Persian Gulf, it was virtually landlocked. The Tigris and Euphrates Rivers merged to flow into the Gulf in what was called the Shatt al-Arab (the Arab River), but Iraq had sovereignty over only the western bank of that river, for the Iran-Iraq boundary ran down the center of the ship channel. For years Iraq had made no secret of its ambition to obtain a real coastline, and with the collapse of the shah and the rise of the Ayatollah Khomeini, Saddam Hussein believed that his moment had come. In September 1980, with America in the throes of anti-Iranian hysteria due to the ongoing hostage crisis, he launched a ground invasion of Iran.[14]

Instead of the easy victory that almost everyone expected, the Iraqi army ran into fanatical resistance. The war lasted through the fall and winter, and then into the hot Gulf summer. And still it continued: into a second year, then a third, and a fourth. By the mid-1980s it had become one of the bloodiest wars of the twentieth century, with hundreds of thousands killed and no end in sight. Desperate to achieve a breakthrough, both sides adopted irregular tactics. The clerics who ruled Iran urged their poorly supplied soldiers to carry out human-wave attacks that, however costly, nevertheless won them some tactical victories. For his part, in addition to ordering Scud missile attacks on Tehran, Saddam Hussein authorized the use of poison gas on the battlefield as well as at home, where his regime was threatened by a Kurdish uprising.

Iraq began the naval war in the Persian Gulf barely two weeks into the fighting when, on October 7, 1980, it declared the waters off Iran a "prohibited war zone" and announced that any vessel inside that zone was subject to destruction—not just Iranian vessels but those of any nationality that visited an Iranian port. This was similar to Imperial Germany's declaration of a "war zone" around the British Isles in 1914, but while Germany had relied on submarines to enforce its declaration, Iraq relied on the airplane. As the war began to turn against Iraq, Iraqi air attacks on Gulf shipping escalated and focused particularly on tankers in order to deprive Iran of the money it needed to continue the war. The goal was to frighten neutral shipping away from Iranian ports, and during 1982, Iraqi Mirage fighters conducted twenty-one attacks on tankers, most of them neutrals, in the Persian Gulf.[15]

Iran countered with the declaration that it would "not allow any merchant ship to carry cargo to Iraqi ports." There was an obvious threat in the announcement that "the Iranian government will not take responsibility for those vessels which do not pay consideration to this notice."[16] But despite that threat, the Iranians made no effort to interfere with maritime traffic in the Gulf during the first three years of the war. In part this was because it had its hands full fending off the Iraqi army and in part because it would have been a waste of resources since Iraq exported most of its oil overland by pipeline and was therefore less dependent on tanker traffic.

But in 1984, a year during which Iraqi planes made fifty-three attacks on neutral tankers in the Gulf, Iran at last retaliated. It had become clear that in addition to using the oil pipeline into Syria and Turkey, Iraq also relied on the tankers of both Saudi Arabia and Kuwait to export its oil. More importantly, both of those countries acted as conduits to supply Iraq with war materials from abroad. The Saudis accepted shipments of tanks, artillery, and other war materials at its Red Sea port of Jidda, then shipped the material by truck through Kuwait to Iraq. If not quite Iraqi allies, neither country was genuinely "neutral." That year, therefore, Iran began attacking the tankers of Saudi Arabia and especially Kuwait using small high-speed attack boats armed with machine guns and rocket-propelled grenade launchers, a particularly low-tech threat in an increasingly high-tech war.[17]

This conflict had little direct connection to the Cold War, which was still America's dominant concern, but historically the United States had always been a champion of freedom of the seas. Consequently, at the outbreak of the Iran-Iraq War, President Carter had declared, "Freedom of navigation in the Persian Gulf is of primary importance to the whole international community. It is imperative that there be no infringement of that freedom of passage of ships to and from the Persian Gulf region." Similarly, Carter's secretary of state, Edmund Muskie, declared to the United Nations that "the freedom of navigation to and from the Persian Gulf . . . must not be infringed upon in any way." But despite these statements, the United States directed its principal efforts at halting Iranian seaborne attacks and ignored Iraq's airstrikes on Iranian shipping.[18]

In January 1981 Ronald Reagan replaced Jimmy Carter in the White House, and in a deliberate slap at the departing president, Iran released the American hostages the same day.* Like his predecessors, Reagan focused most of his foreign policy attention on the Cold War rivalry with the Soviet Union, which the new president called an "evil empire." Indeed, efforts by the Reagan administration to strengthen the U.S. military—

---

* Conspiracy theorists argue that officials of the Reagan-Bush campaign team deliberately colluded with the Khomeini regime to keep the hostages imprisoned until after the election to avoid giving Carter a diplomatic victory that might have aided his reelection. Though there is strong circumstantial evidence of such a plot, no clear evidence has been found to substantiate it.

including a plan to increase the U.S. Navy to six hundred ships—were directed exclusively at the Soviets. Reagan's secretary of defense, Casper Weinberger, was especially focused on the Soviet issue; one administration insider noted that Weinberger's "whole world was Moscow." Despite such single-minded focus, other issues intruded. In 1982 the United States sent eight hundred Marines into Lebanon as part of a peacekeeping force, and in October of the following year 241 of them died when a terrorist drove a truck bomb into their barracks. In 1986, the United States executed an air raid against Libya in retaliation for a series of terrorist acts against Americans and others. That same year the number of attacks on tankers in the Gulf jumped to 111, and Reagan sounded very much like his predecessor in announcing that "the United States has a vital interest in maintaining freedom of navigation in the gulf and stability in the region generally."[19]

In the midst of this sudden acceleration in the number of attacks, Kuwait sought protection for its tanker fleet by appealing first to the Gulf Cooperation Council and soon thereafter to the United States. At first the Reagan administration resisted entanglement in a lengthy and bloody war in the Persian Gulf, especially after the loss of the Marines in Lebanon. The United States was naturally and genuinely concerned by the menace to trade, but accepting responsibility for the security of the Gulf seemed to many to be a slippery slope and a distraction from the country's focus on countering Soviet ambitions. Then the State Department learned that Kuwait had also appealed to the Soviet Union for help and that the Soviets were giving it serious consideration. In fact, the Soviets had already chartered three Kuwaiti tankers and re-flagged them as Soviet vessels. To the Reagan administration, the only scenario worse than putting U.S. forces in the middle of a shooting war halfway around the world was one that allowed the Soviet Union to become the patron of the oil-rich countries of the Persian Gulf. "Once we knew that the Kuwaitis were negotiating with the Soviets," an American official admitted, "it sped up the process tremendously and we said 'Let's do it all!'" As a result, the United States advised the Kuwaiti government in March 1987 that it would accept responsibility for escorting Kuwaiti tankers in and out of the Persian Gulf.[20]

To justify an American escort, the first step was to reflag the Kuwaiti tankers as American vessels. Only after the Reagan administration had committed itself did someone think to ask the Coast Guard about the legal ramifications of such a move. As the Coast Guard representative began to explain the rules at a meeting in the White House, Weinberger became visibly agitated, finally bursting out: "Are you telling me we can't do this?" It could, in fact, be done, but it would require a lot of work. The ships would have to be refitted to meet U.S. standards, American skippers had to be found, and it all had to be accepted by the Kuwaitis. "We had to scurry around and get the Kuwaitis to agree," recalled Admiral William J. Crowe Jr., the chairman of the Joint Chiefs of Staff, "and they were very reluctant .... They were grumbling all the way."[21]

Nor was that the only complication. Revelations that the Reagan administration had been engaged in secretly (and illegally) selling arms to Iran in order to obtain funds that it funneled into Central America to support a revolution there not only triggered a political firestorm in the United States but dramatically weakened the administration's Gulf policy as well, since it was at least possible to argue that some of the weapons Iran was using to attack neutral shipping had been provided by the United States. Indeed, the United States continued to deliver missiles clandestinely to Iran as late as October 1986.

Then on May 17, 1987, an Iraqi fighter jet put two Exocet missiles into the USS *Stark*, and an angry Congress voted to put the escort mission on hold. The nation found itself entangled in a policy web so complex that even experts had difficulty sorting it out. As policy makers wrestled with the alternatives, there seemed to be three options: (1) the United States could back away from its emerging role as the cop on the beat and pull its naval assets out of the Gulf, conceding the field to the Soviets; (2) it could invite other nations to join it in establishing a multinational maritime force to protect trade; or (3) it could aggressively reinforce its own position in the Gulf and attempt to do the job alone. The Reagan administration considered the first option completely unacceptable. The United States might have opted for a multinational approach if it had been able to convince other nations to participate, but America's NATO partners did not see Gulf security as a NATO issue despite the fact that in 1986 Western

European countries obtained 46 percent of their oil from the Gulf. In the end, therefore, the United States settled on option three.[22]

The Reagan administration determined to proceed with the convoy program partly because any alternative suggested a kind of retreat and partly because the habit of standing up to the Soviets had become irresistible. It is unlikely that those who contributed to the decision had any intention of carving out a new foreign policy doctrine for the nation; Caspar Weinberger stated bluntly that "our ships are not there as referees." That same week, however, a *Newsweek* article observed that the new challenge for the United States was "how to act as a neutral gendarme." In any event, two days after the *Stark* disaster, Reagan declared, "We remain deeply committed to supporting the self-defense of our friends in the gulf and to insuring the free flow of oil through the Strait of Hormuz."[23]

To do that, of course, the United States would have to increase its naval presence dramatically and modify the rules of engagement to allow captains more leeway to defend their commands. Within days the United States sent additional surface forces into the Persian Gulf, and the carrier *Constellation* moved into Camel Station in the northern Arabian Sea. Altogether, the United States committed thirty warships to the operation, with more to follow. In addition, although the rules of engagement remained officially unchanged, Admiral Crowe made a visit to the Gulf to encourage commanders to interpret "hostile intent" more broadly. In particular, he told them that they did not have to be shot at first before they acted in self-defense. "If you are locked on, and you think you are under threat, you do what you need to do to protect your ship." That included shooting first. "If you make a mistake," he told them, "I'll support you."[24]

More than a few in Congress and in uniform worried about the new policy. By acting to protect Kuwaiti tankers trading with Iraq, the United States appeared to be openly choosing sides in the war. Others wondered if by acting unilaterally, the United States was not assuming too high a profile. Lee Hamilton, chairman of the House Foreign Affairs committee, asked "if an international force would have been more appropriate," and Admiral Wesley McDonald in the semiofficial U.S. Naval Institute *Proceedings* expressed a concern about America becoming the "policeman of the world." Finally, of course, the decision would put U.S. ships and sailors in peril. The *New York Times* quoted one Iranian firebrand who declared, "Those who think that by flying the U.S. flag they can help the aggressor, are making a mistake and should know that we will set those flags on fire." In spite of all these concerns, however, the U.S. Navy prepared to fulfill the mission it was assigned: to escort Kuwaiti tankers through the war zone of the Persian Gulf in what was officially code-named Operation Earnest Will.[25]

—

The first convoy of Earnest Will got under way on July 22, 1987, in the middle of the searing Gulf summer. The escort was a strong one, consisting of three U.S. Navy warships: the guided missile cruiser *Fox*, the destroyer *Kidd*, and the frigate *Crommelin* (a sister ship of the *Stark*), under the overall command of Captain Dave Yonkers. Their assignment was to escort two vessels, the 400,000-ton supertanker *Bridgeton* (formerly the *Al Rekkah*) and the much smaller *Gas Prince*, a liquid petroleum gas transport ship, from the Gulf of Oman through the Strait of Hormuz to the Al Ahmadi oil terminal near Kuwait City at the head of the Persian Gulf, a two-day journey. The *Bridgeton*'s new American captain, Frank Seitz, assured his Kuwaiti crew that they had nothing to fear on the trip through the Gulf because they would be under the protection of the U.S. Navy, and when the American flag broke at the *Bridgeton*'s masthead, the crew offered a round of applause.[26]

Yonkers had originally planned to take the convoy through the Strait at night. It was there, where the main ship channel was only twelve miles from Iranian territory, that the danger would be greatest. Yonkers knew that the Iranians had Chinese-made Silkworm missile batteries on the north side of the strait, and with their thousand-pound warheads, not only could those missiles cripple a tanker, they could very likely sink his warships. But Navy officials wanted to minimize the possibility of another error in identification such as the one that had nearly doomed the *Stark* and directed Yonkers to make the run in daylight. Consequently, the convoy got under way at 9:30 in the morning, with the temperature already topping a hundred degrees. Over the ship's loudspeaker, Captain Bill Mathis of the *Fox* set the tone: "Remember—this is the real thing—this is not a drill. We are going to be ready—we will make sure that these ships get to Kuwait on time and unharmed."[27]

All three U.S. warships set Condition One Alpha, in which two-thirds of the crew remained at battle stations, and they stayed in that condition throughout the seven-hour transit through the Strait. The *Fox* led, with the two tankers next in line, and the small frigate *Crommelin* in the rear. The destroyer *Kidd* took the flank, alternating from one side to the other depending on where the danger seemed greatest. The crew was on high alert, the men in the air-conditioned CIC bent low over their radar repeaters, and the lookouts topside in the baking sun were more intent than usual as they searched the Iranian shoreline with their binoculars for any sign of approaching small craft. On the escorts, the chaff and Phalanx systems were set in automatic mode; in the air, AWACS planes kept the escorts apprised of air activity over the Gulf; at Camel Station in the Gulf of Oman, A-6 attack planes and F/A-18 fighters sat in launch positions on the deck of the *Constellation*. As the convoy passed into the Strait of Hormuz the warships detected Iranian missile-control radar tracking them. A petty officer on the *Fox* confided to an onboard journalist: "Everybody has the feeling that something is going to happen."[28]

But it didn't. Despite all the threats made by the Iranians that they would not tolerate American interference in the Gulf War, the convoy passed through the strait not only unscathed but largely ignored. Once into the southern Gulf, two Iranian F-4 aircraft approached the convoy at 5,000 feet, but when warned off by the *Kidd*, they disengaged and departed the area. With a straight run to the oil-loading pier off Kuwait City, it seemed that the United States had successfully called Iran's bluff. Then on July 24, with the convoy just 120 miles from its destination, Captain Seitz, on the *Bridgeton*, felt a sudden jarring blow. He recalled later, "It felt like a 500-ton hammer hit us up forward." A shock wave rippled down the twelve-hundred-foot length of the giant ship, and when it reached the bridge near the stern, it snapped the guy wires on the ship's radar mast and nearly knocked Seitz off his feet. The *Bridgeton* had struck a Soviet-made

The 400,000-ton supertanker *Bridgeton* (formerly the *Al Rekkah*) rides high in the water with most of its rudder exposed in its unburdened (empty) state. The Kuwaiti tanker had to be reflagged as an American vessel and assigned an American captain in order to justify an escort by the U.S. Navy. (U.S. Navy)

The thirty-by-fifteen-foot hole in the bow of the *Bridgeton* created by the detonation of a Soviet-made M-08 contact mine. (U.S. Navy)

M-08 mine, an old-fashioned contact mine: a bottom-moored sphere with projecting horns not significantly different from the mines that the Spanish had dumped in Manila Bay in the hope of deterring Dewey. Although it was a particularly low-tech weapon in this new age of electronic warfare, it had blown a thirty-by-fifteen-foot hole in the forward hull of the *Bridgeton*.[29]

Seitz ordered all stop, but a 400,000-ton tanker steaming at sixteen knots cannot stop in a hurry. Even ordering full astern had a minimal effect in halting the ship's inertia. As far as Seitz knew, there were more mines ahead, but if so, there was nothing he could do about it as the *Bridgeton* continued forward for another three miles before it slowed, finally, to a halt. Seitz ordered an inspection of the damage. The giant hole in the forward hull was less critical than it first appeared. Because the tanker's storage tanks were compartmented, the structural damage was limited to one section, and the *Bridgeton* was in no danger of sinking. Moreover, because it was traveling north, it was unburdened—that is, empty—though in fact crude oil is remarkably stable, and in most attacks on tankers the cargo failed to ignite. Seitz recalled later, "After about five minutes, we knew the ship was in no real danger." After hearing Seitz's report, Yonkers decided to continue the voyage, though at reduced speed.[30]

It was now evident, however, that in addition to Iranian speedboats, Silkworm missiles, and Iraqi fighter jets, there was a new peril in the Persian Gulf. Mines—silent and impersonal—could be lurking anywhere in its narrow, crowded confines. The mine threat caught the United States by surprise. It was not that Americans had failed to imagine it; instead policy makers had doubted Iran's willingness to employ mines, expecting (actually hoping) that the large U.S. naval presence would deter Iran's rulers from escalating the naval conflict. As a result, the U.S. Navy was simply unprepared for mine warfare, and its impressive fleet seemed suddenly very vulnerable. The *Bridgeton* had demonstrated that it could survive contact with a mine, but the same explosion that tore a thirty-by-fifteen-foot hole in the bottom of the 400,000-ton *Bridgeton* would very likely be fatal to the 3,600-ton *Crommelin* or even the 6,500-ton *Fox*.[31]

Quickly appraising the new circumstances, and aware that where there was one such mine there were almost certainly others, Seitz recommended to Yonkers that each of the escorts "get in behind the *Bridgeton*." Yonkers agreed, and in that moment the protectors suddenly became the protected. As the convoy proceeded north at a reduced speed of eight knots with the American escorts trailing the giant *Bridgeton* like so many ducklings, Seitz took a good deal of ribbing from his crew for his earlier assurance that the voyage would be a safe one because they were being escorted by the U.S. Navy.*

The United States took steps to dramatically improve its minesweeping capability. Giant Air Force C-5 transport planes flew eight RH-53D Sea Stallion minesweeping helicopters from the United States to the tiny island of Diego Garcia in the Indian Ocean, and from there the helicopters flew under their own power to the deck of the helicopter carrier *Guadalcanal*. In addition, the United States anchored two enormous barges (named *Hercules* and *Winbrown*) in the Gulf and used them as immobile helicopter carriers. Leased from the Houston, Texas, firm of Brown & Root, these heavy-lift barges essentially fulfilled the role that many felt should have been assumed by Saudi Arabia and Kuwait, both of which refused to allow the United States to use its bases for minesweeping helicopters. Later, the United States added half a dozen old minesweepers built in the 1950s and called into service from the reserve fleet.[32]

Eventually these Gulf convoys became more or less routine. Two or three American destroyers or frigates would rendezvous with between two and four tankers at one end or the other of the Persian Gulf and escort them through the combat zone. During the passage it was not uncommon for other ships of any nationality to join the convoy, though they did so without authorization, shouldering their way into the formation and causing headaches for the convoy commander. One convoy ended up with a total of twenty-one ships, most of which were uninvited hangers-on. As one convoy commander recalled, they barged into the formation "like

---

* The experience of the *Bridgeton* led to a morbidly humorous exchange between a Navy official and a group of reporters. When the reporters asked how many minesweepers the U.S. Navy had in the Gulf, the Navy official at first replied, "None." Then, after pausing, he changed his answer to eleven: the number of Kuwaiti tankers the U.S. had pledged to escort.

Mama Cass at an all-you-can-eat buffet . . . there was nothing we could do about it."[33]

Eventually U.S. naval forces conducted a total of 136 convoys in the Persian Gulf, escorting 270 ships through the war zone. Of those, 188 (70 percent) were reflagged Kuwaiti tankers. In the end, only the unlucky *Bridgeton* suffered any damage. America's debut as the policeman of the Persian Gulf in Operation Earnest Will was a success. In a larger sense, however, what was important in all this was the nation's initial decision to accept responsibility for the control and direction of Gulf traffic. The convoys themselves, as Michael Palmer has pointed out, were largely symbolic. What was historically significant was America's willingness, and the Navy's ability, to turn the Persian Gulf into a kind of American lake.[34]

—

To this point, American involvement in the Iran-Iraq War was peripheral, but it nevertheless caused the Iranians serious concern, for if it chose to do so, the U.S. Navy could easily dominate the naval war. Iran did have a substantial surface navy: it was essentially the navy that the Khomeini regime had inherited from the shah, much of it supplied by Britain and the United States.* But the Iranian navy, like the Iranian army, had suffered greatly in the wake of the 1979 revolution, and in any case it could not come close to matching up to the U.S. Navy. Whenever Iranian warships ventured out of port, the U.S. Navy made it clear that they were to keep their distance. "We would just illuminate them with our fire control radar," one officer recalled, "and that would be enough to keep them outside the range of our missiles."[35]

Iran's most sophisticated antiship weapon was the Chinese-made Silkworm missile, which had a range of eighty miles. But using a Silkworm

---

* The shah's military buildup was still under way at the time of the revolution that drove him from power. He had recently contracted with the United States for the delivery of four new, specially modified *Spruance*-class destroyers. After the shah's fall, the United States halted delivery of these vessels, bought them from the builder, and commissioned them as U.S. Navy warships. The USS *Kidd*, which participated in the first Gulf convoy, was the namesake of the class. Despite their official designation as *Kidd*-class destroyers, sailors routinely called them "Khomeini-class destroyers."

against tankers turned out to be like shooting elephants with a .22 rifle. They could punch a hole in a tanker, but they seldom proved fatal or even particularly serious. Moreover, Silkworm missiles were expensive. As defense analyst Norman Friedman noted at the time, "It cost less to repair a tanker than to buy another anti-ship missile on the international market." In short, firing Silkworm missiles at tankers was a losing proposition.[36]

A more unpredictable element of Iran's naval capability was the seagoing arm of what was called the Islamic Revolutionary Guards Corps (or just the Guard), a semiautonomous cadre of religious fanatics who were not only self-appointed guardians of Iran's internal morals and religious purity but also virtual free agents in the war with Iraq. The Guard's "navy" consisted of a score or so of small rubber Zodiac boats armed with machine guns and rocket-propelled grenade (RPG) launchers. Just as the Iranians embraced low-technology warfare on land—launching human-wave attacks against the Iraqi army—so, too, did the Islamic Revolutionary Guards Corps adopt a low-technology naval effort in the Gulf. These dedicated fanatics put to sea in vessels so tiny they could hide behind navigational buoys; even in the open sea they didn't show up on radar. The notion of attacking a 400,000-ton tanker in a rubber boat may have looked like a mosquito assaulting a rhinoceros, but these vessels could still do damage. Their usual procedure was to approach a tanker and politely ask its nationality and port of embarkation. Receiving the information, they would then leave, only to return at night and shoot up the bridge and living quarters with small-arms fire. They couldn't sink ships, but they could kill people, and their presence created anxiety for U.S. warship commanders. "A lot of the time there'd be small boats, whether they were smuggling, fishermen, or whatever," one U.S. officer recalled. "They'd come by and we'd man the .50-caliber and 25 mm guns. . . . It was very unsettling. There's a war going on with people shooting and killing each other on land and air and sea. We're not an active belligerent in that war, but at the same time there are commercial airliners, merchant shipping, fishermen, and others, and it was stressful to distinguish among all these. It was very nerve wracking."[37]

But Iran's most dangerous low-technology weapon was mines. Iran turned to mine warfare because it simply lacked the assets to fight a traditional naval war against the U.S. Navy. Just as the Confederacy turned to ironclads in 1862 and Germany to submarines in 1914, so in 1987 did Iran seek an alternative to the conventional weapons of naval warfare. Cheap and easy to put in place, mines caused the U.S. Navy special problems in the confined and crowded waters of the Persian Gulf because they did not distinguish among targets and were difficult to remove and destroy.

From the moment of impact, the Americans had assumed that the mine that damaged the *Bridgeton* had been laid by Iranian forces. Iran's government made no secret of its determination to target the shipping of both Saudi Arabia and Kuwait. The Iranians contended that both countries, though officially neutral, were effectively supporting Iraq in what was, after all, an unprovoked war of aggression. As far as Iran was concerned, that made Saudi and Kuwaiti vessels fair game, and if the United States chose to put itself in harm's way by escorting them through a war zone, the United States, too, was fair game, though Iran was reluctant to challenge the United States directly. For that reason, Iran did not publicly claim credit for damaging the *Bridgeton*, instead attributing the incident to "invisible hands." Nevertheless, the location of the mine, only eighteen miles from Iranian-controlled Farsi Island, was suspicious, and most Americans assumed that Iran was the culprit. Still, it was hard to prove who was responsible for sowing any particular mine, and to hold Iran accountable, it would be necessary to catch them in the act.[38]

Americans found the smoking gun in September. As one example of an emerging tendency toward interservice cooperation (or jointness), Admiral Crowe arranged for a few U.S. Navy frigates in the Gulf to carry U.S. Army Special Forces MH-6 helicopters, which fit easily into the hangers that had been designed for the Navy's ASW helicopters. Despite initial resistance by Navy personnel to the whole idea of hosting Army Rangers on Navy ships, the small, two-seater Army helicopters soon proved their value. What made them especially desirable was that they were remarkably quiet and were equipped with the latest in night-vision technology. Because they flew only at night, the Navy crews called them "Sea Bats." The pilots, Army Special Forces warrant officers, stayed aboard the ships during the day in quarters that the Navy men quickly labeled the "Bat Cave" and ventured out at night when the Iranians believed they were protected by the veil of darkness. On the night of September 21, two of these small but lethal helicopters from the USS *Jarrett* spotted a vessel in a ship channel northeast of Bahrain. Through their night-vision goggles, they could clearly see sailors on the fantail dropping mines over the side.[39]

Prior to their deployment to the Gulf, the Army pilots had been briefed personally by Admiral Crowe, himself a former commander of the Middle East Forces, who had emphasized that laying mines was "a hostile act" and told them that if they observed any vessel so engaged, they could open fire without warning. Consequently, the Sea Bats immediately swooped down and laced the stern of the vessel with their 7.62-millimeter Gatling guns. The crew members threw themselves to the deck, but when the helicopters flew past, they resumed dropping mines in the water. The Army helicopters came around for another run, and this time they fired 3.75-inch rocket pods filled with fléchette rounds—hundreds of tiny nails. The ship's crew jumped over the side, and the vessel caught fire. The next morning a Navy SEAL team boarded the abandoned vessel, which proved to be the Iranian transport vessel *Iran Ajr*, and found ten mines still on board along with their fuses and timers.[40]

Dead and living Iranians were plucked from the water nearby and taken aboard the U.S. command ship *LaSalle*, a converted transport dock that was serving as the flagship of the Commander Middle East Force. The dead were stored rather awkwardly in the ship's freezer, those who needed hospital attention were flown to the *Guadalcanal*, and the rest were bound with plastic handcuffs and detained aboard the *LaSalle*. Their legal status was a bit murky. "We're not at war," a U.S. Defense Department spokesman declared, "so they really couldn't be called prisoners. For now they're being called detainees." It was a new term for a new kind of conflict, and it would not be the last time the United States would find occasion to use it.[41]

The Sea Bats soon made nighttime mine laying a dangerous business for the Iranians. On October 8 a night-flying MH-6 helicopter sank an

Iranian Boghammer gunboat and damaged two other craft.* Iran protested these attacks and called for a mutual withdrawal of forces from the Gulf. Instead, the United States warned Iran that continued mine laying would provoke even harsher responses. In a press interview, Secretary of the Navy James Webb declared, "There comes a time when a different sort of reaction could be necessary in order to make it clear what our objectives are."[42]

With the night-flying Sea Bats interrupting their mine-laying efforts, and Sea Stallions sweeping the mines ahead of the convoys, the Iranians tried a new tactic. Their reconquest of the Faw Peninsula, just east of the Shatt-al-Arab, put them within missile range of Kuwait, and on October 15, 1987, they fired a Silkworm missile at a Liberian-registered tanker near the Al Ahmadi oil terminal. The next day they fired another into the bridge of the reflagged supertanker *Sea Isle City*. Technically, because the oil terminal was in Kuwaiti waters, the *Sea Isle City* was no longer under American protection, but because it had been previously reflagged as an American vessel, the Reagan administration decided that some kind of retaliation was needed. Despite the administration's public disdain for the kind of incremental escalation that had drawn the United States into Vietnam, Reagan sought a measured response. The key word in the administration was "proportionality." What would constitute a proportional response for a missile attack on the *Sea Isle City*?[43]

Rather than sink an Iranian warship, which some in the administration feared would provoke a dangerous escalation, administration planners decided instead to target an Iranian oil platform. The justification for this was that the Iranians used these platforms to monitor maritime trade in the Gulf and to conduct surveillance of U.S. warships. The particular plat-

---

* One of the Iranian "detainees" from this confrontation said that he had attempted to shoot down the attacking American helicopter with a Stinger missile but could not get the tone that indicated the missile was locked on. The container for the Stinger was found by one of the U.S. patrol boats from the barge *Hercules*, but not the missile itself. Navy dive teams tried three times to recover the missile because of the possibility that it was one of the weapons shipped to Iran as part of the Iran-Contra scandal in which Lieutenant Colonel Oliver North, USMC, played such a conspicuous role. Ironically, North's younger brother Tim was an officer on board the *Thach* at the time of this recovery effort.

form selected was the Rashadat platform in the southern Gulf, from which the Iranians had fired (though unsuccessfully) at a U.S. helicopter the year before.

To ensure overwhelming firepower superiority, the United States assigned no fewer than six warships to the mission: one cruiser, four destroyers, and the small frigate *Thach*, named in honor of Jimmy Thach, who had commanded VF-3 in the Battle of Midway. Their orders were to steam up to the Rashadat platform, warn the Iranians to evacuate, and then destroy it with gunfire. To ensure that the rest of the world (including the American public) witnessed this expression of American displeasure, a film crew also came on board with orders to photograph the entire operation.[44]

The attack took place on October 19, 1987. One of the two platforms caught fire almost immediately, but the other proved remarkably resilient; it was like trying to destroy a spiderweb with rifle fire. After an hour and a half, although the U.S. ships had fired more than a thousand rounds of high-explosive ordnance into its skeleton, the second platform stubbornly refused to collapse. Finally, the *Thach* sent an ordnance disposal team over to it; the team planted munitions and returned. When the ordnance was detonated, "the platform disappeared."[45]

The purpose of the raid was to make a clear statement not only to the Iranian government but also to the international community. The commanding officer of the *Thach* recalled, "The real payoff . . . was the film of the U.S. ships firing as a demonstration of U.S. power and resolve, not the actual destruction of an oil platform." Without a doubt, it got the Iranians' attention. The Iranian ambassador to the United Nations wailed that the United States "has opened an all-out war against my country." But there was concern within the U.S. Navy, too. A relatively large U.S. naval squadron had expended more than a thousand rounds of high explosive and fragmentation shells to cripple an oil platform. A cartoon that was reprinted in the *Navy Times* depicted a Navy gunner reporting to his superiors: "That's ONE THOUSAND high-explosive five inch rounds fired at close range, target sort of destroyed, sir!" To which the officer replied: "Dam' fine shooting, gunner. Good thing that oil platform wasn't moving!" And another officer added: "Or firing back!" One critic calculated the cost of a thousand shells and concluded that the operation had cost the United States more than it had the Iranians.[46]

In February 1988 U.S. Naval forces in the Gulf got a new commander. He was Rear Admiral Anthony "Tony" Less, a fifty-year-old, blond, blue-eyed naval aviator with more than six thousand flight hours under his belt, including several combat tours in Vietnam and a stint as flight leader of the Blue Angels Flight Demonstration Squadron. He had also commanded a carrier battle group. Now in his new job he would wear two hats: he was commander of the Middle East Force, but he was also commander of the Joint Task Force Middle East. Reflecting a new concern for effective inter-service cooperation, the United States for the first time would have one person who was responsible for all military operations in the Arabian Sea, the Gulf of Oman, and the Persian Gulf. Before he left Washington, Less met personally with Admiral Crowe, who emphasized to him the importance of effective joint operations. It was clear that, in Crowe's view at least, success in the complex environment of the Persian Gulf meant that the U.S. Navy had to act in close coordination with the other services.[47]

And indeed, the Gulf was a complex environment that winter. With Iran in control of the Faw Peninsula, Saddam Hussein began to fear that he might actually lose the war he had started. He therefore ordered a renewal of the airstrikes against tankers in the Gulf. To prevent another *Stark* disaster, U.S. and Iraqi officials worked out a series of procedures, but Iraqi pilots did not always observe the protocols. "Those Iraqi cowboys in F-4s just turned, closed their eyes, and fired," one officer recalled. "Then they turned north to go home." In any given watch period it was more than likely that at least one Iraqi jet would fly through Gulf airspace en route to targets off Iran. "Because of the AWACS, we would know as soon as they lifted off," recalled Lieutenant James Smith, the weapons officer on the *Thach*, whom everyone called "Red" because of his hair. "We were really prepared because nobody wanted a repeat of the *Stark* event. Our air controllers used certain code words to talk to these aircraft as they were inbound. If we asked them to adjust their course, they did." In spite of these protocols, however, several times in early 1988 Iraqi planes flew dan-

gerously close to U.S. Navy ships. The closest call took place on February 12
when an Iraqi jet actually fired two missiles at the American destroyer
Chandler but missed.[48]

—

Despite the renewed threat from the air, it was the mine threat that provoked the next crisis. On April 14 the *Samuel B. Roberts*, a sister ship of the
unlucky *Stark*, was heading southward. As always, AWACS planes as well as
the *Roberts*'s own air search radar kept a wary electronic eye on the air traffic, while topside lookouts scanned the sea with binoculars for Iranian
speedboats or mines. No new mines had been discovered for a week, however, and when a few floating objects off the bow caught the lookouts'
attention, at least one of them thought they might be sheep carcasses. In
addition to tankers, other vessels routinely plied the shipping lanes,
including giant Australian cargo ships that carried thousands of live sheep.
Whenever one or two of the sheep died, as inevitably happened, they were
tossed unceremoniously over the side. American sailors had gotten used to
seeing their bloated carcasses float past with the legs sticking up out of the
water. But a second look showed that these were no sheep carcasses—they
were the real thing. Quickly the lookouts reported the sighting to the
bridge. The skipper of the *Samuel B. Roberts*, Paul Rinn, ordered all stop.
Finding himself in the middle of a new minefield, Rinn decided to reverse
engines and back out slowly the way he had come. Relatively rough seas
made this difficult, and the *Roberts* was suddenly rocked by a huge underwater explosion directly beneath the engine room that lifted the ship's
stern completely out of the water.[49]

The blast opened a twenty-five-foot hole in the bottom of the *Roberts*,
jarred the ship's two gas turbine engines off their mounting blocks, bent
the main shaft, and ignited a fire that fed on the spilled fuel oil and started
spreading through the ship. But as on the *Stark*, heroic damage control
saved the ship. Indeed, lessons learned from the *Stark* disaster meant that
the *Roberts*'s damage control teams were better supplied with oxygen
masks and canisters for firefighting. The crew showed remarkable inven-
tiveness. The mine had nearly broken the *Roberts* in half, and to prevent

the ship from literally breaking apart, the crew used wire cables to effectively tie it back together.[50] Eventually the *Roberts* made it into port using its auxiliary engines.*

Unlike the *Stark* disaster, the mining of the *Roberts* did not produce banner headlines in the United States. One reason was that on the same day the *Roberts* hit the mine, the Soviet Union, after a decade of futility, signed an agreement to withdraw from Afghanistan, an event that pushed the *Roberts* disaster off the front page. In addition, and rather remarkably, no Americans had died on the *Roberts*, though ten were wounded, including seven who had to be treated for second-degree burns. Still, the event was a turning point. A search of the area afterward led to the discovery of several more mines. U.S. teams secured them and flew photographers from the press out to take pictures before the mines were destroyed. These images proved beyond any doubt that the mines were Iranian in origin.

What no one in the American camp knew at the time was that although the mines were indeed Iranian, they had been sown by the Islamic Revolutionary Guard, and almost immediately afterward the regular Iranian navy had put to sea in an effort to sweep them up, thus demonstrating the wide gulf between the goals of the Guard fanatics and Iran's more pragmatic government leaders who sought to avoid a direct confrontation with the American superpower. But U.S. policy makers either failed to make the distinction or were unsure how to respond to challenges from an enemy operating outside government sanction. If Iranians had laid the mines, then Iran must pay the consequences.[51]

At a meeting held on Friday afternoon, April 15, the day after the *Roberts* was damaged, the President ordered his Department of Defense team to compile a list of possible targets, then he left for Camp David for the weekend. While he was gone, Defense Department personnel put together a plan. Crowe, the only uniformed member of the team, wanted to sink a ship. "My general theory was that if we were going to take any

---

* The *Roberts* was carried to the United States piggybacked on top of the Dutch heavy-lift vessel *Mighty Servant II*, which the United States leased from the Netherlands. Like the *Stark*, the *Roberts* was repaired and returned to service.

retaliatory measures at all, we should destroy targets that would reduce the Iranians' ability to harm us." "I pushed hard," he wrote later, "for hitting a warship." In particular, Crowe wanted to sink the Iranian frigate *Sabalan*,* whose captain had built a well-earned reputation for ruthlessness and was known throughout the Gulf as "Captain Nasty." His modus operandi was to stop a tanker or cargo vessel, query its captain and crew, then shoot up the bridge and living spaces. Afterward he would call out "Have a nice day!" before steaming off. Frank Carlucci, the new secretary of defense, "kind of liked the idea" of hitting a warship, but almost everyone else in the room was opposed, fearing that such an act would escalate the conflict; they argued instead that the United States should target another oil platform.[52]

In the end, Reagan opted for a compromise: U.S. Navy forces would strike at several Iranian oil platforms—larger and more important platforms known as gas and oil separation platforms (GOSPs). But, the president said, if the Iranian navy ventured out in an attempt to defend them, the Navy "could engage and sink them."[53] Crowe interpreted this to mean that if the *Sabalan* came out of port, the U.S. Navy could send it to the bottom. This time Reagan made a special effort to inform congressional leaders of the plan. Robert Dole of Kansas reported to his colleagues that "the President . . . intends to keep us fully informed and involved as this action evolves," and Lee Hamilton declared, "I do not see a renewed debate on Persian Gulf policy." Having lined up the political support and selected the targets, Reagan gave the "go" order on April 16 to execute what was codenamed Operation Praying Mantis.[54]

—

On the receiving end of that order, Tony Less organized his forces into three strike teams called surface action groups, or SAGs, and assigned each of them a specific target. SAG Bravo was to destroy the Sassan platform and SAG Charlie the Sirri platform, and SAG Delta was to be ready to

---

* Variously spelled *Sabalan*, *Savblan*, and *Zabalon*, the spelling used here was the one most widely used at the time.

intercept any attempt by the Iranians to interfere. In addition, the planes of the *Enterprise,* which had replaced the *Constellation* on Camel Station, stood ready to join in the fight if an opportunity presented itself. Altogether, more than a dozen warships were committed to the operation. Less himself remained aboard the command ship *Coronado* at Bahrain to direct the overall operation from a distance. The three SAG groups would attack simultaneously but independently.

SAG Bravo was led by Captain James B. Perkins, and it was his job to destroy the Sassan GOSP. His orders required him to warn the Iranian crew of the GOSP before he fired, which made him uncomfortable because the Sassan platform was not merely an oil and gas separation plant but a well-armed outpost of the Iranian military, armed with .20- and .50-caliber machine guns as well as larger guns, and intelligence sources indicated that it was manned in part by elements of the fanatical Republican Guard.

The Sassan gas and oil separation platform (GOSP) prior to the attack by U.S. forces. (U.S. Navy)

Perkins later argued that "warning an armed GOSP . . . prior to opening fire may register high on the humane scale, but it clearly ranks low in terms of relative tactical advantage." Still, orders were orders.[55]

Just past dawn on April 18, at about 6:00 A.M., the ships of SAG Bravo steamed up to the Sassan platform. It was an enormous structure—over an acre in size and with several levels, appearing to some rather like a Hollywood version of a futuristic city. While the two sides studied one another, a Farsi linguist on the USS *Merrill* broke the silence to announce over the radio in both Farsi and English: "You have thirty minutes to get everybody off; we are going to destroy this platform."[56]

Watchers on the U.S. Navy ships then saw a lot of activity. Men ran about from place to place; some seemed to be getting ready to leave, while others just seemed to be "running around." Listeners on the radio net heard the GOSP occupants frantically ask their bosses in Tehran for orders, then radio to the Americans to beg for more time. Perkins and his staff denied all requests for an extension, and at 8:04 A.M. the designated deadline expired. With a last look at his watch, Perkins ordered, "Weapons free," and a five-inch high-explosive shell flew toward the Sassan platform.[57]

It was a curious form of naval combat in the age of electronic warfare. Normally in a confrontation with an armed combatant, the captain of the ship would occupy the padded chair in the combat information center. From that darkened room deep in the ship, where the monitors and TV screens reported all the relevant information from a variety of sensors, he would direct both the ship's movements and its weapons systems, using radar directors to aim his weaponry. But on this day the captain of the *Merrill* and the task group commodore both stood on the bridge wing to watch the fall of shot. Lieutenant Commander Henry "Hank" Sanford, the *Merrill*'s executive officer, actually manned the ship's "big eyes," the oversize binoculars on the bridge, so that he could assess the impact of the gunfire more accurately. "Everything," he said later, "was done visually."[58]

Almost everything. A second-class petty officer sitting at the gun console in the *Merrill*'s CIC used a joy stick and a tiny TV screen, just like a video game, to aim the ship's five-inch guns. He managed to put an air-burst round directly above the gun mount, and it virtually wiped out the Iranian gun crew. That proved to be decisive. After a few more air-burst rounds, the Iranians came on the radio and announced that they had decided to evacuate. Perkins ordered his ships to cease fire. Again the platform resembled an ant farm that had been prodded with a stick as men ran, seemingly randomly, over the platform. Soon, however, they made for the ladders and began to climb down into a few boats that were tied up at the base. Sanford counted them off as they departed, losing count after thirty. He was glad to see them go: "We didn't want any prisoners." A few of the men were carrying some wounded and had trouble making the climb, but eventually they all got into the boats and left.[59]

After the Iranians cleared the area, helicopters from the *Trenton* hovered over the target, and Marines fast-roped down onto the platform. In

The badly damaged Sassan GOSP occupied by U.S. Marines who rappelled down from helicopters from the USS *Trenton* to search for intelligence and set explosives. (U.S. Navy)

thirty minutes the Marines recovered whatever papers might be of value and planted their charges. The ships of SAG Bravo moved away from the platform, and the Americans "pulled the trigger." Those standing on the bridge of the *Merrill* felt the air concussion from five miles away. It was, one recalled, "the most powerful explosion I've ever seen."[60]

The attack on the Sirri platform by SAG Charlie unfolded similarly. This task group was headed by the *Belknap*-class cruiser *Wainwright*, a sister ship of the *Fox*, which had participated in the first Earnest Will convoy. The *Wainwright*, a guided-missile cruiser with a two-armed missile firing system forward and a five-inch gun aft, was a handsome vessel with a bluff-faced superstructure. Unlike the *Spruance*-class destroyers, the *Wainwright* had not been designed for ASW. Its basic mission was antiair warfare, but its triple-ring missile battery and Mark 76 control system could also fire the Navy's standard missile (SM-1 or SM-2) at surface targets, which made it a ship-killer. SAG Charlie also had the small frigates *Simpson* (a sister ship of both the *Stark* and the *Roberts*) and *Bagley*, a slightly larger vessel with similar armament. The senior officer of SAG Charlie was Captain James Chandler, a career Navy officer who had spent nearly all his professional life in cruisers and destroyers. In war gaming exercises at both Newport and Norfolk, Chandler had specialized in missile warfare.[61]

The sailors on the *Wainwright* had heard rumors for days of a forthcoming mission, and they looked forward to it. "We knew something was going to happen," recalled a first-class petty officer. "There was a lot of tension. . . . The crew all around the ship were all pretty, you know . . . , well, they were mad actually. Because of what happened to the *Roberts*. And we hadn't done nothing about it." Then on the afternoon of April 17 Chandler held a "captain's call" on the helicopter deck of the *Wainwright*. With the crew gathered around him, he explained the coming operation, telling his men exactly what their jobs would be and how he intended to execute his orders. Then he invited questions. At the end of it, he told them to "make sure your battle stations are ready to go to war in the morning." He told them he was confident in them, that he was sure they would "carry the day." Then he asked the ship's chaplain to lead a prayer.[62]

The guided-missile cruiser USS *Wainwright* shown with a missile "on the rail," ready to shoot. The missiles loaded without being touched by human hands from the wedge-shaped magazine astern of the missile firing arms. The ship's 5-inch gun is aft, astern of the helicopter deck. (U.S. Navy)

Reveille on April 18 was at 5:30, and when general quarters sounded at 7:00, one officer recalled that "it was the fastest muster we ever had." Chandler himself went down into the darkened CIC, where more than sixty people crowded around the various screens and monitors. During combat operations, it was Chandler's policy to turn the bridge over to his executive officer, while he took the chair of the tactical action officer in CIC. To his right was Lieutenant Marty Drake, the ship's weapons officer. In front of him, sitting at an elaborate panel of screens and switches, including the launch key for the ship's Harpoon missile system, were the senior enlisted men who operated the electronics. That morning, the petty officers on duty were Operations Specialist Chief Paul McCullough and thirty-two-year-old Operations Specialist First Class Reuben Vargas, who had enlisted in the Navy as a teenager in Puerto Rico. Now Vargas sat with his fingers literally on the trigger, so close to Chandler that, as he recalled later, "his hand was actually on my shoulder."[63]

The *Wainwright* and its consorts slowly circled the Sirri platform. At precisely 7:55 a U.S. intelligence officer on board radioed the first warning to the Iranians: "Gas and oil separation platform, this is U.S. Navy warship. You have five minutes to evacuate your platform. Any actions other than evacuation will result in immediate destruction." This announcement was duplicated in Farsi, and repeated. Then, in mocking imitation of the Iranian captain of the *Sabalan*, he intoned: "Have a nice day." The Iranians on the platform radioed back excitedly that five minutes was not enough time, but they began to evacuate at once. Three American helicopters were aloft, and the pilots reported that they could see men making their way down the ladders onto a small tug. "It was clear they were abandoning the GOSP," Chandler said later, "but they just needed more time. I called the *Bagley* and the *Simpson* and told them to hold fire."[64]

The tug pulled away from the GOSP at about 8:15, but not everyone had evacuated; the helicopter pilots reported that there were uniformed men manning the guns. Some of the Iranians, at least, intended to fight it out. The three ships of SAG Charlie opened a coordinated fire just after 8:30 with five-inch and seventy-six-millimeter guns. The Iranians returned small-arms fire for a few minutes until one U.S. shell hit a compressed gas tank, which ignited a secondary explosion that incinerated the gun crew and set the whole platform ablaze. After that, the Iranians lost the will to fight and agreed to leave. The ships of SAG Charlie held their fire while the Iranian tug returned to pick up the survivors. By now the platform was burning so ferociously it was impossible (and unnecessary) to insert the SEAL team.[65]

So far the mission had been a success: both of the targeted platforms had been completely destroyed, U.S. forces had suffered no casualties, and the earlier embarrassment of expending a thousand rounds to destroy an immobile target had been expunged. But the operation was not yet complete. From the beginning, the senior American officers had hoped that the attacks on the oil platforms would incite the Iranian navy to sortie. It had been almost half a century since U.S. surface combatants had tangled with warships from another navy, and almost to a man, the Americans hoped they would have a chance to retaliate for the *Roberts* by sinking an Iranian frigate. As one sailor expressed it, "We wanted to kick ass." On the other hand, few imagined that it would happen, for surely the Iranians were aware that their tiny navy was no match for the U.S. squadron.[66]

Then at 11:30, the signals exploitation team reported to Chandler in CIC that an Iranian surface combatant was closing the formation.

—

The Iranian decision to sortie its surface navy on April 18 is inexplicable. It is possible that the commander of the Islamic Revolutionary Guard, Mohsen Reza'i, demanded that Iran's navy respond to the American attacks. If so, it suggests, as one authority has posited, "that the Guard was in de-facto command of the regular Navy."[67] Another possibility is that the Iranians concluded that the United States had finally decided to ally itself openly with Iraq, for, as it happened, Iraqi ground forces had launched a massive counterattack that same morning, and the Iranians likely believed this simultaneous assault was not a coincidence—that the United States had at last sided openly with the Iraqis. Whatever factors contributed to the Iranian decision, it was a horrible miscalculation.*

Chandler radioed Admiral Less to apprise him of the situation. Less ordered him to get a positive identification on the approaching vessel, and Chandler ordered the *Simpson* to send its Light Airborne Multi-Purpose System (LAMPS) helicopter up for a visual ID. The LAMPS pilot radioed back that the surface contact was "a frigate-sized Iranian warship with a mast and radar amidships and two missiles astern of the mast."[68] It was, in fact, the *Joshan*, a 154-foot Iranian gunboat. But small as it was, the *Joshan* packed a punch, for it carried a seventy-six-millimeter gun amidships (the same size gun as on the American frigates), as well as a forty-millimeter machine gun. More importantly, it could fire both surface-to-air missiles

---

* The Iranians were not the only ones who were suspicious about the coincidence of the simultaneous Iraqi ground attack and American naval attack. Administration spokesman Charles Redman declared, "There is no linkage or connection between these two events," and no evidence has ever emerged to suggest otherwise, though a number of analysts conclude that given America's intelligence capability in the region, it is hard to see how the United States could have been ignorant of the attack, and very likely the Iranians drew the same conclusion.

and the deadly surface-to-surface American-made Harpoon missile.*
Chandler knew this because, as at Midway, the United States had superior
intelligence about the enemy. In fact, the intelligence team that had been
put on board for this operation had a complete file on every Iranian ship.
Chandler recalled, "The officer in charge of the signal intercept group
came down with his book and showed me just what the *Joshan* was—gave
me a short bio of the commanding officer, and showed me his picture."[69]

Before challenging the contact, Chandler ordered the *Wainwright's*
weapons officer to put an SM-1 on the rail and advised the ships in his
command "to prepare for an SM-1 engagement." Then he sent the *Joshan* a
radio message: "Iranian patrol frigate, this is United States Navy warship.
Do not interfere with my actions. Remain clear or you will be destroyed.
Over." When the *Joshan* did not respond to that challenge and continued
to close, Chandler tried again, demanding that the *Joshan* send its hull
number. This time the *Joshan* replied, giving its hull number (255) and
declaring that it would "commit no provocative acts."[70]

To Chandler, however, actions were louder than words, and the *Joshan*
continued to close at high speed. Chandler radioed the *Joshan* twice more,
ordering it to stop its engines. There was no response either time. Chandler then notified the other ships in the task group: "He has not stopped
his engines. And those canisters [on the stern] are probably Harpoon canisters, and I believe that there is one Harpoon remaining that is operational. He has it on board."

He warned the *Joshan* again: "Heed my warning. Stop your engines. If
you do not stop, I will take you under fire." Receiving no reply, he tried
again: "If you do not stop, I will take you under fire." Chandler's next message was terse: "Iranian patrol ship, this is U.S. Navy warship. Stop and
abandon ship. I intend to sink you."[71]

At that moment, Chief McCullough, sitting just in front of Chandler in
the CIC, announced, "Captain, I have separation!" Simultaneously, the

---

* The Iranians had a total of nine Harpoons, all sold to them by the United States, but only one that
was operational—the one on the *Joshan*. The *Joshan's* bold decision to take on the ships of SAG
Charlie may have been motivated by that fact.

electronic warfare specialist announced, "I have an emitter!" A homing device had locked onto the *Wainwright*. "After that," Vargas recalled, "all hell broke loose." Marty Drake, the TAO, called out, "Launch chaff!" though the electronics warfare technician, Petty Officer Third Class Hall, had already anticipated the order, punching the button that fired a cloud of aluminized plastic confetti off to the starboard side. Chandler ordered the task group to open fire: "This is Wainwright. I am launching chaff. I am being locked on. Batteries released! Batteries released! Fire!" The weapons officer ordered: "Let's go. Launch 'em."[72]

Then every man on board heard what one called "this big whoosh going down the starboard side from forward to aft." The Harpoon missile from the *Joshan* flew so close to the *Wainwright* that the men on the bridge could feel the heat of the propellant as it passed. It missed the *Wainwright* by a matter of feet before splashing harmlessly into the sea some seventy-five yards astern. Down in the CIC, the weapons controller turned the key on the ship's weapons console. "Birds free," he reported.[73]

The *Wainwright*'s first missile blew the mast off the *Joshan*, while the

A U.S. Navy standard missile (SM-1) being launched. (U.S. Navy)

Simpson's smashed into its superstructure. On the radar screen, however, the *Joshan* still appeared to be moving. "I think I'm gonna have the *Simpson* feed him another," Chandler announced.

"Simpson, this is Wainwright. Are you prepared for another attack?"

"That's affirmative."

"Birds free."

"Roger out."

"This is Simpson. Evaluate a hit."

Altogether, SAG Charlie fired four missiles into the *Joshan*, and all four were hits. By then the *Joshan* was on fire from stem to stern and sinking.[74]

For Tony Less on the *Coronado* it was both electrifying and frustrating. Like Nimitz at Pearl Harbor during the Battle of Midway, he had to monitor unfolding events by interpreting the calls he overheard on the radio. "The most tense moment of my tour," he recalled later, was "when I received the transmission . . . that the *Joshan* had fired a Harpoon missile."[75] All he could do was wait for the next transmission that told him "the Harpoon had missed." Then Less contacted Chandler again:

"Did you sink him?" he asked.

"Negative," Chandler replied. "He's dead in the water and on fire."

Less switched phones and spoke briefly to Admiral Crowe in Washington. Then he got back on the phone to Chandler to order him to sink the *Joshan*—it had not been the original target of the operation, but a ship was a ship.[76]

Crowe had been monitoring the radio chatter himself from the basement Navy Command Center at the Pentagon along with Secretary of Defense Frank Carlucci. They heard Chandler's report that the *Joshan* had fired a Harpoon and the report that SAG Charlie was engaging. "We heard the message traffic all day," Crowe recalled. "But we didn't interfere much." As he put it, "I've always had an aversion to the Pentagon giving orders to operational commanders."[77]

With orders to finish off the *Joshan*, Chandler closed to within gun range of the smoking hulk and ordered each of the ships under his command to open fire. With Marine spotters in helicopters to report the fall of the shot, the *Wainwright* fired one round long, one short, and landed the third on target. Then the ships of SAG Charlie fired for effect. The *Wainwright* aimed six rapid-fire five-inch rounds into the burning hulk. After the sixth round, the spotter in the helicopter radioed for the task group to cease fire. When Chandler asked him why, the spotter reported that the *Joshan* had disappeared. "There were bodies everywhere," Vargas recalled. "The hardest thing was shutting it off."[78]

On the bridge of the *Wainwright*, someone asked Chandler if they should sweep the area for survivors. Chandler was quiet for a moment, then replied: "No." There were a number of Iranian fishing dhows in the area that could pick up any survivors, and Chandler feared that if he closed the wreckage, the Iranians might later claim that it was for the purpose of killing the survivors. As it happened, they made this claim anyway, reporting that American ships had machine-gunned survivors in the water. "It certainly wasn't a brilliant move on my part," Chandler said later, "but I still think it was the smart thing to do."[79]

In response to the panicked calls from the two GOSPs and the sinking *Joshan*, the Iranians had scrambled a few F-4 fighter aircraft from the airfield near Bandar Abbas on the Strait of Hormuz. In midafternoon, as the one-sided fight with the *Joshan* was winding down, the *Wainwright* got a report that an F-4 was approaching at high altitude. Chandler warned the F-4 to stay clear; getting no response, he fired two standard missiles in air mode and scored at least one hit, though the crippled F-4 managed to make it back to its base, missing part of its wing.

That proved to be the last encounter of the day for SAG Charlie. After ten hours of combat, the men could finally stand down. They had been at general quarters since seven that morning; some had been at their posts since midnight the night before. "It was pretty tense to be sitting in that seat for seventeen hours," Vargas recalled later. "It was something you don't ever forget." Almost as soon as it was over, the men on the *Wainwright* began to appreciate how close they had come to being on the receiving end of a Harpoon missile. "The chaplain was very busy that night," one officer recalled. "We had a lot of scared young sailors who [realized that] they'd almost bought it."[80]

The reality of that came home to the crew of the *Wainwright* when they

A smiling Admiral William Crowe, chairman of the Joint Chiefs of Staff (left), congratulates Captain James Chandler, commanding officer of the *Wainwright,* for his ship's performance in Operation Praying Mantis. (Courtesy James Chandler)

learned that a Cobra helicopter gunship that had refueled on their after deck that afternoon was overdue—long overdue, and presumed missing. Much later, long after the fighting was over, the Navy employed sonar technology to find the wreck of the missing bird, resting on the bottom of the Persian Gulf. Navy divers sent to explore the site discovered the pilot and copilot still strapped into their seats, victims, apparently, of vertigo: a sense of dizziness and loss of balance that occasionally strikes helicopter pilots. Though not the consequence of hostile action, they were the only American casualties of Praying Mantis.

All this time, the men of the first group—SAG Bravo—were listening in on the radio net but also keeping a close watch on their own electronic sensors. In the middle of the battle between SAG Charlie and the *Joshan,* the surface search radar on the *Merrill* identified a high-speed surface contact with the signature of a large surface combatant. It had a profile similar to the Iranian frigate *Sabalan* and was approaching at twenty-five knots. Perkins decided to send up a helicopter and "get a visual."[81]

The morning had been clear and sunny, but by midafternoon the weather had turned hazy over the Gulf as the heat mounted. The Marine helicopter pilot from the *Merrill* could not positively identify the contact. It was a warship and had the general size and configuration of a destroyer or frigate, but in the thick haze he could not see more than that. Perkins tried raising the contact on the radio, but for whatever reason it did not respond. After that, while Perkins stayed on the bridge, the *Merrill*'s captain went down to the CIC to take the chair of the tactical action officer. "Now we were getting excited," the *Merrill*'s executive officer remembered. "We needed to prep the Harpoon, because if this is what we think it is, we don't know if he had a Harpoon or not." Perkins, however, still wanted a positive identification, and he ordered the Marine helicopter to move in closer. At this, Colonel Bill Rakow, the senior Marine officer, expressed his concern that the men in the helicopter might be sacrificed. "We had a kind of discussion," Sanford recalled. "The captain is down in combat plotting Harpoon solutions. He had the key around his neck, and was getting ready to go." But the Marine colonel did not want his pilots to be placed in more danger than necessary.[82]

Sanford got on the radio to the helicopter pilot and asked him if he could see a hull number.

"Well," came the reply, "it's three numbers, but it's back a little bit."

American warships carried their hull numbers on the bow, so this was clearly not an American vessel. The bridge team pulled out a copy of *Jane's Fighting Ships* and quickly thumbed through it looking at the Iranian order of battle. The Iranians didn't have any ships with a three-digit hull number either.

Then Sanford recalled that on the way into the Gulf some months back, the *Merrill* had passed a Soviet warship heading out of the Gulf whose hull number was 767. He told Perkins that this was probably a Soviet vessel. "The ship was in close, the captain in Combat had a Harpoon solution and the key was in the lock," he recalled later. "It was just a matter of turning the key." But Perkins held his fire, and eventually a Soviet *Sovremenny*-class guided-missile destroyer steamed past within three thousand yards, apparently oblivious. Perkins pointedly asked him his intentions, and the Soviet captain radioed back, speaking in heavily accented English: "I vant to take peectures for heestory."[83]

—

For the ships and men of the third combat group—SAG Delta—it had been a frustrating day. Since dawn they had listened in on the radio traffic while SAG Bravo and SAG Charlie had fulfilled their missions, and they had cheered when they heard that the *Joshan* had been sunk. But there was disappointment mixed with their celebration, for they had hoped to find and sink the Iranian frigate *Sabalan*, and instead it was SAG Charlie that had an opportunity to engage an Iranian warship. In fact, SAG Delta had yet to locate the *Sabalan*, though it was not for lack of trying. All day the three ships of SAG Delta had pursued electronic leads looking for Iran's premier combat vessel; at the same time a squadron composed of one A-6E Intruder and two F-14 Tomcats from the *Enterprise* searched the periphery of the Gulf. The pilots thought the *Sabalan* might be hiding among the merchant shipping that crowded the Strait of Hormuz; other reports indicated it was in port at Bandar Abbas with engine trouble. Indeed, there was little evidence that suggested the Iranians were even paying much attention to the American attacks.[84]

But the Iranians *were* paying attention. Late in the morning a small squadron of Iranian Boghammer gunboats attacked an oil platform and several merchant vessels near the Mubarek oil fields off Sharjah in the southern Gulf. The attack may have been a coincidence, or the Iranians may have decided to attack an oil platform in an effort to respond "proportionately" to the American attacks on Sassan and Sirri. Whatever their motives, the Boghammers were out in international waters, and two A-6 Intruders from the *Enterprise* requested permission to hit them. Admiral Less was willing enough, but the ships were near Iranian territorial waters and they might simply dart back across that invisible line. He sought guidance up the chain of command. Could U.S. forces "chase Iranian forces out of international waters and hot pursue them into territorial waters?" His request was flashed by satellite to General Crist in Tampa, and from there to the Pentagon, and finally to the desk of Lieutenant General Colin Powell at the White House. Powell took the request personally to President Reagan, who responded, "Do it!" and the attack order was delivered back down the chain of command to the pilots in the A-6s. The whole circuit took "less than three minutes." The Intruders attacked, sinking one Boghammer and driving the rest aground on nearby Abu Musa Island.[85]

Soon afterward American sensors detected an Iranian *Saam*-class frigate—the same class as the *Sabalan*—heading for the area. An A-6 sought to identify the contact using its forward-looking infrared radar (FLIR), while an accompanying F-14 Tomcat employed its onboard TV camera. Aware of the close call that SAG Bravo had had with the Soviet destroyer that afternoon, Less wanted a positive visual identification. The A-6 therefore swooped in low to eyeball the vessel, which turned out to be not the *Sabalan* but its sister ship, the *Sahand*. As the Intruder passed low over the *Sahand*, the Iranian ship opened fire with both triple-A and surface-to-air missiles. The A-6 dropped flares to confuse the tracking radar of the *Sahand*'s missiles, then counterattacked, firing a Harpoon, several rockets, and a Mark 82 laser-guided bomb that tracked along the laser beam to hit the *Sahand* precisely on target. By the time SAG Delta arrived on the scene, the *Sahand* was dead in the water and on fire.[86]

SAG Delta consisted of the *Adams*-class guided-missile destroyer *Joseph Strauss*, the *Spruance*-class destroyer *O'Brien*, and the *Perry*-class frigate *Jack Williams*. In addition to these surface assets, the air boss on the *Enterprise* had launched a strike force as soon as he heard that the *Sahand* had fired on an American aircraft. Even as the ships of SAG Delta closed on the crippled and burning *Sahand*, six A-7 attack planes and another A-6 were also streaking toward the target. The *Straus* fired a surface-to-surface Harpoon at almost the same time that an A-6 fired an air-to-surface Harpoon, and both missiles smashed into the *Sahand*, exploding nearly simultaneously. Altogether more than a dozen warheads struck the burning vessel, including several thousand-pound laser-guided bombs. By then the

The Iranian *Saam*-class frigate *Sahand* on fire from stem to stern as a result of multiple hits by both surface- and air-launched missiles. (U.S. Navy)

Sahand was already sinking. Within minutes its magazine exploded and it disappeared.[87]

It had been a spectacular day for American arms. Granted, the United States had overwhelming superiority in both numbers and technology, but the American strike force had destroyed three armed oil platforms and sunk two warships while suffering only the loss of the two men on the missing Cobra helicopter.

Then, late in the afternoon, American forces found the *Sabalan*. An A-6 investigating a suspicious contact in the Strait of Hormuz near Bandar Abbas identified what appeared to be a *Saam*-class frigate that subsequently proved to be the much-despised *Sabalan*. As the American Intruder approached, the ship sent up a stream of antiaircraft fire; having been fired on, the pilot immediately counterattacked, dropping a five-hundred-pound laser-guided bomb right down the stack. It exploded inside the *Sabalan*'s engine room. The ship seemed to expand like a balloon from the internal explosion, then the hull relapsed and the ship went dead in the water. At last U.S. naval forces had the *Sabalan* right where they wanted it: exposed and immobile—a sitting duck for more airstrikes or surface-launched Harpoons. SAG Delta and a fresh squadron of attack planes were already en route. By now, of course, the whole notion of "proportionality" had been blown to bits, and back in the Navy Command Center in Washington, Secretary of Defense Carlucci turned to Admiral Crowe to ask, "What should we do?" Crowe shook his head: "We've killed enough people." With Carlucci's approval, Crowe issued orders to call off the hunt and allow the *Sabalan* to limp back into port.* Operation Praying Mantis was over.[88]

—

The events of April 18 did not end hostilities in the Gulf—there was one more scene in the drama. Ten weeks later, in early July, the *Ticonderoga*-class cruiser USS *Vincennes* escorted the crippled *Samuel B. Roberts* through the Strait of Hormuz on the first leg of its long trip home. The *Vincennes* was one of the newest ships in the Navy and was equipped with the AEGIS fire control system, a cutting-edge integrated computer system that allowed a single ship to monitor and engage multiple surface and air targets simultaneously. Not entirely in admiration, the men of more conventional cruisers called it "Robocruiser." In its darkened CIC, the computers projected illuminated maps of the region on four giant screens, allowing the decision makers to monitor virtually all air and surface traffic in the area, each contact indicated on the screen by a tiny symbol showing the contact's course and speed. The computers also fed targeting information directly to the guns and missile systems so that it was no longer necessary to compute a target solution before engaging.[89]

The *Vincennes* replaced the *Wainwright* in May. Its skipper was a Texas-born career officer with the all-American name of Will Rogers, though, as he often had to tell people, he was not related to the famous humorist.

---

* The Iranians repaired the *Sabalan*, and it was still operational in the first decade of the twenty-first century.

Returning back through the strait that evening after seeing the *Roberts* on its way, the *Vincennes* picked up a distress call from a Danish tanker that was under attack by Iranian Boghammers. Heading back into the Gulf, Rogers ordered the U.S. frigate *Elmer Montgomery* to lob a star shell at the Boghammers, chasing them back into Iranian waters.

Rogers then shaped a course for Bahrain, but before the *Vincennes* was more than halfway there he received another distress call. The Boghammers were at it again. Racing back to the scene of the trouble, Rogers sent a helicopter aloft to get a clear view of what was going on. As the helicopter approached the Boghammers, they opened fire on it. Rogers immediately ordered flank speed and closed on the offending gunboats in order to put them inside the envelope of his weapons. Rogers showed remarkable

The combat information center (CIC) on board the USS *Vincennes*. (U.S. Navy)

restraint in not opening fire at once. One Iranian Boghammer passed between the *Vincennes* and the *Elmer Montgomery*; the guns of the *Vincennes* tracked it as it passed, but because "it didn't show hostile intent," Rogers allowed the little open motorboat to pass unmolested. Not long afterward, however, seven of the small gunboats gathered for what looked like a "swarm attack," where the enemy presented so many high-speed targets that the object of the assault could not respond effectively. Rogers requested permission to open fire, and Less radioed him to "take with guns." The AEGIS system allowed the men in the *Vincennes*'s CIC to aim the ship's guns at multiple targets, even after the forward gun slipped a pawl and became inoperative. At 10:42 A.M., as the officers and men in the crowded CIC concentrated on the multiple pips on their radar repeaters, they also picked up an air contact.[90]

The plane that appeared on the large air-search display in the CIC had flown out of the Iranian airport at Bandar Abbas and was approaching at high speed. Rogers knew there was a squadron of Iranian attack planes at Bandar Abbas, and he immediately sent out a challenge on the emergency frequency ordering the contact to turn away from the combat area. There was no response. Nor was there a clear signal from the plane's transponder—the electronic device designed to indicate whether it was a civilian or a military aircraft.* The contact was assigned a tracking number, and with the fate of the *Stark* in the back of his mind, at 10:51 Rogers declared the contact "presumed hostile."[91]

Meanwhile the fight with the Boghammers was intensifying; small-arms ammunition struck the bridge of the *Vincennes* as it maneuvered to unmask its five-inch gun astern. The air contact was still closing, and the officer reading the air plot screen reported that it appeared to be descending as well, as if preparing to launch a missile. In his mind, Rogers had

---

* All aircraft send out an electronic signature called a "squawk," indicating whether it is civilian or military. Subsequently, investigators surmised that because the receivers in the *Vincennes* were collecting signals from a variety of aircraft—the Iran Airbus, an AWACS and Navy E2-C Hawkeye, and an Iranian P-3—this may have confused the team in the CIC. In addition, the flat panel depicting the air traffic showed only a two-dimensional picture, and it is possible that the tactical information officer may have confused the decreasing *range* of Iran Airlines flight 655 with descending *altitude*.

decided to fire if the contact came within twenty miles (the Iraqi F-1 that
had nearly sunk the *Stark* had fired from twelve miles). But when the contact crossed that twenty-mile limit, Rogers still hesitated. He tried the
radio one more time. Receiving no reply, at 10:54 A.M. he ordered the
weapons officer to fire two standard missiles in air mode. By then the contact was only nine miles away.[92]

Nine thousand feet above the Gulf, Iran Airlines flight 655, a commercial airliner with 290 people on board, was heading for Dubai in the
United Arab Emirates on a scheduled flight. The pilot, Captain Mohsen
Reza'i, was monitoring flight information from both Bandar Abbas and
Dubai and was not tuned in to the emergency radio circuit. He never
heard any of Captain Rogers' seven warnings. When two U.S. Navy Standard missiles struck the fuselage, the plane broke apart at once. There were
no survivors.

—

The events of April 18 were decisive in the Iran-Iraq War. This was not so
much because of Operation Praying Mantis as because of Iraq's massive
ground attack on the Faw Peninsula that same day. Of course, the U.S.
Navy's near destruction of the Iranian navy played its own role in convincing Tehran that it was time to accept an end to hostilities. On July 18—
three months to the day after Praying Mantis (and fifteen days after the
loss of Iran Airlines 655)—Iran accepted the terms of United Nations Resolution 598. Three weeks after that, a cease-fire went into effect only weeks
before what would have been the eighth anniversary of the third bloodiest
war of the twentieth century.

The events of April 18, 1988, were decisive for the United States, too, for
they illuminated not only the dramatic changes that had taken place in the
nature of naval warfare since World War II but also the front edge of what
would become a new philosophy about the role that the United States and
the U.S. Navy should play in the world. Several aspects of those changes
are evident in hindsight.

First there was the American decision to act as an armed enforcer in a
war between two nations (neither of which was a particular friend)

halfway around the globe. After some ambivalence, the Reagan administration accepted the responsibility to act as a kind of regional policeman in the Persian Gulf even though, in the end, it found impartiality impossible. Convinced that U.S. interests were tied up in protecting the export of oil shipments from the Gulf and preventing the expansion of Soviet influence in the region, the United States put itself in the middle of the conflict.

That decision created a difficult environment for Navy commanders. They could defend themselves if fired upon, but much of the time they were never sure who the enemy was or what they were allowed to do. Ambiguity in war was not new, of course. As far back as the American Revolution or as recently as Vietnam, ambiguity and uncertainty were central elements in many of America's wars. What was new in the Persian Gulf was that the latest generation of electronic weapons so compressed the decision making process that commanders had only minutes, and sometimes seconds, to make life-and-death decisions. Brindel, in the *Stark*, erred in demonstrating too much restraint; Rogers, in the *Vincennes*, was determined not to make the same mistake.

Indeed, those weapons systems constituted the most dramatic aspect of this changed paradigm of war. Praying Mantis was the first large-scale surface action involving U.S. naval forces since the end of World War II. In those four-plus decades, several generations of weapons systems had come and gone. The sophisticated, electronically based weapons systems used in Praying Mantis, though they had been tested in development and in training, had never been used in combat with a hostile force. The *Wainwright* was the first U.S. warship ever to fire missiles at both surface and air targets in the same engagement and also the first to fire an SM-2 missile in combat; the *Joseph Strauss* and an A-6 from the *Enterprise* participated in the first ever coordinated surface/air attack in sinking the *Sahand*. In that sense, Praying Mantis was a testing ground. The U.S. chief of naval operations, Admiral Carlisle Trost, remarked, "We spent a lot of effort and taxpayer's dollars . . . to achieve the level of readiness that we enjoy today. What our people saw was an opportunity for the first time under hostile conditions to use both their sensors and weapons; and they worked as advertised."[93]

Equally dramatic was the changed environment in military communications. It took weeks for Oliver Hazard Perry to communicate with his superior at Sackett's Harbor, and once George Dewey left Hong Kong, he was out of touch with his superiors altogether. At Midway, Jack Waldron and Wade McClusky made decisions on the spur of the moment while operating under radio silence. But the chain of command during Praying Mantis extended from the bridge of a warship (or the cockpit of an A-6) all the way to the White House. Twice on that April 18, operational commanders received instructions from literally the highest level. To many Navy people this was both good news and bad news. It was great to have globe-circling, real-time communications. But it also meant that a president, a defense secretary, or a chief of naval operations in Washington might become the tactical decision maker in a battle taking place six thousand miles away, and not every U.S. Navy officer was comfortable with that. One hundred years earlier a senior American naval officer had complained that the telegraph cable had reduced him to "a damned errand boy at the end of a telegraph wire." One can only imagine his reaction to the communications network of the late twentieth century.[94]

Praying Mantis was also a model of what defense policy analysts were calling "jointness." Powerful as the U.S. Navy was in 1988, it was even more powerful when linked to Air Force and Army assets as well as its Marine Corps partners. Air Force AWACS airplanes maintained an intelligence picture for Navy surface assets; Army Sea Bats helicopters, flying off Navy frigates, identified and attacked Iranian mine layers; Marines, SEALs, and Army Rangers all participated in the carefully selected proportional responses chosen for them by their civilian masters. Presiding over all of it was a marine general in Florida, who gave orders to a Navy admiral in the Persian Gulf, who then gave orders to what was called the Joint Task Force Middle East.

Moreover, Operation Praying Mantis demonstrated rather dramatically how impersonal naval warfare had become in the electronic age. The men manning the guns on Perry's *Lawrence* could see into the faces of their foes; Dewey's gunners could at least see the ships of their opponents; if Spruance never saw the carriers his pilots attacked, the pilots themselves confronted the enemy in a very personal way. But in the Persian Gulf, dangerous as it was, the enemy was always faceless. Those who "turned the key" on their weapons consoles to fire the missiles that sank the *Joshan* never left the air-conditioned environment of the CIC. The only time Chandler saw the face of his enemy was when intelligence specialists opened a classified folder and showed him a photograph.

And finally, Praying Mantis demonstrated the extent to which America's technological and operational superiority had outpaced the rest of the world. As subsequent events in the Persian Gulf would demonstrate, the events of April 18, 1988, offered only the first glimpse of the stunning technological revolution, already under way, that over the next decade and a half would make the United States not merely a "superpower," not merely the greatest military power on earth, but the greatest military power the world had ever seen. Ironically, this new capability did not just evoke awe from America's partners (and its adversaries); it also contributed to a new sense of wariness. In the absence of the Soviet rivalry after 1989, the United States represented such a dominant military force, possessed of such a futuristic technology, that its actions took on a new, and to some very frightening, significance. The very success of that new technology fed an assumption among many that American weapons were infallible and that the shooting down of the Iran Airlines Airbus must therefore have been a deliberate act. A decade later, when three U.S. missiles fired at Bosnian assets in the former Yugoslavia instead hit the Chinese embassy, U.S. diplomats found it impossible to convince the Chinese that it had been a genuine mistake. The very technical dominance that was supposed to undergird American policy goals also provoked fear, skepticism, and even hatred in certain quarters.

The United States would discover that there would be little gratitude, even from its traditional allies, for its new assumption of authority as the world's cop.

EPILOGUE

—

Naval Battles and the Twenty-first Century

The five naval battles described in this volume highlight the dramatically changed roles played by the men (and, more recently, women) who commanded the ships and operated the weapons of the U.S. Navy over the past two hundred years. In 1813, when Oliver Hazard Perry was desperate for manpower, he cared little about the education or training of his prospective recruits—he wanted bodies. He eagerly accepted any able-bodied souls, including soldiers and militiamen, who were willing to abide the confined quarters, the fierce discipline, and the dangerous work aboard Navy warships. What he needed was the brute muscle necessary to manhandle the guns over the decks, to wind up the anchors, or to haul on whatever rope was pointed out to them by the sailing masters.

Fifty years later in Hampton Roads, at least some crewmen on both the *Virginia* and the *Monitor* had to understand and maintain the steam engines, but most of the crew was assigned to work the guns, and once again any soldier who volunteered was eagerly accepted. Steam moved the ironclads around the roadstead (albeit rather slowly), but ships—even ironclad ships—were still essentially floating platforms for heavy guns.

By 1898, when Dewey steamed into Manila Bay, the engine plants had become more complex and much more efficient; the range of the naval artillery had expanded from one to several miles, and men needed more experience and training to make the ships function efficiently. Even so, whatever expertise might be needed to maintain the engines or point the guns could still be learned on board. Moreover, Dewey's ships, like those of most late-nineteenth-century navies, had a large number of international crewmen on board, few of whom had any real training as sailors, and many of whom could not even read or write English.

A bigger sea change took place in the forty-four years between Manila Bay and Midway. While Dewey's gunners aimed their ordnance as best they could at targets two and a half miles away (and missed most of the time), at Midway the ordnance was flown out to a target nearly two hundred miles away by highly trained Navy pilots, most of whom were officers. Brute labor was still needed on board America's carriers—the planes had to be pushed from place to place, and the bombs and torpedoes were hauled out by hand trucks to be attached to the planes. But it was becoming increasingly evident that specialized training was essential to operational success, not only to fly the planes but to operate the radar systems, man the radio nets, and exercise effective damage control. The training necessary to produce such men was extensive. Although airplanes could be made relatively quickly, especially once America's astonishing industrial capacity reached its potential, the training of a carrier pilot took time. Indeed, one of the reasons that the U.S. Navy carrier force was able to assert itself so dramatically over its Japanese foe after Midway was that the United States sent its best pilots stateside to train more pilots while Japan tended to keep its best pilots on the front line, and as a result, Japan soon ran out of skilled pilots altogether. The skill and training of the crew, even more than the increased sophistication of the weapons systems, was the key element of naval success.

By the time of Praying Mantis in 1988 (another forty-six years later) the entire crew on America's combat warships, officers and enlisted alike, was composed of specially trained and often highly educated personnel. Virtually all of the men on board the *Wainwright,* as well as the other ships of the Persian Gulf force, had worked their way through a number of service schools in order to develop the expertise necessary to operate the array of sophisticated electronic gadgetry in the ship's combat information center. One dramatic element of the sea change in naval warfare, therefore, was the specialized training and education of the officer corps, and more particularly the enlisted force, that manned the ships.*

In addition to that, however, the five naval battles profiled here also reflect the dramatic changes in America's conception of itself as a nation and its proper role in the world. These changes were both multidimensional and interconnected. Just as the two-masted brigs of Perry's squadron on Lake Erie gave way first to ironclad steamships, then to seagoing battleships, aircraft carriers, and finally highly technical missile warfare, so too did the dominant concern of Americans about the security of the frontier give way to a passionate confrontation over the issue of national union, then to debates about overseas empire, international involvement and alliances, and finally the responsibilities of superpower status. They mark, in short, milestones in national culture and outlook as well as technology and training.

The naval battles discussed here did not cause these changes. Still, at some level, the national policy of any era of American history depends in part on the capability of the nation's military arsenal, as well as its intentions, good or bad. What a nation decides to do depends very much on what it *can* do. The United States decided not to go to war with Spain in 1873 in the wake of the *Virginius* affair partly because it lacked the means to do so; similarly, fifteen years later after the destruction of the *Maine*, it did go to war in part because it could. Technology and resources are therefore integral elements in national policy planning and execution. At no time is that more evident than in the early years of the twenty-first century, when America's military technology has become globally dominant.

―――

* In another kind of sea change, women were authorized to go to sea on a limited number of Navy logistics ships beginning in 1978. Indeed, women were aboard the USS *Acadia*, the repair ship that came to the aid of the *Stark* after it was struck by Iraqi missiles in May 1987. Not until 1993, however, did Congress repeal the law banning women from service on combat ships. Consequently, although no women were aboard any of the ships that participated in Operation Praying Mantis, women pilots flew combat missions over Iraq to enforce the no-fly zone after Gulf War I, and they served in a wide variety of combat roles during Gulf War II.

In 1648, at the end of the Thirty Years' War, the exhausted nations of Europe signed an agreement—the Treaty of Westphalia—in which they essentially agreed to coexist with one another. That agreement established the nation-state system in which a number of nations, each with a sovereign government, agreed to occupy the planet together. It did not abolish war—war, it seems, is a permanent characteristic of the human condition—but it rationalized war to the extent that governments exercised control over national armies and employed them to compete with one another for territory, trade, or some other tangible advantage. Occasionally one nation or another—one person or another—would attempt to overwhelm its neighbors and become dominant (Napoleon and Hitler being the obvious examples), but in every case the nation-state system survived. In time, a kind of balance of national power prevented any fundamental challenge to this system.

Then only months after Operation Praying Mantis, the world balance of power not only shifted tracks but fell completely off the rails when the Soviet Union, strained literally to the breaking point by forty years of Cold War rivalry, began to implode, starting a process that within a few years caused it to collapse entirely, dissolving eventually into its constituent parts. It was an astonishing development.* For nearly half a century the U.S. military, including the Navy, had measured itself against the vaunted Soviet juggernaut. During the 1980s the Reagan administration had poured billions of dollars into an effort to build a six-hundred-ship navy that could support a "Maritime Strategy," the principal goal of which was to confront the Soviet Navy on its own doorstep. This program was still under way when the Soviet Union collapsed.[1]

The iconic moment in this historic phenomenon was the fall of the Berlin Wall on November 9, 1989. The world watched live as television cameras recorded the historic image of citizens from East and West Berlin hacking at the wall with hammers and crowbars, literally tearing down the

---

* The extent to which the collapse of the Soviet Union caught the United States by surprise is evident in the 1982 National Intelligence Estimate, declassified twenty years later, which stated: "We believe this [Soviet] wartime strategy will remain essentially unchanged over the next 15 to 20 years."

most widely recognized symbol of the Cold War. But five months before that incredible scene another iconic moment, little noted at the time, took place when, in recognition of the thaw in U.S.-Soviet relations, the chairman of the Joint Chiefs of Staff, Admiral William Crowe, accepted an invitation to visit the new flagship of the Soviet Navy, the 45,000-ton *Kirov*. As Crowe reached the deck of the giant *Kirov*, the Soviet navy band struck up "The Star-Spangled Banner" and an American flag broke out overhead. "Suddenly the weight of the moment swept over me," Crowe recalled. "Truly we were in the midst of a sea change."[2]

The collapse of the Soviet Union marked a watershed moment not only in the history of the United States but in the history of the world. If it did not immediately supplant the nation-state system established at Westphalia nearly three and a half centuries earlier, it at least produced what President George H. W. Bush called a "new world order." In that new order, the United States emerged as the single dominant military power on the globe. Some Americans thought the time had come for the United States to shoulder the responsibility of world management, for it certainly had the military power to do so. The United States stood alone as the one great superpower on earth. The U.S. Navy, too, stood alone: unchallenged, and indeed unchallengeable, as master of the world's oceans. By the end of the century, a single U.S. Navy carrier battle group and its embarked air wing carried more potential firepower than the rest of the world's navies combined. An article in the *Washington Post* in 2003 declared unequivocally that "all other nations have conceded the seas to the United States. . . . The naval arms race—a principal aspect of great power politics for centuries— is over." More than Rome at its height or Victorian Britain at its peak, the United States had emerged as a power of unprecedented supremacy. It had become *arbiter mundi*, the power of the world—an astonishing circumstance for a republic that a mere nine score years before had strained its resources to build two twenty-gun brigs on Lake Erie.[3]

Though the United States stood unchallenged as the dominant economic and military power in the world, it also stood at a crossroads, because the part it would play in these new circumstances had not yet been decided. So much thought, energy, and money had been poured into the forty-five-year struggle with the Soviets that relatively few had considered the character of U.S. policy in a post–Cold War world. Over the next dozen years, however, two wars in Iraq would illuminate the possible alternatives. In the first of them, the United States led an international coalition to repel aggression and restore order to the Persian Gulf region after an Iraqi invasion of Kuwait; in the second, a dozen years later, it chose a different path, asserting that its unchallenged military power and moral certainty gave it the right to overthrow the government of Iraq and attempt to remake the Middle East in its own image. Rather than two chapters of a single conflict, America's wars in Iraq marked distinct and dramatic alternatives for the United States in the post–Cold War era.

—

As if to prove that no good deed goes unpunished, Saddam Hussein rewarded Kuwait for the staunch support it had provided him during the war with Iran by invading it in August 1990. If Hussein could not extend Iraq's coastline at the expense of Iran, he would do so at the expense of the smaller and weaker Kuwait. Hussein very likely assumed that the United States would benignly accept Iraq's rapid conquest of what he proclaimed to be "Iraq's nineteenth province." After all, not only had the George H. W. Bush administration continued to supply Iraq with arms during and after its war with Iran, it had signaled through diplomatic channels that the United States had "no opinion" on conflicts between Arab states and would therefore have no problem with an "adjustment" of the Iraq-Kuwait border. From the beginning, however, American policy in the Gulf had been a product less of genuine support for Iraq than of opposition to Iran because of lingering bitterness over the hostage crisis. To most Americans, Iraq's invasion of Kuwait looked much like the kind of naked aggression that Hitler had inflicted on Poland in 1939, or the North Koreans on South Korea in 1950. Perceiving an opportunity to reassert American leadership as well as his own political fortunes, Bush declared that the Iraqi conquest of Kuwait "will not stand," and he successfully mobilized both domestic and international support for a war to repel the Iraqi invaders from Kuwait.[4]

That war, officially Operation Desert Storm, but subsequently called the First Gulf War or Gulf War I, was an astounding success. President Bush assembled an international coalition that included not only America's traditional NATO allies but also (and crucially) a number of Arab nations, and he secured at least benign acceptance by Russia, no longer the Soviet Union. He sought and received the backing of both the U.S. Congress and the United Nations. Then he assembled the military forces that drove the Iraqi army out of Kuwait.

Though a genuine international coalition won the victory in Iraq, American money, American technology, and American sea lift capability were keys to victory. During the buildup phase (Operation Desert Shield), the United States moved more than half a million people and ten million tons of supplies to the Gulf. This logistic phenomenon could not have been achieved without American sealift capability. It took more than a thousand of the Air Force's largest transport planes to match the tonnage capacity of a single U.S. Navy transport ship, and in the end, 95 percent of all the cargo used to support the war came by sea. It was, as one commentator noted, "equivalent to moving the entire city of Atlanta—its people and all their food, cars, and other possessions—to the Middle East."[5]

Then, after this lengthy buildup, the United States applied overwhelming force to achieve a decisive result. The use of overwhelming force—subsequently labeled the Powell Doctrine after General Colin Powell, chairman of the Joint Chiefs—was in part a reaction to the Army's frustration with the incremental approach used in Vietnam during the 1960s and '70s. U.S. ground forces spearheaded the attack that smashed Saddam Hussein's military, including its much-vaunted Republican Guard, and inflicted an estimated one hundred thousand deaths on the Iraqis, all at an astonishingly modest cost to the United States and its allies. Though U.S. Marines played an important role in the ground war, there were no naval battles in Gulf War I because Iraq had no force that could even pretend to contest the seas with the powerful U.S. Navy. The Navy was, however, a full partner in the air war that preceded the ground attack.

Two elements of that air war deserve mention here because they illuminate the evolving character of naval warfare at the end of the twentieth century. The first of these (indeed, the dominant image that emerged from

Gulf War I) was the dramatic success of so-called smart bombs. Though coalition forces expended hundreds of tons of conventional bombs on the Iraqi front lines in Kuwait, the unchallenged media star of the air war was the new technology that featured the use of laser-guided ordnance. During the air bombardment of Baghdad that preceded the ground attack, the United States unveiled the newest generation of precision ordnance. The first phase of that air assault was dominated by U.S. Air Force radar-resistant "stealth" airplanes and sea-launched cruise missiles.* Both of these new technologies allowed the United States to put ordnance on target without serious risk to American pilots.

One key was the increased range of the Navy's new generation of missiles. The SM-1 standard missile used in Praying Mantis had a range of thirty miles, and the ship-to-ship Harpoon missile had a range of fifty-six miles, but the ship-to-ground Tomahawk Land Attack Missile (TLAM) used in Desert Storm carried its thousand-pound warhead up to seven hundred miles, which allowed U.S. Navy ships well out in the Persian Gulf to attack targets in downtown Baghdad. The Tomahawk also demonstrated an unprecedented accuracy for an unpiloted weapon thanks in large part to a terrain-contour guidance system (TERCOM) that allowed the missile's internal computer to match the signals it received from its active radar to a three-dimensional map built into its computer memory so that it could guide itself (theoretically, at least) to within eighteen meters of a predetermined target. The Navy fired some 282 Tomahawks into Iraq during Desert Storm, 170 of them in the first two days of the war.[6] At a million dollars a shot, it was a profligate use of ordnance, but the Tomahawks allowed the United States to strike Iraqi targets in daytime without risking a pilot, and they quickly gained a reputation for astonishing accuracy. On one occasion, an American TV reporter was giving a live report from downtown Baghdad when both he and his viewing audience were startled by a Navy Tomahawk missile as it flew past him down one of Baghdad's streets en route to its preassigned target.

---

* Unlike rockets, which rely on solid or liquid fuel that can burn in the absence of oxygen, cruise missiles have jet engines that breathe air, making them essentially unmanned jets.

Air-launched ordnance was, if anything, even more impressive. Though Air Force planes carried the lion's share of the air war, U.S. Navy pilots flew a total of 18,303 sorties during Desert Storm, with Marines flying another 10,683.[7] Tiny television cameras in the noses of the projectiles they delivered allowed Americans in their living rooms to ride the ordnance all the way to the target—like Slim Pickens in *Dr. Strangelove*—watching the target expand on their viewing screens until it disappeared in a blur of visual static. Since the Pentagon had to approve each film clip before it could be shown publicly, only the most accurate attacks made it to the airways, and the overwhelming impression was that American weapons had become infallible. A *Saturday Night Live* skit portrayed a U.S. smart bomb pursuing Saddam Hussein down a hallway and into a bathroom, where it knocked on the door. If U.S. bombs were not quite as smart as that, they nevertheless demonstrated a dramatic change in the nature of warfare and proved again that the United States was at least a full generation ahead of the rest of the world in the sophistication of its weapons systems.

The second element of the air war that illuminated the continuing evolution of warfare was the tight control that the military planners placed on the warriors who deployed and triggered these weapons. The targets of the Tomahawk missiles fired from Navy warships in the Persian Gulf were determined not on board those warships but at Central Command (CENTCOM) in Riyadh, Saudi Arabia, or even in Washington. Likewise, many of the pilots who flew their F/A-18s, A-6s, or A-7s from carriers in the Red Sea as well as the Persian Gulf felt restricted by the very specific and precise targeting instructions they received. Unlike the Battle of Midway, where Jack Waldron and Wade McClusky used a kind of seat-of-the-pants intuition to locate the Japanese carrier force, the pilots in Gulf War I received detailed instructions concerning their launch time, flight path, ordnance package, target selection, and virtually every other aspect of the operation. The air tasking order (ATO) for each day's air operations ranged from three hundred to six hundred pages, and because transmission of such a document by electronic means would have choked the fleet's capacity, the five- or six-pound orders had to be flown out to the carriers by helicopter. Though President Bush and his advisers sought to avoid involving themselves in the conduct of the war, Gulf War I nevertheless demonstrated that decision making in naval warfare continued to move up the chain of command from individual ship or unit commanders to staff officers and technocrats hundreds or even thousands of miles away.[8]

The new template of warfare suggested by Gulf War I was that of a very precise, highly technical, and relatively bloodless (for Americans) application of force on behalf of a world consortium directed at aggressors and rogue nations. Indeed, the outcome surprised even some Pentagon planners. As one expert noted, the results of the war proved that "even the most 'optimistic' estimates turned out to be overly 'pessimistic.'"[9] Moreover, U.S. consultation and cooperation with the United Nations, as well as support from the nations most concerned, cast an international legitimacy over the effort that allowed the United States to emerge from the war as the world's white knight. The very success of the war, however, provoked concern in some quarters that, if it wished, the United States could act unilaterally, and that if it chose to act alone, there was little the rest of the world could do about it.

—

Military supremacy proved to be no guarantor of security, as became evident on October 12, 2000. On that date, the Arleigh Burke–class guided-missile destroyer USS Cole (DDG-67) was in the port of Aden on the coast of Yemen making a routine refueling stop en route to the Persian Gulf. Seizing a target of opportunity, a handful of anti-American terrorists in a small rubber boat, not unlike those used by the Iranians in the Gulf, maneuvered their little craft alongside the Cole and detonated a bomb. The resulting explosion blew a giant hole in the side of the Cole, killed seventeen Americans, and wounded thirty-nine more. This was no accident like the attack on the Stark, nor was it random like the mining of the Roberts; it was a deliberate act of sabotage and terrorism conducted by men who were willing to give up their lives to hurt the United States. U.S. intelligence analysts attributed it to continuing resentment by Arabs, and especially Islamic fundamentalists, of America's pro-Israel stance. President Bill Clinton called it "a despicable and cowardly act" and redoubled efforts both to find the presumed leader of the terrorists, the multimillionaire Osama bin Laden, and to broker a solution to the Israeli-Palestinian struggle.[10]

Much worse was to come. A year later, in a coordinated assault on September 11, 2001, nineteen fanatical followers of bin Laden hijacked four commercial airliners, flew two of them into the twin towers of the World Trade Center in New York City, and smashed a third into the Pentagon. A fourth plane, very likely intended for the Capitol, crashed instead into the Pennsylvania countryside when the passengers attempted to retake the plane from the hijackers. Almost as much as the collapse of the Soviet Union, the terror attacks of 9/11 (as it came to be called) marked a historic milestone in American and world history.

The attack galvanized Americans. In many ways 9/11 was essentially an escalation, albeit a dramatic one, of the several previous attacks that had been aimed at American icons worldwide, from the 1983 bombing of the Marine barracks in Lebanon and the 1988 destruction of Pan American flight 103, which exploded over Lockerbie, Scotland, to the USS *Cole*. Nev-

The USS *Cole* in the port of Aden in Yemen shows the results of the suicide attack in October 2000 that killed 17 and wounded 39. (U.S. Navy)

ertheless, for many Americans 9/11 marked a watershed. In part this was because of the sheer horror of the televised images of that day: the second plane crashing into the south tower of the Trade Center, the desperate men and women jumping from the upper floors, the dedication and heroism of the rescue teams, and the searing memory of the moment the buildings themselves collapsed in a giant cloud of dust and debris that roiled through the streets of Manhattan. It was a horror epic become real. But another factor in the American reaction was that unlike any of those other events, this terrorist act occurred on American soil. Americans perceived at once that their insulating oceans no longer protected them from a dangerous world.

Americans reacted as they always had to attacks on their country. Much like the response to the destruction of the USS *Maine* one hundred years earlier, or the Japanese attack on Pearl Harbor forty-three years after that, Americans after 9/11 were united in their desire for justice and revenge. The events of 9/11 provoked an outpouring of patriotic anger. American flags, often accompanied by the declaration "United We Stand," blossomed on front porches, lapels, and car bumpers.

The news was a shock overseas as well. The immediate international response to the disaster was an outpouring of international sympathy for the United States. *Le Monde*, the leading French daily newspaper, carried a headline on September 13 that read "Nous Sommes Tous Américains" (we are all Americans).* President George W. Bush delivered a moving address to a joint session of Congress and rode the wave of American anger by promising retaliation against terrorists and a final victory in what soon came to be called a "war on terror."[11]

The first American strike in that war was directed at the fundamentalist Islamic Taliban government in Afghanistan, a country that had provided terrorists with a safe haven and which served as a base of operations for

---

* American anger at the unwillingness of the French to support the U.S. invasion of Iraq (which included renaming french fries as "freedom fries" in the congressional cafeteria) is ironic in light of the fact that French president Jacques Chirac not only made a trip to the United States after 9/11 to express French sympathy and support but visited ground zero in New York to pay his respects before President Bush did.

bin Laden's followers.* Though the Soviets had struggled unsuccessfully for ten years to suppress the Afghans in the 1980s, the U.S. war effort there in 2002 was a marvel of efficiency. As in Gulf War I, a principal reason for America's success was its ability to apply precision ordnance from the sky, and in fact the war in Afghanistan demonstrated a dramatic improvement, even a revolution, in the effectiveness of such ordnance. Whereas during Gulf War I the Navy had devoted ten aircraft to each target in order to ensure target destruction, in Afghanistan each aircraft was assigned two targets. The Navy's EA-6B Prowlers jammed Taliban communications, F-14 Tomcats passed global positioning satellite information to the attack aircraft, and Navy and Air Force attack planes so dominated the skies above the battlefield that even though Americans and their Afghan allies on the ground were outnumbered by as much as two to one, they soon overran the country. As Vice Admiral Mike Mullen noted, "For thousands of years the conventional wisdom has required a five to one advantage of offense to defense, [but] we rewrote the rule book in Afghanistan." The campaign ended so quickly that it was over before the United States had time to negotiate basing rights in neighboring countries, rights it ended up not needing.[12]

Having disposed of the Taliban in Afghanistan, the George W. Bush administration then turned its attention to Iraq.

———

More than Gulf War I, which was a response to a specific provocation, the American invasion of Iraq in 2003 marked another sea change for the United States and its military. Earnest Will, Praying Mantis, and Desert Storm had all demonstrated America's willingness to act as a global policeman, but Gulf War II (officially Operation Iraqi Freedom) was a dramatic escalation, even a redefinition, of that role. Despite attempts by adminis-

---

* In many respects, the Taliban government in Afghanistan was the creation of the United States. Throughout much of the 1980s, the CIA had funneled arms and supplies to the Afghan "freedom fighters" (as President Reagan labeled them), who were resisting Soviet occupation. As noted in Part Five, the Soviet retreat from Afghanistan, which left the Taliban in control, was treated in Washington as a great victory.

tration spokesmen to imply a connection between the events of 9/11 and the government of Iraq, the only suggestion of such a link was that Iraq was one of only three countries (the others being China and Libya) that refused to lower its flag to half mast after the 9/11 disaster, and the unconfirmed testimony of the expatriate Iraqi Ahmed Chalabi (who had motives of his own and whose testimony proved unreliable), who claimed that there were terrorist training camps in Iraq. Nevertheless, the events of 9/11 created a new public climate in the United States that allowed the George W. Bush administration to propose and execute a dramatically new doctrine for the exercise of American military power abroad.*

Though Gulf War I had been a model of international cooperation, a segment of the American defense establishment had argued, even at the time, that international cooperation was vastly overrated. Some members of the Reagan and first Bush administrations were uncomfortable with cooperative efforts under the aegis of either the United Nations or NATO, preferring when possible to go it alone so as not to have to convince reluctant or skeptical allies to accept the American vision of what needed to be done. Long before the 9/11 disaster, and even before the events of Praying Mantis, some members of the Reagan administration were expressing the view that "foreign alliances may hinder America's global might."[13]

More than any other single individual, Paul D. Wolfowitz was the architect of this view. The number three man in the Department of Defense at the end of the first Gulf War, Wolfowitz was a Ph.D. out of the University of Chicago who had taught briefly at both Yale and Johns Hopkins. Some administration officials called him the "resident egghead." In 1992, in the wake of Gulf War I, Wolfowitz offered a position paper in which he addressed the role the United States should play in the "new world order." Wolfowitz discounted the value of collective security through the United Nations and argued that as the world's only superpower, the United States

---

* The official report of the bipartisan congressional committee that investigated the events of September 11, 2001, subsequently concluded that there was no collusion or collaboration between the government of Iraq and bin Laden's al-Qaeda organization, though public opinion polls continued to show that most Americans believed there was a connection.

should assume unilateral responsibility for the maintenance of world stability. In September 2002, ten years after he first proposed it, the United
States publicly announced a new national security policy that embraced
Wolfowitz's views: "Our forces will be strong enough to dissuade potential
adversaries from pursuing a military build-up in hopes of surpassing, or
equaling, the power of the United States." The United States thus not only
acknowledged its global military supremacy but also asserted its determination to maintain that supremacy. By implication, at least, this meant that
it was no longer necessary for the United States to compromise, or for that
matter even to negotiate, with its rivals or its allies.* If another power
demonstrated either the willingness or the capability to challenge American supremacy, the United States would be justified in striking first in
order to maintain its global domination. It was, in short, a doctrine of preemptive or preventive war.[14]

Liberal critics of the second Bush administration pointed out that the
United States had never before espoused such a policy. "This goes much
further than the notion of America as the policeman of the world," Hendrick Hertzberg wrote in the *New Yorker*. "It's the notion of America as
both the policeman and the legislator of the world." The historian Arthur
Schlesinger, Jr. noted that the United States was espousing a policy of
"anticipatory self-defense" that was disturbingly similar to the one
advanced by Japan as a justification for its attack on Pearl Harbor. And the
liberal gadfly Noam Chomsky stated bluntly that the new policy was an
"imperial strategy" that suggested a "quest for global dominance."[15]

Dismissing such criticism, the George W. Bush administration determined soon after the 9/11 disaster to go to war against Iraq for the second
time in a dozen years. Though the administration tried hard to connect

---

* The notion that the United States would be better off without allies can be traced back to George
Washington, who warned of "entangling alliances" in his Farewell Address. Washington's warning
derived from the assumption that the United States was so geographically isolated, the great powers of the world would leave it unmolested if Americans simply stayed out of their way. The Wolfowitz Doctrine, by contrast, assumed that the United States had become so dominant it could do
whatever it wanted, and that partnership with allies would only complicate and hinder U.S. execution of its policies.

Iraq and Saddam Hussein to the events of 9/11, three other factors actually led the United States to war in 2003. The first was that Saddam Hussein represented unfinished business. Despite the lopsided American victory in Gulf War I, the first President Bush had ended hostilities after the headlong retreat of the Iraqi army from Kuwait in 1991. Fulfilling a pledge he had made to the Arab states participating in the coalition, the elder Bush announced that Kuwait was liberated, and since that had been the original object of the war, he declared hostilities at an end. He very likely expected that Hussein's humiliation would lead to his collapse in any case, and in pursuit of that, American operatives encouraged the Shiite Muslims in southern Iraq and the Kurds in the north to rise against him. But when Hussein's armed forces ruthlessly crushed both uprisings, the United States did not interfere, and Saddam Hussein survived. Consequently, some members of the second Bush administration were urging a renewal of military operations in order to bring about a "regime change" in Iraq even before the events of 9/11.[16]

The second reason for an American invasion of Iraq, and the one that commanded most of the prewar (and postwar) dialogue, was American insistence that Saddam Hussein possessed "weapons of mass destruction"—defined as nuclear, chemical, or biological weapons. If so, not only would this justify an attack under the Wolfowitz Doctrine of preempting any challenge to American supremacy, it also would have been a breach of the agreement Hussein had been forced to accept at the end of the 1991 war, for his possession of such weapons would have constituted a kind of international parole violation. Though United Nations inspection teams had found no such weapons, Hussein was spectacularly (and stupidly) uncooperative with the inspectors, and Bush administration spokesmen declared repeatedly and categorically that the United States had proof that such weapons existed. The remarkable efficiency of U.S. electronic gadgetry demonstrated in Gulf War I and during the Afghan War led most Americans to conclude that the United States had special capabilities for detecting such weapons—capabilities that the United Nations inspectors lacked—and they were willing to accord their president the benefit of any doubt. Bush made a connection between Iraq's purported weapons and the "war on terror" by raising the specter that Hussein might make some of these weapons available to terrorists.

Months after the war was officially declared over and it became evident that Saddam Hussein had no connection with the 9/11 attacks and that Iraq did not, in fact, have any weapons of mass destruction, a third justification was advanced for the war. Regime change in Iraq had been necessary, the Bush administration argued, because Saddam Hussein was an evil man. He had terrorized his own people, killed thousands of Iraqi Kurds during the war with Iran, and was a ruthless dictator. This fact alone, the United States now declared, was sufficient justification for the war to depose Saddam Hussein. It was a claim reminiscent of the U.S. argument in 1898 that even if the Spanish had not blown up the *Maine*, their misrule in Cuba was sufficient grounds for a war to liberate the Cuban people. Whatever the motives, the Bush administration swept aside opposition from NATO allies and expressions of concern from the United Nations and took the United States to war in Iraq in the spring of 2003.

Once again, the star of the war was the suite of sophisticated weapons delivered primarily by air in a blitz described by Secretary of Defense Donald Rumsfeld as a campaign of "shock and awe." Inspired, perhaps, by the ease of American success in Afghanistan, the administration planned a more streamlined war in 2003 than the one in 1991. Some hoped that the application of American air-launched weapons would cause the Iraqi regime to collapse almost at once. Impressed by the assurances of expatriate Iraqis, Vice President Cheney and others in the administration insisted that all the United States had to do was kick in the door and the whole rotten structure would come crashing down.[17]

It was not quite as easy as that. Though badly overmatched—and completely unable to respond to American air superiority—the Iraqis demonstrated surprising tenacity in the ground fighting, especially in southern Iraq around Basra. Nevertheless, U.S. and British forces soon overwhelmed the Iraqi army, and U.S. forces entered Baghdad on April 7, 2003.

But just as Dewey's apparently easy victory in Manila Bay had been followed by a long and bloody war in the Philippines, the swift march to Baghdad was followed by a long and wasting guerilla campaign, especially in the so-called Sunni triangle in central Iraq. In this second Gulf War, the United States abandoned the Powell Doctrine of overwhelming force and instead sought to win the war by a surgical application of precise munitions and a minimum number of ground troops in accordance with Secretary Rumsfeld's view that the United States could do more with less. In the aftermath of the initial victory, however, it soon became evident that U.S. planners were completely unprepared to fill the vacuum caused by the collapse of Iraq's government, and much of the country descended into chaos. Resistance continued after Hussein himself was captured, pulled ignominiously from a "spider hole" near Baghdad in December 2003; even after the handover of official sovereignty to Iraqis in June 2004, sporadic and deadly attacks on American forces continued.[18]

The cost of the war multiplied. As in the Philippines a hundred years earlier, the United States became involved not only in an ugly guerilla-style war but also with the burdens of a lengthy "nation-building" campaign. After the fall of Baghdad and the formal declaration that "major combat operations" had ended, Bush asked Congress for a budget supplement of $87 *billion* to rebuild the Iraqi economy, and another $82 billion in February 2005. In addition, the continued violence strained the capacity of the American armed forces, compelling the United States to call up an unprecedented number of reservists and, in what was called a "stop-loss" order, require soldiers whose terms of service had expired to stay in Iraq beyond that term. Finally, American unilateralism in Iraq cost it the goodwill of much of the rest of the world. By choosing to prosecute the war despite widespread world opposition, the United States demonstrated its resolve, but it also weakened the Cold War–era alliances—NATO in particular—that had helped secure victory over the Soviet Union. Public opinion polls outside the United States showed widespread hostility toward the United States. When photos were published depicting the mistreatment of Iraqi prisoners by American forces in the notorious Abu Ghraib prison in Baghdad, some Iraqis declared angrily, if hyperbolically, that U.S. occupation was no better than Saddam's tyranny. It was evident that superpower status and a policy of preemptive war came with a price, both tangible and intangible.

It remains to be seen which of the two Gulf Wars will serve as a model for future U.S. policy: the international cooperation of Gulf War I or the unilateralism of Gulf War II. A "war on terror" has no geographical boundaries or chronological limits, and the long-term cost of sustaining an open-ended and unilateral commitment may in the end prove unsustainable. Indeed, almost as soon as the active phase of the war was officially over, the George W. Bush administration began efforts to persuade as many countries as possible to share in the burden of the occupation, both financially and with ground troops, in part perhaps to demonstrate its willingness to revive a sense of international partnership, but also in belated recognition of the enormous costs—financial and political—of sustaining a lengthy American occupation.

—

In the first decade of the twenty-first century, the United States polices the world through five global commands. It has more than half a million troops deployed around the world in 120 countries on five continents, and its naval forces patrol every ocean on the globe. Moreover, it does so with a decreasing dependence on allies or foreign bases. To increase flexibility, the Navy has modified the regular rotation of carrier battle groups at predictable intervals to allow the nation to respond ("surge") to trouble spots on demand. Moreover, the ability of U.S. Navy surface ships to strike deep within an enemy's territory using Tomahawk cruise missiles prompted another sea change with the establishment of something called the Expeditionary Strike Group, a force not built around the carriers but centered on an amphibious assault ship (LHA or LHD), essentially a helicopter carrier designed to insert troops onto hostile shores, accompanied by half a dozen other ships including guided-missile cruisers and destroyers. A Navy spokesman described the new policy as necessary in order to provide the president of the United States with a full quiver of arrows "ready to go" whenever the need called.[19] Implicit in such a basing plan is the assumption that the United States will be ready to act not only quickly but unilaterally. One supporter of the policy called it "the Doctrine of the Big

Enchilada" and concluded matter-of-factly that "power breeds unilateral-ism. It's as simple as that."[20]

One clear lesson of history, however, is that no single nation has ever risen to dominance and stayed there. As George Kennan wrote in 1999, "Purely military power, even in its greatest dimensions of superiority, can produce only short term successes." One reason is that unilateral global policing is enormously expensive. And another is that the wielding of great power inevitably breeds resentment. Even when it is not intended to be deliberately imperious, policy decisions that overlook or ignore the views of other nations are perceived as imperial in character. In a speech to the graduating class at West Point in May 2003, President G. W. Bush declared that "America has no empire to extend or utopia to establish," and in a subsequent talk to veterans at the White House he reiterated that "we don't seek an empire." But to much of the world, the United States in the twenty-first century looked very much like an empire: "always threatening, always demanding," and nearly always humiliating. It is not an empire in the tra-ditional sense of that term. Indeed, as Michael Ignatieff has noted, "it is an empire without consciousness of itself as such, constantly shocked that its good intentions arouse resentment abroad."[21]

The collapse of the Soviet Union and the advent of the "war on terror" have redefined the mission of the U.S. Navy. No longer charged with con-fronting the Soviet Navy on its maritime doorstep or tracking Soviet sub-marines in the deep places of the earth, the Navy in the post-9/11 era focuses instead on patrolling the sea lanes of the world in an effort to break up and shut down efforts by America's stateless enemies to deliver arms to places where American lives or American interests could be imper-iled. In August 2002 the United States announced that its ships would begin inspecting vessels of any nationality deemed to be suspicious, and later, in May 2003, President Bush announced (while in Poland) that the United States claimed the right of its warships to stop vessels of any nationality anywhere in the world, to inspect their cargoes, and to impound any ships or cargoes found to be suspicious. In 1812 the United States went to war, in part at least, to protest similar policies carried out by the Royal Navy. But two hundred years later the U.S. Navy has become the new cop on the beat: not only in wartime, but also in the ubiquitous twilight of the "war on terror," and not only in the Persian Gulf but everywhere on earth.

Whether that commitment represents a conscious effort at global empire, as its critics charge, or merely reasonable caution in a dangerous time, as its defenders insist, it is a far cry from the frontier squadron of Oliver Hazard Perry or even the gray steel armada that fought its way across the Pacific Ocean to the shores of Japan. It marks one more dramatic milestone in the history of the Navy, the history of the United States, and ultimately the history of the world.

[NOTES]

PROLOGUE: NAVAL BATTLES AND HISTORY

1. Burke Davis, *The Campaign That Won America: The Story of Yorktown* (New York: Dial Press, 1970), 149; Harold A. Larrabee, *Decision at the Chesapeake* (New York: Clarkston N. Potter, 1964), 185–86.

2. Cornwallis to Graves, July 26, 1781, in French Ensor Chadwick, ed., *The Graves Papers and Other Documents Relating to the Naval Operations of the Yorktown Campaign, July to October 1781* (New York: Naval History Society, 1916), 98–99 (hereafter *The Graves Papers*).

3. Davis, *The Campaign That Won America*, 59.

4. "Translation of the French Account of the Action Off the Chesapeake," November 27, 1781, printed in *The Graves Papers*, 253.

5. Larrabee, *Decision at the Chesapeake*, 189.

6. Hood to George Jackson, September 16, 1781, *The Graves Papers*, 86–87.

7. Ibid., plus "Enclosure 1," 89.

8. Graves to Stephens, September 14, 1781, and "Addendum," both in *The Graves Papers*, 68, 69–70.

9. "Enclosure 1" in Hood to Jackson, September 16, 1781, *The Graves Papers*, 91; Larrabee, *Decision at the Chesapeake*, 213.

10. *The Graves Papers*, 92–93.

11. "Translation of the French Account," *The Graves Papers*, 255.
   Graves to Stephens, September 26, 1781, *The Graves Papers*, 111; Larrabee, *Decision at the Chesapeake*, 193.

PART ONE: THE BATTLE OF LAKE ERIE

1. David Bunnell, *The Travels and Adventures of David Bunnell* (Palmyra, NY: F. E. Grandin, 1831), 111.

2. W. W. Dobbins, *History of the Battle of Lake Erie* (Erie, PA: Ashby Printing Co., 1876), 29.

3. Usher Parsons, *The Battle of Lake Erie* (Providence: Benjamin T. Albro, 1854), 8.

4. Alexander Slidell Mackenzie, *The Life of Oliver Hazard Perry* (New York: Harper & Brothers, 1840), 1:225.

5. Max Rosenberg, *The Building of Perry's Fleet on Lake Erie, 1812–1813* (Harrisburg: Pennsylvania Historical and Museum Commission, 1997), 11–14.

6. James F. Zimmerman, *Impressment of American Seamen* (New York: Columbia University Press, 1925), appendix.

7. Bradford Perkins, *Prologue to War: England and the United States, 1805–1812* (Berkeley: University of California Press, 1961), 140–49.

8. Ibid.; Reginald Horsman, *The Causes of the War of 1812* (Philadelphia: University of Pennsylvania Press, 1962); Donald R. Hickey, *The War of 1812: A Forgotten Conflict* (Urbana: University of Illinois Press, 1989), 20–24.

9. Sandy Antal, *A Wampum Denied: Procter's War of 1812* (Carleton, ON: Carleton University Press, 1997).

10. R. David Edmunds, "Tecumseh's Native Allies: Warriors Who Fought for the Crown," in W. J. Welsh and David C. Skaggs, *War on the Great Lakes* (Kent, OH: Kent State University Press, 1991), 56–57; David C. Skaggs and Gerard Altoff, *A Signal Victory: The Lake Erie Campaign, 1812–1813* (Annapolis: Naval Institute Press, 1997), 20.

11. *Niles Weekly Register*, March 7, 1812.

12. Clay to Thomas Bodley, December 18, 1813, *The Papers of Henry Clay*, ed. Thomas F. Hopkins (Lexington: University of Kentucky Press, 1959), 1:842.

13. *Annals of Congress*, 12th Congress, 1st session, 978.

14. Skaggs and Altoff, *A Signal Victory*, 7.

15. Samuel Taggert was the congressman, quoted in Antal, *A Wampum Denied*, 14.

16. The phrase "frontier constabulary" is borrowed from Skaggs and Altoff, *A Signal Victory*, 7.

17. Skaggs and Altoff, *A Signal Victory*, 8–9.

18. Antal, *A Wampum Denied*, 36.

19. Richard V. Barbuto, *Niagara, 1814: America Invades Canada* (Lawrence: University Press of Kansas, 2000), 28; Antal, *A Wampum Denied*, 51.

20. Hickey, *War of 1812*, 80–84.

21. Madison to Dearborn, October 7, 1812, quoted in Hickey, *War of 1812*, 128.

22. Hamilton to Chauncey, August 31 and September 4, 1812, in William S. Dudley, ed., *The Naval War of 1812: A Documentary History* (Washington, DC: Naval Historical Center, 1985), 1:297–300, 302. Italics in original.

23. Charles O. Paullin, "Jesse Duncan Elliott," *Dictionary of American Biography*, 3:96–97; Allan Westcott, "Commodore Jesse D. Elliott: A Stormy Petrel of the Navy," U.S. Naval Institute *Proceedings*, September 1928, 773–78.

24. Elliott to Chauncey, September 14, 1812, in Dudley, ed., *The Naval War of 1812*, 1:313.

25. Ibid.

26. Elliott to Hamilton, October 9, 1812, in Dudley, ed., *The Naval War of 1812*, 1:328–31.

27. Christopher McKee, *A Gentlemanly and Honorable Profession: The Creation of the U.S. Naval Officer Corps, 1794–1815* (Annapolis: Naval Institute Press, 1991), 297.

28. Dobbins, *Battle of Lake Erie*, 9–10.

29. Hamilton to Dobbins, and two letters from Hamilton to Chauncey, all dated September 11, 1812, in Dudley, ed., *The Naval War of 1812*, 1:307–10.
30. Elliott to Dobbins, October 2, 1812, ibid, 1:321.
31. None of the full-length biographies of Perry is fully satisfactory. The earliest is John M. Niles, *The Life of Oliver Hazard Perry* (Hartford: William S. Marsh, 1820), followed by Alexander Slidell Mackenzie, *The Life of Commodore Oliver Hazard Perry*, 2 vols. (New York: Harper & Brothers, 1831). Mackenzie was Perry's friend and is very much an advocate as well as biographer. James Cooke Mills' *Oliver Hazard Perry and the Battle of Lake Erie* (Detroit: John Phelps, 1913) is a centennial biography that is also largely hagiographic. Charles J. Dutton's *Oliver Hazard Perry* (New York: Longmans, 1935) is better, as is Richard Dillon, *We Have Met the Enemy: Oliver Hazard Perry, Wilderness Commodore* (New York: McGraw-Hill, 1978). But none of these books employs either footnotes or a comprehensive bibliography. The best short overview is John K. Mahon, "Oliver Hazard Perry, Savior of the Northwest," in James C. Bradford, ed., *Quarterdeck and Bridge: Two Centuries of American Naval Leaders* (Annapolis: Naval Institute Press, 1997), 59–75.
32. Perry to Jones, January 29, 1813, and February 11 and 17, 1813, all in "Letters Received by the Secretary of the Navy from Commanders, 1804–1886," National Archives, Record Group 45, microfilm reel 5 (hereafter "Commanders Letters").
33. Dobbins, *History*, 71–72; Mackenzie, *Life*, 127–30.
34. Samuel Hambleton Diary, April 1, 1813, Maryland Historical Society.
35. Dobbins, *History*, 17–18; Hambleton Diary, April 1, 1813.
36. Hambleton Diary, May 16, 1813.
37. Dobbins, *History*, 75.
38. Ibid., 19–23, 32. The best general history of the building of Perry's squadron is Max Rosenberg, *The Building of Perry's Fleet on Lake Erie, 1812–1813* (Harrisburg: Pennsylvania Historical and Museum Commission, 1997).
39. Ibid., 28.
40. Hambleton Diary, June 9 and 25, 1813.
41. Ibid., July 19, 1813.
42. Perry to Jones, June 19, 1813; Jones to Perry, July 3, 1813; and Perry to Chauncey, July 27, 1813, all in Dudley, ed., *The Naval War of 1812*, 2:482, 487, 530; Perry to Jones, July 23, 1813, "Commanders Letters," reel 5. For detailed information about Perry's manning problems see Gerard T. Altoff, *Deep Water Sailors, Shallow Water Soldiers: Manning the United States Fleet on Lake Erie* (Put-in-Bay, OH: Perry Group, 1993).
43. Chauncey to Perry, July 30, 1813, in Dudley, *The Naval War of 1812*, 2:530; Skaggs and Altoff, *Signal Victory*, 78–79.
44. Perry to Jones, August 10, 1813; and Jones to Perry, August 18, 1813, both in Dudley, ed., *The Naval War of 1812*, 2:532–33.
45. Richard Henry Dana, *Two Years Before the Mast: A Personal Narrative of Life at Sea* (1843; reprint, New York: Penguin Books, 1981), 124; George Stockton to

Perry, September 5, 1813, Perry Papers (No. 50), Clements Library, University of Michigan.

46. Report dated July 23, 1813; Smith to Perry, August 23, 1813; Perry's General Orders dated August 23 and September 9, 1813, all in Perry Papers (No. 42).

47. Skaggs and Altoff, *Signal Victory*, 84–86.

48. Dobbins, *History*, 45–46; William V. Taylor, "Journal of the Sloop [*sic*] of War *Lawrence*," August 3–4, 1813, Newport Historical Society.

49. Hambleton Diary, August 3–5, 1813; Affidavit of William Taylor, June 23, 1818, Perry Papers (No. 144).

50. Perry to Jones, August 4, 1813, in Dudley, ed., *The Naval War of 1812*, 2:546.

51. Hambleton Diary, August 8, 1813.

52. Ibid., August 22, 1813. David Skaggs and Gerard Altoff estimate that with the addition of Harrison's men, Perry had 356 sailors, 34 marines, and 195 soldiers and landsmen, for a total of 585. Skaggs and Altoff, *Signal Victory*, 83.

53. Skaggs and Altoff, *Signal Victory*, 53.

54. Ibid., 61–68. The *Queen Charlotte* formerly carried eighteen guns, but swapped four of her 24-pounders for three 12-pounders. See ibid., 186.

55. Barclay to Yeo, September 1, 1813, in Dudley, ed., *The Naval War of 1812*, 2:551–52.

56. Barclay to Prevost, July 16, 1813; and Prevost to Barclay, July 21, 1813, both in Dudley, ed., *The Naval War of 1812*, 2:545.

57. Barclay to Yeo, September 1 and September 12, 1813, in Dudley, ed., *The Naval War of 1812*, 2:551, 555; Harrison to Perry, September 4, 1813, Perry Papers (No. 49).

58. Bunnell, *Travels and Adventures*, 112–13; Parsons, *Battle of Lake Erie*, 9–10.

59. Hambleton Diary, October 12, 1813.

60. Mackenzie, *Life*, 229–30; Anonymous Affidavit, Perry Papers (No. 183).

61. Affidavit by Thomas Holdup Stevens, June 10, 1818, Perry Papers (No. 142).

62. Mackenzie, *Life*, 233.

63. Parsons, *The Battle of Lake Erie*, 12–13.

64. Mackenzie, *Life*, 241; Bunnell, *Travels and Adventures*, 114.

65. Mackenzie, *Life*, 238–39.

66. Bunnell, *Travels and Adventures*, 114.

67. Mackenzie, *Life*, 244; Dulaney Forrest to M. C. Perry, January 29, 1821, Perry Papers (No. 167).

68. Taylor to his wife, September 15, 1813, in Dudley, ed., *The Naval War of 1812*, 2:559–60.

69. Mackenzie, *Life*, 250.

70. Ibid.

71. Barclay to Yeo, September 12, 1813, in Dudley, ed., *The Naval War of 1812*, 2:556.

72. Mackenzie, *Life*, 252–53.

73. "Surgeon Usher Parsons's Account," n.d., in Dudley, ed., *The Naval War of 1812*, 2:563.

74. Perry to Harrison, August 5, 1813, D. E. Clanin, ed., "The Correspondence of William Henry Harrison and Oliver Hazard Perry, July 5, 1813–July 31, 1815," *Northwest Ohio Quarterly* 60 (1988): 165; Skaggs and Altoff, *Signal Victory*, 147.

75. Perry to Harrison, and Perry to Jones, both dated September 10, 1813, in Dudley, ed., *The Naval War of 1812*, 2:553–54.

76. Mackenzie, *Life*, 263–64.

77. Perry to Jones. September 13, 1813, in Dudley, ed., *The Naval War of 1812*, 2:557–58.

78. Perry to Elliott, June 18, 1813, *Documents in Relation to the Difference Which Subsisted Between the Late Commodore O. H. Perry and Captain J. D. Elliott* (Washington, 1821), 21–22; *Niles Weekly Register*, December 4, 1813, in E. Cruikshank, *The Documentary History of the Campaign upon the Niagara Frontier in the Year 1813* (Welland: Tribune Office, 1905), 3:148.

79. Affidavit of Dr. Parsons, n.d., *Documents in Relation to the Difference*, 17; Affidavit of Usher Parsons, July 2, 1818, Perry Papers (No. 145).

80. Affidavit of Stephen Champlin, June 19, 1818, Perry Papers (No. 143).

81. Statement of W. H. Breckinridge, n.d., and Elliott to Perry, n.d., both in *Documents in Relation to the Difference*, 18–19.

82. Perry to Elliott, June 18, 1818, ibid., 8–15

83. Perry to Benjamin Hazard, June 6, 1819, and Hambleton to Perry, May 26, 1814, both in Perry Papers (No. 160 and No. 89).

84. Westcott, "Commodore Jesse D. Elliott: A Stormy Petrel of the Navy," 773–78.

PART TWO: THE BATTLE OF HAMPTON ROADS

1. Quoted in William C. Davis, *Duel Between the First Ironclads* (Baton Rouge: Louisiana State University Press, 1975), 85, italics added; William Keeler to his wife, May 7, 1862, in Robert W. Daly, *Aboard the USS Monitor: 1862* (Annapolis: Naval Institute Press, 1964), 106.

2. Background on Franklin Buchanan is in Craig L. Symonds, *Confederate Admiral: The Life and War of Franklin Buchanan* (Annapolis: Naval Institute Press, 1999), 1–3, 128–40.

3. Buchanan to Du Pont, May 20, 1861, Du Pont Letters, Hagley Museum and Library, Wilmington, Delaware.

4. Mallory to Buchanan, February 24, 1862, *Official Records of the Union and Confederate Navies in the War of the Rebellion* (Washington: Government Printing Office, 1894–1917), series I, 6:776–77 (hereafter cited as *ORN*); John R. Eggleston, "Narrative of the Battle of the Merrimac," *Southern Historical Society Proceedings* 41 (1916): 168.

5. The best discussion of the causes of the Civil War is David M. Potter, *The Impending Crisis, 1848–1861* (New York: Harper & Row, 1976); for a discussion of the war and historical memory, see David Blight, *Race and Reunion: The*

Civil War in American Memory (Cambridge and London: Harvard University Press, 2001).

6. Richmond *Examiner*, July 13, 1861.

7. The quotation is from James Chesnut, husband of the famous diarist Mary Chesnut, and is in James M. McPherson, *Battle Cry of Freedom: The Civil War Era* (New York: Oxford University Press, 1988), 238.

8. For background on the technological developments in naval warfare in this era, see Robert Gardiner, ed., *Steam, Steel & Shellfire: The Steam Warships, 1815–1905* (London: Conway Maritime Press, 1992).

9. Lincoln's "Proclamation of a Blockade," April 19 and April 27, 1861, in Roy S. Basler, ed., *The Collected Works of Abraham Lincoln* (New Brunswick: Rutgers University Press, 1953), 4:338–39, 346–47.

10. Mallory to his wife, August 31, 1862, Stephen Mallory Letters, P. K. Yonge Library, University of Florida; Mallory to Congress, May 8, 1861, *ORN*, series II, 1:742.

11. John M. Brooke, "The Plan and Construction of the *Merrimac*" in *Battles and Leaders of the Civil War* (New York: Century, 1887–89), 1:715–16 (hereafter *B&L*); John L. Porter, untitled essay, *B&L*, 1:716–17; J. Thomas Scharf, *The Confederate States Navy* (New York: Rogers & Sherwood, 1887), 1:145–47. See also Craig L. Symonds and Harold Holzer, "Who Designed the CSS *Virginia*," *Military History Quarterly*, Fall 2003, 6–14.

12. Investigation of the Navy Department, February 26, 1863, *ORN*, series II, 1:783–84; Scharf, *Confederate States Navy*, 1:147.

13. John Quarstein, *CSS Virginia: Mistress of Hampton Roads* (Appomattox: H. E. Howard, 2000), 36–39; Scott Nelson, *Iron Confederacies: Southern Railways, Klan Violence, and Reconstruction* (Chapel Hill: University of North Carolina Press, 1999), 39.

14. Mallory to Conrad, May 8, 1861, *ORN*, series II, 1:742; Quarstein, *CSS Virginia*, 36; Charleston *Mercury*, October 30, 1861.

15. John Niven, *Gideon Welles* (New York: Oxford University Press, 1973), 365–66.

16. Bushnell to Welles, March 9, 1877, *B&L*, 1:748.

17. Ibid.; Robert Schneller, *Quest for Victory: A Biography of Rear Admiral John A. Dahlgren* (Annapolis: Naval Institute Press, 1996), 183–89.

18. Bushnell to Welles, March 9, 1877, in *B&L*, 1:748.

19. Ibid., 749.

20. Ibid.

21. Smith to Worden, January 11, 1862, *ORN*, series I, 6:515; Gideon Welles, "The Building of the *Monitor*," *B&L*, 1:731n; Worden to Smith, January 13, 1861, *ORN*, I, 6:516.

22. Keeler to his wife, February 28, 1862, in Daly, *Aboard the USS* Monitor, 18.

23. Ibid.; George Geer to his wife, March 2, 1862, in William Marvel, ed., *The Monitor Chronicles* (New York: Simon & Schuster, 2000), 20.

24. Keeler to wife, serial letter dated March 6, 1862, in Daly, *Aboard the USS* Monitor, 27.

25. Davis, *Duel Between the First Ironclads*, 49.

26. Geer to his wife, March 2, 1862, in Marvel, *The* Monitor *Chronicles*, 21.

27. John Ericsson, "The Building of the *Monitor*," *B&L*, 1:741; Keeler to his wife, serial letter dated March 6, 1862, in Daly, *Aboard the USS* Monitor, 27–28.

28. Samuel Greene, "In the *Monitor* Turret," *B&L*, 1:721; Keeler to his wife, March 6, 1862, in Daly, *Aboard the USS* Monitor, 28–30.

29. Louis N. Stodder (as told to Albert Stephens Crockett), "Aboard the U.S.S. *Monitor*," *Civil War Times Illustrated* 1 (1963): 32; Greene, "In the *Monitor* Turret," 1:721; Keeler to his wife, serial letter dated March 6, 1862, in Daly, *Aboard the USS* Monitor, 30–31.

30. H. Ashton Ramsay, "The Most Famous of Sea Duels," *Harper's Weekly*, February 10, 1912, 11; E. A. Jack, *Memoirs of E. A. Jack* (White Stone, VA: Brandywine Publishers, 1998), 14.

31. Thomas O. Selfridge, *Memoirs of Thomas O. Selfridge, Jr.* (New York: G. P. Putnam's Sons, Inc., 1924; reprint, Columbia: University of South Carolina Press, 1987), 44.

32. [Richard Curtis], *History of the Famous Battle Between the Iron-Clad* Merrimac, *C.S.N., and the Iron-Clad* Monitor *and the* Cumberland *and* Congress *of the U.S. Navy* (Hampton, VA: Houston Printing and Publishing House, 1957), 5; Jack, *Memoirs*, 14; Symonds, *Confederate Admiral*, 163.

33. [Curtis], *History*, 8.

34. Selfridge, *Memoirs*, 50.

35. Morris to Radford, March 9, 1862, and Kennison to Welles, March 18, 1862, both in *ORN*, series I, 7:721, 722; Symonds, *Confederate Admiral*, 164; Selfridge, *Memoirs*, 58.

36. Davis, *Duel Between the First Ironclads*, 99–100.

37. William H. Parker, *Recollections of a Naval Officer*, ed. Craig L. Symonds (Annapolis: Naval Institute Press, 1985), 277; Davis, *Duel Between the First Ironclads*, 100.

38. John R. Eggleston, "Narrative of the Battle," Southern Historical Society *Proceedings* 41 (1916): 173.

39. Ramsay, "The Most Famous of Sea Duels," 12.

40. John Taylor Wood, "The First Fight of Iron-Clads," *B&L*, 1:700.

41. Gideon Welles, *Diary of Gideon Welles*, ed. Howard K. Beale (New York: W. W. Norton, 1960), 1:62–64.

42. McClellan to Wool, March 9, 1862, in Stephen W. Sears, ed., *The Civil War Papers of George B. McClellan* (New York: Ticknor & Fields, 1989), 199.

43. Davis, *Duel Between the First Ironclads*, 116; Symonds, *Confederate Admiral*, 170.

44. An excerpt of Catesby Jones's report is in Buchanan to Mallory, March 27, 1862, *ORN*, I, 7:46.

45.   Welles to Marston, March 5 and 7, 1862, and Van Brundt to Welles, March 10, 1862, all in *ORN*, series I, 6:681, 687, 7:11.

46.   Keeler to wife, serial letter dated March 6, 1862, in Daly, *Aboard the USS* Monitor, 32–33.

47.   Ibid.

48.   Welles, "The Building of the *Monitor*," 1:734; Greene, "In the *Monitor* Turret," 1:722. Ericsson's original plan called for a viewing slit only 5/8 inch wide, but it was enlarged to 7/8 inch during construction. I am indebted to Francis J. DuCoin of Stuart, Florida, for information about the design of the *Monitor*'s pilothouse.

49.   Keeler to his wife, serial letter dated March 6, 1862, in Daly, *Aboard the USS* Monitor, 34.

50.   Ibid.; Greene, "In the *Monitor* Turret," 722; Quarstein, *CSS Virginia*, 108.

51.   Davis, *Duel Between Ironclads*, 122; Greene, "In the *Monitor* Turret," 1:723.

52.   E. V. White, *The First Iron-Clad Engagement in the World* (New York: J. S. Ogilvie, 1906), 6; Ramsay, "The Most Famous of Sea Duels," 12.

53.   Greene, "In the *Monitor* Turret," 1:725.

54.   Ibid.

55.   Ibid.

56.   Wood, "The First Fight of Iron-Clads," 1:703.

57.   Ramsay, "The Most Famous of Sea Duels," 12.

58.   [Curtis], *History*, 12.

59.   Greene, "In the *Monitor* Turret," 1:725.

60.   Van Brunt to Welles, March 10, 1862, *ORN*, series I, 7:11.

61.   Wood, "The First Fight of Iron-Clads," 1:701.

62.   Keeler to his wife, serial letter dated March 6, 1862, in Daly, *Aboard the USS* Monitor, 38.

63.   Ibid.

64.   Davis, *Duel Between the First Ironclads*, 133.

65.   Jack, *Memoirs*, 16.

66.   Keeler to his wife, March 30, 1862, Daly, *Aboard the USS* Monitor, 63.

67.   James Tertius deKay, *Monitor: The Story of the Legendary Civil War Ironclad and the Man Whose Invention Changed the Course of History* (New York: Walker and Co., 1997), 227.

68.   Nathaniel Hawthorne, "Chiefly About War Matters," *Atlantic Monthly*, July 1862, 43–62.

PART THREE: THE BATTLE OF MANILA BAY

1.   Quoted in John D. Hayes and John B. Hattendorf, eds., *The Writings of Stephen B. Luce* (Newport, RI: Naval War College, 1975), 1. The Oscar Wilde story was first published in 1890, the same year that Mahan published his influential book.

2. Alfred Thayer Mahan, *The Influence of Sea Power upon History, 1660-1783* (Boston: Little, Brown, 1890).

3. Lt. C. G. Calkins, USN, "The Naval Battle of Manila Bay," in *The American-Spanish War: A History by the War Leaders* (Norwich, CT: Charles C. Haskell & Son, 1899), 110; Cdr. Nathan Sargent, USN, *Admiral Dewey and the Manila Campaign* (Washington, DC: Naval Historical Foundation, 1947), 23; George Dewey, *Autobiography of George Dewey, Admiral of the Navy* (New York: Charles Scribner's Sons, 1913), 207; Joseph L. Stickney, "With Dewey at Manila," *Harper's New Monthly Magazine*, February 1899, 489.

4. John M. Ellicott, "The Naval Battle of Manila Bay," U.S. Naval Institute *Proceedings*, September 1900, 499.

5. Dewey, *Autobiography*, 199.

6. Ibid., 208.

7. Wayne Longnecker to his brother, July 31, 1898, "Wayne [Longnecker], United States Navy, Vessels A-O, USS Olympia," Spanish-American War Survey Collection, U.S. Army Military History Institute (USAMHI), Carlisle, PA; Ellicott, "The Naval Battle of Manila," 499; Stickney, "With Dewey at Manila," 478; Calkins, "The Naval Battle of Manila Bay," 111; Sargent, *Admiral Dewey and the Manila Campaign*, 33.

8. Calkins, "The Naval Battle of Manila Bay," 113; Longnecker to his brother, July 31, 1898, USAMHI.

9. Dewey, *Autobiography*, 211; Stickney, "With Dewey at Manila," 479.

10. The Ostend Manifesto of October 18, 1854, is in House Exec. Doc. 93 (33rd Cong., 2nd sess.), 127–32; Louis A. Perez, *The War of 1898: The United States and Cuba in History and Historiography* (Chapel Hill: University of North Carolina Press, 1998), 5.

11. Richard H. Bradford, *The Virginius Affair* (Boulder: Colorado Associate University Press, 1980). Admiral David Dixon Porter's 1874 report on the state of the Navy declared that most of the nation's monitors "can never be of the least use in peace or war, unless sunk as obstructions to channels."

12. Perez, *The War of 1898*, 12–24.

13. The *New York World*, May 17, 1896, quoted in Harold U. Faulkner, *Politics, Reform, and Expansion* (New York: Harper & Row, 1959), 226.

14. Ivan Musicant, *Empire by Default: The Spanish-American War and the Dawn of the American Century* (New York: Henry Holt, 1998), 38–124; David Trask, *The War with Spain in 1898* (New York: Macmillan, 1981), 1–57.

15. Margaret Leech, *In the Days of McKinley* (New York: Harper & Brothers, 1959), 161–65.

16. Detailed diagrams of the *Maine*'s design are in Charles D. Sigsbee, "Personal Narrative of the 'Maine,'" Part II, *Century*, December 1898, 250–51.

17. Sigsbee, "Personal Narrative," Part I, *Century*, November 1898, 84; Musicant, *Empire by Default*, 126, 129.

18. Quoted in Musicant, *Empire by Default*, 132–33.

19. Ibid., 165.

20. Hyman G. Rickover, *How the Battleship* Maine *Was Destroyed* (Washington, DC: Naval History Division, 1976), 91.

21. Leech, *In the Days of McKinley*, 168; Sandburg is quoted in Perez, *The War of 1898*, 26. Italics in original.

22. See Table 1 in Benjamin Franklin Cooling, *Gray Steel and Blue Water Navy: The Formative Years of America's Military-Industrial Complex, 1881–1917* (Hamden, CT: Archon Books, 1979), 222; Leech, *In the Days of McKinley*, 169.

23. Leech, *In the Days of McKinley*, 181–90.

24. Long to Dewey, April 24, 1898, in Sargent, *Admiral Dewey and the Manila Campaign*, 22n.

25. See diary entries of January 11, February 25, and February 26 in *The Journal of John D. Long*, ed. by Margaret Long (Rindge, NH: Richard R. Smith, 1956), 212–13, 216–17.

26. Theodore Roosevelt, *An Autobiography* (New York: Charles Scribner's Sons, 1913), 210–11.

27. Sargent, *Admiral Dewey and the Manila Campaign*, 8.

28. Trask, *The War with Spain in 1898*, 75–76. See also John A. S. Grenville, "American Preparations for War with Spain, 1896–1898," *Journal of American Studies*, April 1968, 33–47.

29. Sargent, *Admiral Dewey and the Manila Campaign*, 5.

30. Ibid., 11.

31. Musicant, *Empire by Default*, 198–99; Sargent, *Admiral Dewey and the Manila Campaign*, 10; Dewey, *Autobiography*, 191.

32. Sargent, *Admiral Dewey and the Manila Campaign*, 10.

33. Calkins, "The Naval Battle of Manila Bay," 105; Stickney, "With Dewey at Manila," 482.

34. Black to Dewey, April 24, 1898, in Sargent, *Admiral Dewey and the Manila Campaign*, 19n–20n.

35. Dewey, *Autobiography*, 170.

36. Sargent, *Admiral Dewey and the Manila Campaign*, 19; Calkins, "The Naval Battle of Manila Bay," 107; Wayne Longnecker to his brother, July 31, 1898, USAMHI.

37. Calkins, "The Naval Battle of Manila Bay," 106; Sargent, *Admiral Dewey and the Manila Campaign*, 30; Dewey, *Autobiography*, 230; Long to Dewey, April 24, 1898, in Sargent, 22n.

38. Quoted in Ernest May, *Imperial Democracy: The Emergence of America as a Great Power* (New York: Harcourt Brace, 1961), 86.

39. Archbishop Davila's broadside is printed in Sargent, *Admiral Dewey and the Manila Campaign*, 30–31, n. 7.

40. Montojo to the commandant at Cavite, April 24, 1898, in Adelbert Dewey, *The Life and Letters of Admiral Dewey* (New York: Woolfall Company, 1899), 274.

41.   Ibid.

42.   Ibid.

43.   Musicant, *Empire by Default*, 207; Ellicott, "The Defenses of Mobile Bay," U.S. Naval Institute *Proceedings*, June 1900, 279–85; Montojo's report, printed in Dewey, *Life and Letters*, 285.

44.   Montojo's report, printed in Dewey, *Life and Letters*, 287.

45.   Calkins, "The Naval Battle of Manila Bay," 114.

46.   Dewey, *Autobiography*, 212; Sargent, *Admiral Dewey and the Manila Campaign*, 35.

47.   Sargent, *Admiral Dewey and the Manila Campaign*, 36; Dewey, *Autobiography*, 214; Charles H. Twitchell, quoted in Dewey, *Life and Letters*, 373.

48.   Dewey, *Autobiography*, 214; Sargent, *Admiral Dewey and the Manila Campaign*, 36; Twitchell in Dewey, *Life and Letters*, 373.

49.   Calkins, "The Naval Battle of Manila Bay," 116; George P. Colvocoresses to Dewey, May 3, 1898, in Dewey, *Life and Letters*, 367.

50.   Calkins, "The Naval Battle of Manila Bay," 115–16, 125; Bradley A. Fiske, "Why We Won at Manila," *Century*, November 1898, 131–32. The description of loading and firing during the battle is from Fiske, who was a gunnery officer on the *Petrel* during the fight.

51.   Stickney, "With Dewey at Manila," 38; Hugh Rodman, *Yarns of a Kentucky Admiral* (Indianapolis: Bobbs-Merrill, 1928), 78.

52.   Ellicott, "The Naval Battle of Manila," 505; Ensign W. Pitt Scott, quoted in Louis Stanley, *The Life of Admiral Dewey* (Philadelphia: P. W. Zingler & Co., 1899), 138; Twitchell quoted in Dewey, *Life and Letters*, 373–74; Rodman, *Yarns of a Kentucky Admiral*, 243–44.

53.   Stickney, "With Dewey at Manila," 476.

54.   Calkins, "The Naval Battle of Manila," 117; Dewey, *Autobiography*, 220; Ellicott, "The Naval Battle of Manila," 503.

55.   Dewey, *Autobiography*, 218.

56.   Stickney, "With Dewey at Manila," 476–77.

57.   Ibid.; Dewey, *Autobiography*, 218–19.

58.   Calkins, "The Naval Battle of Manila," 116; Dewey, *Autobiography*, 221; Ellicott, "The Naval Battle of Manila," 504–5; Stickney, "With Dewey at Manila," 480.

59.   Calkins, "The Naval Battle of Manila," 118.

60.   Ibid., 119; Dewey, *Autobiography*, 221.

61.   Sargent, *Admiral Dewey and the Manila Campaign*, 40; Ellicott, "The Naval Battle of Manila," 511.

62.   "Calkins, "The Naval Battle of Manila," 120.

63.   Sargent, *Admiral Dewey and the Manila Campaign*, 42–43.

64.   Dewey to Long, May 1, 1898, in ibid., 44n; see also 54.

65.   Quoted in May, *Imperial Democracy*, 246.

66.   Dewey, *Autobiography*, 234; Dewey to his brother, October 6, 1898, in Dewey, *Life and Letters*, 413.

67. Sargent, *Admiral Dewey and the Manila Campaign*, 93.

68. Musicant, *Empire by Default*, 591.

69. Trask, *The War with Spain in 1898*, 257–69; French Ensor Chadwick, *The Relations of the United States and Spain: The Spanish-American War* (New York: Russell & Russell, 1919), 2:142–77.

70. Musicant, *Empire by Default*, 198.

71. Brian Linn, *The Philippine War, 1899–1902* (Lawrence: University of Kansas Press, 2000), 20–22.

72. Ibid., 22.

73. Henry Corbin to Wesley Merritt, August 13, 1898, quoted in Linn, *The Philippine War*, 26.

74. Long diary entry, November 4, 1898, *The Journal of John D. Long*, 229.

75. U.S. State Department, *Foreign Relations of the United States* (1898), 937–38; Musicant, *Empire by Default*, 602–4; Trask, *The War with Spain in 1898*, 441.

76. Linn, *The Philippine War*, 31.

77. McKinley is quoted in Perez, *The War of 1898*, 118.

78. Linn, *The Philippine War*, 315.

79. Max Boot, *The Savage Wars of Peace: Small Wars and the Rise of American Power* (New York: Basic Books, 1902), 123–24. See also Glenn A. May, "Why the United States Won the Philippine-American War, 1899–1902," *Pacific Historical Review* 52 (1983): 353–77.

80. Linn, *The Philippine War*, 315–17.

81. Ibid., 31; Boot, *The Savage Wars of Peace*, 124–25.

82. Trask, *The War with Spain in 1898*, ix; Charles M. Thompson, *History of the United States* (Chicago: B. H. Sanborn, 1922), 474. Proctor is quoted in H. Wayne Morgan, *America's Road to Empire: The War in Spain and Overseas Expansion* (New York: John Wiley, 1965), 83; Frank Prebery, "To Lands Across the Sea," *Harper's New Monthly Magazine*, May 1899, 1; Henry Cabot Lodge, "The Spanish War," *Harper's New Monthly Magazine*, February 1899, 447; Rudyard Kipling, "The White Man's Burden," *McClure's*, February 1899, 12.

83. Quoted in Warren Zimmerman, *First Great Triumph* (New York: Farrar, Straus & Giroux, 2002), 327.

84. Julius W. Pratt, *Expansionists of 1898: The Acquisition of Hawaii and the Spanish Islands* (Baltimore: Johns Hopkins University Press, 1936), 317–26. As Pratt wrote: "The annexation of Hawaii was a by-product of the war with Spain" (317).

85. David W. Taylor, "Our New Battleships and Armoured Cruisers," U.S. Naval Institute *Proceedings*, December 1900, 593.

86. London *Times*, May 2, 1898, quoted in May, *Imperial Democracy*, 221.

PART FOUR: THE BATTLE OF MIDWAY

1. Samuel Eliot Morison, *Coral Sea, Midway, and Submarine Action (May 1942–August 1942)* (Boston: Little, Brown, 1949), 52–56; E. B. Potter and Chester Nimitz, eds., *Sea Power: A Naval History* (Englewood Cliffs, NJ: Prentice-Hall, Inc., 1960), 662–68; John B. Lundstrom, *The First Team: Pacific Naval Air Combat from Pearl Harbor to Midway* (Annapolis: Naval Institute Press, 1984), 155–306.

2. Gordon W. Prange with Donald M. Goldstein and Katherine V. Dillon, *Miracle at Midway* (New York: McGraw-Hill Book Company, 1982), 111; interview of Captain Joseph J. Rochefort, USN (ret), by Etta-Belle Kitchen, October 5, 1969, U.S. Naval Institute Oral History Collection, Special Collections, Nimitz Library, U.S. Naval Academy, 1:225.

3. Prange, *Miracle at Midway*, 111; Joseph J. Rochefort interview, October 5, 1969, 1:225.

4. *Dictionary of American Naval Fighting Ships* (Washington, DC: Naval History Division, 1963, 1969), 8:533–38.

5. W. J. Holmes, *Double Edged Secrets: U.S. Naval Intelligence Operations in the Pacific During World War II* (Annapolis: Naval Institute Press, 1979), 53.

6. Edwin T. Layton, *"And I Was There": Pearl Harbor and Midway—Breaking the Secrets* (New York: William Morrow and Company, 1985), 405; interview of Captain Thomas H. Dyer, USN (ret), by Paul Stilwell, September 14, 1983, U.S. Naval Institute Oral History Collection, Nimitz Library, U.S. Naval Academy, 247; Ronald W. Russell to Otis Kight, June 27, 2004, letter forwarded to the author by Otis Kight.

7. Joseph J. Rochefort interview, October 5, 1969, 1:249.

8. Ibid., 211. Rochefort himself did not send the signal. Years later he suggested that perhaps Edwin T. Layton sent it, but Jasper Holmes, the civilian academic on the Hypo team, claimed authorship in his memoir. See Thomas Dyer interview, September 14, 1983, 241; and Holmes, *Double-Edged Secrets*, 90. Hugh Bicheno asserts that the purpose of the message was mainly to show up rivals within the code-breaking community and "was not the breakthrough of myth and movie." Bicheno, *Midway* (London: Cassell, 2001), 85.

9. Morison, *Coral Sea, Midway, and Submarine Actions*, 70–72.

10. Mitsuo Fuchida and Masatake Okumiya, *Midway: The Battle That Doomed Japan, the Japanese Navy's Story* (Annapolis: Naval Institute Press, 1955), 34–46.

11. Prange, *Miracle at Midway*, 11; E. B. Potter, *Nimitz* (Annapolis: Naval Institute Press, 1976); the quotation is from Joseph J. Rochefort interview, October 5, 1969, 1:223.

12. Potter, *Sea Power*, 800–802; Edward L. Beach, *Submarine!* (Annapolis: Naval Institute Press, 1946, 2003), 22–25.

13. Lieutenant Fuchida thought the Kido Butai was wasted in carrying out minor operations all over the Indian and Pacific Oceans when it ought to have been

focused on the main business of eliminating the American carrier force. See Fuchida and Okumiya, *Midway*, 44–47.

14. Potter, *Nimitz*, 91–92.

15. The decrypted messages are in Appendix III of the Edwin T. Layton Collection, Spruance Papers, Naval War College, Newport, R.I., 287–93. The quotations are from Rochefort interview, October 5, 1969, 217–19.

16. Rochefort interview, October 5, 1969, 1:220.

17. E. B. Potter, *Bull Halsey* (Annapolis: Naval Institute Press, 1985); Thomas B. Buell, *The Quiet Warrior: A Biography of Raymond A. Spruance* (Boston: Little, Brown, 1974).

18. Potter, *Nimitz*, 86.

19. Action Report, Commander in Chief, U.S. Pacific Fleet (Nimitz), June 28, 1942, from "U.S. Navy Action and Operational Reports from World War II, Pacific Theater," Part I: CINCPAC (Bethesda, MD: University Publications of America microfilm, 1990), reel 2. Hereafter cited as "Action Reports microfilm." All references are to Part I.

20. Lundstrom, *The First Team*, 315–20; Bicheno, *Midway*, 116–17.

21. Statement of Captain P. R. White, USN, June 6, 1942, Action Reports microfilm, reel 3.

22. Interview of Lieutenant Commander John S. "Jimmy" Thach, August 26, 1942, microfilm NRS 527, Nimitz Library, U.S. Naval Academy; interview of Admiral John S. Thach, USN (ret), by Etta-Belle Kitchen, November 6, 1970, U.S. Naval Institute Oral History Collection, Special Collections, Nimitz Library, U.S. Naval Academy, 1:218, 223.

23. John S. Thach interview, August 26, 1942, 5; author's interview of Captain John W. "Jack" Crawford, USN (ret), May 5, 2004.

24. George Gay, *Sole Survivor: The Battle of Midway and Its Effects on His Life* (Naples, FL: Midway Publishers, 1980), 122. Jimmy Thach, who was bitterly critical of the performance characteristics of American planes compared to their Japanese counterparts, claimed that the Devastator cruised at no more than 80 knots, or "with the nose down, maybe 110." Thach interview, November 6, 1970, 1:231.

25. Thomas Wildenberg, *Destined for Glory: Dive Bombing, Midway, and the Evolution of Carrier Air Power* (Annapolis: Naval Institute Press, 1998); Daniel Hernandez, *SBD-3 Dauntless and the Battle of Midway* (Torrent, Spain: Aeronaval Publishing, 2003).

26. Fuchida and Okumiya, *Midway*, 105–6.

27. Several histories of the battle offer the number 272 as the number of available Japanese aircraft at Midway. But this number is based on the maximum load rather than the actual number of planes aboard ship. In addition, some two dozen planes were disassembled Zeros intended for use on Midway's captured airfields. While some of these got into the fighting at Midway, the total num-

ber of available combat aircraft in the Kido Butai was nearer 250 than 270. The number given here (249) is from Ikuhiko Hata and Yasuho Izawa, *Japanese Naval Aces and Fighter Units in World War II* (Annapolis: Naval Institute Press, 1989), 148; and Lundstrom, *The First Team*, 331.

28. Fuchida and Okumiya, *Midway*, 60.

29. Ibid., 125–27.

30. Ibid., 130.

31. Ibid., 125–70.

32. Prange, *Miracle at Midway*, 162–64.

33. Ibid., 170.

34. Ibid., 225–27.

35. Dick Knott, "Night Torpedo Attack," *Naval Aviation News*, June 1982, 10–13; Prange, *Miracle at Midway*, 174–76.

36. Bicheno, *Midway*, 60–61.

37. Fuchida and Okumiya, *Midway*, 146–48.

38. Ibid., 152–54; Prange, *Miracle at Midway*, 184–84.

39. Fuchida and Okumiya, *Midway*, 148. Dallas Isom argues that the late takeoff by the *Tone*'s second search plane was actually fortuitous for the Japanese. The late departure, he argues, encouraged the pilot to begin his dogleg to the north sooner than scheduled in order to make up for the late start, and that enabled him to sight Spruance's Task Force 16 sooner than he would have if he had left on time and adhered to the original course. See Dallas W. Isom, "The Battle of Midway: Why the Japanese Lost," *Naval War College Review*, summer 2000, 88–89.

40. Action Report, Commander Task Force 17 (Fletcher), June 14, 1942, Action Reports microfilm, reel 2.

41. Communication Log Relative to Midway Attack, Action Reports microfilm, reel 2; Crawford interview, May 5, 2004.

42. Action Report, Commanding Officer Task Force 17 (Fletcher), June 14, 1942, Action Reports microfilm, reel 2.

43. Alan Schom, *The Eagle and the Rising Sun: The Japanese-American War, 1941–1945* (New York: W. W. Norton, 2004), 285; Action Report, Commanding Officer USS *Enterprise* (Murray), June 13, 1942, Action Reports microfilm, reel 2.

44. Otis Kight to the author, June 28, 2004.

45. Action Report, Commanding Officer USS *Hornet* (Mitscher), June 13, 1942, Action Reports microfilm, reel 2.

46. Action Report, Commanding Officer Task Force 16 (Spruance), June 16, 1942, Action Reports microfilm, reel 2; Morison, *Coral Sea, Midway, and Submarine Actions*, 114.

47. Interview of Captain James R. Ogden by Paul Stilwell, March 16, 1982, U.S. Naval Institute Oral History Collection, Nimitz Library, 76–78.

48. Interview of Lieutenant Colonel Ira Kimes, USMC, August 31, 1942, Action Reports microfilm, reel 2.

49. Prange, *Miracle at Midway*, 206; Fuchida and Okumiya, *Midway*, 156.

50. Fuchida and Okumiya, *Midway*, 160.

51. The precise timing of the *Tone*'s message is a matter of some uncertainty. The message was dispatched at 7:28 but may not have been received aboard the *Akagi* until nearly 8:00 after being relayed en route. See Prange, *Miracle at Midway*, 217; Fuchida and Okumiya, *Midway*, 165; and Isom, "Battle of Midway," 68–70.

52. Action Report, Commanding Officer Marine Scout-Bombing Squadron 241, June 12, 1942, Action Reports microfilm, reel 3.

53. Prange, *Miracle at Midway*, 216–230; statements of Captain Leon M. Williamson, USMC, Second Lieutenant Thomas F. Moore, USMC, and Private Charles W. Huber, USMC, all dated June 7, 1942, Action Reports microfilm, reel 3; Fuchida and Okumiya, *Midway*, 168.

54. Fuchida and Okumiya, *Midway*, 168, 170.

55. Gay, *Sole Survivor*, 93–95; Lundstrom, *The First Team*, 324. See also "Memorandum for the Commander-in-Chief," by Ensign George Gay, June 7, 1942, in Action Reports microfilm, reel 2.

56. Gay, *Sole Survivor*, 116.

57. Memorandum of Stanhope Ring, March 28, 1946, in Bruce R. Linder, "Lost Letter of Midway," U.S. Naval Institute *Proceedings*, August 1999, 32; Action Report, Commanding Officer, USS *Enterprise* (Murray), June 13, 1942, Action Reports microfilm, reel 2.

58. Gay, *Sole Survivor*, 119.

59. Ibid., 120–21; "George Gay's Fisheye View of Midway," *Naval Aviation News*, June 1982, 18–21.

60. Gay, *Sole Survivor*, 127–29.

61. Action Report, Commanding Officer, *Yorktown* Air Wing (Pederson), June 14, 1942, Action Reports microfilm, reel 2.

62. John S. Thach interview, November 6, 1970, 1:246; Action Report, Commanding Officer, VF-3 (Thach), June 4, 1942, Action Reports microfilm, reel 3.

63. John S. Thach interview, November 6, 1970, 1:248.

64. Prange, *Miracle at Midway*, 1:257.

65. John S. Thach interview, November 6, 1970, 1: 251.

66. Fuchida and Okumiya, *Midway*, 177.

67. Action Report, Commander in Chief U.S. Pacific Fleet (Nimitz), June 28, 1942, Action Reports microfilm, reel 2.

68. Action Report, Commanding Officer, *Yorktown* Air Wing (Pederson), June 14, 1942, Action Reports microfilm, reel 2.

69. John S. Thach interview, November 6, 1970, 1:252.

70. Action Report, Commanding Officer VB-3 (Shumway), June 8, 1942, Action Reports microfilm, reel 2.

71. Action Report, Commanding Officer *Yorktown* Air Wing (Pederson), June 14,

1942, Action Reports microfilm, reel 2; Fuchida and Okumiya, *Midway*, 178.

72.   Fuchida and Okumiya, *Midway*, 179.

73.   Action Report, Commanding Officer USS *Yorktown* (Buckmaster), June 18, 1942, Action Reports microfilm, reel 3.

74.   Interview of Lieutenant Commander C. C. Ray, USN, Communications Officer on the *Yorktown*, July 15, 1942, Action Reports microfilm, reel 2.

75.   Message traffic is from Enclosure C of Action Report, Commander in Chief. U.S. Pacific Fleet (Nimitz), June 28, 1942, Action Reports microfilm, reel 3.

76.   John S. Thach interview, November 6, 1970, 1:264.

77.   Message traffic is from Enclosure C of Action Report, Commander in Chief U.S. Pacific Fleet (Nimitz), June 28, 1942, Action Reports microfilm, reel 3.

78.   Action Report, Commanding Officer USS *Yorktown* (Buckmaster), June 18, 1942, Action Reports microfilm, reel 3.

79.   Ibid.; John W. Crawford interview, May 5, 2004.

80.   John S. Thach interview, November 6, 1970, 1:269; Prange, *Miracle at Midway*, 235–36.

81.   John S. Thach interview, November 6, 1970, 1:269; Action Report, Commanding Officer USS *Yorktown* (Buckmaster), June 18, 1942, Action Reports microfilm, reel 3.

82.   John W. Crawford interview, May 5, 2004.

83.   Action Report, Commanding Officer USS *Yorktown* (Buckmaster), Action Reports microfilm, reel 3.

84.   Fuchida and Okumiya, *Midway*, 194; Bicheno, *Midway*, 174.

85.   Message traffic is from NRS 547 microfilm on the Battle of Midway, Nimitz Library, U.S. Naval Academy.

86.   Action Report, Commanding Officer USS *Yorktown* (Buckmaster), June 18, 1942, Action Reports microfilm, reel 3.

87.   John W. Crawford interview, May 5, 2004; interview of Rear Admiral Ernest M. Eller, USN (ret), by John T. Mason, August 25, 1977, U.S. Naval Institute Oral History Collection, Nimitz Library, U.S. Naval Academy, 542.

88.   Action Report, Commanding Officer USS *Yorktown* (Buckmaster), June 18, 1942, Action Reports microfilm, reel 3.

89.   Fuchida and Okumiya, *Midway*, 231; James Schlesinger, "Underappreciated Victory," *Naval History*, October 2003, 21; Stimson is quoted in Prange, *Miracle at Midway*, 365.

PART FIVE: THE PERSIAN GULF

1.   "A Tragedy in the Gulf," *Newsweek*, June 1, 1987, 19.

2.   Michael Vlahos, "The Stark Report," U.S. Naval Institute *Proceedings*, May 1988, 64–65.

3.   "A Tragedy in the Gulf," 16–20.

4. Ibid., 21.

5. *Navy Times,* October 26, 1987, 28. All the *Navy Times* articles cited in this section were written by staff writer William Matthews, who covered the Gulf for the *Navy Times* in 1987–88. See also Jeffrey L. Levinson and Randy L. Edwards, *Missile Inbound: The Attack on the Stark in the Persian Gulf* (Annapolis: Naval Institute Press, 1997).

6. *Navy Times,* October 12, 1987, 18, and October 26, 1987, 1.

7. *New York Times* editorial, May 27, 1987, A22; *Newsweek,* June 1, 1987, 20.

8. *Navy Times,* August 10, 1987, 26.

9. Michael A. Palmer, "The U.S. Navy and the Persian Gulf: The Origins of the Commitment, 1945–1953," in William R. Roberts and Jack Sweetman, eds., *New Interpretations in Naval History* (Annapolis: Naval Institute Press, 1991), 146, 156n.

10. Ibid., 147.

11. Report of the USS *Greenwich Bay* (APV-41), August 12, 1948, in ibid., 149.

12. Stephen Kinzer, *All the Shah's Men: An American Coup and the Roots of Middle East Terror* (New York: John Wiley & Sons, 2003).

13. Michael A. Palmer, *Guardians of the Gulf: A History of America's Expanding Role in the Persian Gulf, 1833–1992* (New York: Free Press, 1992), 106.

14. Martin S. Navias and E. R. Hooton, *The Tanker Wars: The Assault on Merchant Shipping During the Iran-Iraq Crisis, 1980–1988* (London: Taurus Academic Studies, 1996), 15–22.

15. Ibid., 50.

16. Ibid., 31.

17. William J. Crowe Jr., *The Line of Fire: From Washington to the Gulf, Politics and Battles of the New Military* (New York: Simon & Schuster, 1993), 173; Ronald O'Rourke, "Gulf Ops," U.S. Naval Institute *Proceedings,* May 1989, 43; Wesley L. McDonald, "The Convoy Mission," U.S. Naval Institute *Proceedings,* May 1988, 37.

18. Navias and Hooton, *The Tanker Wars,* 39.

19. The insider was the chairman of the Joint Chiefs of Staff, Admiral William Crowe, from author's interview of Admiral William J. Crowe Jr. (ret), Annapolis, Maryland, August 13, 2003; the Reagan quotation is from Michael A. Palmer, *On Course to Desert Storm: The United States Navy and the Persian Gulf* (Washington: Naval Historical Center, 1992), 109–10.

20. McDonald, "The Convoy Mission," 37; *New York Times,* May 26, 1987, A5.

21. William Crowe interview, August 13, 2003.

22. "Why Europe and Japan Won't Help," *Newsweek,* June 8, 1987, 35; Palmer, *On Course to Desert Storm,* 116.

23. The Weinberger quotation is from a speech before the American Defense Preparedness Association on May 20, 1987, quoted in Levinson and Edwards, *Missile Inbound,* 4; *Newsweek,* June 1, 1987, 20; *New York Times,* May 19, 1987, A10.

24. *Navy Times,* October 12, 1987, 18; W. Hays Parks, "Righting the Rules of

Engagement," U.S. Naval Institute *Proceedings,* May 1989, 83; William Crowe interview, August 13, 2003.

25. *New York Times,* May 19 and July 24, 1987, A10; McDonald, "The Convoy Mission," 43.

26. Frank B. Seitz, "SS *Bridgeton*: The First Convoy," U.S. Naval Institute *Proceedings,* May 1989, 56.

27. *Navy Times,* August 10, 1987, 10.

28. *Navy Times,* August 3, 1987, 37–38, and August 10, 1987, 10.

29. Seitz, "SS *Bridgeton*," 52.

30. Ibid.

31. Crowe, *The Line of Fire,* 186.

32. *Navy Times,* August 10, 1987, 10; *New York Times,* July 25, 1987, 5; William Crowe interview, August 13, 2003.

33. *Navy Times,* September 14, 1987, 13; Commander Alfred Eakins, USN, to Commander Tom Schaefer, USN, January 18, 2000, author's collection.

34. Palmer, *Guardians of the Gulf,* 135–37.

35. Author's interview with Captain James "Red" Smith, USN, Annapolis, MD, May 2, 2003.

36. Norman Friedman, "World Naval Developments, 1987," U.S. Naval Institute *Proceedings,* May 1988, 220.

37. Kenneth Katzman, *The Warriors of Islam: Iran's Revolutionary Guard* (Boulder, CO: Westview Press, 1993), 134; Anthony Cordesman, *Iran's Military Forces in Transition: Conventional Threats and Weapons of Mass Destruction* (Westport, CT: Praeger, 1999), 192–93; "Guerilla War on the Water," *Newsweek,* June 15, 1987, 41; James Smith interview, May 2, 2003.

38. *New York Times,* July 25, 1987, A1.

39. William Crowe interview, August 13, 2003; James Smith interview, May 2, 2003.

40. *Navy Times,* October 5, 1987, 30.

41. Ibid., 16.

42. *Navy Times,* October 19, 1987, 2.

43. Crowe, *The Line of Fire,* 200.

44. Jerry O'Donnell to the author, July 29, 2003; James Smith interview, May 2, 2003.

45. James Smith interview, May 2, 2003; *Navy Times,* November 2, 1987, 4.

46. O'Donnell to the author, July 29, 2003; *Navy Times,* November 2, 1987, 4; cartoon reprinted in U.S. Naval Institute *Proceedings,* June 1988, 80.

47. "Mideast Perspective: Interview with RADM Anthony A. Less," *Wings of Gold,* Spring 1990, 50.

48. O'Rourke, "Gulf Ops," 43–44; author's interview with Captain Henry Sanford, USN (ret), Annapolis, Maryland, June 6, 2003; James Smith interview, May 2, 2003.

49. *New York Times,* April 15, 1988, A3; *Navy Times,* April 25, 1988, 3; Crowe, *The Line of Fire,* 200.

50. *Navy Times*, May 2, 1988, 6; Crowe, *The Line of Fire*, 200.

51. Katzman, *The Warriors of Islam*, 134.

52. *New York Times*, April 19, 1988, A1, A10; Crowe, *The Line of Fire*, 201; William Crowe interview, August 13, 2003.

53. Crowe, *The Line of Fire*, 201.

54. *New York Times*, April 19, 1988, A10.

55. J. B. Perkins, "Operation Praying Mantis," U.S. Naval Institute *Proceedings*, May 1989, 70.

56. Henry Sanford interview, June 6, 2003.

57. Ibid.

58. Ibid.

59. Ibid.

60. Perkins, "Operation Praying Mantis," 70; Henry Sanford interview, June 6, 2003.

61. James Chandler interview, November 1, 2003.

62. Interview of Chief Petty Officer Reuben Vargas, USN, by Lieutenant Commander Donald Donegan, USN, on board USS *Carl Vinson*, May 30, 2003; James Chandler interview, November 1, 2003.

63. Author's interview of Lieutenant Commander Leo Carling, USNR (ret), Annapolis, Maryland, October 5, 2003; James Chandler interview, November 1, 2003; Reuben Vargas interview, May 30, 2003.

64. Transcript of tape recording from the CIC of USS *Wainwright*, April 18, 1988, tape in author's possession; James Chandler interview, November 1, 2003.

65. Perkins, "Operation Praying Mantis," 69; *New York Times*, April 19, 1988, A11; James Chandler interview, November 1, 2003.

66. Reuben Vargas interview, May 30, 2003.

67. Katzman, *The Warriors of Islam*, 134.

68. Transcript of tape recording from the CIC of USS *Wainwright*, April 18, 1988; James Chandler interview, November 1, 2003.

69. James Chandler interview, November 1, 2003.

70. Transcript of tape recording from the CIC of USS *Wainwright*, April 18, 1988.

71. Ibid.; James Chandler interview, November 1, 2003.

72. Reuben Vargas interview, May 30, 2003; James Chandler interview, November 10, 2003; transcript of tape recording made in CIC of USS *Wainwright*, April 18, 1988.

73. Reuben Vargas interview, May 30, 2003; transcript of tape recording made in CIC of USS *Wainwright*, April 18, 1988.

74. Transcript of tape recording made in CIC of USS *Wainwright*, April 18, 1988.

75. "Mideast Perspective: Interview with RADM Anthony A. Less," 52.

76. James Chandler interview, November 1, 2003.

77. William Crowe interview, August 13, 2003.

78. James Chandler interview, November 1, 2003; Reuben Vargas interview, May 30, 2003.

79. James Chandler interview, November 1, 2003.

80. Reuben Vargas interview, May 30, 2003; Leo Carling interview, October 5, 2003.

81. Henry Sanford interview, June 6, 2003.

82. Ibid.

83. Ibid.; Perkins, "Operation Praying Mantis," 69.

84. Bud Langston and Don Bringle, "Operation Praying Mantis: The Air View," U.S. Naval Institute *Proceedings*, May 1989, 58.

85. Ibid.; Secretary of State Colin Powell to the author, September 2, 2003, author's collection.

86. Perkins, "Praying Mantis," 70; Langston and Bringle, "The Air View," 58–59.

87. Palmer, "Operation Praying Mantis," 394.

88. Ibid.; William Crowe interview, August 13, 2003.

89. *New York Times*, July 6, 1988, A6; Norman Friedman, "The Vincennes Incident," U.S. Naval Institute *Proceedings*, May 1989, 72; Leo Carling interview, October 5, 2003; William M. Fogarty, *Investigation Report: Formal Investigation into the Circumstances Surrounding the Downing of Iran Air Flight 655 on 3 July 1988* (Washington, DC: Department of Defense, 1988).

90. Michael Agresti, "The REAL Story about 3 July 1988," USS *Vincennes* Web site, posted August 2, 2001, at www.military.com/HomePage/UnitPageHistory.

91. Friedman, "The Vincennes Incident," 75; *New York Times*, July 5, 1988, A1.

92. Ibid.

93. Langston and Bringle, "The Air View," 65.

94. The senior American officer was Caspar Goodrich. He is quoted in William N. Still Jr., *American Sea Power in the Old World: The United States Navy in European and Near Eastern Waters* (Westport, CT: Greenwood Press, 1980), 13.

Epilogue

1. John B. Hattendorf, *The Evolution of the U.S. Navy's Maritime Strategy, 1977–1986* (Newport, RI: Naval War College Press, 2004).

2. William J. Crowe Jr., *In the Line of Fire: From Washington to the Gulf, Politics and Battles of the New Military* (New York: Simon & Schuster, 1993), 20–21.

3. George Easterbrook, "American Power Moves Beyond Mere Super," *Washington Post*, April 30, 2003.

4. On the origins of Gulf War I, see Edward Marolda and Robert J. Schneller Jr., *Shield and Sword: The United States Navy and the Persian Gulf War* (Washington: Naval Historical Center, 1998); and Anthony H. Cordesman and Abraham R. Wagner, *The Lessons of Modern War*, Vol. IV: *The Gulf War* (Boulder, CO: Westview Press, 1996).

5. Cordesman and Wagner, *The Lessons of Modern War*, 784; "U.S. Military Logistics," *The Atlantic*, May 2003, 50.

6. Cordesman and Wagner, *The Lessons of Modern War*, 797–98.

7.   Ibid., 785.

8.   Marolda and Schneller, *Shield and Sword*, 183–96.

9.   Cordesman and Wagner, *The Lessons of Modern War*, 399.

10.   "Terrorist Attack on USS Cole," *Navy Times*, October 23, 2000, 8–11.

11.   *Le Monde*, September 13, 2001.

12.   Lisa Troshinsky, "Navy Pilots Set Flying and Target Records in Afghanistan," *Navy News & Undersea Technology*, January 22, 2002, 1.

13.   *Newsweek*, June 1, 1987, 25.

14.   The White House, "The National Security Policy of the United States," September 17, 2002.

15.   Hendrick Hertzberg, "Manifesto," *The New Yorker*, October 14–21, 2002, 64; Arthur Schlesinger Jr., "Good Foreign Policy a Casualty of War," *Los Angeles Times*, March 23, 2002; Noam Chomsky, *Hegemony or Survival: America's Quest for Global Dominance* (New York: Metropolitan Books, 2003), 17.

16.   Richard Clarke, *Against All Enemies: Inside America's War on Terror* (New York: Free Press, 2004), 231–46; Bob Woodward, *Plan of Attack* (New York: Simon & Schuster, 2004), 9.

17.   On March 16, 2003, Vice President Cheney declared on *Meet the Press*, "There is no question but that they [the Iraqi people] want to get rid of Saddam Hussein and they will welcome as liberators the United States when we come to do that."

18.   America's unreadiness for the postwar chaos is detailed in James Fallows, "Blind into Baghdad," *Atlantic Monthly*, January-February 2004. See also Rick Atkinson, *In the Company of Soldiers: A Chronicle of Combat* (New York: Henry Holt and Co., 2004), 297–303.

19.   Vernon Loeb, "Navy Plans to Increase Carrier Readiness," *Washington Post*, June 29, 2003, A9.

20.   Max Boot, "The Doctrine of the Big Enchilada," *The Washington Post*, October 14, 2002, A29.

21.   George Kennan is quoted in Ronald Steel, "George Kennan at 100," *The New York Review of Books*, April 29, 2004, 9; Michael Ignatieff, "The Burden," *New York Times Magazine*, January 5, 2003, 24.

[INDEX]